THE AFTERLIVES OF
EIGHTEENTH-CENTURY FICTION

The Afterlives of Eighteenth-Century Fiction probes the adaptation and appropriation of a wide range of canonical and lesser-known British and Irish novels in the long eighteenth century, from the period of Daniel Defoe and Eliza Haywood through to that of Jane Austen and Walter Scott. Major authors including Jonathan Swift, Samuel Richardson, Henry Fielding, and Laurence Sterne are discussed alongside writers, such as Sarah Fielding and Ann Radcliffe, whose literary significance is now increasingly being recognized. By uncovering this neglected aspect of the reception of eighteenth-century fiction, this collection contributes to developing our understanding of the form of the early novel, its place in a broader culture of entertainment then and now, and its interactions with a host of other genres and media, including theatre, opera, poetry, print caricatures, and film.

DANIEL COOK is Lecturer in English at the University of Dundee. He is the author of *Thomas Chatterton and Neglected Genius, 1760–1830* (2013), the editor of *The Lives of Jonathan Swift* (2011), and the co-editor (with Amy Culley) of *Women's Life Writing: Gender, Genre, and Authorship, 1700–1850* (2012). He has published essays on a variety of topics ranging from Pope to Wordsworth in such journals as *The Library*, *Philological Quarterly*, and *The Review of English Studies*.

NICHOLAS SEAGER is Senior Lecturer in English at Keele University. He has published essays on authors ranging from John Bunyan to Oliver Goldsmith, and his work appears in journals including *Modern Language Review*, *The Library*, *Philological Quarterly*, *Eighteenth-Century Fiction*, and *The Eighteenth-Century Novel*. He is the author of *The Rise of the Novel: A Reader's Guide to Essential Criticism* (2012) and a forthcoming monograph, *Daniel Defoe and the History of Fictional Form*.

THE AFTERLIVES OF EIGHTEENTH-CENTURY FICTION

EDITED BY

DANIEL COOK AND NICHOLAS SEAGER

CAMBRIDGE
UNIVERSITY PRESS

CAMBRIDGE
UNIVERSITY PRESS

University Printing House, Cambridge CB2 8BS, United Kingdom

Cambridge University Press is part of the University of Cambridge.

It furthers the University's mission by disseminating knowledge in the pursuit of
education, learning and research at the highest international levels of excellence.

www.cambridge.org
Information on this title: www.cambridge.org/9781107054684

© Cambridge University Press 2015

First published 2015

Printed in the United Kingdom by Clays, St Ives plc

A catalogue record for this publication is available from the British Library

Library of Congress Cataloguing in Publication data
The afterlives of eighteenth-century fiction / edited by Daniel Cook and Nicholas Seager.
pages   cm
Includes bibliographical references and index.
ISBN 978-1-107-05468-4 (Hardback)
1. English fiction–18th century–History and criticism.   2. English fiction–Irish authors–18th
century–History and criticism.   3. English fiction–Adaptations–History and criticism.
I. Cook, Daniel, 1981– editor.   II. Seager, Nicholas, 1982– editor.
PR851.A37 2015
823'.509–dc23   2014050297

ISBN 978-1-107-05468-4 Hardback

Contents

List of Illustrations

Notes on Contributors

DAVID A. BREWER is Associate Professor of English at The Ohio State University. He is the author of *The Afterlife of Character, 1726–1825* (2005) and the editor of Richard Brinsley Sheridan's *The Rivals* and George Colman the Elder's *Polly Honeycombe* (2012).

MICHAEL BURDEN is Professor of Opera Studies and Fellow in Music at New College, University of Oxford, and former President of the British Society for Eighteenth-Century Studies. He has edited Henry Purcell's *The Fairy-Queen* (2009) and is currently heading The London Stage Project, 1800–1900.

DANIEL COOK is Lecturer in English at the University of Dundee. He is the author of *Thomas Chatterton and Neglected Genius, 1760-1830* (2013), the editor of *The Lives of Jonathan Swift* (2011), and (with Amy Culley) the co-editor of *Women's Life Writing: Gender, Genre, and Authorship, 1700-1850* (2012).

JILL HEYDT-STEVENSON is Associate Professor of English at the University of Colorado, Boulder. She is the author of *Austen's Unbecoming Conjunctions: Subversive Laughter, Embodied History* (2005) and co-editor of *Recognizing the Romantic Novel: New Histories of British Fiction, 1780-1830* (2008).

ROBERT MAYER is Professor of English at Oklahoma State University. He is the author of *History and the Early English Novel: Matters of Fact from Bacon to Defoe* (1997) and editor of *Eighteenth-Century Fiction on Screen* (2002) and *Historical Boundaries, Narrative Forms* (2007).

MICHAEL MCKEON is Board of Governors Distinguished Professor of Literature at Rutgers University and is the author of *Politics and Poetry in Restoration England* (1975), *The Origins of the English Novel,*

1600–1740 (1987), and *The Secret History of Domesticity: Public, Private, and the Division of Knowledge* (2005).

M-C. NEWBOULD teaches English at the University of Cambridge, where she is Bowman Supervisor in English and College Research Associate at Wolfson College. She is the author of *Adaptations of Laurence Sterne's Fiction: Sterneana, 1760–1840* (2013) and an editor of Sterne journal *The Shandean*.

LEAH ORR is Assistant Professor of English at the University of Louisiana, Lafayette. She has published on eighteenth-century fiction, book history, and the classical tradition. She is currently completing a book-length project on fiction and the British book trade in the period 1690–1730.

DAHLIA PORTER is Assistant Professor of English at the University of North Texas. She is the co-editor of Wordsworth and Coleridge's *Lyrical Ballads, 1798 and 1800* (2008) and her articles have appeared in *Romanticism, European Romantic Review, The Eighteenth Century: Theory and Interpretation*, and the essay collection *Charlotte Smith and British Romanticism*.

SARAH RAFF is Associate Professor of English at Pomona College. She has published essays on Jane Austen and on didactic novels in the eighteenth century in journals, including *The Eighteenth-Century Novel* and *Comparative Literature Studies*, and is the author of *Jane Austen's Erotic Advice* (2014).

PETER SABOR is Professor of English and Canada Research Chair at McGill University. He has edited Samuel Richardson, Sarah Fielding, John Cleland, Horace Walpole, Frances Burney, Jane Austen, and Thomas Carlyle and is the author (with Thomas Keymer) of *'Pamela' in the Marketplace* (2005).

NICHOLAS SEAGER is Senior Lecturer in English at Keele University. He has published essays on authors ranging from John Bunyan to Oliver Goldsmith, and he is the author of *The Rise of the Novel: A Reader's Guide to Essential Criticism* (2012) and a forthcoming monograph, *Daniel Defoe and the History of Fictional Form*.

DAVID FRANCIS TAYLOR is Associate Professor in the Department of English and Comparative Literary Studies at the University of Warwick. He is the author of *Theatres of Opposition: Empire, Revolution, and Richard Brinsley Sheridan* (2012) and co-editor of *The Oxford Handbook of the Georgian Theatre, 1737-1832* (2014).

Introduction

Daniel Cook and Nicholas Seager

An adaptation is not vampiric: it does not draw the life-blood from its source and leave it dying or dead, nor is it paler than the adapted work. It may, on the contrary, keep that prior work alive, giving it an afterlife it would never have had otherwise.[1]

Linda Hutcheon

The choice of this metaphor [afterlife] creates a relation between the source-text and its avatars that is quite different from those considered in the study of influences, sources, or intertextual echoes, which give priority and power to the source-text; speaking in terms of afterlives shifts the balance further down the line towards new figures, new openings, new chances.[2]

Terence Cave

Hutcheon's insistent nots and nors attest to a lingering defensiveness in what has become a seminal study in its field, *A Theory of Adaptation* (2006, revised 2013). After all, adaptation theorists continue to grapple with critical questions that seem old-fashioned in an age of fervent fan fiction, multimedia crossovers, mash-ups, remakes, and swedings: Is it faithful to the source? Is it as good as the original? Although it is a wide-ranging and increasingly diverse field, adaptation studies still privileges investigations into the transfer of novels (typically in the realist tradition) to films (typically in the narrative tradition), a sign of the continued influence of studies such as Brian McFarlane's *Novel to Film* (1996) and Deborah Cartmell and Imelda Whelehan's anthology *Adaptation: From Text to Screen, Screen to Text* (1999).[3] But the second edition of Hutcheon's study, which includes a timely epilogue on new media by Siobhan O'Flynn, makes a powerful case for the importance of pursuing creative adaptation across a range of platforms alongside film and theatre, such as video games, pop music, and theme parks. Bakhtinian theorists like Robert Stam have compellingly argued for the dynamic flux of adaptation as an ongoing process within a larger matrix of allusion and invocation rather than a product, a move away from its treatment as one-directional, the simple 'transport of form and/or content *from* a source *to* a result, such as from novel to film'.[4] The expansiveness opened up by the intertextual turn in adaptation studies is highly appealing, but it circles back to an important, disquieting question posed by Hutcheon: 'What is *Not* an adaptation?'[5]

The term 'afterlives', as Terence Cave suggests, helps us to move beyond axiological defensiveness, inhibiting taxonomy, and simplistic linearity because it levels distinctions of value and priority, takes as its object of study the set of mutual relations between 'versions' of works, and flexibly accommodates a range of creative and other efforts by which works persist and are transformed. Afterlives, Anna Holland and Richard Scholar assert, 'do not suggest a series of increasingly etiolated existences, or shadow-lives, but rather an astonishingly vital sequence of incarnations or lives made anew'.[6] *The Afterlives of Eighteenth-Century Fiction* addresses the range of ways in which novels originally published in the century from Haywood and Defoe to Austen and Scott were adapted, appropriated, and otherwise re-presented. These novels were transferred into new genres and fora, in the eighteenth century and beyond, including stage versions, visual texts, and film. They have been modified and re-presented in different textual states, occasioned by anthologization, abridgement, serialization, and continuation. And the motifs, conventions, and techniques of eighteenth-century fiction have been taken up by later artists, including subsequent novelists.[7] This aspect of the early novel, its susceptibility to creative responses across time and genre, has received only limited attention, largely focused on eminent examples: typically *Robinson Crusoe* (1719), *Pamela* (1740), *Tristram Shandy* (1759–67), *Frankenstein* (1818), and of course Jane Austen's novels. The diffuse nature of the subject – and its delving into 'non-canonical' genres (staged melodramas and graphic novels), 'derivative' works (opportunistic sequels and screen adaptations), or 'debased' versions (bastardized texts or irreverent pastiches) – might account for the relative critical neglect of imaginative responses to eighteenth-century fiction. They have certainly received less attention than the influence of the nineteenth-century novel – the persistence of Dickens, the Brontës, and Hardy in modern culture, their influence on the genre's development, and of course reworkings of their novels are much better known than those of Richardson, Fielding, and Sterne.

This collection begins to redress this state of affairs. Daniel Cook's essay interrogates eighteenth-century conceptions of authorship in order to re-orient our understanding away from the rise of the proprietary, original author. Mimicry, vamping, and other techniques borrowed from the theatre, along with the pervasive collaborative practices of the period, he argues, agitate any serious claims to absolute or singular ownership over literary property. Michael McKeon similarly revisits the origins of the novel in his contention that a longstanding convention of romance – the trope of discovered noble parentage – had a varied afterlife in *Pamela*, *Joseph Andrews* (1742), *Evelina* (1778), and *Pride and Prejudice* (1813), which cumulatively marks the move from nobility as an outward manifestation of rank to an interior signifier of merit.

Leah Orr is also concerned with the afterlife in the eighteenth-century novel of traits from older forms of fiction. She provides a new explanation for the novel's picaresque heritage through publication and reading practices, contending that chapbook abridgements of rambling, plot-focused picaresque in the late seventeenth and early eighteenth centuries provided a market for criminal and rogue narratives focused on a charismatic central character, such as *Moll Flanders* (1722) and *Captain Singleton* (1720). Sarah Raff considers the influence of a model of guardianship and authorship advanced in Richardson's *Sir Charles Grandison* (1753–54), picked up by Dickens a century later in *Bleak House* (1852–53). *Bleak House*, Raff contends, extended Richardson's model of author/reader relations, in which an author is imagined as 'living on in the affective experiences of his readers, appropriating their love lives as part of his own afterlife'.[8]

Continuing the attention to publication practices and shifting reading tastes, Nicholas Seager charts the early novel's post-publication history in early-century newspapers. He argues not just that this episode in the history of serial fiction extended the readership for prose fiction, but that readers became accustomed to the pleasures of reading digressive, interruptive, and episodic fiction through such protraction. M-C. New-bould moves our focus to the second half of the century with a detailed look at *Beauties* anthologies of Sterne and Fielding. These collections outwardly repackaged two bawdy and irreverent authors (by reputation, at least) for a specific audience: young, sentimental readers of the 1780s and 1790s.

In addition to issues of genre, authorship, audience, and influence, the essays that follow explore fictional afterlives in terms of remediation: the textual (poetry, prose, and playtexts), the performative (film, opera, and theatre), and the visual (caricatures, illustrations, and photographs). Original poetry published in 1790s novels, Dahlia Porter suggests, went places that prose sometimes could not. These poems were subsumed into collections of the author's verse, separating if not always divorcing them from the 'source' novel; reviews of novels often quoted the poetry as representative, meaning that it stood, by synecdoche, for the larger work. The novel's poetic afterlife continued into the nineteenth century, providing specific afterlives for the original novels. David A. Brewer, meanwhile, considers ways in which the concept of fiction as non-referential discourse (developed in the novel's movement from depictions of 'Somebodies' to depictions of 'Nobodies') is complicated by puppet theatre, an often overlooked entertainment on which novelists like Fielding and Haywood were regular commentators. The dizzying games puppet theatre played with referentiality challenge basic assumptions about how the category of fiction was worked out in this period. Turning his gaze to seemingly more legitimate theatre, Michael Burden traces some of the notable trends in the reworking of prose fiction for stage musicals, including opera. He takes *Pamela*, William Godwin's *Caleb Williams* (1794), Walter Scott's *Ivanhoe* (1819), and Mary Shelley's *Frankenstein* as his examples to show how the adapters rendered the novels' themes of sentimentalism, politics, history, and horror. Shifts in taste, gauged by reviews and viewers' accounts, indicate that the afterlives of these and other novels on stage can reveal much about contemporary audiences, as well as the techniques used to appease them, including the use of spoken dialogue, all-sung recitative, melodrama, and ballad.

David Francis Taylor next attends to an important period in graphic satire by contextualizing James Gillray's retrieval of Jonathan Swift's *Gulliver's Travels* (1726) in a caricature depicting George III holding a belligerent Bonaparte in the palm of his hand. Caricatures, Taylor argues, became an important vehicle for the expression and consolidation of patriotism amid the hostilities between Britain and France, and Swift's narrative provided a potent and versatile frame of reference for political propaganda. Whereas Taylor examines Swift's posthumous influence on visual culture in a specific medium, Robert Mayer traces the enduring cultural influence of Defoe's novels by looking primarily at screen versions, but also at exhibitions, photography, and travel books. As Mayer demonstrates, Defoe's novels have been put to a variety of uses by modern artists and filmmakers across the world, including Anglo-American feminism, protesting against government responses to the SARS epidemic in Asia and AIDS in the West, and exposing the social consequences of Britain's post-industrial decline. Jillian Heydt-Stevenson extends the examination of filmic adaptations of canonical authors by comparing the embodiments of happiness in two screen versions of *Sense and Sensibility* (1811). Recovering Austen's conception of happiness as more proximate to virtue than self-fulfilment or pleasure, Heydt-Stevenson shows that revisions to major characters like Edward and Marianne represent a fundamental reconceptualization of Austenian happiness. Peter Sabor, in our final chapter, extends our reach further still in his account of the reception of Austen's juvenile 'The History of England', a parodic national history. As Sabor argues, Austen's work had a notable influence on the early twentieth-century mock-history *1066 And All That*, by W. C. Sellar and R. J. Yeatman, indicating that Austen's influence extends beyond the novel to include fictive history.

Further studies might move beyond these textual, performative, or visual boundaries to consider in detail the use of fictional works in marketing, tourism, merchandise, and other facets of modern living, drawing indeed on the appropriation of fiction in the eighteenth century by makers of printed handkerchiefs, commemorative busts, pottery, and other forms of souvenir. The contributors to this collection build on the principle that eighteenth-century fiction is inherently adaptive both in the sense that it adopts other forms (romance, travel writing, conduct books, poetry, and the like) and lends itself to remediation in other formats (films, theatre, graphic novels, and so on). Future investigations into popular culture's absorption of literary works will need to move away from what we might call narrative and narrative qualified media and develop a grammar of immersive experience in order to make sense of theme parks, apps, gaming, toponymy, fan culture, museums, stately homes, and themed bars and restaurants.[9] In any case, we advocate an inclusive approach to literary afterlives. 'Afterlife' is a capacious term that includes critical reception, remediation, and creative appropriation. Accordingly, the following essays touch on the impact of eighteenth-century authors on writers from the period itself through to the twenty-first century, but more remains to be said. Defoe and Sterne in particular have attracted the attention of graphic novelists, while Fielding and Austen continue to influence writers of comedy and satire. Adaptation still carries connotations of authorial hierarchy and legitimacy, notwithstanding Hutcheon's appealing assertion that even if adaptations arrive *secondarily*, they must not be treated as *secondary*. 'Afterlife' as a term extends Hutcheon's challenge to the tyranny of the original insofar as it gestures towards the extended, open-ended legacy of a work – what Cave calls 'new openings' and 'new chances'.

Afterlives of 'long' eighteenth-century works of fiction are not always concerned with straightforwardly keeping the original alive. Many reworkings of *Gulliver's Travels*, from nineteenth-century versions for children to the Gulliver's Land theme parks and the most recent studio film (directed by Rob Letterman in 2010), tend to limit themselves to the first two voyages, jettisoning the third and fourth voyages. John Moore's *Zeluco* (1789) had a major influence on Byron's *Childe Harold's Pilgrimage* (1812–18) via popular stage productions, but it fell out of print between 1827 and 2008. But even when a novel's reputation is not especially high, its afterlives may keep it in the larger cultural consciousness, allowing for a later recuperation. Acknowledging his 'Debt' to the late Aphra Behn in the dedication to his 1695 stage adaptation of *Oroonoko* (1688), Thomas Southerne wrote that 'She had a great Command of the Stage; and I have often wonder'd that she would bury her Favourite Hero in a *Novel*, when she might have reviv'd him in the *Scene*.'[10] At this point in history, adaptation seemed able to save a good story from the still-disreputable genre of prose fiction. Behn's noble slave is figuratively killed (buried) in fiction but brought back to life ('reviv'd') on stage. Southerne's *Oroonoko* became one of the most frequently printed and performed – and in turn reworked – plays of the eighteenth century, leading Clara Reeve to declare in 1785 that 'Mrs. *Behn* will not be forgotten, so long as the Tragedy of *Oroonoko* is acted.'[11] Indeed, Southerne's decision to change Imoinda to a white woman made that character a popular figuration for Behn herself, just as the homodiegetic narrator of the novel has served this biographical function in Behn's afterlife. Biyi Bandele's 1999 play based on *Oroonoko* retained the black Imoinda but wrote out the white female character, whereas Joan Anim-Addo's libretto *Imoinda, or She Who Will Lose Her Name* (2008) concentrates on the experiences of the female slave from Behn's narrative. Before these postcolonial revisitations, as Jane Spencer has shown, *Oroonoko* was '[c]o-opted for the abolitionist movement', such as in James Ferriar's 1788 play, *The Prince of Angola*.[12]

The eighteenth-century novel's afterlives are often politically motivated, then, as writers revisit its identity politics from postcolonial and feminist vantages. One example is Erica Jong's 'mock-eighteenth-century novel', *Fanny* (1980), an audacious retelling of John Cleland's *Memoirs of a Woman of Pleasure* (1747–48) – often referred to as *Fanny Hill* – that references much else along the way, as its Defovian *faux* title page suggests:

THE TRUE HISTORY
OF
THE ADVENTURES
OF
FANNY
HACKABOUT-JONES

IN THREE BOOKS

COMPRISING HER LIFE AT LYMEWORTH, HER
INITIATION AS A WITCH, HER TRAVELS WITH
THE MERRY MEN, HER LIFE IN THE BROTHEL,
HER LONDON HIGH LIFE, HER SLAVING VOYAGE,
HER LIFE AS A FEMALE PYRATE, HER EVENTUAL
UNRAVELLING OF HER DESTINY, ET CETERA.

Printed for G. Fenton in The Strand

MDCCLI

Fanny's name conjures Tom Jones and Moll Hackabout, as well as Fanny
Hill. The mimicry continues with the orthography, typography, style, and
diction of the narrative, and its synoptic chapter titles and imitation of
eighteenth-century fiction's formal features. *Fanny* comprises rambling,
miscellaneous adventures, interpolated life stories, and a stand-alone history

of piracy spliced into the narrative; and the final three chapters playfully play out a protracted conclusion. Fanny finds time for some 'Animadversions' on 'the dastardly Mr. Cleland', whom she says stole her story, 'but being a Man . . . he could not but sentimentalize my History'. 'Only a Man', Fanny reflects, '(and an indiff'rently-endow'd one at that) would dwell so interminably upon the Size and Endurance of sundry Peewees, Pillicocks, and Pricks – for a Woman hath better Things to do with her Reason and her Wit'. In her Afterword, Jong actually defends Cleland, but that hardly neutralizes Fanny's criticisms of the heroines created by male novelists: 'Neither Pamela Andrews, with her incessant Scribbling of her "Vartue," nor tiresome Clarissa Harlowe, with her insuff'rable Weeping and Letter-writing, nor yet the gentle Sophia Western of whom Mr. Fielding so prettily writes, nor the wicked Moll Flanders of whom Mr. Defoe so vigorously writes, shines out as an Example upon which a Flesh-and-Blood Female can model her Life.' Jong's *Fanny* pays homage to eighteenth-century sexual candour, revelling in the self-determinacy available to a woman before more constrictive domestic ideology took shape; but Jong subjects to the critique of second-wave feminism the attitude that 'Men see us either as the Embodiment of Virtue or the Embodiment of Vice'.[13]

Fanny Hill received fairly sanitized BBC treatment in a television mini-series in 2007, with a screenplay by Andrew Davies, whose credits include *Pride and Prejudice* (1995), *Moll Flanders* (1996), and *Northanger Abbey* (2007). In Martin Rowson's graphic novel, *The Life and Opinions of Tristram Shandy, Gentleman* (1996) and Michael Winterbottom's movie *A Cock and Bull Story* (2005), the conventions of the 'heritage' film adaptation associated with Davies are gently mocked, a tendency also evident in some recent film versions of the genre's perennial favourite, Jane Austen.[14] These recent versions of *Tristram Shandy* mark a self-conscious, postmodern return to remediations of Sterne's novel, which had lain dormant as far as adapters were concerned for about 150 years. And yet, as recent studies have established, *Tristram Shandy* and *A Sentimental Journey* (1768) were extensively adapted for the stage and appropriated by visual artists in the late eighteenth and early nineteenth centuries, and they elicited a wide variety of textual responses.[15] The recent versions replicate the famously self-reflexive qualities of Sterne's novel to reflect on the art of adaptation. Rowson's is a graphic novel about the writing of a graphic novel about a novel about the writing of a novel; it subversively plays with the linear progression demanded by pictorial frames and mimics artistic styles from Albrecht Dürer to Aubrey Beardsley. Equally, Winterbottom's is a film about adapting Sterne, somewhat in the vein of Terry Gilliam's Quixotic *Lost in La Mancha* (2002); it depicts a film crew making *Tristram Shandy*, with Steve Coogan portraying a burlesqued version of himself playing both father and son, Walter and Tristram. Both Rowson's and Winterbottom's works respond to the challenges of 'rewriting' Sterne, making inventive use of the 'media affordances' of the comic and the movie, respectively. So in the novel the indescribable beauty of the Widow Wadman remains undescribed, as the reader is invited to 'call for pen and ink' and 'paint her to your own mind —— as like your mistress as you can —— as unlike your wife as your conscience will let you –'tis all one to me – please but your own fancy in it'.[16] The film within the film of *A Cock and Bull Story* pleases its own fancy by casting the established Hollywood actress Gillian Anderson, but we see Anderson's consternation when it turns out her scenes have not made the final cut. Rowson meanwhile follows Sterne's refusal to describe the Widow by drawing her with a fan concealing her face, a nice hint at her modesty. *Tristram Shandy* stages a tension between the described and the depicted, between the verbal and the visual; the primarily visual forms of cinema and graphic novel engage with that tension in roundabout ways.

Film adaptations of eighteenth-century novels have been treated most fully in *Eighteenth-Century Fiction on Screen*, edited by Robert Mayer, containing essays on screen versions of such major works as *Moll Flanders*, *Gulliver's Travels*, *Tom Jones* (1749), *Clarissa* (1747–48), and *Rob Roy* (1817). Mayer makes an important case for getting beyond evaluative approaches to film adaptations that assess them against the 'original' by using theories of reading that conceive of reception as an act of 'concretization', by which readers creatively reconstruct a text afresh.[17] The point extends beyond film to all creative responses to prior works. Adaptations, Mayer reminds us, are themselves context-bound, responding to pressing social questions of their moment, and engaging with the aesthetic norms of their own medium, genre, and era. For example, Ernest C. Warde's 1917 silent film of *The Vicar of Wakefield*, produced by the American company Thanhouse, is committed to the construction of a pastoral and pleasant England at a time when that idyll was threatened by an industrial war to which America had just committed; its use of direct quotations from Oliver Goldsmith's 1766 novel on its caption cards indicates that it places a premium on fidelity. This is not to say that the film is to be judged by that standard alone: it of course makes use of affordances germane to film, not literature, including music, acting styles, and mise-en-scène. The point to be made here is that viewers' horizons of expectation and the filmmakers' aims determine the nature of its intertextual relation to the novel, in this case privileging fidelity.

Patricia Rozema's 1999 film of *Mansfield Park* (1814), by contrast, is an instance of licence being taken with a 'source': in the film, Tom Bertram's illness is a consequence not of his dissolute lifestyle, but of trauma following his experience on his father Sir Thomas's slave plantation in Antigua. Sir Thomas's Caribbean interests are a 'silence' within Austen's 1814 novel brought to critical attention by Edward Said's 'contrapuntal' reading in 1993.[18] Rather than her cheerful questions about Antigua ominously receiving no reply, as in Austen's novel, a horrified Fanny Price discovers Tom's sketches of abused slaves, including William Blake's print 'A Negro Hung Alive by the Ribs to a Gallows'. This is a significant moment, not just because it marks a newly politicized take on Austen in adaptation, moving away from the more submerged politics of nostalgia embodied in heritage films, but also because an iconic anti-slavery image is conscripted in a rather complex manner. To some degree, Jane Austen (Rozema's Fanny *is* a figuration of the young Austen, a budding writer whose efforts include Austen's own 'History of England') is situated in the abolitionist movement more obviously represented by her contemporary Blake. But if the viewer recognizes the image as actual, Tom's sketches may or may not be taken as derived from his experience: wrenching the book from Fanny, Sir Thomas announces that Tom is mad. It is a moment that exemplifies Mayer's insistence, following Harold Bloom, that adaptations can take the form of 'creative correction' and even wilfully misconstrue a precursor, and it illustrates the emphasis Mayer and others place on context-bound audiences as complicit in the construction of meaning.

An instance of such creative re-reading and response comes in *The Fan. A Heroi-Comical Poem* (1749), which describes a misplaced fan depicting affecting scenes from *Tom Jones*. The pretence is that the 'fair Lydia' has lost this 'favourite Fan', which is particularly regrettable because she is a devotee of the recently published novel: 'She lov'd the Toy, because she lov'd the Tale.' *The Fan* is an ekphrastic poem, '*In Imitation of* ACHILLES*'s Shield, so nobly describ'd by* HOMER', so follows the spirit of Fielding's mock-epic style. These stanzas take us from the fan's graphic rendering of Tom's banishment to an early escapade on the road:

> The painter next a mournful Tale had wrought,
> Where colours labour'd with expressive thought.
> An awful foe to vice *Allworthy* stands;
> *Jones* pale and trembling hears his fixt commands,
> Acquits his judge, himself accuses most,
> Grieves at his fate, but more *Sophia* lost.

> The robber suppliant next demands his life,
> And pleads a starving family and wife;
> *Jones* melts at this, you'd see his pity rise,
> His purse he gives him, and his wants supplies.
> A pale-fac'd comic figure lies hard by,
> And *Partridge* trembling dies, or seems to die.[19]

The Fan, suitably for the subject of Fielding's novel, moves at will between heroic and mock-heroic and sentimental and comic modes. It suggests that what was worth dwelling on in a favourite novel were the 'highlights', and it indulges as well as derides the poem's other 'fan', Lydia. Describing imaginary illustrations, it is certainly no straightforward poetic rendering of Fielding's novel. Indeed, relatively few prose fictions were versified in the eighteenth century, though *Don Quixote* (1605–15) was 'Merrily Translated into Hudibrastick Verse' by Ned Ward in 1711, George Bennet's aborted serial *Pamela Versified* (1741) aimed for a time to capitalize on Richardson's success, and Pushkin's 'The Wanderer' ('Strannik', 1835) is a versification of the opening of John Bunyan's *The Pilgrim's Progress* (1678), the entirety of which Francis Hoffman had 'done into VERSE' in 1706.[20] William Cowper's 'Verses' in the voice of Alexander Selkirk is in conversation with *Robinson Crusoe*, and thus an example of poetry supposedly written by a character from a novel, a mode illustrated more purely by Gulliveriana like 'The Lamentation of Glumdalclitch for the Loss of Grildrig' and 'Mary Gulliver to Capt. Lemuel Gulliver; An Epistle' (both 1727).[21] Recent critics have emphasized that poetry and the novel developed in conjunction, a move away from theories of the rise of the novel that propound generic displacement. Novels incorporated poetry, both within their plots and as paratexts (mottos, for example), and the formal developments of poetry and prose fiction informed one another throughout the period.[22] But poetry also furnished novels with afterlives.

The Fan reminds us that reworkings of eighteenth-century novels extend to visual media. Novels of this period were rarely illustrated in as full a sense as those of Dickens and Thackeray in the next century, but case studies of later illustrations of *Robinson Crusoe* and *Gulliver's Travels*, as well as the novels of Smollett and Sterne, have contributed to our understanding of this aspect of their reception and imaginative re-creation.[23] Illustration and painting are arts whose interrelations with the novel require more attention. Lynn Shepherd argues that Richardson, after negotiating the illustrations by Joseph Highmore to the sixth edition of *Pamela* in 1742, developed an interest in portraiture that influenced not only his own representational practices in *Clarissa* and *Sir Charles Grandison* but also continued to inform the novel at least until Austen.[24] And eighteenth-century novels have inspired fine art: nineteenth-century paintings of *The Vicar of Wakefield* such as Marcus Stone's *Olivia* (1880), derived from the 1878 stage version, provide one example. *Clarissa* furnished a subject for Theodor von Holst's *Clarissa Harlowe in the Prison Room of the Sheriff's Office* (1833–37, the cover image of this book) and Louis Edouard Dubufe's *Lovelace Abducting Clarissa Harlowe* (1867).

So whereas we have long known that the novel did not develop in isolation from other forms of writing, recent research has considered ways in which it took shape in conjunction with visual and performative arts too. The theatre is an important instance of this intergeneric development. Focusing on Haywood, Burney, Inchbald, and Edgeworth, Emily Hodgson Anderson notes that these writers 'were especially devoted to both literary forms [novel and drama], and they often repositioned elements – characters, plots – from one genre into another: they often recast characters from their plays into their novels, rewrite their plays as novels, or (in the case of Inchbald) rewrite their novels as plays'.[25] Novels of the eighteenth century were promptly adapted for the stage, *Pamela* being a well-documented example.[26] *Tom Jones* also became a play and was more loosely used by dramatists, such as George Colman the Younger in *The Jealous Wife* (1761). Haywood's *The History of Miss Betsy Thoughtless* (1751) was recast by Robert Hitchcock as *The Coquette; or, Mistakes of the Heart* (1777). Gothic fiction proved especially irresistible to playwrights. Among the adaptations of Walpole's *The Castle of Otranto* (1765), Robert Jephson's *The Count of Narbonne* (1781) is the most noteworthy. James Boaden's *Aurelio and Miranda* (1798) adapted Matthew Lewis's *The Monk* (1796). Ann Radcliffe's novels inspired numerous plays: in the 1790s, opera- and theatre-goers could have seen Boaden's *Fontainville Forest* (1794) based on *The Romance of the Forest* (1791), Henry Siddons's *The Sicilian Romance; or, the Apparition of the Cliffs* (1794) based on *A Sicilian Romance* (1790), Miles Peter Andrews's opera *The Mysteries of the Castle* (1795) based on *The Mysteries of Udolpho* (1794), and Boaden's *The Italian Monk* (1797) based on *The Italian* (1797).[27] Late eighteenth- and early nineteenth-century fiction in general furnished material for new plays, which Philip Cox connects with the profusion of novels and their countervailing tendency to bear only one reading while inciting audiences' desires for more: staged versions prolonged readers' pleasure when novels started to permeate culture to the extent that people moved promptly to the next novel after finishing the last.[28] And operas based on eighteenth-century novels, starting in earnest with operas based on *Pamela* like Piccini's *opera buffa*, *La buona figliuola* (1760), continued with such nineteenth-century instances as Offenbach's *opera comique* of *Robinson Crusoé* (1867). *Ivanhoe* was one of the most adapted novels in the nineteenth century: in his catalogue of dramatizations of Scott's work, Richard Ford lists an astonishing thirty-seven stage plays, musicals, and burlesques based on the novel between 1820 and 1913.[29] The ascendancy of the novel may be gauged by its saturation of other genres.

In a recent study, Ann Rigney 'explains how Scott's *oeuvre* became such an all-pervasive point of reference, and how it ceased to be one'. Rigney defines the period from 1814 (when *Waverley* was first published) to 1932 (the centenary of the author's death) as 'the Scott century', when he was a ubiquitous cultural presence. But the decline of Scott's status since then, according to Rigney, indicates the 'transience of his canonicity'.[30] Attention to their afterlives, then, can enrich our understanding of authors' fluctuating cultural significances. Only a small number of fictions from the long eighteenth century have attained the status of cultural myth that guards them (for now) against obsolescence or neglect – stories of castaways, of miniature people, and of over-reaching scientists evoke *Crusoe*, *Gulliver*, and *Frankenstein* largely without being tethered to the originals. *The Mysteries of Udolpho* does not enjoy the popularity it once did, but it endured as an intertextual presence, invoked not just opportunistically in T. J. Horsley Curties's *The Monk of Udolpho* (1807) and knowingly in Austen's *Northanger Abbey* (1818), but as a convenient shorthand for a type of fiction (and heroine) as late as Henry James's *The Turn of the Screw* (1898). In popular culture Jane Austen's star is presently in the ascendancy among the period's novelists, and the screen adaptations, modern continuations, fan cultures, new media presence, and commercial power of her novels have attracted much scholarly attention.[31] Re-imagining Austen's corpus is big business and perhaps socially urgent.

What Anne Humphreys terms 'afterings' – modern reworkings, writing back, and 'novels about novels' – represent an important part of the eighteenth-century novel's modern reincarnation.[32] Upton Sinclair's *Another Pamela, Or, Virtue Still Unrewarded* (1950) and Carlos Fuentes's Shandean *Christopher Unborn* (*Cristóbal Nonato*, 1987) are important examples fuelled by particular social agendas.[33] But 'afterings' are far from new. *Robinson Crusoe* was copied, imitated, abridged, and rewritten almost from the moment it first appeared, giving rise to an entire sub-genre called 'the Robinsonade', which includes Johan David Wyss's Romantic education-in-nature *The Swiss Family Robinson* (1812), Victorian children's fiction like R. M. Ballantyne's *The Dog Crusoe* (1860), and postmodern critiques like J. M. Coetzee's *Foe* (1986). Whereas *Crusoe*'s 'afterings' have burned long and slow, Richardson's *Pamela* inspired dozens of almost-immediate parodies and mimicries in verse, prose, and theatre, all of which were embedded in an insistent material culture. Following William B. Warner, recent scholars have viewed *Pamela* as a 'media event'.[34] Not only does this allow us to understand the extent of the novel's reach, it also frees up one of the most inventive works of fiction produced in its wake – Fielding's *Shamela* (1741) – to be read not merely as a parody, or even a plagiarism, of *Pamela* in isolation. As Thomas Keymer and Peter Sabor have outlined, '*Pamela* inspired a swarm of uninvited appropriations, a Grubstreet grabfest in which a hungry succession of entrepreneurial opportunists and freeloading hacks – "these Poachers in Literature," a book-trade colleague of Richardson called them – moved in for a slice of the action.'[35] Clara Reeve declared that 'the word *Novel* in all languages signifies something new',[36] but an awareness of the way in which novels drew on their predecessors unsettles this definition. Reeve in *The Old English Baron* (1778) declared: 'This Story is the literary offspring of the Castle of Otranto', employing a metaphor of filiation rather than of purloining or devouring.[37] Some novels respond playfully to other novels, but some are outright antagonistic. William Godwin, for one, satirized what he perceived to be the decadence of sensibility by rewriting Henry Mackenzie's *The Man of Feeling* (1771) as *Fleetwood: or, The New Man of Feeling* (1805).

The language of theft ('poachers') employed in the wake of *Pamela*'s widespread appropriation reminds us that many authors in the eighteenth century were thinking in increasingly proprietary terms, looking to protect their commercial interests and their artistic right to control the shape of their text. And yet the realities of copyright law and actual practice meant that 'derivative' or imitative writing was as valuable (in every sense) as 'original' work. Romanticism linked the value of art to originality, but novels have always responded to and cannibalized other works of fiction. Before he wrote *Robinson Crusoe*, Defoe added a *Continuation* (1718) to Giovanni Paolo Marana's *Letters Writ by a Turkish Spy* (1684–97). Some of the women who read *Clarissa* in manuscript as it was composed wrote their own endings.[38] *A Sentimental Journey*, itself a spin-off from *Tristram Shandy*, attracted numerous sequels after Sterne's death.[39] Daniel Defoe, Jane Barker, Samuel Richardson, and Sarah Fielding were among those who wrote sequels to their own novels. Betty Schellenberg contends that sequels in this period are 'part of a culture of progressive textual production'. For Schellenberg, this comfort with proliferation and accretion points to a tradition in formation, in much the same way that novels insistently anchor themselves with reference to forebears or models – Burney's invocation in *Evelina* of precedents including Fielding, Richardson, and Smollett; Sterne's nods to Cervantes and Rabelais; and Reeve's debt to Walpole.[40] Gérard Genette helpfully distinguishes between a 'continuation' and a 'sequel' on the basis that the former is premeditated and necessary to bring a work to a close, whereas the latter re-opens a work already once closed. Austen's unfinished novels, *The Watsons* (abandoned in 1805) and *Sanditon* (unfinished at Austen's death in 1817), were extended first by her family in the nineteenth and early twentieth centuries and thereafter by numerous others, qualifying them as continuations, whereas the plethora of sequels, prequels, and spin-offs to Austen's completed novels work the other way, aiming to prolong pleasures even at the risk of marring a satisfying closure and subjecting pristine economical prose to disposable verbosity.[41] Austen's continuers often inadvertently deflate the qualities of her novels, but this can be done deliberately too: Thackeray's *Rebecca and Rowena* (1850) is a parodic continuation of *Ivanhoe* that humorously drags romance down to the quotidian and domestic and restores 'poetic justice' by killing off Rowena and marrying Ivanhoe to Rebecca.

An aspect of literary afterlives often separated rather sharply from studies that focus on adaptation and appropriation is textual history. But a full understanding of the afterlives of eighteenth-century fiction should take stock of the processes of editing, censorship, abridgement, and republication in new forms, formats, and venues by which novels have reached readers. Defoe in the nineteenth century was often read in altered versions; *Memoirs of a Woman of Pleasure* was not legally available in many countries for much of its existence; and readers encounter eighteenth-century novels in specific publishing contexts, like newspapers, magazines, and series. In an important critical treatment of the anthology genre, in which exemplary excerpts from novels were collected, largely divested of their narrative context, Leah Price contends that 'the novel could not have become respectable without the tokenism embodied in the anthology'.[42] More focused studies have been conducted, such as Catherine Parisian's publishing history of Burney's *Cecilia* (1782), which considers in close detail its editing, abridgement, serialization, illustration, incorporation into an established series, and translation in the 230 years since its publication.[43]

Such scholarship is vital for a more complete understanding of the afterlives of fiction. Translation in the eighteenth century, for instance, was as creative an activity as adaptation. As Mary Helen McMurran puts it: 'Novels did not simply move from the source to target language, and one nation to another, but dangled between cultures and languages.' So novels reached more people via translations, but the versions produced were not as bound by 'fidelity' as were later conceptions of translation; amplification and addition were common, with the 'original' treated as a source more than an authoritative text to be replicated.[44] Desfontaines excised parts he found objectionable from *Gulliver's Travels*; Prévost reduced and augmented Richardson's novels; and as late as 1815, Isabella de Montolieu's *traduction libre* of *Sense and Sensibility* drastically altered the ending, having Marianne choose Brandon over Willoughby and redeeming the latter by marrying him to Eliza, Brandon's ward, legitimating their child. Eighteenth-century British and Irish fictions have been reprinted globally and translated into many languages, generating responses and commentary outside of their home countries.[45] Adapters of all kinds have kept familiar stories and characters alive ever since they appeared in the expansive print culture of the long eighteenth century. The period bookended by Defoe and Austen witnessed a particularly high outbreak of pirating, plagiarism, parodies, pastiches, official and unofficial prequels and sequels, engraftments, abridgements, anthologies, keys, and the like, whereas remediations starting in the period extend to the present day. The kind of materials considered in the following chapters is varied, but the contributors share the conviction that where a text goes and by whom it is received matters as much as whence it originated.

Notes

1 Linda Hutcheon with Siobhan O'Flynn, *A Theory of Adaptation*, 2nd edn (London and New York: Routledge, 2013), p. 176.
2 Terence Cave, *Mignon's Afterlives: Crossing Cultures from Goethe to the Twenty-First Century* (Oxford University Press, 2011), p. 36.
3 Brian McFarlane, *Novel to Film: An Introduction to the Theory of Adaptation* (Oxford: Clarendon Press, 1996); *Adaptation: From Text to Screen, Screen to Text*, eds. Deborah Cartmell and Imelda Whelehan (London: Routledge, 1999).
4 Jørgen Bruhn, Anne Gjelsvik, and Eirik Frisvold Hanssen, '"There and Back Again": New Challenges and New Directions in Adaptation Studies', in *Adaptation Studies: New Challenges, New Directions*, eds. Jørgen Bruhn et al. (London: Bloomsbury, 2013), pp. 1–16 (9).
5 Hutcheon and O'Flynn, *Adaptation*, p. 170.
6 *Pre-Histories and Afterlives: Studies in Critical Method for Terence Cave*, eds. Anna Holland and Richard Scholar (London: Legenda, 2009), p. 5.

7 Character is an important example: see David A. Brewer, *The Afterlife of Character, 1726–1825* (Philadelphia: University of Pennsylvania Press, 2005).

8 Sarah Raff, 'Ghosts of the Guardian in *Sir Charles Grandison* and *Bleak House*', in *The Afterlives of Eighteenth-Century Fiction*, eds. Daniel Cook and Nicholas Seager (Cambridge University Press, 2015), pp. 91–110 (91).

9 For an account of video games that follow the self-reflexive style inherited from eighteenth-century fiction, especially of the 1750s and 1760s, see Christina Lupton and Peter McDonald, 'Reflexivity as Entertainment: Early Novels and Recent Video Games', *Mosaic: A Journal for the Interdisciplinary Study of Literature*, 43:4 (2010), 157–73.

10 Thomas Southerne, *Oroonoko: A Tragedy* (London: H. Playford, B. Tooke, and S. Buckley, 1696), sig. A2^v.

11 Clara Reeve, *The Progress of Romance*, 2 vols. ([Colchester]: W. Keymer, 1785), vol. 1, p. 118.

12 Jane Spencer, *Aphra Behn's Afterlife* (Oxford University Press, 2001), p. 225.

13 Erica Jong, *Fanny* (London: Granada, 1980), pp. 492, 3, 173–74, 21.

14 Ariane Hudelet, 'Austen and Sterne: Beyond Heritage', in *A Companion to Literature, Film, and Adaptation*, ed. Deborah Cartmell (Oxford: Blackwell, 2012), pp. 256–71.

15 Warren Oakley, *A Culture of Mimicry: Laurence Sterne, His Readers and the Art of Bodysnatching* (London: MHRA, 2010); M–C. Newbould, *Adaptations of Laurence Sterne's Fiction: Sterneana, 1760–1840* (Farnham: Ashgate, 2013).

16 Laurence Sterne, *The Life and Opinions of Tristram Shandy, Gentleman* (1759–67), eds. Melvyn New and Joan New (London: Penguin, 1997), p. 388.

17 Robert Mayer, 'Introduction: Is there a Text in the Screening Room?', in *Eighteenth-Century Fiction on Screen*, ed. Robert Mayer (Cambridge University Press, 2002), pp. 1–15.

18 Edward Said, *Culture and Imperialism* (New York: Knopf, 1993), pp. 80–97.

19 *The Fan. A Heroi-Comical Poem, in Three Cantos* (Norwich: James Carlos, 1749), pp. 6, 8.

20 Edward Ward, *The Life and Notable Adventures of that Renown'd Knight, Don Quixote de la Mancha* (London: T. Norris et al., 1711); [Francis Hoffman], *The Pilgrim's Progress . . . now done into VERSE* (London: R. Tookey, 1706).

21 Jonathan Swift, *Gulliver's Travels* (1726), ed. David Womersley, The Cambridge Edition of the Works of Jonathan Swift (Cambridge University Press, 2012), pp. 576–78, 582–86.

22 G. Gabrielle Starr, *Lyric Generations: Poetry and the Novel in the Long Eighteenth Century* (Baltimore: Johns Hopkins University Press, 2004); *Eighteenth-Century Poetry and the Rise of the Novel Reconsidered*, eds. Kate Parker and Courtney Weiss Smith (Lewisburg: Bucknell University Press, 2014).

23 David Blewett, *The Illustration of 'Robinson Crusoe', 1719–1920* (Gerrards Cross: Smythe, 1995); Robert Halsband, 'Eighteenth-Century Illustrations of *Gulliver's Travels*', in *Proceedings of the First Münster Symposium on Jonathan Swift*, eds. Hermann J. Real and Heinz J. Vienken (Munich: Wilhelm Fink, 1985), pp. 83–112; Julian Fung, 'Eighteenth-Century Illustrations of the Novels

of Tobias Smollett', *Eighteenth-Century Life*, 38:1 (2014), 18–62; W. B. Gerard, *Laurence Sterne and the Visual Imagination* (Farnham: Ashgate, 2006). For a database containing entries for over 1,500 illustrations of Scott's novels, see http://illustratingscott.lib.ed.ac.uk/ (accessed 10 September 2014).

24 Lynn Shepherd, *Clarissa's Painter: Portraiture, Illustration, and Representation in the Novels of Samuel Richardson* (Oxford University Press, 2009).

25 Emily Hodgson Anderson, *Eighteenth-Century Authorship and the Play of Fiction* (London: Routledge, 2009), p. 2.

26 *The Pamela Controversy: Criticisms and Adaptations of Samuel Richardson's 'Pamela', 1740–1750*, eds. Thomas Keymer and Peter Sabor, 6 vols. (London: Pickering and Chatto, 2000), vol. 6.

27 Radcliffe adaptations continued into the nineteenth century: Bertrand Evans, *Gothic Drama from Walpole to Shelley* (Berkeley: University of California Press, 1947), pp. 90–115; Diego Saglia, '"A Portion of the Name": Stage Adaptations of Radcliffe's Fiction, 1794–1806', in *Ann Radcliffe, Romanticism, and the Gothic*, eds. Dale Townshend and Angela Wright (Cambridge University Press, 2014), pp. 219–36.

28 Philip Cox, *Reading Adaptations: Novels and Verse Narratives on the Stage, 1790–1840* (Manchester University Press, 2000), pp. 2–3.

29 Richard Ford, *Dramatisations of Scott's Novels: A Catalogue* (Oxford Bibliographical Society, 1979).

30 Ann Rigney, *The Afterlives of Walter Scott: Memory on the Move* (Oxford University Press, 2012), pp. 2–4.

31 Among recent books, see *Janeites: Austen's Disciples and Devotees*, ed. Deidre Lynch (Princeton University Press, 2000); *Jane Austen & Co.: Remaking the Past in Contemporary Culture*, eds. Suzanne R. Pucci and James Thompson (Albany: State University of New York Press, 2002); Sue Parrill, *Jane Austen on Film and Television* (Jefferson: McFarland and Co., 2002); *Uses of Austen: Jane's Afterlives*, eds. Gillian Dow and Clare Hanson (Basingstoke: Palgrave Macmillan, 2012); Kylie Mirmohamadi, *The Digital Afterlives of Jane Austen* (Basingstoke: Palgrave Macmillan, 2014).

32 Anne Humphreys, 'The Afterlife of the Victorian Novel: Novels about Novels', in *A Companion to the Victorian Novel*, eds. Patrick Brantlinger and William B. Thesing (Oxford: Blackwell, 2002), pp. 442–57.

33 Elizabeth Kraft, 'Writers that Changed the World: Samuel Richardson, Upton Sinclair, and the Strategies of Social Reform' and Michael Hardin, 'Nativity and Nationhood: Laurence Sterne's *Tristram Shandy* and Carlos Fuentes's *Christopher Unborn* as Critiques of Empire', in *On Second Thought: Updating the Eighteenth-Century Text*, eds. Debra Taylor Bourdeau and Elizabeth Kraft (Newark: University of Delaware Press, 2007), pp. 141–57, 174–92.

34 William B. Warner, *Licensing Entertainment: The Elevation of Novel Reading in Britain, 1684–1750* (Berkeley: University of California Press, 1998), p. 177.

35 Thomas Keymer and Peter Sabor, *'Pamela' in the Marketplace: Literary Controversy and Print Culture in Eighteenth-Century Britain and Ireland* (Cambridge University Press, 2005), p. 2.

36 Reeve, *Progress of Romance*, vol. i, p. 110.

37 Clara Reeve, *The Old English Baron: A Gothic Story* (London: Edward and Charles Dilly, 1778), sig. A2^r.

38 Ruth Perry, 'Clarissa's Daughters; Or, the History of Innocence Betrayed. How Women Writers Rewrote Richardson', in *Clarissa and Her Readers: New Essays for the Clarissa Project*, eds. Carol Houlihan Flynn and Edward Copeland (New York: AMS Press, 1999), pp. 119–41.

39 W. B. Gerard, '"Betwixt One Passion and Another": Continuations of Laurence Sterne's *A Sentimental Journey*, 1769–1820', in *On Second Thought*, pp. 123–40.

40 Betty A. Schellenberg, '"The Measured Lines of the Copyist": Sequels, Reviews, and the Discourse of Authorship in England, 1749–1800', in *On Second Thought*, pp. 25–42. See also Schellenberg, '"To Renew Their Former Acquaintance": Print, Gender, and Some Eighteenth-Century Sequels', in *Part Two: Reflections on the Sequel*, eds. Paul Budra and Betty A. Schellenberg (University of Toronto Press, 1998), pp. 85–101.

41 Deidre Lynch, 'Sequels', in *Jane Austen in Context*, ed. Janet Todd (Cambridge University Press, 2005), pp. 160–68; www.pemberley.com/sequels/sequels_02. html (accessed 10 September 2014).

42 Leah Price, *The Anthology and the Rise of the Novel: From Richardson to George Eliot* (Cambridge University Press, 2000), p. 7.

43 Catherine M. Parisian, *Frances Burney's 'Cecilia': A Publishing History* (Farnham: Ashgate, 2012).

44 Mary Helen McMurran, *The Spread of Novels: Translation and Prose Fiction in the Eighteenth Century* (Princeton University Press, 2010), p. 2.

45 See *The Reception of Laurence Sterne in Europe*, eds. Peter de Voogd and John Neubauer (London: Thoemmes, 2004); *The Reception of Jonathan Swift in Europe*, ed. Hermann J. Real (London: Thoemmes, 2005); *The Reception of Sir Walter Scott in Europe*, ed. Murray Pittock (London: Thoemmes, 2006); *The Reception of Jane Austen in Europe*, eds. Anthony Mandal and Brian Southam (London: Thoemmes, 2007).

CHAPTER I

On Authorship, Appropriation, and Eighteenth-Century Fiction

Daniel Cook

The long eighteenth century abounded in appropriative texts. Giles Jacob's *The Rape of the Smock* (1717) smuggles Pope's *The Rape of the Lock* (1712, revised 1714) into bawdier territory. Attributed jointly to Colley Cibber and the late Sir John Vanbrugh, *The Provok'd Husband; or, A Journey to London* (1728) absorbs the latter's unfinished play *A Journey to London* while simultaneously speaking back to an older work, Vanbrugh's *The Provok'd Wife, a Comedy* (1697). Frances Burney's *Evelina* (1778) recasts significant aspects of *Caroline Evelyn* (1767), an early work burned by the author at the age of fifteen. Adaptations freely crossed the boundaries of media and genre. So-called Lilliputian verses colonized small corners of the periodical press soon after the appearance of *Gulliver's Travels* in 1726. Within a year of its publication in 1740, *Pamela* begat *Shamela*, *Anti-Pamela*, *The True Anti-Pamela*, and *Pamela Versified*. Not long after the arrival on stage and in print of Henry Giffard's theatrical adaptation of *Pamela* – *Pamela. A Comedy* (1741) – Joseph Dorman repurposed it as *Pamela; or, Virtue Rewarded. An Opera* (1742). Many British and Irish novels outwardly followed 'in the manner of' popular models, most conspicuously *Don Quixote* (1605–15), as in Henry Fielding's *Joseph Andrews* (1742) and Charlotte Lennox's *The Female Quixote* (1752).[1] The fictional archive, to adopt David A. Brewer's term, lay prone to – yet encouraged – plunder by named and unnamed assailants alike.[2]

Anonymity, as Robert J. Griffin reminds us, 'was at least as much a norm as signed authorship' in the eighteenth century.[3] The sheer volume of novels that were published without reference to the legal name of the writer certainly bears out this claim. However, a narrowed focus on the legality of authorship obscures and even demonizes the ongoing pseudonymous gamesmanship at play in the period. Pseudonymity was just as common as unsigned authorship, especially if we factor in the proprietary branding of important works such as 'By the Author of the NEW ATALANTIS' (in *The Court Legacy*, a misattribution to Delarivier

Manley) or even 'By the Editor of PAMELA and CLARISSA' (in *Sir Charles Grandison*). Even if Eliza Haywood's legal name appears nowhere in *The History of Jemmy and Jenny Jessamy* (1753), the phrase 'By the AUTHOR of the HISTORY of *Betsy Thoughtless*' (itself published anonymously in 1751) establishes an incorrigible link between the novels and gives the prospective reader some hints up front about its style. To be sure, many appropriators, including unauthorized continuers, hid behind established pseudonyms or allonyms, but, in doing so, they thereby participated in the generic masking established by Defoe, Swift, Richardson, and others, as well as the anonymity favoured by Haywood, Burney, and scores of other authors in the period. Novelists habitually gesture towards possible insertions, extensions, and spin-offs, even as they close their stories.[4] At the end of *Love in Excess* (1719–20), Haywood leaves Count D'Elmont and Melliora, and Frankville and Camilla, 'still living' – in the present tense – 'blest with a numerous and hopeful issue'.[5] In a posthumously published last work of fiction, *Conclusion of the Memoirs of Miss Sidney Bidulph* (1767), Frances Sheridan belatedly returns to, and completes, her popular sentimental novel, *Memoirs of Miss Sidney Bidulph* (1761). Set eight years after the original work, the continuation largely follows the schemes of Sophy and Edward Audley, who are intent on tricking Sidney's daughter into marriage with Edward.

Even when their literary domains were openly challenged, some writers seemed to concede that misattribution and misappropriation were endemic to pseudonymous writing. Swift added a prefatory letter to the 1735 Faulkner edition of *Gulliver's Travels* written in the guise of the wearied eponymous hero addressing his cousin: 'you are loading our Carrier every Week with Libels, and Keys, and Reflections, and Memoirs, and Second Parts'.[6] 'I find likewise', continues Gulliver, 'that the Writers of those Bundles are not agreed among themselves; for some of them will not allow me to be Author of mine own Travels; and others make me Author of Books to which I am wholly a Stranger'. Richardson turns *Pamela* into *Clarissa* (1747–48), perhaps in tacit acknowledgement that the former has been wrested from his control by opportunistic adapters and continuers. *The Life of Pamela* (1741) brazenly rebooted, in third-person narrative, Richardson's original and (in later instalments) John Kelly's unofficial continuation, *Pamela's Conduct in High Life* (1741), by rectifying 'a thousand more Mistakes that have been made in that Work'.[7] In *Shamela*, one of the most stinging of the *Pamela* reworkings, Fielding's Parson Tickletext (himself a borrowing from Aphra Behn's *The Feign'd Curtizans* [1679]) hints at a further continuation with vivid plot details:

'*P.S.* Since I writ, I have a certain Account, that Mr. *Booby* hath caught his Wife in bed with *Williams*; hath turned her off, and is prosecuting him in the spiritual Court.'[8]

A reappraisal of the often dubious, often ingenious ways in which authors and adapters extended the fictional archive reminds us that the period used different types of collaborative writing, including co-labour (Jane Collier and Sarah Fielding's *The Cry* [1754]), interpolation (Sarah Fielding's ghostwritten letter from Leonora to Horatio in *Joseph Andrews*), correction (Henry Fielding's intrusive alterations to Sarah Fielding's *David Simple* [1744]), counterfeiting (Francis Noble's substantial engraftments on and deletions to Defoe's *Roxana* [1724]), or mimicry (Seth Grahame-Smith and Jane Austen's nominal co-authorship of *Pride and Prejudice and Zombies* [2009], to use a recent example).[9] By re-orientating the mechanics of writing around the persistent strategies of adapters, continuers, editors, and other types of secondary authors, I hope to illuminate the conflicted contribution of eighteenth-century fiction to a modern treatment of adaptation as 'repetition, but repetition without replication', as defined by Linda Hutcheon.[10] Parodists and pasticheurs alike relocated the fluid text in a range of new formats and fora, often in response to other responses, 'enriching rather than "robbing" them', as Julie Sanders says.[11] My approach to secondary authorship dissents from Mark Rose's influential account of the professionalization of authorship. 'The distinguishing characteristic of the modern author', for Rose, 'is proprietorship; the author is conceived as the originator and therefore the owner of a special kind of commodity, the work'.[12] When considered in the purview of the novelists' inheritance of appropriative techniques from the theatre, such as mimicry and vamping, as well as counterfeiting and other common publishing practices, we can see that the widespread resistance to closure in major and minor works of fiction unsettles any serious claims to absolute ownership.

Particularly useful for my purposes is Simon Stern's historically grounded distinction between the economy of scarcity and the economy of abundance. In the former category, writers act as though their works were under threat. By contrast, in the latter, 'plots, characters, and techniques circulate freely without any threat of depletion'. 'This view of the literary economy', he continues, 'may be discerned in the etymology of "copy", from *copia*, "transcript, duplicate" (an extension of the word's root sense, "copiousness, plenty"); analogously, "author" derives from *augere*, "augment, increase". Here the author is a principle of multiplication, not merely recycling the resources in the literary commons but expanding their range.'[13] Whereas Fielding might be placed in the economy of abundance, after a fashion, Richardson is the major exemplar of the economy of scarcity in the period. Richardson preferred his readers to be 'authorially governed' (in Thomas Keymer's phrase), but this model simply could not survive amid the appropriating habits of an expansive readership.[14] Novels, as J. Paul Hunter puts it so well, are 'additive, digressive, lumpy, and resistant to closure'.[15] Mimics, counterfeiters, continuers, and adapters of all kinds sought purchase in the literary commons.

Proprietary Editors

Authors often moved quickly to produce sequels to saleable works. Near the end of *Robinson Crusoe* (1719) the narrator hurriedly describes a return journey to the new world, even after he has settled safely in England. 'All these things, with some very surprizing Incidents in some new Adventures of my own, for ten Years more', he teases, 'I may perhaps give a farther Account of hereafter'.[16] Defoe duly turned *Robinson Crusoe* into a trilogy within a year when he added *The Farther Adventures of Robinson Crusoe* (1719) and *Serious Reflections During the Life and Surprising Adventures of Robinson Crusoe* (1720). Jane Barker spun *A Patch-Work Screen for the Ladies* (1723) into a continuation, *The Lining of the Patch-Work Screen* (1726), to form what has become known as the Galesia trilogy with her well-known Jacobite novel *Love Intrigues* (1713). Sarah Fielding produced a trilogy of sorts around her 1744 novel *The Adventures of David Simple*, if we include the formally divergent *Familiar Letters between the Principal Characters in David Simple, and Some Others* (1747) along with *Volume the Last* (1753).[17] Popular works were rapidly reworked, even reset. Defoe, we might say, redoes Haywood's *Idalia; or, The Unfortunate Mistress* (1723) within a year of its publication with *The Fortunate Mistress; or, A History of the Life and Vast Variety of Fortunes of Mademoiselle de Beleau, Afterwards Called the Countess de Wintselsheim, in Germany, Being the Person known by the Name of the Lady Roxana, in the Time of King Charles II* (known as *Roxana* after 1742). In *Amelia* (1751), Henry Fielding finally tells the tale of married life and maturity, having glossed over this aspect of Tom and Sophia's story in *Tom Jones* (1749).

Defoe's *Captain Singleton* (1720) and many other notable works were serialized in newspapers and periodicals across the political spectrum almost as soon as they were first published. By embracing the 'opportunistic seriality and shameless repetition' of the critically maligned, seemingly formulaic novel of amorous intrigue in the 1720s, Eliza Haywood thrived in 'an urban print market of diverse buyers ready to pay cash for entertainment', as William B. Warner demonstrates.[18] Laurence Sterne kept pace with, and responded to, novels of the 1760s through his masterful 'improvisatory serialization' (to use Keymer's term) of *Tristram Shandy* (1759–67) over an eight-year period.[19] As Nicholas Seager argues in his essay in the present collection, authors before Dickens increasingly tailored their writing to the narrative opportunities opened up by the interruptive serial format. Tobias Smollett's Quixotic *Sir Launcelot Greaves* (1760–61), for one, seemed ideally suited to *The British Magazine*, the monthly paper in which it first appeared. Compilers of chapbook editions, moreover, cared little about taking liberties with established texts such as *Robinson Crusoe* where it suited their immediate political or commercial purposes.[20] The Statute of Queen Anne, *An Act for the Encouragement of Learning, by Vesting the Copies of Printed Books in the Authors or Purchasers of such Copies, during the Times therein mentioned* (1710), formally recognized in statute law for the first time the importance of proprietary rights in copies. Tellingly, though, in the 1761 case of *Dodsley v. Kinnersley*, Samuel Johnson's publisher unsuccessfully sued the owners of the *Grand Magazine of Magazines* for reprinting *Rasselas* (1759) with the moral reflections excised. A book in its entirety could be protected from piracy – in theory at least – but not from abridgement, alteration, or even parody and pastiche.

Not until the Berne Convention of 1886 would the moral rights of authors be fully acknowledged: 'Independently of the author's economic rights, and even after the transfer of the said rights, the author shall have the right to claim authorship of the work and to object to any distortion, mutilation or other modification' (Article 6bis). In an article in the *Review* (2 February 1710), Defoe freely acknowledges that literary property can be sold – and is therefore not tied to the writing process – but fears that secondary authors could unfairly seize his literary offspring:

> A Book is the Author's Property, 'tis the Child of his Inventions, the Brat of his Brain; if he sells his Property, it then becomes the Right of the Purchaser; if not, 'tis as much his own, as his Wife and Children are his own – But behold in this Christian Nation, these Children of our Heads are seiz'd, captivated, spirited away, and carry'd into Captivity, and there is none to redeem them.[21]

Richardson resorted to using similarly incendiary rhetoric when he heard an unofficial sequel to *Pamela* was due to appear before he had himself concluded the work: his commodity had been 'Ravished out of my Hands, and, probably my Characters depreciated and debased, by those who know nothing of the Story, nor the Delicacy required in the Continuation of the

Piece'.[22] Implicit in Defoe's and Richardson's paternal claims over literary property is an authorial complaint that goes back to at least Martial: plagiarism (from *plagiarius*, 'kidnapper, slave-stealer'). Such claims restrict eighteenth-century print culture to Stern's economy of scarcity:

> On this view, writers are trapped in a zero-sum economy in which an increased demand for one title translates into a corresponding decline for its competitors, however they are defined. This is the economic logic underlying the language of 'literary theft' and 'plagiarism' ... These terms, often applied to various forms of imitation other than verbatim reproduction, treat copying as a form of seizure, an abduction of the author's brainchild. Talk of misappropriation and pilfering suggests that texts are diminished through copying, as if the novelist who 'borrows' a plot has removed something from the book, leaving it incomplete.[23]

Richardson, as a printer and author, felt the sting of the respective crimes of piracy and plagiarism when printers in Dublin issued an unlicensed edition of *Sir Charles Grandison* in 1753.[24] In an impassioned pamphlet, he retaliates with an insular view of authorship: 'Never was Work more the Property of any Man, than *this* is his.'[25] The tetchy attack on fellow bookmen belies an implicit acknowledgement that literary property exists on a spectrum from negligible to absolute ownership, at the latter end of which Richardson (as author, editor, and printer) places his novel. Property rights, to put it another way, had to be forcibly asserted.

Moreover, Richardson's sense of proprietorship recalls John Locke's classic liberal discourse on possessive individualism in *Two Treatises of Government* (1690): 'The *Labour* of his Body, and the *Work* of his Hands, we may say, are properly his.'[26] Locke continues, 'Whatsoever then he removes out of the State that Nature hath provided, and left it in, he hath mixed his *Labour* with, and joyned to it something that is his own, and thereby makes it his *Property*.' Within a Lockean purview proprietary authorship would include the nominal role of editor that Richardson had publicly claimed, but it would deliberately exclude the alteration, serialization, or continuation undertaken by secondary authors and adapters of all kinds. As endorsement of his work, Richardson added a prefatory letter (probably by the Reverend William Webster) addressed 'To my worthy Friend, the Editor of *Pamela*, &c.', in which the contributor asks him to present *Pamela* 'as *Pamela* wrote it; in her own Words, without Amputation, or Addition'.[27] The economy of scarcity treats outsider appropriation such as John Kelly's *Pamela's Conduct in High Life*, which continued Pamela's correspondence beyond where the original volumes ended, as an act of destruction rather than as a legitimate form of creative expansion. An alternative approach to the relationship between authors and property instead links paternity with secondary labour – that is, re-appropriation – in more positive, if cautious terms. As early as 1366, Petrarch pre-empted Linda Hutcheon's repetition-with-a-difference, as the 'proper imitator should take care that what he writes resembles the original without reproducing it', since resemblance is like 'a son to his father'.[28] The Petrarchan distinction between acceptable, necessary imitation and slavish copying runs prominently throughout the seventeenth and eighteenth centuries. Even Edward Young, the populist of a seemingly new investment in the doctrine of originality in 1759, describes the classical form of imitation as a 'noble Contagion'.[29]

In *Tom Jones*, Fielding famously ironizes the discrepancy between ancient allusion and modern copying by sarcastically conflating economic and literary value in terms consonant with the respective economies of Parnassian abundance and Grub Street scarcity. The writings of the 'wealthy Squires' (Ancients) 'may be considered as a rich Common, where every Person who hath the smallest Tenement . . . hath a free Right to fatten his Muse', but if one were to plunder from a living author, the 'Poor of *Parnassus*' (Moderns), it would be 'highly criminal and indecent; for this may be strictly stiled defrauding the Poor'.[30] Secondary authorship that invades the time-worn literary commons has long been considered acceptable, even gentlemanly behaviour, whereas an unacknowledged use of more recent works leaves the appropriator vulnerable to irremediably prejudiced charges of piracy and profiteering. It is in this semantic slippage between imitation and plagiarism that Sterne fell in the second half of the century. As is well known, *Tristram Shandy* absorbed dozens of works of fiction and non-fiction alike, including Robert Burton's *The Anatomy of Melancholy* (1621), a text that shadows volumes five and six in particular.[31] To take a noted example from the beginning of the fifth volume of Sterne's novel, Tristram muses on the futility of scholarly pursuits while watching the London coach being hauled up a hill by the 'main strength' of the horses: 'Tell me, ye learned, shall we for ever be adding so much to the *bulk*—so little to the *stock*?'[32] He continues, 'Shall we for ever make new books, as apothecaries make new mixtures, by pouring only out of one vessel into another? Are we for ever to be twisting, and untwisting the same rope? for ever in the same track—for ever at the same pace?' Wittily, this wearied denunciation of derivative composition closely mimics a famous passage in Burton's *Anatomy*:

> As apothecaries we make new mixtures every day, pour out of one vessel
> into another; and as those old Romans robbed all the cities of the world to

set out their bad-sited Rome, we skim off the cream of other men's wits, pick the choice flowers of their tilled gardens to set out our own sterile plots ... [W]e weave the same web still, twist the same rope again and again.[33]

In the 1790s, years after his death in 1768, Sterne was outed as a plagiarist by John Ferriar. As an admirer of Sterne, Ferriar had been keen to assure his audience in 1791 that 'I do not mean to treat him as a Plagiarist ... If some instances of copying be proved against him, they will detract nothing from his genius'.[34] But by 1798, in an expanded version of his essay, Ferriar had decided that the word 'plagiarism' was indeed an apt description.[35] By the end of the century the marketplace had seemingly come to vilify the art of imitation in which Sterne was a late master. Youngian critics like Ferriar had lost sight of a key influence on Sterne's style: the appropriative practices of seventeenth- and eighteenth-century theatre. As a cleric and writer Sterne was a habitual mimic, after all. He inhabits Hamlet's soliloquies, among other literary commons, and stretches them into a larger pastiche of materials:

> ... or a worse thought in the middle of it than *to be—or not to be,*—the entering upon a new and untried state of things,—or, upon a long, a profound and peaceful sleep, without dreams, without disturbance.[36]

The typographical division between authors was a curious feature of post-Restoration theatre where playwrights faced increasing pressure to acknowledge their sources even as they touted themselves as proprietary authors, as Paulina Kewes convincingly argues.[37] In *The Tragical History of King Richard III* (1700), for example, Colley Cibber draws a clear distinction between his writing and Shakespeare's own. Here he inverts the dynamic between primary and secondary author: 'to satisfie the curious, and unwilling to assume more praise than is really my due, I have caus'd those that are intirely *Shakespear's* to be Printed in this *Italick Character*; and those lines with this mark (') before 'em, are generally his thoughts, in the best dress I could afford 'em'.[38] Cibber and Sterne mark out Shakespeare's material as both extractable from yet intrinsic to their new texts. Collaboration after the fact travesties the bond between authorship and ownership.

Mimicry and Vamping

Like *Tristram Shandy*, Fielding's *The Tragedy of Tragedies; or the Life and Death of Tom Thumb the Great* (1731) – a main piece that began as an

afterpiece – compulsively absorbed numerous texts. (As indicated in
his footnotes, under the mock-pseudonymous guise of H. Scriblerus
Secundus, Fielding plundered in excess of forty tragedies while working
on his play; Sterne cited 208 named authors in his novel). By acknowledging his sources Fielding stays within an expansive economy rather than a
destructive one. But is it a work of mimicry or vamping? Mimics not only
impersonated their material; they also inhabited and therefore moved
beyond it. Boswell, for one, remarked to Johnson that 'it is amazing how
a mimick can not only give you the gestures and voice of a person whom
he represents; but even what a person would say on any particular
subject'.[39] Another theatrical term, vamping, had far less impressive connotations. Vamped texts nevertheless sell well, as we learn in *The Adventures of an Author* (1767): 'though the trade have given it the invidious
appellation of vamping, it is well known, that there never want purchasers
for a saleable commodity'.[40] If mimicry dramatizes imitation, vamping is
a performance-based form of plagiarism. The anonymous author of
The New Modern Story-Teller (1772) uses the common analogy of tailoring
to suggest that vamping entails the artful, partial hiding of seams, just as a
plagiarist would hide his or her sources:

> Impose old cloaths vampt up for new:
> Now in our trade too, Moll, I swear,
> We arts employ to vend our ware;
> Like those whom we presum'd to quote,
> Oft sell for new a vampt up coat.[41]

Fielding toys with similar imagery in *The Author's Farce* (1730, revised
1734), a satirical play in which Marplay junior (a fictionalized version of
Theophilus Cibber, son of Colley Cibber) defends his hackery:

> Was you to see the Plays when they are brought to us, a Parcel of crude,
> undigested Stuff. We are the Persons, Sir, who lick them into Form,
> that mould them into Shape—The Poet make the Play indeed! The
> Colour-man might be as well said to make the Picture, or the Weaver the
> Coat: My Father and I, Sir, are a Couple of poetical Tailors; when a Play is
> brought us, we consider it as a Tailor does his Coat, we cut it, Sir, we cut it:
> And let me tell you, we have the exact Measure of the Town, we know how
> to fit their Taste. (Act I, Scene VI)[42]

The poetical tailors exemplify a demented version of Lockean proprietary
authorship insofar as their labour subsists in the cutting and altering of
other people's pre-fabricated materials. Not merely do they rely on the
freely accessible literary commons, they work over the primary authorship

of others. If mimicry extends the fictional archive, vamping tampers with it. We can trace the parody-in-progress in *The Tragedy of Tragedies*, as Maurice Johnson puts it, in such lines as 'your Eyes, | That, like two open Windows, us'd to shew | The lovely Beauty of the Rooms within, | Have now two Blinds before them' (Act II, Scene IV).[43] These lines, we see on the printed page, deflate Nathaniel Lee's pompous phrasing (as given in the footnote), 'Dost thou not view Joy peeping from my Eyes, | The Casements open'd wide to gaze on thee[?]' But formally speaking it is an unusual kind of parody-through-vamping as Fielding's noticeably flabbier lines stretch and thereby mock the pretensions of his rival, rather than flatter him (directly or otherwise) through mimicry.

Like *Tristram Shandy* and *The Tragedy of Tragedies*, *Shamela* – or *An Apology for the Life of Mrs. Shamela Andrews* – creatively vamps a range of texts, most immediately *Pamela* and *Pamela in Her Exalted Condition*, the autobiography of Fielding's theatrical rival, *An Apology for the Life of Mr. Colley Cibber, Comedian*, Conyers Middleton's *Life of Cicero* (both 1740), and even fan letters included by Richardson in later editions of *Pamela*.[44] Fielding extensively tailors the original material of his notional hypotext, *Pamela*, in what Thomas Lockwood calls a 'contemptuous abbreviation' of Richardson's primary authorship.[45] Read within the context of vamping, we can more readily appreciate Fielding's bold use of a cut-and-pasting technique in order to excavate the hypocrisy buried amid Richardson's own words. In Letter VI of *Shamela*, Mr Booby's gratuitous, pointed invective – 'Hussy, Slut, Saucebox, Boldface' – consists entirely of words used by his counterpart, Mr B., throughout *Pamela*: 'What a foolish Hussy you are …' (Letter XI), 'I believe this Slut has the Power of Witchcraft …' (Letter XXII), 'by such a Sawcebox as you …', 'Very well, Boldface …' (both Letter XV). In Letter VI, Mr Booby mock-bashfully sexualizes the girl's body ('I know not whether you are a Man or a Woman, unless by your swelling Breasts'), an erotic reworking of Mr B.'s contradictory claim that 'I know not, I declare (beyond this lovely Bosom), your Sex' at the point at which he confesses to harbouring 'the worst Designs' on her (Letter XXXII). We might characterize *Shamela* as a sort of insincere mimicry of *Pamela* if we allow that it impersonates and then extends beyond the original novel. Shamela herself is an actress who fakes the role of a virtuous woman ('I counterfeit a swoon'), an on-stage recasting of Cibber's nonchalant exposure of the 'strings, wires, and clock-work' behind the scenes of the theatrical stage in his *Apology*. Syrena, too, 'counterfeited Faintings' in the face of her would-be seducer Mr L. in Haywood's *Anti-Pamela* (1741) so as to 'raise her market value', as Peter

Sabor suggests.[46] Haywood and Fielding alike invade the sentimental novel in order to challenge its implicit, specious countering of amatory fiction.

If Boswellian mimicry displaces the original outright, it veers into the dubious realm of counterfeiting, or vamping as revamping, a permanent and disguised alteration. A plagiarist is a book-thief who, in the words of John Bullokar, 'fathers other mens [sic] works upon himself'.[47] *Plagiat*, an Old French word, still carried connotations of fraudulent impersonation; 'counterfeit also means a more tangible impersonation or impostor – unto the womb', as Nick Groom puts it, 'counterfeit children being those fathered in adultery'.[48] A spate of novels in the second half of the eighteenth century certainly played up to their invented heritage, as in Thomas Cogan's baggy, metafictional extension of Thomas Amory's popular Irish novel *The Life of John Buncle* (1756–66), *John Buncle, Junior* (1776). (It is the counterfeiting – rather than the kidnapping – of literary offspring that should have alarmed Defoe and Richardson.) In 1762, *Tristram Shandy* even gave birth to his own grandfather, *Christopher Wagstaff*, a novel that largely rehashed John Dunton's *Voyage Round the World* (1691), one of Sterne's sources. In *Joseph Andrews*, an extension of the life of Pamela Andrews through her fictional brother, Fielding even jokes about the dubious ancestry of characters borrowed from rival writers when he supposes that his eponymous hero 'had no Ancestors at all, but had sprung up ... out of a Dunghill'.[49] Critics have typically argued that Fielding actively demotes the presence of *Pamela* in *Joseph Andrews*, as he loses sight of his nominal hypotext as early as Chapter Ten. Jill Campbell writes: '[as] Joseph is released from a genealogical relation to Richardson's heroine by the revelations of the novel's conclusion, so Fielding's work itself gain[s] a form of autonomy from its predecessor in the course of the novel'.[50] Campbell's choice of rhetoric strikes me as an over-anxious attempt to expunge Fielding's appropriative practices from his art. Even if the novel pointedly turns on the fact that Joseph is not related to Pamela, the title of the novel cynically continues the false claim in print. Joseph is, as Claude Rawson astutely observes, '*in effect* Pamela's brother for the bulk of the novel', the pages of which encompass his entire lifespan as an invented character.[51] So Fielding both encroaches upon Richardson's property *and* rejects it even as he retains a notional connection between their works. He mimics *Pamela* precisely in order to move – publicly – beyond its limitations.

Fielding, in turn, attracted imitators who intruded upon his literary estate. As the title suggests, *Tom Jones in His Married State* (1749) would invariably draw in fans of the recently published *Tom Jones*. But the author of the sequel openly states in the Preface that 'Henry Fielding, Esq. is not the Author of this Book, nor in any Manner concerned in its Composition or Publication'.[52] He even has the audacity to pitch his novel at the primary author in the hope that he may 'engage the warm Recommendation' of 'That Gentleman' – presumably in the manner of Fielding's endorsement of his sister's work in the second edition of *David Simple*. A few months later, in *Charlotte Summers* (1750), a novel sometimes attributed to Sarah Fielding, the narrator-author presents himself as the illegitimate son of Fielding's narrator-author: 'You must know then, I am the first Begotten, of the poetical Issue, of the much celebrated Biographer of *Joseph Andrews*, and *Tom Jones*'. He continues in a playful, Fielding-esque tone: 'I dare not pretend to be legitimately begotten ... therefore I am afraid I should scarce be able to fix a Marriage upon the Squire, especially as the Ceremony of poetical Espousals is so much controverted by the Priests of *Parnassus*, that it's next to impossible to settle the Ritual, that would convey the Privilege of Legitimacy to the Offspring of the Poets'.[53] Although it riffs on Fielding's sarcastic distinction between Parnassian allusion and Grub Street plagiarism, the speech more readily concedes that the economy of scarcity wins out: the author fears his 'borrowed wit' will become yet duller as others imitate his copy of a copy. Both novels, *Tom Jones in His Married State* and *Charlotte Summers*, feed off Fielding's acclaimed authorship while openly drawing attention to the faulty, cloying artifice of such an enforced filial connection.

Other continuers hid their handiwork by effectively counterfeiting the design of the original publications. In February 1727, barely a few months after the first edition of *Gulliver's Travels* appeared (October 1726), a youngish Samuel Richardson printed (at least) the first part of the spurious *Volume III*, which as Nicholas Seager has shown, cynically copied the appearance of Swift's book.[54] (Like many printers in the period, Richardson routinely helped compile cut-and-paste publications from an array of mismatched or left-over texts.)[55] Most of the seemingly new material in *Volume III* comes from Denis Vairasse's *History of the Sevarites or Sevarambi* (1675–79), itself a likely source for Swift's original work. A similar, if more invasive case, is Defoe's *Roxana*.[56] There were six distinct editions that feature a continuation that takes the narrative beyond the point at which the original author left off, in 1740, 1745, 1750, 1755, 1765, and 1775. Many of these editions engraft a new plot dénouement, either rewarding the penitent prostitute or punishing her maternal and marital failures in the body of the novel. Astonishingly, a 1740 edition has an additional 150 pages mainly filled with material lifted from Haywood's *The British*

Recluse (1722) and a freely adapted Restoration conduct book, William de Britaine's *Humane Prudence* (1680).[57] More egregious still is the 1775 edition often referred to as *The New Roxana* (*The History of Mademoiselle de Beleau; or, the New Roxana, the Fortunate Mistress*). It was the first edition to showcase Defoe's name, even though the publishers Francis Noble and Thomas Lowndes made, or commissioned, significant alterations to the earlier versions of the text.

A year later Noble worked the same trick on *Moll Flanders* (1722). In the editorial note to *The History of Laetitia Atkins, Vulgarly called Moll Flanders* (1776), the adapter claims that he was surprized by Defoe's vulgarities in both *Moll Flanders* and *Roxana*, but as he 'came in possession' of manuscript versions much altered by the original author he 'thought it proper, in their new dress, to introduce them for the entertainment of those who are admirers of nature'.[58] This is an audacious case of revamping – new clothes flaunted in place of the original, tattered rags – that further extends the claim in Defoe's preface to *Moll Flanders* that his novel is a dressed-up version of a memorandum. Ostensibly restoring a damaged text, Noble creates a new work for a new kind of readership. Moll is no longer a pickpocket and Roxana is strikingly more maternal as the adapter 'restores' the children, as the preface to *The New Roxana* asserts. In short, as Robert J. Griffin argues, Noble transforms 'a realistic novel into a genteel, sentimental one'.[59] Rather than restrict the text to a specific milieu, I would add, the adapter actually opens it up to potential spin-offs and continuations. After all, in the 1775 preface he refers to 'some part of her history [that] lay abroad, and cannot so well be vouched as the first'. Noble's Moll, though, is killed off at the age of seventy-five, five years after we leave her in penitent retirement at the end of the 1722 edition. Defoe's texts, plots, and characters were especially prone to extension and destruction, mimicry and vamping, in equal measure.

To be continued?

In *Gulliver's Travels*, Swift seems to be wary of the uncertain ways in which a literary text could be altered or appropriated once it appeared in print. As Seager observes, 'the frequent rhetorical claim to incompleteness, in both Swift's narrative and its paratexts, is another sense in which the story is extendable and resistant to closure'.[60] *Gulliver's Travels* certainly invited further excursions away from an environment that the protagonist had grown to loathe by the end of the fourth voyage. But Swift's prefatory letter from 'The Publisher to the Reader' merits further scrutiny in the context of the competing economies of abundance and scarcity: 'This Volume would have been at least twice as large, if I had not made bold to strike out innumerable Passages'.[61] Here Swift-as-editor mingles the language of extension and destruction: he destroys unwritten material that only existed in a fictional universe. Such material could be restored, rewritten (that is, written), either by the author himself or self-appointed appropriators. The vagueness of the phrase 'innumerable Passages' even entices potential adapters to find creative ways in which to counterfeit the seemingly missing pieces.

Other authors sought to close their texts in more definitive terms. No doubt stung by the continuations that appeared within weeks of *Pamela*, Richardson pleadingly hopes readers of *Sir Charles Grandison*, 'when you consider the circumstances of the Story', will be satisfied 'that it ends very properly where it does'.[62] Fourteen years earlier Richardson had attempted to close Pamela's story at the end of volume two: 'Here end the Letters of the incomparable PAMELA to her Father and Mother'.[63] At this point in the text there follows a lengthy list of fragmented summaries of the characters' fictional afterlives (Pamela is happily married; Miss Goodwin finds an honourable husband; the honesty and integrity of Mr and Mrs Andrews is finally rewarded). 'But the ragged ending of *Pamela*, the serial-like present-tense excitements of the story, and its great popularity', as Ian Donaldson observes, 'were to lead to a number of unauthorized continuations of the novel by other hands; and Richardson was driven to think that he would resume the story himself'.[64] The contagion of continuation soon crept into the novel. The fifth edition (September 1741) concluded with the teasing words: 'Here end, *at present*, the Letters of Pamela' (emphasis added). By December of that year Richardson had rapidly produced two more volumes of the heroine's life as a married woman, *Pamela in Her Exalted Condition*. In a thinly veiled attack on the unofficial sequels that had appeared in the interim, Richardson 'flatters himself, that [the new volumes] may expect the good Fortune, which *few Continuations* have met with, to be judg'd not unworthy the *First*'.[65] Fielding perhaps picked up on this self-aggrandizing claim at the end of *Joseph Andrews*, where the narrator cheekily claims his hero will not be 'prevailed on by any Booksellers, or their Authors, to make his Appearance in *High-Life*', a clear allusion to the extension that most readily spurred Richardson's return to *Pamela*, John Kelly's *Pamela's Conduct in High Life*.[66]

Fielding is also responding to a larger anxiety among authors about the quality of sequels in the period. In *The Farther Adventures of Robinson Crusoe*, for one, Defoe pledges to his readers that the 'Second Part . . . is (contrary to the Usage of Second Parts,) every Way as entertaining as the First'.[67] The preface to Sarah Fielding's *Volume the Last* admits that 'Sequels to Histories of this kind are so generally decried, and often with such good Reason, that a few Words seem necessary towards an Explanation of the following Design'.[68] There follows a loose plot summary of *David Simple* insofar as the writer of the preface (probably Jane Collier) outlines the ways in which the author sought to illustrate the social truism that 'The Attainment of our Wishes is but too often the Beginning of our Sorrows' and that, further, every evil may be overcome. The preface openly acknowledges that a continuation of this theme could be carried out with a new set of characters, with new names at least, but this would amount to a 'pretended Appearance of Novelty'. Such a novel, in other words, would be a derivative recasting. The preface-writer also concedes that there is a risk in bringing established characters back to the stage 'if not done with equal Humour and Spirit'. But, she insists, it is not the characters that make a novel fresh and original, but the plot, the putting of 'known and remarkable Characters into new Situations'. Such a move speaks to what Terry Castle identifies as the readerly insistence 'that the sequel be different, but also *exactly the same*'.[69] The start of Book 5 further defends Fielding's deployment of her old eponymous hero in a new adventure:

> That *David Simple*, having been for some Years retired from the World, and when all his Transactions had been so long buried in Oblivion, should again appear on the Stage, is owing to his having undergone a Variety of Accidents; and some as remarkable as any in his former Story. I therefore doubt not, but those Persons who were then pleased with his Character, will be no less pleased with knowing the Remainder of so very uncommon a Life: and for those who are yet unacquainted with our Hero, we hope his Character will in the following Pages appear strong enough to need no formal Description, in the Beginning of this Book.[70]

The author has it both ways: the new volume builds on the previous story and yet can stand alone for uninitiated readers. She declares the story is as interesting, 'as remarkable', as the first novel. Read alone, though, *Volume the Last* foregrounds David's marriage to Camilla as though the story has begun in medias res: '. . . having obtained a Wife his Judgment approves, and his Inclination delights in'. Fielding then skips over eleven years in order to get to what amounts to a relentless series of tribulations and ultimately David's death.

In the final speech, Fielding cleverly lifts the tone a notch above maudlin despair so as to leave the reader emotionally satisfied by cajoling us into empathizing with the faithful friend at the hero's bedside: 'These

Things did *David* speak at various Times, and with such Chearfulness, that *Cynthia* said, the last Hour she spent with him, in seeing his Hopes and Resignation, was a Scene of real Pleasure'. Rather than end there, however, Fielding takes pains to close the trilogy in authoritative rather than authoritarian terms:

> But now will I draw the Veil, and if any of my Readers chuse to drag *David Simple* from the Grave, to struggle again in this World, and to reflect, every Day, on the Vanity of its utmost Enjoyments, they may use their own Imaginations, and fancy *David Simple* still bustling about on this Earth. But I chuse to think he is escaped from the Possibility of falling into any future Afflictions, and that neither the Malice of his pretended Friends, nor the Sufferings of his real ones, can ever again rend and torment his honest Heart.[71]

In this passage Sarah Fielding seems to commingle an economy of abundance, in which she encourages a fecund expansion of her work off the page, and an economy of scarcity, in which her literary property lay prone to misuse and reputational damage. The language of scarcity certainly recurs throughout the trilogy, especially in *Volume the Last*, as part of a compound satire on the fretful pretentiousness of the middling classes.[72] In Book 6, Chapter 2, the snobbish Mrs Orgueil, for one, worries that 'every kind Word' uttered in praise of Cynthia's daughter is a 'Robbery' from her own child, Henrietta-Cassandra.[73] Ultimately, though, the author eschews a Richardsonian claim over her creation as she freely acknowledges that the character belongs to her readers as much as to her, even if she seeks to influence them against the prolonging of David's troubles. The emotional manipulation at work here contrasts, and even redacts, the open-endedness of the final sentence of *David Simple*: 'it is this Tenderness and Benevolence, which alone can give any real Pleasure, and which I most sincerely wish to all my Readers'.[74] Such pleasant feeling ought to be kept alive, and perhaps continued, by the reader or for the readers' sake. In closing the trilogy, Fielding had perhaps become mindful of the creeping rise of fan fiction and unofficial extensions in the mid-century.[75] After all, in a high-profile media spat between Samuel Richardson and the publishers of John Kelly's usurping sequel to *Pamela*, 'The Proprietors of *Pamela's Conduct in High Life*' resorted to killing off the heroine in an advertisement of a forthcoming volume on 18 July 1741 so that 'neither Mr. R—n or his accomplices might be guilty of Murdering Her'.[76] Literary property lay open to theft (or, euphemistically, borrowing) and, in extreme cases, annihilation.

Readers have always inserted new pages into or deleted unsatisfactory ones from their copies of books. But the increased output of fictional works and the intensification of celebrity culture in the second half of the eighteenth century gave rise to a new phenomenon: a reader's intrusive engagement with the author. Lady Bradshaigh and her sister Elizabeth, Lady Echlin, as a notable example, entered into a lengthy correspondence with Richardson about their own happier endings to *Clarissa*.[77] Whereas commonplace books, anthologies, and beauties collections condense favourite or instructive works into manageable pieces, fan fiction extends established literary property by filling in putatively missing scenes, providing new adventures, expanding the timeline, elaborating character background, or shifting attention to incidental characters or scenes. A cheaply printed 1776 abridgement of Tobias Smollett's *Roderick Random* (1748) – *The Comical Adventures of Roderick Random and His Friend Strap* – promoted fan favourite Hugh Strap to second billing and, at the conclusion of the story, rewarded him with £200 and a job as a steward to the protagonist's father.

Of all of the major novelists of our period, Jane Austen has attracted, and continues to attract, the most fan fiction.[78] Many of these works revisit Austen's plots or locales, as in P. D. James's *Death Comes to Pemberley* (2011), set six years after the events in *Pride and Prejudice* (1813). In 2009 a different kind of work – a mash-up – appeared: *Pride and Prejudice and Zombies*.[79] Although the work is credited as a transhistorical collaboration, in effect Seth Grahame-Smith both mimics and vamps (rather than counterfeits) Austen as he writes the interpolative sections on zombies very loosely – and with playful anachronism – in the 'imitated style of Jane Austen'. As much of the novel is lifted from *Pride and Prejudice*, it is not an extension as such, but a much more extreme engraftment than *Joseph Andrews* was a 'lewd and ungenerous engraftment' on *Pamela* (in Richardson's view).[80] Grahame-Smith's book has since been adapted in different media, including a 2010 graphic novel (with text supplied by acclaimed comics writer Tony Lee and art by Cliff Richards) and a forthcoming studio movie. Quirk Books commissioned Steve Hockensmith to write a prequel to Austen and Grahame-Smith's novel within a year of its first printing in order to capitalize on its sudden popularity. Tellingly, *Pride and Prejudice and Zombies: Dreadfully Ever After* (2010) largely covers the early training of Elizabeth Bennet as a zombie killer, and so moves yet further away from Austen's original. Hockensmith even extended the extension a year later when he published a prequel not to Austen's novel but to Grahame-Smith's interpolative adaptation: *Dawn of the Dreadfuls: Pride and Prejudice and Zombies*. We might treat this as a paradigmatic case of the adapter as 'raider' in H. Porter Abbott's terms ('they don't copy, they steal what they want and leave the rest').[81] Or we might consider it as the logical endpoint of eighteenth-century practice.

The fan-fiction theorist Abigail Derecho draws on Derrida's theory of the archive in her taxonomy of what she calls archontic literature, where a text 'allows, or even invites, writers to enter it, select specific items they find useful, make new artifacts using those found objects, and deposit the newly made work back into the source text's archive'.[82] Like many notable and lesser known eighteenth-century adaptations and appropriations of the fictional archive, the alternate versions of Austen's work vamp the original texts with a specific audience in sight. After all, Grahame-Smith's enforced co-authorship is more honest than, if just as self-aggrandizing as, Noble's reworking of *Roxana* after Defoe's death. Where classical imitation gives way to modern copying after Richardson, modern-day fan fiction revisits the mimicry mastered by Fielding and Sterne. We ought to acknowledge more readily that secondary authorship is intrinsic to, and often roused further by, familiar eighteenth-century writing.

Notes

1 See Brean Hammond, 'The Cervantic Legacy in the Eighteenth-Century Novel', in *The Cervantean Heritage: Reception and Influence of Cervantes in Britain*, ed. J. A. G. Ardila (London: Legenda, 2009), pp. 96–103.

2 David A. Brewer, *The Afterlife of Character, 1726–1825* (Philadelphia: University of Pennsylvania Press, 2005), pp. 25–52.

3 Robert J. Griffin, 'Anonymity and Authorship', *New Literary History*, 30:4 (1999), 877–95 (882).

4 See Betty A. Schellenberg, '"To Renew Their Former Acquaintance": Print, Gender, and Some Eighteenth-Century Sequels', in *Part Two: Reflections on the Sequel*, eds. Paul Budra and Betty A. Schellenberg (University of Toronto Press, 1998), pp. 85–101.

5 Eliza Haywood, *Love in Excess; or, The Fatal Enquiry* (1719–20), ed. David Oakleaf, 2nd edn (Peterborough, Ont.: Broadview Press, 2000), p. 266.

6 Jonathan Swift, *Gulliver's Travels* (1726), ed. David Womersley, The Cambridge Edition of the Works of Jonathan Swift (Cambridge University Press, 2012), pp. 7–14 (11).

7 Quoted in Thomas Keymer and Peter Sabor, *'Pamela' in the Marketplace: Literary Controversy and Print Culture in Eighteenth-Century Britain and Ireland* (Cambridge University Press, 2005), p. 52.

8 Henry Fielding, *'Joseph Andrews' and 'Shamela'* (1742 and 1741), ed. Douglas Brooks-Davies, rev. Thomas Keymer (Oxford University Press, 2008), p. 344. Hereafter cited separately as *Joseph Andrews* and *Shamela*. Tickletext also appears in Behn's *The Town-Fopp* (1677), as well as in comedies by D'Urfey, Centlivre, Bullock, and others.

9 On collaborative writing see Dustin Griffin, *Authorship in the Long Eighteenth Century* (Newark: University of Delaware Press, 2014), pp. 49–57.

10 Linda Hutcheon with Siobhan O'Flynn, *A Theory of Adaptation*, 2nd edn (London and New York: Routledge, 2013), p. 7.

11 Julie Sanders, *Adaptation and Appropriation* (London and New York: Routledge, 2006), p. 41.

12 Mark Rose, *Authors and Owners: The Invention of Copyright* (Cambridge, MA: Harvard University Press, 1993), p. 1.

13 Simon Stern, '"Room for One More": The Metaphorics of Physical Space in the Eighteenth-Century Copyright Debate', *Law and Literature*, 24:2 (2012), 113–50 (119).

14 Thomas Keymer (published as Tom Keymer), *Richardson's 'Clarissa' and the Eighteenth-Century Reader* (Cambridge University Press, 1992), p. 72.

15 J. Paul Hunter, 'Serious Reflections on Farther Adventures: Resistances to Closure in Eighteenth-Century English Novels', in *Augustan Subjects: Essays in Honor of Martin C. Battestin*, ed. Albert J. Rivero (Newark: University of Delaware Press, 1997), pp. 276–94 (278).

16 Daniel Defoe, *Robinson Crusoe* (1719), ed. Thomas Keymer (Oxford University Press, 2008), p. 258.

17 See Allen Michie, 'Far from Simple: Sarah Fielding's *Familiar Letters* and the Limits of the Eighteenth-Century Sequel', in *On Second Thought: Updating the Eighteenth-Century Text*, eds. Debra Taylor Bourdeau and Elizabeth Kraft (Newark: University of Delaware Press, 2007), pp. 83–111.

18 William B. Warner, *Licensing Entertainment: The Elevation of Novel Reading in Britain, 1684–1750* (Berkeley: University of California Press, 1998), p. 116.

19 Thomas Keymer, *Sterne, the Moderns, and the Novel* (Oxford University Press, 2002), p. 9.

20 See Andrew O'Malley, 'Poaching on Crusoe's Island: Popular Reading and Chapbook Editions of *Robinson Crusoe*', *Eighteenth-Century Life*, 35:2 (2011), 18–38; Pat Rogers, 'Classics and Chapbooks', in *Book and Their Readers in Eighteenth-Century England*, ed. Isabel Rivers (New York: St Martin's Press, 1982), pp. 27–45.

21 Quoted in Rose, *Authors*, p. 39. Rose suggests that authors often invoked the language of paternity to describe their relationship with the text: 'the author as begetter, and the book as child' (pp. 38–41).

22 Richardson to James Leake, August 1741, *Selected Letters of Samuel Richardson*, ed. John Carroll (Oxford: Clarendon Press, 1964), p. 43.

23 Stern, 'Room for One More', p. 119.

24 See Kathryn Temple, *Scandal Nation: Law and Authorship in Britain, 1750–1832* (Ithaca and London: Cornell University Press, 2003), pp. 20–72. On Richardson's dual role as author and printer see Laura Maruca, *The Work of Print: Authorship and the English Text Trades, 1660–1760* (Seattle: University of Washington Press, 2007), pp. 127–57.

25 *The Case of Samuel Richardson, of London, Printer; With Regard to the Invasion of His Property in The History of Sir Charles Grandison* (London: S. Richardson, 1753), p. 2.

26 Quoted in Rose, *Authors*, p. 5.

27 Samuel Richardson, *Pamela; or, Virtue Rewarded* (1740), ed. Albert J. Rivero, The Cambridge Edition of the Works and Correspondence of Samuel Richardson (Cambridge University Press, 2011), p. 7.

28 Quoted in Robert W. McHenry, Jr, 'Plagiarism and Paternity in Dryden's Adaptations', in *Originality and Intellectual Property in the French and English Enlightenment*, ed. Reginald McGinnis (New York: Routledge, 2009), pp. 1–21 (1).

29 Edward Young, *Conjectures on Original Composition* (London: A. Millar and J. Dodsley, 1759), p. 24. See Daniel Cook, 'On Genius and Authorship: Addison to Hazlitt', *The Review of English Studies*, 64 (2013), 610–29.

30 Henry Fielding, *Tom Jones* (1749), ed. Sheridan Baker, 2nd edn (New York and London: W. W. Norton, 1995), p. 401.

31 See Richard Terry, *The Plagiarism Allegation in English Literature from Butler to Sterne* (Basingstoke: Palgrave Macmillan, 2010), pp. 152–68.

32 Laurence Sterne, *The Life and Opinions of Tristram Shandy, Gentleman* (1759–67), eds. Melvyn New and Joan New (London: Penguin, 2003), pp. 309–10.

33 Quoted in Terry, *Plagiarism Allegation*, pp. 162–63.

34 'Comments on Sterne', *Memoirs of the Literary and Philosophical Society of Manchester*, 5 vols. (London and Manchester: T. Cadell, 1793), vol. 4, pp. 45–86 (47).

35 On Ferriar's conflicted outing of Sterne as a plagiarist see H. J. Jackson, 'Sterne, Burton, and Ferriar: Allusions to the *Anatomy of Melancholy* in Volumes Five to Nine of *Tristram Shandy*', *Philological Quarterly*, 54:2 (1975), 457–70. See also Warren Oakley, *A Culture of Mimicry: Laurence Sterne, His Readers and the Art of Bodysnatching* (London: MHRA, 2010).

36 Sterne, *Tristram Shandy*, p. 332.

37 Paulina Kewes, *Authorship and Appropriation: Writing for the Stage in England, 1660–1710* (Oxford: Clarendon Press, 1998), p. 8.

38 Quoted in Kewes, *Authorship and Appropriation*, p. 93.

39 James Boswell, *The Life of Samuel Johnson*, 2 vols. (London: Charles Dilly, 1791), vol. 1, p. 357.

40 *The Adventures of an Author*, 2 vols. (London: Robinson and Roberts, 1767), vol. 2, p. 164. Compiled by William Oldys and Edmund Curll from the papers of Thomas Betterton, *The History of the English Stage* (London: E. Curll, 1741) equates vamping with hack writing in the case of Benjamin Griffin as he 'commence[d] Dramatic-Poet by vamping up an old play or two of Massinger and Decker, and scribbling a few farces, all of which met with the deserved contempt of such trifling performances' (p. 151).

41 *The New Modern Story-Teller*, 2 vols. (London: J. Williams, 1772), vol. 1, p. 84.

42 Henry Fielding, *Plays*, ed. Thomas Lockwood, 3 vols., The Wesleyan Edition of the Works of Henry Fielding (Oxford University Press, 2004–11), vol. 1, pp. 314–15. This passage comes from the revised edition of 1734.

43 Fielding, *Plays*, vol. I, p. 565; Maurice Johnson, *Fielding's Art of Fiction: Eleven Essays on 'Shamela', 'Joseph Andrews', 'Tom Jones', and 'Amelia'* (Philadelphia: University of Pennsylvania Press, 1961), p. 21.

44 For detailed textual comparisons see Charles B. Woods, 'Fielding and the Authorship of *Shamela*', *Philological Quarterly*, 25:3 (1946), 248–72.

45 Thomas Lockwood, '*Shamela*', in *The Cambridge Companion to Henry Fielding*, ed. Claude Rawson (Cambridge University Press, 2007), pp. 38–49 (41).

46 *The Pamela Controversy*, vol. 3, p. xvii. This volume comprises *Anti-Pamela* and *Memoirs of the Life of Lady H—*.

47 *An English Expositor, or Compleat Dictionary* (1695), quoted in Terry, *Plagiarism Allegation*, p. 19.

48 Nick Groom, *The Forger's Shadow: How Forgery Changed the Course of Literature* (London: Picador, 2002), p. 45.

49 Fielding, *Joseph Andrews*, p. 17.

50 Jill Campbell, *Natural Masques: Gender and Identity in Fielding's Plays and Novels* (Stanford University Press, 1995), p. 71.

51 Claude Rawson, 'Henry Fielding', in *The Cambridge Companion to the Eighteenth-Century Novel*, ed. John Richetti (Cambridge University Press, 1996), pp. 120–52 (134).

52 *The History of Tom Jones the Foundling, in His Married State* (London: J. Robinson, [1749]), preface.

53 *The History of Charlotte Summers, the Fortunate Parish Girl*, 2 vols. (London: Printed for the author, 1750), vol. I, p. 3.

54 Nicholas Seager, 'Samuel Richardson and the Third Volume of *Gulliver's Travels*', *Swift Studies*, 28 (2013), 128–36.

55 See John A. Dussinger, 'Fabrications from Samuel Richardson's Press', *Papers of the Bibliographical Society of America*, 100:2 (2006), 259–79.

56 See Ashley Marshall, 'Did Defoe Write *Moll Flanders* and *Roxana*?', *Philological Quarterly*, 89:2–3 (2010), 209–41; Robert J. Griffin, 'The Text in Motion: Eighteenth-Century *Roxanas*', *English Literary History*, 72:2 (2005), 387–406; P. N. Furbank and W. R. Owens, 'The "Lost" Continuation of Defoe's *Roxana*', *Eighteenth-Century Fiction*, 9:3 (1997), 299–308.

57 Nicholas Seager traces in detail the textual presence of different editions of *Humane Prudence* (particularly the seventh, eighth, and ninth) in the Applebee *Roxana*: 'Prudence and Plagiarism in the 1740 Continuation of Defoe's *Roxana*', *The Library*, 7th series, 10:4 (2009), 357–71.

58 *The History of Laetitia Atkins, Vulgarly called Moll Flanders* (London: F. Noble, and T. Lowndes, 1776), p. viii.

59 Griffin, '*Roxanas*', p. 396.

60 Nicholas Seager, '*Gulliver's Travels* Serialized and Continued', in *Reading Swift: Papers from the Sixth Münster Symposium on Jonathan Swift*, eds. Kirsten Juhas et al. (Munich: Wilhelm Fink, 2013), pp. 543–62 (551).

61 Swift, *Gulliver's Travels*, pp. 15–16.

62 'Copy of a Letter to a Lady, who was solicitous for an additional volume to the History of Sir Charles Grandison' (15 March 1754): the letter, printed as a pamphlet to be distributed gratis, is reproduced in *The History of Sir Charles Grandison* (1753–54), ed. Jocelyn Harris, 3 vols. (Oxford University Press, 1972), vol. 3, pp. 467–70.

63 Richardson, *Pamela*, p. 457.

64 Ian Donaldson, 'Fielding, Richardson, and the Ends of the Novel', *Essays in Criticism*, 32:1 (1982), 26–47 (33).

65 Samuel Richardson, *Pamela in Her Exalted Condition* (1741), ed. Albert J. Rivero, The Cambridge Edition of the Works and Correspondence of Samuel Richardson (Cambridge University Press, 2012), p. 3.

66 Fielding, *Joseph Andrews*, p. 303.

67 Daniel Defoe, *The Farther Adventures of Robinson Crusoe* (London: W. Taylor, 1719), sig. A3^r (italics reversed).

68 Sarah Fielding, *The Adventures of David Simple* (1744), ed. Malcolm Kelsall (Oxford University Press, 1994), p. 309–11. On *Volume the Last* see Betty A. Schellenberg, *The Conversational Circle: Re-Reading the English Novel, 1740–1775* (Lexington: University Press of Kentucky, 1996), pp. 116–30.

69 Terry Castle, *Masquerade and Civilization: The Carnivalesque in Eighteenth-Century English Culture and Fiction* (Stanford University Press, 1986), p. 134.

70 Fielding, *David Simple*, p. 313.

71 Fielding, *David Simple*, p. 432.

72 See Simon Stern, 'Speech and Property in *David Simple*', *English Literary History*, 79:3 (2012), 623–54.

73 Fielding, *David Simple*, p. 346.

74 Fielding, *David Simple*, p. 305.

75 See Elizabeth F. Judge, 'Kidnapped and Counterfeit Characters: Eighteenth-Century Fan Fiction, Copyright Law, and the Custody of Fictional Characters', in *Originality and Intellectual Property in the French and English Enlightenment*, pp. 22–68.

76 *The Pamela Controversy*, vol. 4, p. xxi. Volumes 4 and 5 of this edition comprise Kelly's novel.

77 See Janice Broder, 'Lady Bradshaigh Reads and Writes *Clarissa*: The Marginal Notes in Her First Edition', in *Clarissa and Her Readers: New Essays for the 'Clarissa' Project*, eds. Carol Houlihan Flynn and Edward Copeland (New York: AMS Press, 1999), pp. 97–118. On Richardson's influence on female contemporaries see Jerry C. Beasley, '*Clarissa* and Early Female Fiction' and Ruth Perry, 'Clarissa's Daughters; Or, the History of Innocence Betrayed. How Women Writers Rewrote Richardson', in *Clarissa and Her Readers*, pp. 69–96, 119–41.

78 On the many Austen-inspired novels produced in the 2000s, see Juliette Wells, 'New Approaches to Austen and the Popular Reader', in *Uses of Austen: Jane's Afterlives*, eds. Gillian Dow and Clare Hanson (Basingstoke: Palgrave Macmillan, 2012), pp. 77–91.

79 See Tiffany Potter, 'Historicizing the Popular and the Feminine: *The Rape of the Lock* and *Pride and Prejudice and Zombies*', in *Women, Popular Culture,*

and the Eighteenth Century, ed. Tiffany Potter (University of Toronto Press, 2012), pp. 5–24 (esp. 16–21).

80 Richardson to Lady Bradshaigh, November/December 1749, *Selected Letters of Samuel Richardson*, p. 133.

81 H. Porter Abbott, *The Cambridge Introduction to Narrative* (Cambridge University Press, 2002), p. 105.

82 Abigail Derecho, 'Archontic Literature: A Definition, A History, and Several Theories of Fan Fiction', in *Fan Fiction and Fan Communities in the Age of the Internet: New Essays*, eds. Karen Hellekson and Kristina Busse (Jefferson: McFarland and Co., 2006), pp. 61–78 (64–65).

CHAPTER 2

The Afterlife of Family Romance

Michael McKeon

'The Afterlives of Eighteenth-Century Fiction' is a rich topic that can be approached from several directions. I would like to conceive it as a question of the afterlives of fictional *conventions* in order to emphasize both the collective and the temporal nature of the phenomenon. More specifically, my guiding question will be: how and why did the ancient convention of family romance enter into the formation of the novel genre in seventeenth- and eighteenth-century Britain? The British novelists on whom I will focus when I engage this question in the latter part of the essay are Richardson, Fielding, Burney, and Austen.

I

The convention of family romance was given its name by Sigmund Freud, who observed that it was extraordinarily common not only in literary works, such as romances and novels, but also in less consciously regulated fictions: folk tales, fairy tales, daydreams, and nocturnal dreams. To Freud, this gave evidence that family romance possesses a universal fascination, which was confirmed for him by what seemed the universal significance of its content. Liberation from parental authority being essential to normal development, family romance plays an important role in facilitating this separation by expressing a young child's earliest capacity to distance himself (Freud's paradigm is male experience) from them. The form taken by the child's critical detachment is a 'feeling of being slighted' (*Zurücksetzung*), a dissatisfaction with his parents for being poor, vulgar, distracted, or in other ways inadequate to the child's sense of self-importance and to his wish to be closely attended to and cared for. Over time the child becomes convinced that these inadequate and unworthy figures cannot be his real parents, that he must have been adopted by them or at least must be no more than their stepchild. The feeling of being slighted is expressed through 'a phantasy in which both his parents are

43

replaced by others of better birth'. One day the real, 'new and aristocratic' parents, resplendent in every way, will appear or be discovered, and they will free their child from the undeserved mediocrity of its existence. Developmentally speaking, this is the first stage of the family romance. As yet, the child knows nothing of how children are produced, although 'the influence of sex' is already evident in the boy's greater hostility toward and greater need to be freed from his father than his mother. The fantasy that defines the second stage of family romance is marked by sexual awareness. Now the boy imagines that his father alone is an impostor and soon to be replaced: his mother is authentic and the boy's adulterous progenitor, immoral but also the object of his own sexual desire.[1]

In his interpretation of this second stage we can see how the family romance helped Freud concretize his theory of the Oedipal Complex. And in the name that he gave to this ancient narrative Freud of course embedded a profound interpretation of its meaning. I will continue to use 'family romance' to name that story but will also use, as frequently, 'discovered parentage' as a more neutral description of just what all these narratives and narrative fragments have in common.

For thousands of years before Freud wrote his essay, family romance was being put to varied purposes, the earliest of which serve to single out, unlike Freud's modern and universalizing reading, extraordinary figures as the rightful founders of tribes, races, and communities. In these ancient versions, the feelings and wishes of the child are of little interest; what matters is the fact that they have been chosen by a higher power to do great things and therefore must be taken up into great families. But to speak of family romance specifies the discursive form of romance, which, whether we regard it as a genre or a mode, imposes a structure on the myths of ancient gods, kings, and heroes, marked for singular achievements by the discovery or contrivance of elevated kinship.[2] The term applies more loosely to rationalized myths concerned with seasonal death, revival, and regeneration personified in successions of divine and heroic figures.[3] What we call the family romance of discovered parentage has the ordered shape of a story that has been disembedded from the vast cycles of oral myth, whose principal function is mnemonic, and whose principle of organization is therefore the repetition of actions, themes, and motifs that are metaphorically and metonymically connected to each other. The figure of Oedipus, for example, weaves in and out of mythic material in which discovered parentage mixes with child abandonment, banishment, entombment of the living and survival of the dead, patricide, matricide, incest, suicide, and metamorphosis between gods, humans, animals, and monsters.[4] The story of Oedipus, after which Freud named his theory of early psychic development, has the structured form neither of myth nor of family romance, but of Sophoclean drama, which radically rationalizes the myth by providing the hero with an independent will that leads him to substitute his own wishes for the will of higher powers, thereby unwittingly substituting for his supposedly low parents his fantastically elevated but actual ones.

Lending support to Freud's claim of its universality, family romance pervades not only pagan but also monotheistic faiths. The oldest religion in the West is based on the story of the infant Moses, hidden by his mother to avoid persecution but found and adopted by the Egyptian royal family and destined by the Hebrew God to do great things. The Christian Gospel renounced the patriarchal tradition of paternal lineage that Moses had established, and instead it encouraged true believers to forsake their kinship ties and to embrace their spiritual Father in heaven. But this spiritualization of family romance in turn became anthropomorphized. Jesus himself, seemingly a child of the lowest descent, is discovered by marks and signs to be the son of the King of Kings and ascends at the end of his lowly life to assume his proper place beside his true father.

This quick review reminds us of the convention's antiquity. How did it become central to the modernity of the novel genre? And given the range of uses to which it was put over the intervening centuries, can we really speak of it as the same convention? The answer to the first question, at least, lies most immediately not in England's Judeo-Christian character but in the Norman Conquest and its consequences.

II

The Conquest disrupted Anglo-Saxon England first of all by creating the demographic chaos of mass migration. Within two decades the Anglo-Saxon earls and thanes were almost entirely displaced by an alien aristocracy, and the heterogeneous peasantry was conglomerated within the single category 'serf'.[5] But the great demographic shifts caused by the Conquest's migrations also brought with them the more subtle and long-term social disruption wrought by the advent of feudalism. With the breakup of the ancient Mediterranean world, Europe underwent a process of feudalization whose regional variations had in common the basic result of decentralized power and authority. Local rulers maintained the possession of their territories through military forces bound to their service by grants of land and a customary and legal system of reciprocal rights and obligations. Analogous but hierarchical levels of land and knight tenure loosely held the system together, allocating authority from the top down by personal bonds of homage and fealty, but also at each level through patrilineal inheritance practices.

Because feudal services to the lord were seen as indivisible in nature, partible methods of inheritance were deemed unacceptable for the passing on of the fief.[6] In England patrilineage replaced the customary partible practices of the past, which had dispersed estates along relatively equal lines, by a stricter standard that allocated heritable property through the paternal line. The relatively hierarchical character of patrilineal practices was crowned by the rule of male primogeniture, whose long-term legacy was the intrafamilial rivalry between the heir and his younger brothers. In the immediate aftermath of the Conquest, this rivalry fuelled romances of disinheritance and exile. In the twelfth-century *Havelok the Dane*, the young princes are obliged to wander in anonymity until their inner worth, demonstrated by noble deeds, confirms their status as rightful heirs to their kingdoms. In the fourteenth-century *Gamelyn*, the eponymous hero's treacherous oldest brother enforces primogenitural disinheritance on him against their dying father's wishes for an equal partition of the estate. But in the end Gamelyn proves his worth and is rewarded by being made heir to the estate of the middle son. Over time the rivalry between the heir male and his younger brothers would become conventionalized as a socially resonant conflict between a priori privilege and unacknowledged merit. More striking in post-Conquest England is the way this problematic conflict internal to the logic of familial inheritance was both contained and recapitulated at a higher level in the disparity between the criteria governing elevation and ennoblement in patrilineage on the one hand and in feudalism on the other – the disparity, that is, between the predetermined honour of blood relations and the demonstrated achievements of tenurial service.

So one effect of the Norman Conquest was the inauguration of an extended and searching, although for the most part inexplicit, debate about the nature of nobility and aristocracy. The convention of family romance clearly participated in this debate, but to do so its form had to be regularized well beyond what had been achieved by earlier adaptations of myth to the conditions of literate objectification. On the one hand, the medieval romances I have been discussing maintain a focus on the discovery of true parentage as a means of vindicating sociopolitical and ethical claims that have been introduced or challenged by historical circumstance. On the other hand, they retain within their narrative dilations a connection to elements that have been, like the convention itself, disembedded from the older mythic substratum but rearranged in quasi-linear sequences. Ideologies of transformation that both explain the past and project the future link social to other modes of change in complex and unstable chains of signifiers for natural-cultural transformation. The most powerful and perdurable of these were generated by twelfth-century elaborations of courtly love and a concept of love service rooted in feudalism, from which issued not only the upwardly mobile chivalric challenge, the neoplatonic critique of carnal love, the *cor gentil* of *fin amor* as well as its *stilnovist* spiritualization, but also theriomorphic descent and its sartorial disguises, demonism and madness. The difference I am describing is intelligible as a matter of both literary and social conventionality. That is, it can be understood both in formal terms – as a difference between myth and romance – and in terms of the long-term historical consequences of the Norman Conquest. The ongoing tendency was to figure status in terms of the social. But within this increasingly social framework, the representation of change was obscured by the static social framework of aristocratic ideology, in which family romance had an important role to play.

III

Much of medieval romance is suffused with the supernatural and incompletely committed to syntactic continuity, but in comparison with myth romance aspires to provide a relatively lineal sequence and a texture of explanatory rationale and motivation. This formal development took place at a time when patrilineal principles of inheritance were gaining greater legal, socioeconomic, and cultural ascendancy, solidified through an 'aristocratic ideology' dedicated to the conviction that social status depends on the possession or non-possession of honour, a quality that points both outward and inward. On the one hand, honour is a function of ancestry, lineage, and the indivisibly genealogical and biological element of noble blood, and it is likely confirmed by other external conditions like wealth and political power. On the other hand, honour is an essential and inward property of its possessor to which the conditional or extrinsic signifiers of honour refer, and in this respect honour is equivalent to an internal element of 'virtue' implicitly coextensive with 'merit'. The belief that birth equals worth, that honour is a unity of outward manifestation and inward essence, is the most fundamental justification for the hierarchical stratification of late medieval society by status, and its grounding in blood and lineage promises a stabilization of social identity.

But aristocratic ideology was vulnerable to the facts of life. One of these is that a patrilineal system of inheritance is not able to generate a male line that will be continuous and self-sufficient over time. This is because demographical constraints ensure that in a stationary population, forty percent of all families will fail to produce a male heir. Attrition in the direct male line is therefore a complication that aristocratic ideology is obliged to accommodate by several means of 'patriline repair', like surrogate heirship and name-changing.[7] Another fact of life is the occasional but ineluctable rise of the extraordinary to great wealth or political power. The royal grant or sale of fictitious genealogies and titles of nobility to ignoble families, if judiciously restrained from overuse, to some extent might reassert the integrity of honour by reuniting status with wealth and power. But the commonplace 'true nobility' was also needed to buttress the laws of correspondence by more frankly allowing for their lapses since it gave sanction to the rise of the humble to worldly eminence by acknowledging that rise to be an expression of singular ability and virtue. Thus true nobility, when invoked with moderation, provided a sort of social safety valve that endorsed the infrequent exception to the rule without really challenging it.[8] And the upward mobility that might result from such social anomalies could be justified in exceptionalist terms comparable to, if more naturalized than, those that in former times had explained the birth of the hero. So like playing cards, the deck of lineal inheritance could be kept in order by prudent expedients like these. But the wild card in the deck was the rule of primogeniture – or more precisely, the younger son whom it displaced, possessed of noble blood but deprived from birth of its external signifiers.

It is fair to say that in England aristocratic ideology reached its ascendancy in the seventeenth century. It is also fair to say that for a number of reasons – demographic attrition, political corruption, religious reform, economic innovation, social mobility, intellectual scepticism – the tacit belief that birth equals worth underwent unprecedented assault during this same period.[9] Ideological ascendancy can have a contradictory character, explicitly affirming what formerly had been taken tacitly to be true and right but thereby opening it up to searching historical and scientific analysis. In 1700 Daniel Defoe went back to the Norman Conquest in expressing his grave doubts about the historical continuity of the great English patrilines:

> Thus from a Mixture of all Kinds began,
> That Het'rogeneous Thing, *An Englishman*:
> . . . .
> A *True-Born Englishman*'s a Contradiction,
> In Speech an Irony, in Fact a Fiction.

But his scorn was even greater for the idea that honour was biologically inherited through noble blood, 'as if there were some differing Species in the very Fluids of Nature ... or some Animalculae of a differing and more vigorous kind'.[10] William Sprigg argued that because miraculous births of the hero have ceased, the laws of nature should take precedence over arbitrary human law:

> The younger Son is apt to think himself sprung from as Noble a stock, from the loyns of as good a Gentleman as his elder Brother, and therefore cannot but wonder, why fortune and the Law should make so great difference between them that lay in the same wombe ... [Would it not be more charitable] to expose or drown these latter births ... then thus to expose them like so many little *Moses*'s in Arks of Bulrushes to a Sea of poverty and misery, from whence they may never expect reprieve, unlesse some miraculous Providence (like *Pharoahs* daughters) chance rescue them into her Court and favour?[11]

The reform of inheritance law was less accessible than the reform of social convention. If the difference between the deserts of the first-born and those of the younger son was subject to rethinking, so too might be the difference between the deserts of the younger son and those of mere true nobility. Edmund Bolton's advice to humble fathers was the same as his advice to the gentle fathers of younger sons: '[P]ut your children to be *Apprentises*, that so as God may blesse their iust, true, and virtuous industrie, they may found a new family, and both raise themselues and theirs to the precious and glittering title of Gentlemen'. According to Defoe it 'was said of a certain tradesman of *London*, that if he could not find the antient race of Gentlemen, from which he came, he would begin a new race, who should be as good Gentlemen as any that went before them'. Defoe refers to the practice of searching for one's family heraldry, or more likely purchasing it new. The two methods by which parentage is thereby 'discovered' are radically different, but to Defoe it does not really matter because what is being discovered – uncovered – is a patriline of merit not honour.[12]

And at a time when social justice and social stability vied for primary importance, legal reform was also possible. Toward the end of the seventeenth century, the legal device of the 'strict settlement' sought to stabilize the landed estate by ensuring the descent of the entail in the male heir, but it also guaranteed provisions for daughters and younger sons. Scholarly debate about the ideological weight of the strict settlement has been lengthy and heated. Perhaps the most that can be said is that by attending closely and explicitly to the mediation of distinct family interests, strict settlement helped make more evident and active the intrafamilial tensions that until now had been perennial but implicit. Along with other developments of the period, it signalled the double-edged ascendancy of aristocratic ideology and thereby raised the question: 'What is the source of the gentle family's gentility?' Of the narrative strategies for engaging this question, I will focus on three sorts of family romance that are particularly significant in extending the convention through the confrontation of lineal and true nobility.

In the first of these, the subversive potential of true nobility is exploited in discovered parentage stories that aim to support aristocratic ideology by confirming that in the end birth really *does* equal worth. The paradigm case involves a young man or woman who is patently possessed of moral virtue but is also recognizable, despite years of penury or strategies of disguise, as possessed of high estate through inexpungible physical marks. In Thomas Deloney's *Thomas of Reading* (1600), the beautiful Margaret is obliged to forsake her 'birth and parentage' and to enter domestic service. Although she pretends humble birth, she is so striking in appearance that she comes to be known as '*Margaret* with the lilly white hand'. In his family memorials twenty years later, Gervase Holles writes that his noble kinsman the Earl of Clare happens upon a young fellow 'as he was playing in the street one day amongst poore boyes' and charitably decides to bring him home. The servants naturally set the young Francis to turning the spit in the kitchen. But as soon as Gervase sees that the boy has 'a very good face and a pure complexion', he digs more deeply and finds not only that Francis belongs to his own extended family, but also that he descends from a line that elevates him even higher than the Earl of Clare himself. But both stories end badly. Plagued by misfortune, Margaret renounces all worldly status and enters a monastery, while Francis proves true to his degraded upbringing rather than to his pedigree, and once bound apprentice steals from his master and runs away.[13]

As the case of Francis Holles makes clear, family romance was not confined to fiction. In 1651, two years after the beheading of his father, Charles Stuart was decisively defeated by Oliver Cromwell at the Battle of Worcester, and for the next few weeks wandered the countryside in disguise to avoid capture. The several royalist accounts of this episode relate that the young prince concealed himself first as a 'Country-Fellow' and then as a 'Serveing-man' and a 'Woodcutter'. The whiteness of his skin he obscured with coarse grey stockings and with a distillation of walnut rind. But despite these expedients, more than once his true identity was suspected and discovered by loyal subjects – 'majestie being soe naturall unto him that even when he said nothing, did nothing, his very lookes . . . were enough to betray him'.[14]

In 1660 Charles's majesty was collectively and ceremonially redis-covered. But the later years of the Stuart dynasty were fraught with challenges to the aristocratic version of discovered parentage. In 1649 Charles's father had been beheaded because of the disjunction between his birth and his worth – between his patrilineal sovereignty and his penchant for absolutist politics and crypto-papist religion. Charles II ruled with greater circumspection, but his younger brother, James, Duke of York, threatened to continue his father's policies so flagrantly that parlia-ment attempted to exclude him from the succession. In 1680 York's status as legitimate heir to the throne was challenged by the putative discovery of true parentage in a secret black box that contained documentary proof that Charles's son James, Duke of Monmouth, putatively a bastard, was truly next in line to succeed his father because at the time that he was born to Charles and one Lucy Walter they were legitimately married. Neither the evidence of that marriage nor the effort to exclude York carried the day. But in 1688, three years after James had ascended the throne, it was announced that the queen had given birth to the Prince of Wales, heir to the throne as well as, presumably, to his father's popery. In an inversion of the replacement conventional in family romance, the king's opponents discovered that the baby's true parentage was not high but low: that the little prince was supposititious, the issue of commoners, and that he had been smuggled into the queen's bedchamber in a warming pan. This discovery, too, failed to find official confirmation (both sides rejected it as 'romance'); but by then plans were underway to depose James and replace him by a dependably Protestant heir whose 'true nobility' was thus far more important than the fact that he was only 57th in line for the throne. True, William's wife Mary was the deposed king's daughter and his legitimate lineal heir. But as a married woman her legal being was subsumed under that of her husband, whose weak lineal legitimacy therefore had to be loudly affirmed. It is not hard to see the Glorious Revolution as a parodic performance of patriline repair on the royal succession itself.[15]

In the second kind of family romance that merits special attention, the ideological implications of the discovery that birth is equal to worth are obscured by the fact that the discovery depends entirely on the worth of a female mediator. The sixteenth-century ballad, the 'Lord of Learne', in the tradition of *Havelok the Dane*, tells the story of a boy who is alienated from his inheritance through the perfidy of a steward who forces him to serve as a stable groom. The 'bonny' but docile Lord of Learne eventually regains his lost status through the enterprising influence of the duke of France's daughter, who is instrumental in discovering his parentage, but more important – in fact the question of the lord's parentage oddly fades into the background – in confirming his virtue by nobly maintaining her own constancy to him ('& as I am a true Ladie | I willbe [sic] trew vnto thee'). In the contemporaneous ballad, 'The Nutt browne mayd', not only the eponymous heroine but we as well are ignorant of the hero's noble birth until the ending discovery. All we know is that he is an outlaw and the beloved of the nut brown maid. She pursues him into the forest, reminding him that 'of anceytrye | a Barrons daughter I bee, | & you haue proved how [I] haue loved | a squier of a Low degree'. On the face of it this is a poor choice on her part and proves, more tellingly, that her birth and worth are incompatible. In fact her beloved confronts her on the unlikelihood of her choice, not to derogate it but to test her constancy to him. And once her virtue is confirmed by her constancy to his virtue, he carelessly remarks, 'Thus you haue woone the Erle of westmoreland sonne, | & not a banished man'.[16]

Both of these texts associate the question of nobility with a theme that is new to this enquiry: the constancy of the noblewoman. The theme itself is traditional to aristocratic ideology. The rule of female chastity (or constancy, its moralized enlargement) is the female equivalent of male honour because it ensures the direct transmission of honour and property in the male line. What is new here is, first, the momentary implication that female constancy has the power to validate nobility even in the absence of noble parentage; second, the scope and meaning of true nobility are altered. No longer the rare exception that proves the rule (nor therefore a social safety valve), true nobility becomes what is in the capacity of the noblewoman to recognize and affirm through her own internal worth.

As a social convention of patrilineal inheritance, female chastity is defined by its quality of passive forbearance. But already in these texts female constancy has become an active virtue, and in others with which they are contemporary the theme undergoes a proleptic sea change. There the attribution or discovery of the woman's external birth is beside the point because female constancy has become the property of a commoner, and her spirited resistance to the nobleman's seductions fully demonstrates her internal worth, especially given the moral corruption with which noble lineage is increasingly associated. Here are two exemplary texts from the same period as the ballads.

Robert Greene tells the story of Calamus, 'a noble man . . . of parentage honourable, as allied to the blood Royall', whose 'voluptuous appetite' is whetted by the sight of a 'countrie huswife' named Cratyna. She resists his efforts to corrupt her and resolves 'rather to taste of any miserie, then for lucre to make shipwracke of her chastitie'. Calamus uses every means to break Cratyna's will – she and her husband are his tenants at will and his means are great – but her constancy is so unshakeable that Calamus is reformed by her example. Ashamed of 'offering violence to so virtuous and chast a mynd', the nobleman instead endows 'her with sufficient lands and possessions, as might very wel maintayne her in the state of a Gentlewoman'. Chaste love is the true nobility of the rustic housewife, whose constancy to virtue is rewarded by being reconciled with wealth consonant with noble birth. But Cratyna's constancy is to virtue and to herself, not to the purity of a male lineage, and the actuality of elevated status has no force in her story. The other story is that of Mercy Harvey, the sister of Edmund Spenser's friend, Gabriel Harvey, who wrote but never published an account of her attempted seduction by a married nobleman. Although Mercy lacked the university education of her two brothers, she was more than literate, and her pert facility is shared with later, novelistic heroines who are greatly over-qualified (like over-educated younger sons) for their modest employments. The main events of Harvey's narrative are much the same as those of Greene's, and like Greene Harvey underscores the contrast between the incorruptibility of the 'plaine cuntrie wench' and the 'great dishonour' of the nobleman. At a certain point Mercy finds herself in greater danger than Greene's Cratyna ever does. But the whole affair comes to an abrupt conclusion when one of the lord's letters is misdirected to brother Gabriel. In both narratives, dynamic constancy is the property of common women, defined against the values of patrilineal inheritance and emblematic of the honour that has been alienated from, but is still pursued by, a corrupt male aristocracy.[17] The convention of discovered parentage has no role to play in this scenario.

The third kind of seventeenth-century family romance that exemplifies innovative experiment with the convention is thoroughly anti-aristocratic in ideology. Here we are concerned less with fully articulated narrative than with the elaboration of a familial metaphor we saw earlier in the Gospels that is now brilliantly extended by Calvinist Protestantism into spiritual kidnapping. In 1640 Thomas Hooker wrote that '[w]e are alive . . . as a child taken out of one family and translated into another, even so we are taken out of the household of Sathan, and inserted into the family of God'. Many Puritans, looking back to the language of the

Gospels, saw the deep relevance of family romance tropes to the terrifying experience of sacred rapture. Caught up in spiritual crisis, the Baptist John Bunyan 'did compare my self in the case of such a Child, whom some Gypsie hath by force took up under her apron, and is carrying from Friend and Country'. For orthodox Calvinists, good works or virtuous behaviour counted for nothing in attaining salvation; divine grace was an unearned virtue, a predetermined and gratuitous gift of God. So when Calvinists counted those who were chosen by divine election within the 'aristocracy of grace', they both imitated the doctrine of aristocratic nobility and criticized it – as being like grace, arbitrary and undeserved, but unlike grace, lacking the only sanction of value. According to Thomas Edwards, 'it is not the birth, but the new birth, that makes men truly noble'.[18]

But if an internal state of grace could not be earned by external works or circumstance, whether Roman Catholic penance or noble birth, the good one did in one's calling glorified God and seemed to confirm the soteriological significance of one's second birth. One paradox of the doctrine of the calling is that its arbitrary basis in the inscrutable will of a higher power harks back to discovered parentage in pagan antiquity, yet the calling also posits an intimate relationship with God lodged in the believer's conscience and susceptible to the moods and rhythms of subjectivity. And although explicitly denied by the doctrine of predestination, the godly service of labour discipline, fed by the stream of tenurial service to one's 'Lord', also helped construct the secular belief that not inherited birth but demonstrated merit was the true index of worth.

IV

One benefit of tracing the convention of family romance, however briskly, across centuries of usage is the lesson that even an epochal literary-historical event like the emergence of the novel can be understood as a difference not only in kind but also in degree. Parody, imitation with a critical distance, is a useful concept for conceiving this doubleness. Yet the question still needs to be asked: when does difference in degree become difference in kind, and how is that decisive distinction to be made? For example, how do we understand the way the divinity that drove the ancient convention of discovered parentage was superseded by the modern *deus ex machina* of self-representation? Does the latter preserve that conventionality or supersede it?

Samuel Richardson's *Pamela* (1740) offers a test case. Prefigured by those Elizabethan tales of female constancy in which the possibility of discovered parentage plays no part, Richardson's novel tells the story of a truly noble common woman through which the thread of that possibility nonetheless weaves a delicate skein. Early on Richardson primes our expectations by recourse to the aristocratic micro-convention we have already seen. One of the neighbouring ladies, observing the adolescent servant girl, remarks: 'See that Shape! I never saw such a Face and Shape in my Life; why she must be better descended than you have told me!' As a lady's maid, Pamela has learned from her benevolent and loving mistress all the accomplishments she would have taught the daughter she never had. Wearing the cast-off clothing her mistress has urged upon her, Pamela's external graces seem to match her internal worth so well that noble birth surely will be found to complete the picture. The novel opens soon after Pamela's mistress has died.[19]

As smart as she is beautiful, Pamela is so beset by her new master's lust – quickly unleashed after his mother's death – that she soon resolves to return to her humble home from the great house where she has been labouring as a servant. Keeping alive the intimation of discovered parentage, Mr B. sneers at this news: '[I]t would be Pity, with these fair soft Hands, and that lovely Skin ... that you should return again to hard Work'. Outraged, Pamela replies: 'I'd have you know, Sir, that I can stoop to the ordinary'st Work of your Scullions, for all these nasty soft Hands ... [I]f I could get Needle-work enough, I would not spoil my Fingers by this rough Work. But if I can't, I hope to make my Hands as red as a Blood-pudden, and as hard as a Beechen Trencher, to accommodate them to my Condition'. Pamela turns on its head the aristocratic ideology of family romance since her point is that it is not noble blood that gives one soft hands; it is being relieved of common labour that makes one look nobly born. 'Here, what a sad Thing it is!' Pamela reflects. 'I have been brought up wrong, as Matters stand'. We come by our appearances through nurture, not nature.[20]

But although Richardson's heroine fits comfortably into the model of Protestant labour discipline, it transpires that Pamela's great work is self-representation. *Pamela* is an epistolary novel comprised of letters written almost entirely by Pamela to her humble parents. But once her master frustrates her resolution to return home by imprisoning Pamela on his estate and depriving her even of the physical mobility entailed in domestic service, she can envision no means of delivering her letters to her parents, and her style modulates into a continuous, expansive, and emotionally affecting novelistic mode. Much later, after Mr B. has been converted to Pamela's pristine standards of ethical propriety, the only obstacle to marriage is their vast difference in social status. And when Mr B. secretly summons Pamela's beloved father and arranges a highly theatrical scene of discovery, we find ourselves viewing a fully enacted parody of discovered parentage that both brings to a head and finally puts paid to hints that we are reading a family romance. Mr B. prepares Pamela (and us): '[Y]ou shall see . . . a Man that I can allow you to love dearly; tho' hardly preferably to me'. Then, 'lifting up my Eyes, and seeing my Father, [I] . . . threw myself at his Feet, O my Father! my Father! said I, can it be!—Is it you? Yes, it is! It is! O bless your happy—Daughter!' Pamela's mock-discovery is that her real parent is her actual parent.[21]

So Richardson disposes of the fantasy of discovered parentage with the tautology of modern life: things are what they seem. At the same time he employs other conventions of family romance to focus our attention on how, if not by gentle birth, the barrier of status inconsistency might be overcome. While still imprisoned, Pamela, strolling one day with her servant guard, is approached by 'a Gypsey-like Body' who offers to tell them their fortunes. By invoking the most familiar literary gypsy trope Richardson augments the demotic alterity of the one we have already encountered – the gypsy as baby-swapper, the human embodiment of extra-human narration and causation. Examining Pamela's hand the gypsy says 'I cannot tell your Fortune; your Hand is so white and fine, that I cannot see the Lines'. But rubbing her hand with the dirt on a tuft of grass, 'Now, said she, I can see the Lines'. The gypsy then tells a distressing fortune: Pamela will never marry and will 'die of your first Child'. But she also makes known to Pamela that she has hidden what turns out to be a 'Bit of Paper' in another tuft, which Pamela retrieves and finds is an anonymous warning that Mr B. plans to trick her into a sham marriage.[22]

The gypsy episode recurs to the trope of fair skin as a signifier of noble blood, but only to deny it: to become legible, Pamela's hand, and its genealogical 'lines', must be returned to the condition that signifies her truly common status. On the matter of marriage, the written 'fortune' does not differ greatly in substance from the traditional, spoken one, but its detailed specificity removes it from the realm of irresistible necessity. And while the paper fortune omits direct reference to childbirth, in this context it alludes to an alternative solution to the problem of status inconsistency. For some time now Pamela has been conducting a secret correspondence with Mr Williams. In order to hide them, Pamela has been secreting on her body the fast-accumulating papers filled with her novelistic account of things (the following day she writes that the latest packet 'I still have safe, as I hope, sew'd in my Under-coat, about my Hips') and periodically leaving them under pre-designated garden plants for the parson to find and transport to safety. The location of Pamela's papers suggests a metaphorical childbirth that is antithetical to the traditional serviceability of the gentle-woman to the noble patriline. Preparing to lay a packet of papers beneath a sunflower, Pamela earlier writes: 'How nobly my Plot succeeds! But I begin to be afraid my Writings may be discover'd; for they grow large! I stitch them hitherto in my Under-coat, next my Linen'. Of course her writings do get discovered. Constant in her resistance to the traditional plot of serving nobility by ensuring the purity of its lineage (a fiction she at one point explicitly refutes), Pamela is also constant in her alternative resolve to create herself by writing her own story and thereby discovering her own parentage of herself. 'Published' clandestinely, Pamela's self-representation persuades its first reader, Mr B, to reconceive the generic plot they are in the process of living as not a romance but a novel, and the solution to status inconsistency as not noble birth but the demonstration of true nobility and upward mobility through marriage.[23] Richardson's parody of family romance fundamentally revalues the convention; is it thereby repudiated? Or is its conventionality a precondition for, even a fundamental component of, the formal revision Richardson conceives?

Although Henry Fielding found many things not to like in the style and morals of Richardson's novel, the parody of family romance was not one of them. And by preserving rather more of its micro-conventions than *Pamela*, *Joseph Andrews* (1742) supersedes family romance more definitively. Early on Fielding gives us signs that his two amatory protagonists, virtuous commoners who love each other to distraction, will be found to be of higher birth. Like Pamela, Joseph and Fanny have the beautiful skin that portends a birth equal to their worth.[24] But in creating the expectation of a climactic discovery of gentle parentage, Fielding goes a good deal further. Halfway through their adventures we meet a trustworthy gentle-man, Mr Wilson, who narrates with pain his loss of his infant boy many years ago, 'stolen away from my Door by some wicked travelling People whom they call *Gipsies*; . . . he should know him amongst ten thousand, for he had a Mark on his left Breast, of a Strawberry'.[25] And at the end of the story, in a bewildering series of revelations and reversals, it appears that the two lovers may be brother and sister and their match therefore unthinkable. But it turns out that Fanny, too, had been abducted – by the same gypsies – and is therefore discovered to be the daughter of Joseph's humble parents. But the infants were switched in their cradles, and Joseph, strawberry mark and all, is revealed in turn to be the son of the gentleman Mr Wilson.

So on the face of it, Fielding's novel would appear to recapitulate the aristocratic version of family romance by representing how worth really *does* bespeak good birth. But Fielding has deeper motives. Throughout this novel, and in opposition to Richardson's pretence that *Pamela* is the documentary history of an actual person, Fielding's highly intrusive narrator has made it clear that the document we are reading is the author's total fabrication. Amidst the incredible double discovery with which the novel ends, Fielding's narrator remarks that Joseph and Fanny 'felt perhaps little less Anxiety in this Interval than *Œdipus* himself whilst his Fate was revealing'. Now, while Sophocles is no doubt the instrument through which works the tragic hand of fate, he takes no responsibility for the causation he only represents. But when Parson Adams remarks to Mr Wilson that 'Fortune hath I think paid you all her Debts in this sweet Retirement', and Wilson replies 'I am thankful to the great Author of all Things for the Blessings I here enjoy', it is hard not to hear Fielding inviting us to recognize that in this universe, the role of Fortune is played by himself.[26]

Since this story has consisted of one after another plot hatched by vicious characters to victimize the virtuous, each plot foiled only in the nick of time by equally incredible contrivances, readers are obliged to see that the family romance ending has no real-world implications. Novels are fictions that human authors create in order to achieve the sort of poetic justice scarcely ever meted out in reality, whether by Fate or human law. But if this is true, we are not invited to see family romance as being any greater a contrivance than the many other literary and social conventions thrown into relief by Fielding's scepticism. *Joseph Andrews* is a revolutionary, ground-clearing manifesto about the nature of aesthetic experience whose point cannot be reduced to, but is congruent with, the caveat that art should not be confused with life. It rubs the reader's nose in the conventional as training for future encounters with conventions that seek to efface their conventionality, their aesthetic nature.

A parody of family romance, *Joseph Andrews* is celebrated more particularly as a parody of *Pamela*. Fielding's premise is that Joseph is the younger brother of Pamela and a pious imitator of her gendered constancy. Although defensibly rationalized as a Christian rather than an aristocratic virtue, Joseph's constancy still seems a bit silly. This is because in the century between 1650 and 1750, gender difference underwent a revolutionary dichotomization, in part through the emergence of what a later age will call (male) homosexuality, a category that helped concretize the opposition between masculinity and femininity through the mediation of what was at once both and neither.[27] Fielding makes nothing of Joseph's 'fine skin' in this respect, but that micro-convention of aristocratic family romance had become vulnerable to the hypothesis that the contemporary corruption of the nobility was the generation of sodomy.[28] The author of a satirical tract of 1747 writes of the male type of 'the pretty gentleman':

> Observe that fine Complexion! Examine that smooth, that Velvety Skin! View that *Pallor* which spreads itself over his Countenance! Hark, with what feminine Softness his Accents steal their Way through his half-opened Lips! Feel that soft Palm! . . . The *Pretty Gentleman* is certainly formed in a different Mould from that of Common Men, and tempered with a purer Flame . . . [I]t looks as if Nature had been in doubt, to which Sex she should assign *Him*.[29]

In this economical formulation, the 'pretty gentleman' is distinct from 'common men' in the sense of both social status and gender difference. Fine skin, increasingly debunked as a sign of nobility, is validated, as in Richardson, as a sign of something else entirely.

V

The literary and social developments I have been describing can be understood in relation to long-term changes in attitudes toward the nature and value of the family. By discovering the true, elevated parentage of the obscure and lowly, family romance marks first the sheer wonder of how higher forces – fate, the gods, divine Providence – intervene in human affairs, and then the symmetry of human greatness, the ultimate correspondence of worth and birth. In medieval and early modern England, the family's vital role in the upper social tiers was the perpetuation of the patriline, the honour and property embodied in the male heir and passed on to future generations. And for this reason great value was accorded to the ties of blood – in the language of kinship, to consanguinity. Toward the end of the eighteenth century these traditional norms were beginning to be replaced by the modern norms of conjugality, which value less the perdurability of the family over time than the affective depth of present family relations created through marriage.[30] This shift is related to another. The novel comes into being with Western modernity, when the imagination of anthropomorphic extra-human powers is waning and the creative force of interiority – human authorship, mentality – is gaining credit. And if novel plots tend to trace a rising trajectory (as the Bildungsroman often does) in which protagonists attain an eminence that was not evident earlier as their just deserts, it is less likely to be because they have always been possessed of an external condition that is only now disclosed and more likely to be the result of a change internal to their characters. Yet the discovery of parentage, even if its causal finality is diminished and its very presence obscured or displaced, remains central to novelistic representation.

Frances Burney's *Evelina* (1778) is ostentatiously committed to preserving the archaism of family romance, but with a parodic obliquity. We and Evelina know from the outset that she is the daughter of Lord Belmont. But we also know that his marriage to Evelina's mother was clandestine and that the marriage certificate has been destroyed. For most of the novel we are therefore asked to condemn Belmont for his cruel disregard of his daughter. But we and she learn toward the end that he has been deceived by an ambitious nursemaid (whose intrusive household authority modernizes the more traditional alterity of the gypsies), who switched the infant Evelina with her own child. So Evelina, having moved to London from the country, learns the ways of city sophistication as a beautiful heiress condemned to subsist on the meagre allowance of her rural guardian.

Burney depicts a teeming London, a heterogeneous mixture of 'strangers'. Suggesting how physical mobility and urbanization have contributed to the centripetal shrinkage of the modern conjugal family, some of these strangers include her own 'relations' (her maternal grandmother and cousins), whom she 'discovers' for the first time and with whom she has nothing at all in common.[31] Evelina values the affective strength of traditional kinship terms, and she soon learns to award them on the non-genealogical basis of sympathetic proximity – and to no one more confidently than her guardian, whom she insistently addresses as her 'father'.[32] This is the principle that guides the convention of discovered parentage in *Evelina*: not lineal filiation but emotional affiliation.[33] Burney writes under the spell of the cult of sensibility, and over the course of the novel Evelina learns to renounce her traditionalist dependence on male protection and to be guided instead by her own acute sense of the vices and virtues of those around her, whose manners and countenances she learns to read with extraordinary sensitivity. And this is a good thing because the men she encounters, from aristocrats to parvenu shopkeepers, are to a man predatory, hypocritical, or at best irredeemably vulgar. An exception is Lord Orville. As he and Evelina fall in love by passionately and wordlessly reading each other's minds in their countenances, we witness a prime instance of the elasticity of conventions. Aristocratic family romance had turned on the evidence of nobility that was visible on the subject's face and body. Burney preserves but supersedes this romance trope by turning visibility into deep legibility, not a recognition of social value on the surface of the body but an internal communion, through the body, with another's mind and soul. Female constancy has become a faculty of psychological insight.

Reading minds is like reading letters; but as Evelina becomes increasingly expert in the former her skill at the latter lags, perhaps because for Burney documents – language itself – are relatively crude and deceptive instruments of communication. Under the false impression that Orville has written her an improper letter (really a forgery), Evelina anxiously anticipates their next meeting with a display of sensibility that is microscopically acute:

> [S]hould the same impertinent freedom be expressed by his looks, which dictated his cruel letter, I shall not know how to endure either him or myself. . . . Surely he, as well as I, must think of the letter at the moment of our meeting, and he will, probably, mean to gather my thoughts of it from my looks . . . If I find that the *eyes* of Lord Orville agree with his *pen*,—

But very soon she learns, by confidently reading Orville's mute response to other people's words and actions, that she has misread the offensive letter: 'I should have been quite sick of their remarks, had I not been entertained by seeing that Lord Orville, who, I am sure, was equally disgusted, not only read my sentiments, but, by his countenance, communicated to me his own'.[34]

Although Evelina has come to realize that family members do not deserve their family names, Burney wants it both ways, and she arranges her novel's closure in a series of scenes that includes both the inheritance of external values (family title and fortune) and the confirmation of internal values (a deep and mutual sympathy). Still, the sequence of revelations leaves us in no doubt about which values have priority. Orville declares his love for Evelina before the romance trope of the switched infants and her rightful inheritance are revealed. And even here priorities are carefully ordered. Two maternal tokens have come into Evelina's possession, a family locket and a letter proving her identity. But once Belmont sees his late and deeply lamented wife in Evelina's face and his tears of recognition show the true motives of his heart, he receives these material and documentary tokens of parentage almost as an afterthought. Evelina's true parentage has been discovered through the lineage of feeling, and by this means she has become the subject of family romance – but in a manner that feels decidedly less romance than romantic.

My final author, Jane Austen, as in other ways, picks up where Burney leaves off. For a century or more, the parodic distance taken from the convention of family romance has increasingly been expressed as a distance between birth and worth, in which the value of internal nobility is a given, and external nobility, dependent on the discovery of external parentage, is in several different scenarios unlikely to be disclosed or even highly valued. Perhaps the conclusion that worth is not entailed in birth is foregone in a culture committed to the explicit analysis of the tacit assumption that it is. For such a culture, worth or true nobility has an ethical grounding that is defined by its autonomy of external conditions and considerations like birth – that is, defined by its subjective integrity. Austen takes us further in this direction by relocating the opposition 'external birth/internal worth' one level down, where the playing field belongs to one of the adversaries and the contest is between two different species of interior will or motive. In *Pride and Prejudice* (1813) these are most commonly expressed as the opposition '(social) design/(individual) feeling', whose permutations figure in all of the novel's amatory relationships. Birth remains an important category, but its former wholeness has become fragmented. The value of titled rank itself can be expressed in terms of the amount of money it usually accompanies, and the assumption of worth has become not only a joke, but also, in the empty pride of Lady Catherine de Bourgh, an old joke.

One part of Austen's purpose, in fact, is to check the emergent counter-assumption that low birth equals worth, which becomes evident in her heroine's prejudiced regard for Mr Wickham. Elizabeth falls for Wickham not only because of his charm and beauty but also because he presents himself as the victim of a frustrated family romance. As he tells the story, Darcy's father 'was my godfather, and excessively attached to me ... He meant to provide for me amply' by giving Wickham a clerical living. However, Darcy senior dies before the living becomes available, and his son – *our* Mr Darcy – jealously refuses to make good on his father's promise: '[H]is father's uncommon attachment to me, irritated him I believe very early in life. He had not a temper to bear the sort of competition in which we stood—the sort of preference which was often given me'. So in this telling, Wickham is the spiritual younger son cheated of a patrimony that would have declared him the good son in all but birth.[35]

So far from possessing true nobility, Wickham turns out to be a rank opportunist who in the end finds other means to scheme his way into Darcy's family. But *Pride and Prejudice* is itself a family romance, the story of a young woman who comes to believe that her mother and father cannot be her real parents. Elizabeth already feels this about her crassly acquisitive mother when the novel opens. Her father is a different matter since Elizabeth has learned to value his coolly amusing cynicism about the social conventions Mrs Bennet vulgarly embraces. If Elizabeth ever marries it will be for love, and not for externals as her best friend Charlotte has done, sacrificing (in Elizabeth's words) 'every better feeling to worldly advantage'.[36] But as the relationships that solicit Elizabeth's most acute attention – Charlotte and Collins, Jane and Bingley, Elizabeth and Wickham, Elizabeth and Darcy – develop and overlap in complex ways, the easy opposition between design and feeling and their cognates becomes increasingly difficult to maintain, and she is compelled to revise the confident judgements she had made about some of the key players in her circle once her perspective on them becomes multiple.

Austen borrows from Burney the illuminating juxtaposition of reading letters and reading characters, but what Elizabeth learns from this is less a reassuring contrast between the stable truth-values of each than the diversity of point of view. Pemberley augments the relativity of judgement mandated by a multiplicity of perspectives: observing the outlying grounds through the house's windows, wandering through its interior, seeking out the one familiar face in the long consanguineal arrangement of the portrait gallery and finding that she was able to coordinate his point of view – she 'fixed his eyes upon herself' – with her own. Soon after Darcy himself suddenly comes into view and Elizabeth, 'overpowered by shame and vexation' at her presence there, impulsively flees into his emotional interior in a similar act of sympathetic identification: 'How strange must it appear to him!'[37] Elizabeth thus sees herself through Darcy's eyes, a rare moment of self-recognition prefigured by Darcy's proposal and the angry confrontation it precipitates.

In *Evelina*, the suspect nature of documentary words is captured by the forged letter from 'Orville' that Evelina must read twice before she can reconcile its existence with the sensible presence of the man himself. Elizabeth's two readings of Darcy's letter allow her to see the 'forged' quality of her part in their face-to-face confrontation, which now goes inward: 'She grew absolutely ashamed of herself. . . . "I have courted prepossession . . . Till this moment, I never knew myself"'. Elizabeth's initial prejudice against Darcy, reinforced by a blinkered reading of his behaviour, has become a habituated 'design' masquerading as 'feeling', the psychological equivalent of the prepossession that external birth determines internal worth. This moment of self-recognition requires a double perspective, the self reflecting on the self, and it leads her to reflect on the nature of her feelings for Darcy with a cautiously empirical self-consciousness: 'She certainly did not hate him. . . . [T]here was a motive within her of good will which could not be overlooked. It was gratitude. . . . She respected, she esteemed, she was grateful to him, she felt a real interest in his welfare'.[38]

Many readers see Austen as seeking a reconciliation of social conflict, even the ideological conflict between birth and worth, through the courtship and marriage of Darcy and Elizabeth. If this includes what Elizabeth refers to above as the 'courtship' of subjective states, I agree. But it is this internal courtship, and the act of reconciliation within Elizabeth's mind – better, the disclosure of psychological conflict in need of reconciliation – that most commands our attention, and the true reconciliation can begin only when the simplistic 'birth vs. worth' formulation has been rejected. Nonetheless its conclusion requires that family romance rise to the surface in the Bennet family narrative through Wickham's parodic courtship of Elizabeth's sister Lydia.

True, family romance might be said to surface much earlier than this. The paradigmatic characterizations of Mrs and Mr Bennet as exemplars, respectively, of social design and individual feeling are masterfully established in the first chapter. Mrs Bennet's characterization alters little over the course of the novel, and her husband's view of her (and therefore his views in general) coincides with and is validated by that of the narrative voice.[39] How and why do we come to know Mr Bennet's defects? This is a surprisingly difficult question to answer. The whole of Volume I contains only two relatively minor instances of his improper behaviour.[40] In Volume II, Darcy's letter to Elizabeth charges that apart from Jane and herself, a '"want of propriety"' is betrayed by all the females in the Bennet family, '"and occasionally even by your father"'. Pondering this letter, Elizabeth painfully reviews in her mind 'the unhappy defects of her family', including her father's failure to correct her sisters' manners. Hoping to persuade him to forbid Lydia's impending trip to Brighton, Elizabeth soon after warns Mr Bennet that the family's 'importance, our respectability in the world, must be affected by the wild volatility, the assurance and disdain of all restraint which mark Lydia's character'. Mr Bennet listens sympathetically but demurs. And in the opening of the final chapter of Volume II, we read at some length that Elizabeth 'had never been blind to the impropriety of her father's behaviour as a husband', a defect that includes his habit of 'exposing his wife to the contempt of her own children'.[41] Propriety is related to property. But although we are told early on the crucial fact that in default of an heir male the Bennet estate is entailed out of the immediate family, not until halfway through Volume III does the narrator address Mr Bennet's chronic failure, and his own awareness of that failure (he 'had very often wished, before this period of his life . . .'), to provide financially for that possibility.[42]

Two points are worth making. First, Austen's narrator withholds from us the knowledge and degree of Mr Bennet's defective parentage (and reciprocally, the rational basis for Mrs Bennet's marital anxieties), of which the family members themselves have long been aware. Second, the revelation of these defects is precipitated by Darcy's letter and Elizabeth's reading of it. The result is that in Austen's hands, not only Mr Bennet's paternal defects but also Elizabeth's feeling of being 'slighted', although hinted at earlier, are brought to the level of narrative consciousness by being brought by Darcy's viewpoint to Elizabeth's consciousness. Why should Darcy be the agent of this?

Elizabeth first hears of Lydia's and Wickham's elopement in two distressed letters from Jane, which firmly establish the importance of epistolary communication in maintaining family connections during this multi-county crisis. Elizabeth's anguish is extreme. Impatient early on, like her father, with the practical imperatives of family designs, Elizabeth has learned, through both Lydia's 'susceptibility to her feelings' and her own, that design has its place.[43] Apparently Mr Bennet, having gone to London to aid in the search for the eloped couple, has learned this too. But his family waits in vain for a letter from him and has to rely instead on bits of news sent by Mr Gardiner, Mrs Bennet's brother, a London lawyer of means who with his wife has enjoyed taking Elizabeth under their wing. Even on his return to Longbourn Mr Bennet is quite incommunicative, and when he receives a letter from his brother-in-law, he diffidently hands it to Elizabeth to read aloud. From this we learn that Mr Gardiner has located the couple and persuaded Wickham to accept an outrageously generous marriage settlement, a modest and official amount to be paid by Lydia's father and a much larger, unofficial one to be financed by Mr Gardiner. All that is needed is Mr Bennet's permission '"to act in your name"', which is to say to act as a surrogate father in default of Mr Bennet himself. As Mrs Bennet exults, '"I knew he would manage every thing"'.[44]

In the latter chapters of the novel, the semantic interchange between 'design' and 'feeling' is rivalled by the polysemy of 'family connections', a single term whose elastic power of designation shifts back and forth between patrilineal and affective propriety. Reading Darcy's letter, Elizabeth comes to see that his 'feelings' regarding 'the inferiority of your connections' concern – or have come to concern – less the Bennets' genealogy than their crude and unfeeling behaviour.[45] From a mindless remark by Lydia succinctly representative of Bennet crudeness, Elizabeth is astonished to discover that Darcy, "'a person unconnected with any of us'", was present at Lydia's wedding to Wickham.[46] And from Mrs Gardiner she learns that Darcy had so strenuously insisted that he, rather than Mr Gardiner, take on the marriage settlement, that the parentage Elizabeth has discovered might justly be said to be that of Darcy himself. Incidentally, although Darcy bargains down Wickham's anticipated payoff, the support he provides reverses his earlier denial of support in the form of the clerical living that Darcy senior was said to have promised Wickham. So Darcy is 'discovered' to be the 'father' of Wickham as well as Elizabeth.

Of the several family romances I have discussed in this essay, only the eighteenth-century versions suggest that the cause responsible for dis-covered parentage resides in the mind and will of the protagonist as much as it might have a transindividual, genealogical-ontological origin. The mysterious core of the phenomenon is to be sought not beyond but within. And it is only Austen's version that fully transforms the convention that the exteriority of marriage is a significant confirmation of interiority by interiorizing that confirmation itself at the level of psychic discovery. This discovery has a crucial ambivalence, which Austen represents through a doubled narrative perspective. On the one hand, her narrator makes us aware from the outset that Elizabeth's parentage is psychosocially problematic, but her father's role in this appears to be no more than reactive to the defects of her mother. On the other hand, at the moment that Elizabeth reads Darcy's letter and learns his motives we begin to realize – both through the medium of Elizabeth's voice, which focalizes the problem in her consciousness, and through the medium of the narra-tor's voice, which informs us that Elizabeth (and to some extent Mr Bennet) has been aware of it for much longer – that the problem is equally her father's behaviour. This differential – between the narrator's and Elizabeth's voice and between the past and the present – marks for us Elizabeth's emotional engagement with Darcy's perspective on her family as the moment her unconscious begins to become conscious. The micro-process by which Elizabeth's unconscious becomes conscious is the same as the macro-process by which Austen's plot discovers to us the deep truth about the Bennet family. In the dynamics of Austen's family romance, Darcy is the initial agent of Elizabeth's emotional alienation from her father, the final agent of her financial alienation from him, and the discovered father who will become her marriage choice. As in the second stage of Freud's family romance, the mother remains known and defective, while the father is found to be the ideal image and model of her husband.

VI

I will conclude with some thoughts about how the idea of a convention's 'afterlife' might shed light on the way we do literary history. So far from quibbling with that idea (as the speculative quality of these thoughts otherwise might suggest to readers), I take it to offer an entry into the always-fruitful topic of the literary period.

There is of course a straightforward and unproblematic meaning to the idea that the eighteenth-century novel has an afterlife, and it would be rewarding to pursue the family romance convention into the nineteenth-century novel. Dickens alone – I am thinking of *Oliver Twist* (1838), *Bleak House* (1852–53), and *Hard Times* (1854), to go no further – wrote striking variations that would richly extend the life of the convention. What justifies having chosen instead to investigate the 'anterior-life' or prehistory of eighteenth-century fiction?

It is salient to this question that it is not entirely accurate. Freud's version of discovered parentage, with which I began and which by consensus gives an umbrella name to the convention, itself exemplifies the afterlife of eighteenth-century fiction, having been shaped not simply by Sophocles but by the modern turn toward psychic interiority that is significantly fuelled by, among other things, the eighteenth-century novel. It is not surprising that the conventionality of family romance in *Pride and Prejudice*, the most modern of our texts, should be amenable to Freud's reading of it, and I think we can assume the broad compatibility of that reading with other modern versions of the convention. Is it also compatible with the pre-eighteenth-century versions I have discussed?

This question – about Austen's past, not her future – seems of greater promise for thinking about the historical existence of literary and social conventions that is bound up with the notion of an afterlife. Freud posits the Oedipal Complex, and by implication the psychosexual meaning of family romance, as universal to all cultures, a position that would preclude compatibility with earlier and non-Western versions except in so far as they result from the transhistorical human mind's censorship of its own unconscious. But if we see Freud's version not as a universal but as a compellingly modern reading, the question remains: is the conventionality of family romance continuous across its several versions of discovered parentage despite the apparent discontinuity, at the level of both action and contextual meaning, of the mythic, the Christian, the post-Conquest, the feudal, the aristocratic, the Protestant, and the novelistic? Is the convention of discovered parentage elastic enough to encompass supernatural fiat, the naturalization of mass migration, the rationalization of worth as an entailment of birth, the material accommodation of spiritual conversion, the reward of worth with the metaphor of kinship, and a crucial stage of psychosexual development? Do the successive versions of family romance preserve or supersede what precedes them?

To approach the question of the afterlife of conventions in this way may also unsettle assumptions about the special nature of the novel genre. We are accustomed to seeing the novel as singularly dynamic in form, unusually given to experiment and innovation compared to more traditional and stable kinds of imaginative writing. On this basis we might expect the novelistic version of family romance to push the convention to its most inventively 'unconventional' fulfilment and thereby to constitute most fully its potential and 'life' as a convention, to be followed then by its afterlife. But are the variety and growth of the novel genre any more luxuriant over its 300-year history than romance has been over two millennia? Is the novel perhaps the afterlife of romance?

By this way of thinking, family romance in the eighteenth-century novel represents in turn the afterlife of aristocratic romance. But we can go further than this. In this essay I have been generalizing about the eighteenth-century novelistic family romance as a totality, but as we have seen on the evidence of *Pamela*, *Joseph Andrews*, and *Evelina* alone, that convention is not a single, self-identical form but a series of widely variant instances. Might we say that each of these successive instances amounts to the afterlife of what came before? The transition from the life to the afterlife of a convention might then be defined by nothing more conventional – that is, communal – than the scrupulously singular version on which we choose to focus our attention. By the same token, the life of a convention might be found, as Freud does, in a universal human motive that lies beyond all communal specificity and generates all formal instances. Between these two extremes – of absolute discontinuity and absolute continuity – lies the territory of historical study.

Notes

1 Sigmund Freud, 'Family Romances', *The Standard Edition of the Complete Psychological Works of Sigmund Freud*, trans. and eds. James Strachey and Anna Freud, 24 vols. (London: Hogarth, 1957), vol. 9, pp. 237, 239.
2 This is what Otto Rank calls 'the myth of the birth of the hero': *The Myth of the Birth of the Hero and Other Writings* (1914), ed. Peter Freund (New York: Vintage, 1959), pp. 14–64 for 'The Circle of Myths'.

3 James Frazer, *The New Golden Bough* (1890), ed. and abr. Theodor H. Gaster (New York: Mentor, 1964), Pts. III–IV.

4 H. J. Rose, *A Handbook of Greek Mythology* (New York: E. P. Dutton, 1959), pp. 182–96.

5 F. W. Maitland, *The Constitutional History of England* (1908; Cambridge University Press, 1965), pp. 37, 156–57; G. O. Sayles, *The Medieval Foundations of England* (New York: A. S. Barnes, 1961), p. 211.

6 F. L. Ganshof, *Feudalism*, trans. Philip Grierson, 3rd Eng. edn (New York: Harper Torchbooks, 1964), pp. 139–40.

7 Peter Laslett, *The World We Have Lost Further Explored*, 3rd edn (New York: Charles Scribner's, 1984), pp. 239–41; Jack Goody, *The Development of the Family and Marriage in Europe* (Cambridge University Press, 1983), p. 44; Lawrence Stone and Jeanne C. F. Stone, *An Open Elite? England, 1540–1880* (Oxford: Clarendon Press, 1984), p. 397.

8 G. M. Vogt, 'Gleanings for the History of a Sentiment: *Generositas Virtus, non Sanguis*', *Journal of English and Germanic Philology*, 24:1 (1925), 102–24.

9 Michael McKeon, *The Origins of the English Novel, 1600–1740* (1987; Baltimore: Johns Hopkins University Press, 2002), pp. 132–33, 150–59, 164–67, 189–211.

10 Daniel Defoe, *The True-Born Englishman* (London: [no publisher], 1700), pp. 20, 22; *The Compleat English Gentleman* (written 1728–29), ed. Karl D. Bülbring (London: David Nutt, 1890), pp. 16–17.

11 William Sprigg, *A Modest Plea for an Equal Common-wealth Against Monarchy* (London: Giles Calvert, 1659), pp. 62–63, 68–69.

12 Edmund Bolton, *The Cities Advocate, in this Case or Question of Honor and Armes; whether Apprentiship extinguisheth Gentry?* (London: William Lee, 1629), p. 52; Defoe, *The Complete English Tradesman*, 2nd edn, 2 vols. (London: Charles Rivington, 1727), vol. 1, p. 311.

13 Thomas Deloney, *Thomas of Reading* (1600), in *Shorter Novels: Elizabethan*, eds. George Saintsbury and Philip Henderson (London: J. M. Dent, 1972), p. 98; Gervase Holles, *Memorials of the Holles Family, 1493–1656*, ed. A. C. Wood, Camden Society, 3rd series, 55 (London: Offices of the Society, 1937), pp. 34–35.

14 *Charles II's Escape from Worcester: A Collection of Narratives Assembled by Samuel Pepys*, ed. William Matthews (Berkeley and Los Angeles: University of California Press, 1966), pp. 40, 50, 88, 94, 96, 107, 160.

15 On the episodes of the Black Box and the Warming Pan, see Michael McKeon, *The Secret History of Domesticity: Public, Private, and the Division of Knowledge* (Baltimore: Johns Hopkins University Press, 2005), pp. 499–503, 549–57. On the preference for internal, 'religious nobility' over external, genealogical nobility in the deposal and replacement of James II see McKeon, *Origins*, pp. 181–82.

16 'Lord of Learne', ll.285–86, 'The Nutt browne mayd', ll.135–37, 199–200, in *Bishop Percy's Folio Manuscript. Ballads and Romances*, eds. J. W. Hales and F. J. Furnivall, 3 vols. (London: N. Trübner, 1868), vol. 1, p. 193; vol. 3, pp. 182, 184.

17 Robert Greene, *Penelope's Web* (1587), second tale ('Calamus and Cratyna'), in *Life and Complete Works in Prose and Verse of Robert Greene*, ed. Alexander

B. Grosart, 15 vols. (1881–86; New York: Russell and Russell, 1964), vol. 5, pp. 203, 204, 215, 216; Gabriel Harvey, 'A Noble Mans Sute to a Cuntrie Maid', *Letter-Book of Gabriel Harvey, 1573–80*, ed. Edward J. L. Scott, Camden Society, n.s., 33 (London: Nichols and Sons, 1884), pp. 144, 145.

18 T[homas] H[ooker,] *The Christians Two Chiefe Lessons* (London: P. Stephens and C. Meredith, 1640), p. 288; John Bunyan, *Grace Abounding to the Chief of Sinners* (1666), ed. Roger Sharrock (Oxford: Clarendon Press, 1962), p. 32; Thomas Edwards, 'The Holy Choice' (1625), quoted in Michael Walzer, *The Revolution of the Saints: A Study in the Origins of Radical Politics* (Cambridge, MA: Harvard University Press, 1965), p. 235.

19 Samuel Richardson, *Pamela; or, Virtue Rewarded* (1740), eds. Thomas Keymer and Alice Wakely (Oxford University Press, 2001), p. 53.

20 Richardson, *Pamela*, pp. 69, 70, 76, 77.

21 Richardson, *Pamela*, pp. 289, 294.

22 Richardson, *Pamela*, pp. 223–25.

23 Richardson, *Pamela*, pp. 227, 130–31. For Pamela's refutation of the purity of lineages, see p. 258. For Mr B. on *Pamela* as a novel, pp. 231–32 (but the terms themselves are not clearly distinguished here).

24 Henry Fielding, *Joseph Andrews* (1742), ed. Douglas Brooks-Davies, rev. Thomas Keymer (Oxford University Press, 1999), pp. 33, 132–33.

25 Fielding, *Joseph Andrews*, pp. 195–96.

26 Fielding, *Joseph Andrews*, pp. 295, 195.

27 See further McKeon, *Secret History*, ch. 6. On the parodic uses Fielding makes of Joseph's 'feminine' chastity, see McKeon, *Origins*, pp. 398–400.

28 See Michael McKeon, 'Historicizing Patriarchy: The Emergence of Gender Difference in England, 1660–1760', *Eighteenth-Century Studies*, 28:3 (1995), 295–322 (309–12).

29 [Nathaniel Lancaster], *The Pretty Gentleman* (London: M. Cooper, 1747), pp. 25–26.

30 Ruth Perry, *Novel Relations: The Transformation of Kinship in English Literature and Culture, 1748–1818* (Cambridge University Press, 2004).

31 Frances Burney, *Evelina or the History of a Young Lady's Entrance into the World* (1778), eds. Edward A. Bloom and Vivien Jones (Oxford University Press, 2002), pp. 51–53, 69–72, 85–87.

32 Burney, *Evelina*, pp. 26, 131, 126, 266.

33 For 'filiation/affiliation', see Richard Braverman, *Plots and Counterplots: Sexual Politics and the Body Politic in English Literature, 1660–1730* (Cambridge University Press, 1993).

34 Burney, *Evelina*, pp. 277–78, 288.

35 Austen, *Pride and Prejudice* (1813), eds. James Kinsley, Frank W. Bradbrook, and Isobel Armstrong (Oxford University Press, 1990), pp. 60, 61.

36 Austen, *Pride and Prejudice*, p. 96.

37 Austen, *Pride and Prejudice*, pp. 189, 191.

38 Austen, *Pride and Prejudice*, pp. 159, 201.

39 Austen, *Pride and Prejudice*, p. 3. The narrator echoes Mr Bennet on Mr Collins: see pp. 48, 53.
40 Austen, *Pride and Prejudice*, pp. 77, 85–86.
41 Austen, *Pride and Prejudice*, pp. 152, 163, 176, 180–81.
42 Austen, *Pride and Prejudice*, pp. 20, 233–34.
43 Austen, *Pride and Prejudice*, p. 215.
44 Austen, *Pride and Prejudice*, pp. 230, 232.
45 Austen, *Pride and Prejudice*, p. 148.
46 Austen, *Pride and Prejudice*, p. 243.

CHAPTER 3

From Pícaro to Pirate: Afterlives of the Picaresque in Early Eighteenth-Century Fiction

Leah Orr

In the 1720s, there was a sudden interest in criminal biographies: lives of pirates, prostitutes, and robbers became a major subgenre of fiction. Some of these, such as *Captain Singleton* (1720), *Moll Flanders* (1722), and *John Sheppard* (1724), have become landmark texts in the history of fiction. Where did this trend come from? Scholars of early fiction, including Michael McKeon and Paul Salzman, have noted how the plots of these works are similar to the episodic picaresque and rogue tales of the seventeenth century.[1] However, the real innovation of the works of the 1720s, the focus on a single character's development and motives, has remained unexplained. In this essay, I argue that the eighteenth-century interest in the criminal character relates directly to the chapbook abridgements of seventeenth-century picaresque and rogue tales, as well as earlier folktales popular as chapbooks. These abridgements pared down the rambling plots of rogue fictions to those events that were important in the life of the main character and eliminated other digressions and subplots. By examining the chapbook afterlives and abridgements of the Spanish picaresque *Don Quixote* (1605–15), the English rogue tale *The English Rogue* (1665), and the English folktale narratives *Robin Hood, Reynard the Fox, Sheffery Morgan, Tom Ladle*, and *Tom Tram*, I shall demonstrate that their concentration on character over plot is the same focus that allows for more extended criminal biographies like those in the 1720s. General interest in the chapbook tales signals the market for crime fiction. While some chapbooks remained popular throughout the eighteenth century, their afterlives became what many modern scholars identify as the novel proper.

Abridgements of Seventeenth-Century Picaresque

Although the term picaresque, as Chad M. Gasta points out, is often loosely defined and problematically applied, it generally indicates a type of narrative that has an episodic plot and features a single main character (the pícaro).[2] The pícaro is a rogue character – that is, one who commits more or less petty crimes rather than pursuing a grand adventure or ambition.[3] The episodic plot relates to this: many picaresque narratives follow the crimes of the main character with no clear plot arc other than the beginning and end of the pícaro's life. In the sort of book-length picaresque narratives that were written in the seventeenth century, the form and the content of the work are inextricably connected: the narrative is shaped by the actions of the main character. In the chapbook abridgements of two popular picaresque works, *Don Quixote* and *The English Rogue*, however, the plot is nearly eliminated to focus on character – redefining the rogue narrative to be an exploration of character development rather than the rambling life of the criminal.

Properly speaking, *Don Quixote* is not really picaresque since Quixote is not a criminal or pícaro, but it is often discussed as such because of its episodic plot.[4] First translated into English in 1612, *Don Quixote* was reprinted regularly in its entirety as well as in part, and two new translations appeared in 1700.[5] The length of the full *Don Quixote* meant that it was an expensive book, only available to readers willing and able to spend considerable money on books. The chapbook abridgement that first appeared in 1686, however, introduced the work to a much wider audience and was part of a series of dramatic, poetic, and humorous abridgements and imitations.[6] Chapbooks were a cheaply printed format of just sixteen to forty-eight pages long sold by 'chapmen' for two to six pence: as Margaret Spufford comments, 'These chapbooks really were priced within the reach of the agricultural labourer'.[7] For many people, then, the chapbook abridgement would have been the only version of *Don Quixote* they knew.

Importantly for my argument here, the author of the chapbook altered the basis of the narrative to make Quixote's character the central element of the work – not the episodic plot following his adventures. In the 1612 translation of *Don Quixote*, Quixote is primarily motivated by external concerns: he starts on his adventures because he was 'spur'd on the more vehemently, by the want which he esteemed his delays wrought in the world, according to the wrongs that he resolved to right'.[8] His reason for leaving home in the first place, then, is a sense of duty prompted by problems in the wider world. Much of his thinking is reported through his interactions with other characters, particularly his squire Sancho, and they offer their perspectives on his actions. In the chapbook abridgements nearly all information about other characters is absent, and Quixote's strange personal sense of chivalry is the driving force behind all the action in the narrative. The shift in focus is evident even in the chapter titles. In the full version of *Don Quixote*, the chapters have titles that describe events, such as 'Of that which befell to our Knight, after he had departed from the Inne'.[9] The titles in the 1686 chapbook focus on Quixote, making him the reason for the events described: the first chapter, for example, is titled 'How *Don Quixote* set out; and of the Lady he chose to fight for'.[10] Most of the subsequent chapters start with the phrase 'How Don Quixote' did something, indicating that he is the driving force behind the actions described, rather than someone who is primarily reacting to the world around him.

The absence of any overarching plot means that the chapters in the chapbook focus on self-contained events, like Quixote's fight with the carriers or his imagining that the mills are giants. All the digressive elements of the original narrative are eliminated, along with episodes that feature other characters such as Quixote's conversation with a group of goatherds or the histories of other characters that Quixote meets (including a captain, a lackey, and a shepherd). The only plot framework given in the chapbook version is that Quixote inexplicably chooses 'to seek Adventures' one day, and the narrative ends abruptly with the comment that 'These are the principal Exploits and Adventures of this Famous Knight-Errant ... who having made his Sancho Governour of an Island, as he promised, was himself carried home as in an Enchanted Cage, and there ended his days'.[11] There is no conflict, resolution, or narrative arc, and the events described in the individual chapters are unconnected except that they feature Quixote. A different chapbook version from around 1695 similarly presents Quixote as 'seeking out Adventures' and concludes that he is simply 'sent home to the Village of the *Mancha*; where Don *Quixote* soon after repented him of his Follies, and ended his Days'.[12] This indication that Quixote 'repented' after returning home does attempt to provide some closure to the narrative: that is, Quixote's adventures have to stop at this point because he realizes that he had been wrong to think as he did. Such a conclusion is unsatisfactory as presented in the chapbook, however, since there is no hint that Quixote is even reconsidering the basis for his actions until this final sentence.

While *Don Quixote* is abridged in such a way that emphasizes character by eliminating plot, chapbook versions of *The English Rogue* focus on the life of the main character by highlighting how his life and death frame the narrative and provide a cohesive narrative arc. The full version of *The English Rogue*, written by Richard Head, was originally published in 1665.[13] The main character, Meriton Latroon, descends into a life of crime (primarily theft) and immoral behaviour (drinking and various sexual adventures). He is eventually arrested and transported, and the last third of the narrative is more about his travels than his crimes. *The English Rogue* was successful enough to warrant three sequels published between 1668 and 1671, each of which replicates some elements of the first volume through digressive stories told to Meriton by other people he meets in his travels.[14] Meriton hardly appears at all in the fourth part, which largely follows the life of a different person only tangentially connected to the story from the first part. Such digressions are absent from the chapbook abridgements of the narrative, which mostly focus only on events found in the first part.

Both of the chapbooks of *The English Rogue* show how Meriton turned to a life of crime and provide a more cohesive narrative than is found even in just the first part of the full version. The first chapbook, published in 1679, is called *The Life and Death of the English Rogue*, emphasizing that the plot is meant to encompass Meriton's entire life.[15] The title page indicates that one purpose of the narrative is to provide 'Directions to all Travellers, how to Know Rogues and how to Avoid them', while the address to the reader (signed 'R. H.') expresses a wish that 'May my Debauch't Life and Sinfull Death be a warning to all that Read this ensuing story'.[16] The plot is greatly simplified: Meriton is a beggar, when he is spotted by a merchant who makes him his servant. He has an affair with his master's wife, other apprentices teach him to be a thief, and he learns to be a pickpocket, conman, and eventually a highwayman. When he is caught and condemned to death, he repents and confesses his crimes. Whereas in the full *English Rogue* Meriton's sentence is commuted to transportation, enabling his adventures to continue, in the chapbook he resigns himself and dies: on his execution day, 'Then did I hear my passing-Bell, every Stroke methought, carried my soul one degree higher; being well satisfied about my eternal state, I willingly imbraced Death'.[17] By altering the story this way, the chapbook provides a clear narrative arc and a reason for ending Meriton's narrative, and also adds a moral that is absent from the longer version where he escapes without punishment. The second chapbook, from 1688, ends with his sentence commuted to transportation and his promise that 'now am I put to my Shifts once again, which shall be related in a Second Part, according as this finds acceptance in the World'.[18] This version was evidently not as successful, as it was not reprinted and no sequel appeared, while *The Life and Death of the English Rogue* was reprinted at least twice.[19]

While *Don Quixote* and *The English Rogue* enjoyed success in various abridgements, other picaresque narratives that were translated into English did not work as well in short form, even if they were successful in their full-length versions. The 600-page *Life of Guzman de Alfarache*, for example, was first translated into English in 1623 and a 'fifth' edition appeared in 1656.[20] *Guzman* would not lend itself to the chapbook form, however. Much of the space in *Guzman* is devoted to his advice, musings, and aphoristic observations on life. His descent into theft and his decision to become a pícaro are preceded by digressions on the human desire to be good, the right amount of alcohol to drink, how church-men keep their reputations, and how porters are often rogues.[21] A 200-page version of *Guzman* from 1685 shortens the narrative by eliminating these digressions and evidently did well enough to be reprinted at least once, and Roger Boyle wrote a play about the main character. But neither these adaptations nor the full version was adapted successfully to the changing tastes of the fiction market of the late seventeenth and early eighteenth centuries.[22] Too much of *Guzman* depends on the philosophical digressions; without them, the plot lacks cohesion and the main character seems unoriginal.

Character was clearly important for abridgers of picaresque narratives, and the very short versions in chapbooks focused on character to the exclusion of other narrative elements or plot devices. Brief versions of *Don Quixote* eliminate the plot altogether, retaining only the basic premise of Quixote's wild imagination leading him to become a knight errant. Abridgers of *The English Rogue* created a more cohesive plot than was found in the full version of the work by eliminating digressions and side characters and showing Meriton Latroon repenting and suffering punishment at the end of his life. These abridgements show recognition of the difference in reading practices between a multi-volume narrative and a chapbook: in a short work there is no room for an elaborate plot, so the characters have to be compelling enough to engage a reader.

Rogue Characters from the English Folklore Tradition

The importance of memorable characters for chapbooks is also apparent from the popularity achieved by English folktales and original new works in the chapbook market of the late seventeenth and early eighteenth centuries. While abridging a long picaresque narrative into a character-focused chapbook by eliminating digressions makes sense from a practical standpoint, the new character-driven chapbooks had no such reasons to stick to a well-known story. There were many chapbooks that did not focus on notable characters, but some of the most frequently reprinted of them did. Many of these characters were successful in chapbooks but were not adapted into any longer versions in the seventeenth century, partly because they employ often coarse humour and violence of a sort found only in chapbook fiction. The type of humour is one way that these chapbooks helped to develop a distinctly English rogue tradition in the late seventeenth century. There are three basic types of roguish characters in the chapbooks derived from the folklore tradition or featuring new stories: rogue-heroes (like Robin Hood); rogue-tricksters (like Reynard the Fox); and rogue-jesters (like Tom Tram).

There are, of course, plenty of character-driven chapbooks that are not about roguish characters. Some are about chivalric heroes (*Guy of Warwick* or *Bevis of Hampton*); some tell of interesting lives or noble deeds of commoners (*The Valiant London-Prentice* or *Jack of Newbery*); and some show saint-like sacrifice (*Patient Grisel*).[23] For the most part, however, these works have unambiguous moral appeal: the reader is invited to admire the main character and perhaps emulate him or her. They are not as problematic as the rogue narratives, which have to create a character with sufficiently compelling personal qualities or a strict sense of fairness and justice that can counteract the unsavoury and criminal behaviour described.

Rogue-heroes are characters whose roguish or criminal behaviour is justified by noble or virtuous ends. They are sometimes, but not always, of noble birth. Robin Hood, the quintessential rogue-hero who steals from the wealthy to give to the poor, was of obscure origins in the original medieval versions of the tale, but he was rewritten as an exiled noble following Anthony Munday's 1598 play about his exploits.[24] The chapbook version of the tale follows Munday in this regard, proclaiming Robin Hood's 'Noble Birth' in the same size font as his name on the title page.[25] It begins with the explanation that 'Robin Hood was descended of the Noble family of the Earl of Huntington; and being Out law'd by Henry the Eighth, for many Extravagancies and Outrages he had committed, he did draw together a company of such bold and Licentious persons as himself'.[26] There is no overarching plot to the chapbook, but rather twelve separate stories mainly connected by their featuring Robin Hood. Many of these show a rather unsavoury side of the hero. In one instance, when he wins an archery contest and his rivals do not want to give him the money he won, he kills fifteen of them without mercy: 'Now to your costs', he declares, 'you have found me to be an Archer'.[27] Such violence seems extreme just to prove his point and receive his winnings. Yet these events are balanced by his acts of kindness, as in another story where he exchanges clothing with a beggar and then saves three men from the gallows.[28] By showing Robin Hood to have a noble background and a generous heart, the author of the chapbook is able to maintain sympathy for him even when he is committing mass murder or stealing outright from the sheriff.

Unlike the rogue-heroes, for whom good ends justify bad behaviour, the rogue-tricksters often act for selfish reasons. Their deceptions and tricks are often in response to provocation, however, so like the rogue-heroes they present the illusion that they would not be driven to immoral acts if the rest of the world behaved properly. The chapbook version of Reynard, for example, shows Reynard tricking the other animals after they complain about him to the king. For instance, Reynard brings Tibert the Cat to a henhouse where he himself had previously stolen a hen and tells the cat that he can get mice there. Predictably, the cat 'sprang quickly in, but was quickly caught fast by the Neck, which as soon as the Cat felt he leapt back again, so that the Snare closed and had like to have strangled him'.[29] To the cat's cries Reynard callously jeers, 'Cousen Tibert, love you Mice?'[30] If Tibert had not been shown to be one of the animals complaining against Reynard when the fox had no chance to defend himself, the scene would appear to be an example of Reynard's cruelty; as it stands in the chapbook, however, it depicts Reynard's justified revenge on his detractor.

Reynard's revenge on Tibert is typical of other deceptions in rogue-trickster tales of the late seventeenth century in that it causes little permanent damage. Tibert escapes, and although he loses an eye, no other lasting harm comes from the episode. Frequently, tricks centre on theft, which is portrayed as a more common, less serious crime than bodily injury. *Sheffery Morgan* provides a typical example of how robbery is justified after a highwayman steals £20 from Sheffery. When he sees the thief later, he tells the man he dropped his purse down a well, and the highwayman proposes to go into the well after the money. This works to Sheffery's advantage: 'off comes the Thiefs apparel, and into the Bucket he gets, while Sheffery was very ready to set him down; which done, but seeing the Road clear, and the Thief safe where he could not come out without help, now is the time, thought Sheffery, to deceive the deceiver'.[31] Sheffery gets away with the highwayman's chest, containing £300, while the thief is eventually rescued and chased away by a group of townspeople.[32] The language of the scene serves to justify Sheffery's act: the other man is consistently called the 'Thief', to remind the reader of his criminality. Sheffery's decision to leave the man in the well is presented as spontaneous ('now is the time') and justified ('to deceive the deceiver') rather than premeditated and dishonest. Although the money was presumably stolen from other hapless victims, Sheffery makes no effort to return it or to use it for charitable ends; instead, he 'resolved if he could to raise his Fortune, and get him a handsome young Woman to his Wife, to the end that he might reap the full enjoyment of his Youth'.[33] In this case, Sheffery is also a thief – and worse than the original highwayman since he stole £300 instead of just £20. Yet the chapbook presents his act as justified revenge, and no more than what he earned by the trouble the robbery caused him. The only person harmed in the end, the highwayman, escapes with no damage other than the loss of his stolen money.

The rogue-jesters, similarly, largely avoid causing permanent harm and instead focus their roguish behaviour on making other people look silly. Like the victims of the rogue-heroes, the dupes of the rogue-jesters often deserve the treatment they receive. Tom Ladle, for example, chiefly targets a barber who is having an affair with Tom's mother. The first time Tom catches them, he takes up a stick 'with which he let drive at the Barber's Posteriors, and not only wounded him, but made him leave his sport to see what enemy gave him that back blow'.[34] When this fails to stop the Barber, Tom puts gunpowder in the man's shop, causing a small fire and startling the Barber: 'the poor Barber lost all the Hair off his Eye-brows, tumbled back, and broke his best Looking-glass, which cut his head; but alas! that was not all, for there stood in the way a Pan of Charcoal; which in the Fall he touching, fell all upon him, and some of it into his best Breeches'.[35] This slapstick scene causes discomfort and embarrassment for the Barber, but no lasting damage, and the Barber eventually gets his revenge by seeing Tom beaten by a parson.[36] Tom Ladle is not really a criminal in the way that Robin Hood is.

Some of the rogue-jesters do commit more serious crimes as well as light-hearted pranks, but they often seem unaware of the relative damage they are doing to their victims. In other words, actions of varying degrees of seriousness to modern sensibilities are often presented as being equal, and the rogue character may appear indifferent to the harm caused to his victims. Simon Dickie has argued that in the mid-eighteenth century readers 'openly delighted in the miseries of others', and some of the chapbook pranksters certainly seem to be appealing to a sense of humour different from modern sensibilities.[37] I would suggest that rogue-jesters also seem like better people partly through their ignorance and lack of intention: they are not presented as careful planners or connivers, but rather they simply create situations for other characters to appear silly.

Tom Ladle did not intend for the Barber to break his mirror, cut his head, and ruin his breeches, but by hiding gunpowder in his shop he knew that *something* would happen.

An example of rogue stories intermingling serious and light-hearted tricks can be found in *Tom Tram of the West*, which relates a series of mostly unrelated anecdotes about Tram's pranks on different people. In one anecdote, when he is in prison, the Mayor annoys him by demanding that the prisoners sing psalms instead of 'bawdy songs'.[38] Tram responds by bribing his fellow prisoners 'so that when the Mayor was gone to bed, the Prison-window being close to his Chamber-window, they began to sing Psalms so loud, that the Mayor could take no rest'.[39] This irritates the Mayor so much that he orders them to be released from prison. Tram could not possibly have known that this would be the Mayor's reaction; like Tom Ladle and the barber, Tom Tram was simply setting events in motion and waiting to see what the outcome would be. Tram also executes more elaborately planned and serious tricks, however. In one instance, he offers to give a group of gypsies a place to stay for the night. He leads them to a house surrounded by a ditch, and once they are inside, he removes the bridge leading to the house and sets it on fire. Tram watches 'till they were all in the Ditch, crying and calling out for help, when by Toms means, most part of the Town stood to see the Jest'. At last, he helps them to a warm house, 'where Tom counsels them that they should never make him believe that they could tell him any thing, that did not know what danger should befall themselves'.[40] Tom Tram thereby manages to make the incident into a lesson for the gypsies (not to try to tell the future) and to the reader (not to be deceitful). This is presented as the justification for his treatment of the gypsies, though he deceived them into thinking they could trust him, and he tried to cause them serious injury and perhaps even death by fire.

The English tales adapted into chapbooks, therefore, demonstrate the recognition that character was central to the success of a short form. They also show that once the focus is on the criminal as a person and his or her motives, crime narratives can include a wider variety of criminal types. By focusing on character, writers of these works had to include some appealing or positive characteristics to keep readers interested; hence their protagonists are heroic, clever, or humorous. The incidents in the plot are designed to expose these qualities in the criminals. In *Don Quixote*, the narrative presents itself as though it is telling all the details of his wandering tale. In *Robin Hood* or *Tom Ladle*, by contrast, the events described are isolated from each other and presented as examples of the kind of adventures these characters have, rather than an exhaustive list of incidents. This selectivity results in a narrative that allows greater exploration of different facets of the character's personality and motives than would a tale of sequential events. The chapbooks have little interiority or psychological realism, but they indicate that the criminal character was the most important part of these narratives.

Criminal Characters in Early Eighteenth-Century Fiction

If some of the most successful chapbook versions of picaresque tales focused chiefly on character, how does this development relate to the longer and more complex crime narratives of the early eighteenth century? Salzman comments in passing that 'The step from these works [seventeenth-century rogue fictions] to Defoe's *Captain Singleton* (1720) and *Moll Flanders* (1722) is a question of development, rather than a dramatic emergence of a new form'.[41] The answer to this 'question of development' is outside of the scope of Salzman's argument, but I would contend that one answer lies in the ways the chapbooks manipulate their stories to focus on a single main character. The success of character-oriented chapbooks demonstrated that readers were interested in reading about immoral or even reprehensible characters. Like the chapbooks, these narratives often have redeeming qualities such as sympathetic motives for crime (rogue-heroes), poetic justice (similar to the rogue-trickster tales), or characters with interesting and unique personal qualities (like the rogue-jesters). As I shall argue here, some of the same qualities that distinguished the chapbook tales about rogue characters also appeared in the most famous criminal fictions of the early eighteenth century, including *Captain Singleton*, *John Sheppard*, *Moll Flanders*, and *Colonel Jack* (1722).

A number of scholars have called due attention to the focus on character in early eighteenth-century fiction as a hallmark that distinguishes it from seventeenth-century fictions. David A. Brewer begins his study of the afterlives of fictional characters with 'the unprecedented proliferation of afterlives for Lemuel Gulliver' (first published in 1726) and argues that the rewritings of Gulliver in other contexts, a topic taken up in David Francis Taylor's essay in this collection, brings the 'first efflorescence' of such writings in Britain.[42] Scholars going back to Ian Watt have argued that the psychological realism and individuality of early eighteenth-century fictional characters is one of the key traits that defines the 'novel' as a genre.[43] More recently, critics such as Ian Newman have connected psychological representation in fiction with broader concepts of personhood and subjectivity.[44] My aim here is to build on these critical conversations by arguing that complex characters such as Singleton and Sheppard shape the form of their works, but that they are guided by the traditions of both picaresque narratives and character-driven chapbooks.

Captain Singleton is clearly in the rogue-hero tradition. Like Robin Hood, Singleton comes from a vaguely 'gentle' background: at the age of two, being 'very well dress'd', he is lost by his nursery maid and sold to a gypsy.[45] He blames his early crimes on his companions and lack of moral education, explaining that 'Thieving, Lying, Swearing, Forswearing, joined to the most abominable Lewdness, was the stated Practice of the Ship's Crew . . . I was exactly fitted for their Society indeed; for I had no Sense of Virtue or Religion upon me'.[46] This careful preparation of Singleton's character makes him seem like a victim rather than a criminal, so that he remains sympathetic. He is not simply swept along with his bad company for long, however. Following a botched mutiny he is marooned on an inhospitable island with a group of fellow sailors. Singleton suggests that they turn pirates rather than merely trying to escape: 'as there were other Vessels at Sea . . . our Business was to cruise along the Coast of the Island, which was very long, and to seize upon the first we could get that was better than our own'.[47] The plan does not work, and they have to rebuild their own boats several times, but this is the beginning of Singleton's increasing leadership. When they come into conflict with native people on mainland Africa, Singleton confides in a 'hint to the Reader' that 'tho' my Comerades were all older Men, yet I began to find them void of Counsel' until he 'was indeed forced to command, as I may call it'.[48] This humble declaration of how he came to be in charge due to his greater resolution and natural leadership helps to make Singleton a hero. Even in desperate circumstances, after he has admitted his crimes to the reader, his innate abilities make him seem admirable.

In the second half of the book, Singleton becomes a pirate captain with his own ship, but his behaviour is never cruel or depraved. Any tendencies to violence are held in check by his friend the Quaker William Walters, 'who was always for doing our Business without Fighting'.[49] In the end, Singleton reforms, feeling that 'As to the Wealth I had, which was immensely great, it was all like Dirt under my Feet; I had no Value for it, no Peace in the Possession of it'.[50] He finally finds peace in giving a large sum of money to William's sister, a deserving widow, and in the end he marries her. Singleton throughout presents himself as a victim of circumstances, and when he finally reflects on his crimes at the end of his narrative, he leaves off piracy and gives away at least some of his stolen wealth to a worthy and honest person. His reflections on money show how it is both a reward and a burden to him – a relative view of wealth that makes money a function of his ongoing moral journey. Much like the rogue-heroes of chapbooks like Robin Hood, Singleton is not punished for his crimes. His retirement at the end of the narrative and his giving some of his wealth to an innocent person make penalty seem unnecessary.

Rogue-tricksters, like John Sheppard, are less fortunate in their fates than Singleton. There are several versions of Sheppard's story, based on the real-life crimes and adventures of Sheppard, and they all tell of his thievery, capture, and series of escapes from prison. The Sheppard narratives are somewhat different from lengthy fictional narratives like *Captain Singleton* because they are 32–64 pages (nearly as short as the longer chapbooks) and based on a real person. These narratives do not show Sheppard to have any higher motives for his actions, nor do they show him attempting to make reparations at the end as Singleton does. Instead, after he makes his final great escape through six locked doors of Newgate prison, he immediately returns to his old habits. When his mother comes to him, 'begging on her bended Knees of me to make the best of my Way out of the Kingdom', he promises to do so, but in fact has no intention of leaving.[51] He is finally recaptured while drunk and executed for his crimes and repeated escapes.[52] The reader is meant to learn by his example what not to do, not to emulate or admire him: he calls his own story 'a Warning to all young Men'.[53] Sheppard's crimes are serious, so he receives justice in the end.

Few crime narratives in English employ the rogue-jester model in the manner of Tom Ladle. Some are translations of foreign works such as Alain René Le Sage's *Gil Blas*, which was first translated into English in 1716 and proved successful enough to be reprinted for decades.[54] English works tend to use elements of the rogue-jester character as a way of ameliorating the harsher realities of a criminal life. In *Moll Flanders*, for example, Moll sometimes commits crimes that seem to have fewer detrimental effects and chiefly show her cleverness. In one notable incident, she steals a gold necklace off the neck of a child, noting that 'I did the Child no harm, I did not so much as fright it', an act she even considers 'a just Reproof' to the child's parents for leaving her to walk alone.[55] While she does rob the child's parents of a necklace worth £12–14 by her estimation, there is little other damage done and she manages to excuse the act as a lesson to careless parents – justifying her crime in a more complex way than Singleton would do. In a different sort of example of a comparatively light-hearted decep-tion, Moll is falsely taken up as a suspect in a robbery, and she presses for damages after her innocence is proven. After some haggling, she and her attorney get the mercer who had accused her to pay £150, 'a Suit of black silk Cloaths', the lawyer's fees, and 'a good Supper'.[56] While this is a considerable sum, the money here is not her reason for telling the story. She describes the incident as one of several 'small Broils' that led to her being known to the courts.[57] This links the incident to the broader plot, explaining why Moll had to start dressing in disguise to continue her theft, as well as emphasizing her perpetual remaking of her life. It also illustrates the opportunistic side of her character and shows that she is willing to take advantage of any scheme that comes her way. Moll is not a rogue-jester like those found in chapbooks, but she relates a number of crimes she commits simply because she had the chance, even if the payoff was small. She analyzes the morality of her actions rather than simply relating them and tries to justify her theft by showing how her actions taught a lesson to her victims to be less careless. Like Meriton Latroon from *The English Rogue*, Moll presents her actions as an aid to readers to learn about the tricks of thieves so they can avoid them.

The form of these crime narratives reflects the focus on character that made the chapbooks cohesive and easy to understand. All three of these examples have episodic plots that centre on the life of the main character, following his or her trajectory of initiation into sin, crimes increasing in magnitude and consequence, and a final reckoning in which the criminal reforms and in some cases is punished. Whereas the chapbooks were short and strictly focused on incidents in the life of the main character, these longer narratives have more space for complexities in the plots, additional digressions, and character development. *Captain Singleton*, for example, devotes a good deal of space to developing the friendship between Singleton and William Walters, and includes a digressive passage outlining the experiences on Ceylon of the castaway Robert Knox.[58] This is clearly marked out as a digression, however, and presented within the main plot of Singleton's life. The 'editor' of *Moll Flanders* explains in the preface that there are two digressive stories that would be interesting to include (the history of Moll's governess and the life of her husband who becomes a highwayman), but that 'they are either of them too long to be brought into the same Volume'.[59] While not expanded fully, the lives of both characters are explained at the length of a few pages as Moll learns about their past adventures. Like the chapbook tales, *Captain Singleton* and *Moll Flanders* focus on character rather than incident, but within the framework of the criminal's life they add contrasting tales, subplots, and narratives of other types of lives by introducing side characters and digressions.

I do not mean to suggest that the criminal narratives all followed this formula, but many of the most successful ones from the 1720s did focus on character in a similar fashion to the chapbooks, rather than the episodic plots of the earlier picaresque. One example of a narrative that did not follow this formula is *A New Voyage Round the World* (1725). *New Voyage* is not a criminal autobiography, but instead it details the adventures of a group of merchants and adventurers who use the excuse of England's war with Spain in 1713 to commandeer Spanish ships they find. The 'pirates' are often the enemy, though the ship featured in the story employs piratical tactics such as flying false colours. *New Voyage* is an extreme case of a first-person narrative from the 1720s that does not focus on character: the narrator is never named, and one almost forgets he is even a character in the story. Many of the incidents are described in the plural: 'we took the innocent *Spaniard* into our Convoy . . . we made a Promise to the *Spanish* Captain', and so forth.[60] At times the narrator is at variance with the rest of the crew because he wants to 'make Discoveries', but he still describes the voyage in the plural.[61] In *New Voyage*, the journey is the main subject, not the life of the narrator. Little information is given about the narrator or other characters before they embark or after they return to England, and the various activities described – piracy, war, trade, exploration – are linked together by the voyage. A serialization of *New Voyage*, of the nature discussed in Nicholas Seager's essay in this collection, appeared in 1725, and Francis Noble produced a three-volume edition in 1787, but the work did not have nearly the success of contemporary pirate narratives that focused on the lives of the criminals.[62]

* * *

As mentioned at the outset of this essay, scholars have long seen English criminal narratives as picaresque or borrowing from the picaresque tradition. *Moll Flanders* is often cited as an example of the English picaresque. Stuart Miller, for example, argues that 'Moll Flanders exhibits the internal instability of the traditional picaro, but only in the second half of the book'.[63] Calhoun Winton comments that it follows the tradition of *The English Rogue* and 'fits well into the picaresque mode'.[64] The problem, however, is that a work like *Moll Flanders* has a focus on character that seems antithetical to the episodic, almost formulaic narratives of picaresque tales, which causes the narration to follow her story even when it is not picaresque. Richard Bjornson, for example, points out that Moll's conversion in prison marks 'The crucial point at which Moll's story diverges from those of the earliest Spanish pícaros', and Tina Kuhlisch has more recently argued that the narrative is 'conditioned by the contemporary circumstances of eighteenth-century England'.[65] The variety of critical views is vividly apparent in discussions of realism. Miller and Alexander Blackburn, among others, have seen picaresque narratives as fundamentally unrealistic, whereas *Moll Flanders, Colonel Jack,* and other works of the 1720s are lauded precisely for their realism.[66] John J. Richetti and Lincoln B. Faller have argued that works like *Moll Flanders* derive from a tradition of English criminal biographies that are separate from the picaresque tradition, and that they are more formally complex and socially acute than the picaresque.[67] Such different arguments about the origins and purpose of longer works of criminal fiction suggest that there is a wide gap in how we read works as different as *The English Rogue* and *John Sheppard,* and what we read them for, that signals that they are different enterprises altogether.

The chapbooks of the late seventeenth and early eighteenth centuries supply the missing link in the changes of form between works like *Don Quixote* and *Captain Singleton.* Picaresque works from the seventeenth century have episodic plots and static characters: the focus is on actions and incidents, not the development of the hero. In chapbooks, digressions and subplots are pared away, leaving only the tale of the main character, whose life and death delineates the beginning and end of the work. The short format of the chapbooks accounts for such pruning, but the selectivity shows that abridgers viewed the life of the main character as the most important element of works like *Don Quixote.* The focus on character in chapbooks extends to those that have stories not originally from longer works, such as the folkloric heroes like Robin Hood and Sheffery Morgan. Brief criminal lives, such as those collected in *The History of the Lives of the Most Noted Highway-men* (1714) and *A General History of the Pyrates* (1724), were of interest in the 1720s, and their use of character to delimit the boundaries of a narrative within a short format reflects the formal qualities of the chapbook tales of criminals.[68] The longer fictional criminal lives of the 1720s keep the focus on character popularized by the chapbooks but take advantage of their longer formats to reintroduce subplots and side characters. Chapbooks, short criminal narratives, and longer works of fiction were reprinted during the same period because they appealed to readers in similar ways, and the longer works of criminal biography from the 1720s were often adapted to shorter formats to reach different readers throughout the eighteenth century. The afterlives of picaresque fictions do emerge as the criminal narratives of the 1720s, but they are mediated through the changes in form pioneered and tested in chapbooks.

Notes

1 Michael McKeon, *The Origins of the English Novel, 1600–1740* (Baltimore: Johns Hopkins University Press, 1987), pp. 96–100; Paul Salzman, *English Prose Fiction, 1558–1700: A Critical History* (Oxford: Clarendon Press, 1985), pp. 202–40.

2 Chad M. Gasta, 'The Picaresque According to Cervantes', *Philological Quarterly*, 89:1 (2010), 31–53 (31).

3 Calhoun Winton argues that the criminality of the pícaro is the defining characteristic of the genre: 'Richard Head and the Origins of the Picaresque in England', in *The Picaresque: A Symposium on the Rogue's Tale*, eds. Carmen Benito-Vessels and Michael Zappala (Newark: University of Delaware Press, 1994), pp. 79–93 (81).

4 Anthony J. Close explains the intersections between *Don Quixote* and the picaresque: 'The Legacy of *Don Quijote* and the Picaresque Novel', in *The Cambridge Companion to the Spanish Novel from 1600 to the Present*, eds. Harriet Turner and Adelaida López de Martínez (Cambridge University Press, 2003), pp. 15–30. On *Don Quixote*'s non-picaresque qualities, see Gasta, 'The Picaresque According to Cervantes', pp. 31–35. Michael Sinding has recently argued that *Don Quixote* blends elements of several genres, including picaresque, to create a new hybrid genre: 'Blending in a *baciyelmo*: *Don Quixote*'s Genre Blending and the Invention of the Novel', in *Blending and the Study of Narrative: Approaches and Applications*, eds. Ralf Schneider and Marcus Hartner (Berlin: De Gruyter, 2012), pp. 147–71.

5 *The History of the Valorous and Wittie Knight-Errant, Don-Quixote of the Mancha*, trans. Thomas Shelton (London: E. Blount and W. Barret, 1612). New translations were done by John Stevens (London: R. Chiswell et al., 1700) and Peter Motteux (London: Samuel Buckley, 1700).

6 *The Famous History of Don Quixote de la Mancha* (London: G. Conyers, 1686). See also a play, Thomas D'Urfey, *The Comical History of Don Quixote* (London: Samuel Briscoe, 1694); for a verse imitation, Edward Ward, *The Life and Notable Adventures of that Renown'd Knight, Don Quixote de la Mancha* (London: T. Norris et al., 1711).

7 Margaret Spufford, *Small Books and Pleasant Histories: Popular Fiction and its Readership in Seventeenth-Century England* (Athens: University of Georgia Press, 1981), p. 48.

8 *Don Quixote* (1612), p. 8.

9 *Don Quixote* (1612), p. 23.

10 *Don Quixote* (1686), sig. A3^r.

11 *Don Quixote* (1686), sigs. A3^v, B5$^{r–v}$.

12 *The History of the Ever-Renowned Knight Don Quixote de la Mancha* (London: W. O. and H. Green, c.1695), pp. 4, 24.

13 Richard Head, *The English Rogue Described in the Life of Meriton Latroon, a Witty Extravagant* (London: Henry Marsh, 1665).

14 See the explanation provided by C. W. R. D. Moseley, 'Richard Head's "The English Rogue": A Modern Mandeville?', *Yearbook of English Studies*, 1

(1971), 102–7. The sequels are *The English Rogue Continued* (London: F. Kirkman, 1668); *The English Rogue Continued . . . The Third Part* (London: F. Kirkman, 1671); and *The English Rogue . . . The Fourth Part* (London: F. Kirkman, 1671). The first editions of the sequels have not been digitized; the earliest digitized editions are printed by Kirkman in 1671, 1674, and 1680, respectively.

15 *The Life and Death of the English Rogue* (London: Charles Passinger, 1679).

16 *English Rogue*, sigs. A1^r, A3^v.

17 *English Rogue*, sig. D2^r.

18 *The English Rogue: Containing a brief Discovery of the most Eminent Cheats, Robberies, and other Extravagancies, by him Committed* (London: J. Blare, 1688), sig. B4^v.

19 Reprints of *The Life and Death of the English Rogue* (London: E. Tracy, c.1700); (London: T. Norris, c.1711).

20 Matheo Alemán, *The Rogue: Or, The Life of Guzman de Alfarache* (London: Edward Blount, 1623); 5th edn in 2 parts (London: Philip Chetwind, 1656).

21 Alemán, *Guzman*, (1656), part 1, pp. 151–52.

22 *The Spanish Rogue, Or, The Life of Guzman de Alfarache* (London: Andrew Thorncomb, 1685); one reprint (London: T. Smith, [1730?]). Roger Boyle, *Guzman: A Comedy* (London: Francis Saunders, 1693). The full version was reprinted just once after 1656: *The Life of Guzman d'Alfarache: Or, The Spanish Rogue*, 2 vols. (London: R. Bonwick et al., 1708).

23 *The History of the Famous Exploits of Guy Earl of Warwick* (London: Charles Bates, [1680?]); *The Gallant History of the Life and Death of that most Noble Knight, Sir Bevis of Southampton* (London: J. Deacon, [1691?]); *The Famous History of the Valiant London-Prentice* (London: J. Back, 1693); *A Most Delightful History of the Famous Clothier of England, Called, Jack of Newbery* (London: W. Thackeray, [1680?]); *The True and Admirable History of Patient Grisel* (London: Eliz. Andrews, 1663). Another category, less relevant here, are those works featuring laughable buffoons, like *The Essex Champion* (London: J. Blare, [1690?]).

24 *Here begynneth a lytell geste of Robyn hode* [London: Wynkyn de Worde, 1506]; Anthony Munday, *The Death of Robert, Earle of Huntington, Otherwise Called Robin Hood of Merrie Sherwodde* (London: William Leake, 1601). On Munday's version and Robin Hood's gentility, see Meredith Skura, 'Anthony Munday's "Gentrification" of Robin Hood', *English Literary Renaissance*, 33:2 (2003), 155–80 (155); and Liz Oakley-Brown, 'Framing Robin Hood: Temporality and Textuality in Anthony Munday's Huntington Plays', in *Robin Hood: Medieval and Post-Medieval*, ed. Helen Phillips (Dublin: Four Courts Press, 2005), pp. 113–28 (114).

25 *The Noble Birth and Gallant Achievements of that Remarkable Outlaw Robin Hood* (London: J. Deacon, 1685), sig. A1^r.

26 *Robin Hood*, sig. A2^r.

27 *Robin Hood*, sig. A3^v.

28 *Robin Hood*, sigs. B2^r–B3^r.

29 *The Most Pleasant History of Reynard the Fox* (London: J. Conyers and J. Blare, [1700?]), p. 13.

30 *Reynard the Fox*, p. 13.

31 *The Life and Death of Sheffery Morgan, Son of Shon ap Morgan* (London: J. Deacon, [1683?]), p. 11.

32 *Sheffery Morgan*, pp. 12–13.

33 *Sheffery Morgan*, p. 14.

34 *The Pleasant History of Tom Ladle* (London: J. Blare, 1682), p. 12.

35 *Tom Ladle*, p. 16.

36 *Tom Ladle*, p. 19.

37 Simon Dickie, *Cruelty and Laughter: Forgotten Comic Literature and the Unsentimental Eighteenth Century* (University of Chicago Press, 2011), p. 1.

38 *Tom Tram of the West, Son-in-Law to Mother Winter* (London: J. Gilbertson, [1690?]).

39 *Tom Tram*, sigs. A3$^{r–v}$.

40 *Tom Tram*, sig. A8^r.

41 Salzman, *English Prose Fiction*, p. 238.

42 David A. Brewer, *The Afterlife of Character, 1726–1825* (Philadelphia: University of Pennsylvania Press, 2005), p. 26.

43 Ian Watt, *The Rise of the Novel: Studies in Defoe, Richardson and Fielding* (London: Chatto and Windus, 1957), pp. 60–92.

44 Ian Newman, 'Property, History, and Identity in Defoe's *Captain Singleton*', *Studies in English Literature 1500–1900*, 51:3 (2011), 565–83.

45 [Daniel Defoe], *The Life, Adventures, and Pyracies, of the Famous Captain Singleton* (London: J. Brotherton et al., 1720), p. 1.

46 *Captain Singleton*, p. 8.

47 *Captain Singleton*, p. 33.

48 *Captain Singleton*, pp. 71–72.

49 *Captain Singleton*, p. 236.

50 *Captain Singleton*, p. 328.

51 *A Narrative of all the Robberies, Escapes, &c. of John Sheppard* (London: J. Applebee, 1724), p. 27.

52 *John Sheppard*, pp. 29–30.

53 *John Sheppard*, p. 29.

54 Alain René Le Sage, *The History and Adventures of Gil Blas*, 2 vols. (London: J. Tonson, 1716); vol. 3 (London: J. Tonson, 1725); vol. 4 (London: J. Nourse and F. Cogan, 1735).

55 [Daniel Defoe?], *The Fortunes and Misfortunes of the Famous Moll Flanders* (London: W. Chetwood and T. Edling, 1721 [for 1722]), p. 238.

56 *Moll Flanders*, p. 310.

57 *Moll Flanders*, p. 296.

58 *Captain Singleton*, pp. 293–306.

59 *Moll Flanders*, pp. xi–xii.

60 [Daniel Defoe?], *A New Voyage Round the World, by a Course Never Sailed Before* (London: A. Bettesworth and W. Mears, 1725), pp. 11–12.

61 *New Voyage*, p. 20.

62 *A New Voyage Round the World* (Chester: W. Cooke, 1725?); an abridgement (London: G. Read, 1730?); *Voyage Round the World*, 3 vols. (London: F. Noble, 1787).

63 Stuart Miller, *The Picaresque Novel* (Cleveland: The Press of Case Western Reserve University, 1967), p. 91.

64 Winton, 'Richard Head and the Origins of the Picaresque', p. 90.

65 Richard Bjornson, *The Picaresque Hero in European Fiction* (Madison, Wisc.: University of Wisconsin Press, 1977), p. 201; Tina Kuhlisch, 'The Ambivalent Rogue: Moll Flanders as Modern Pícara', in *Rogues and Early Modern English Culture*, eds. Craig Dionne and Steve Mentz (Ann Arbor: University of Michigan Press, 2004), pp. 337–60 (338).

66 Miller, *Picaresque Novel*, p. 10; Alexander Blackburn, *The Myth of the Picaro: Continuity and Transformation of the Picaresque Novel, 1554–1954* (Chapel Hill: University of North Carolina Press, 1979), p. 22.

67 John J. Richetti, *Popular Fiction before Richardson: Narrative Patterns, 1700–1739* (Oxford: Clarendon Press, 1969), pp. 27–30; Lincoln B. Faller, *Crime and Defoe: A New Kind of Writing* (Cambridge University Press, 1993), pp. 5–6ff.

68 Alexander Smith, *The History of the Lives of the Most Noted Highway-men* (London: J. Morphew and A. Dodd, 1714); Charles Johnson, *A General History of the Robberies and Murders of the most Notorious Pyrates* (London: C. Rivington, J. Lacy, and J. Stone, 1724).

CHAPTER 4

Ghosts of the Guardian in Sir Charles Grandison *and* Bleak House

Sarah Raff

In 'A Passage in the Life of Mr. Watkins Tottle' (1835), one of the *Sketches by Boz*, Charles Dickens's narrator remarks that his title character 'looked something like a vignette to one of Richardson's novels, and had a clean-cravatish formality of manner, and kitchen-pokerness of carriage, which Sir Charles Grandison himself might have envied'.[1] Dickens's account of sad Watkins Tottle the gentle prig, a 'compound of strong uxorious inclinations, and an unparalleled degree of anti-connubial timidity', exemplifies one salient element of *Sir Charles Grandison*'s (1753–54) literary afterlife.[2] The most obvious allusions to Richardson's last novel in fictions by nineteenth-century British authors use Richardson's portrait of an infatuating 'GOOD MAN'[3] either to explore the erotic appeal of a comprehensive male virtue – witness Jane Austen's juvenilia[4] and George Eliot's *Daniel Deronda* (1876) – or to deny, as Dickens here does, that any woman could find a male virgin alluring. The present essay examines a less conspicuous instance of *Grandison*'s nineteenth-century influence, one focused on reprising not just Sir Charles the character or his virtuous masculinity but the special model of authorship-as-guardianship that Richardson's exemplary hero-guardian made possible. With Sir Charles as his representative Richardson was able to stake out an unexpectedly active role in the romantic lives of readers, a role that later works featuring guardian-characters adopted and adapted.[5] Instead of attempting to trace exhaustively the contours of this tradition, which stretches from Jane Austen's *Mansfield Park* (1814)[6] to Henry James's *Watch and Ward* (1871) and *The Awkward Age* (1898–99), the present essay will explain how one novel, Dickens's masterpiece, *Bleak House* (1852–53), took up *Grandison*'s model of author/reader relations, in which an author is imagined as living on in the affective experiences of his readers, appropriating their love lives as part of his own afterlife.

It is not hard to see why Richardson should have found guardianship a convenient metaphor for the didactic authorship he practised.

The guardian's legally defined duties were to provide for his ward's 'maintenance and education' on one hand and to manage the ward's inherited wealth on the other, both of which tasks involved supervising the ward's decisions concerning whom to marry.[7] Richardson's project was similar: to 'cultivate the Principles of Virtue and Religion in the Minds of the YOUTH of BOTH SEXES', to show women readers how to resist the attempts on their bodies or fortunes of designing men, and to teach single readers what sort of persons to seek in marriage as well as which qualities, once displayed, would be apt to attract an appropriate spouse.[8] Nor was it just in the content of his instruction that an author could be guardian-like with respect to the reader. Aaron Hill's praise of Richardson as the '*Father*' not of bodies but of '*Millions of* MINDS, which are to owe new Formation to the future Effect of his Influence!', points to a logic of priority linking author/reader with guardian/ward relations: an author cannot create readers from scratch as he does his characters, but he can re-make them through lessons in virtue, much as a guardian is not the progenitor but may become the reformer of his ward.[9] In contrast to the 'trope of paternity' that sometimes describes an author's relationship to his characters, a trope implying that the author has 'absolute authority' over his fictional creations, the trope of guardianship describing an author's relation to his readers suggests merely provisional authority, for the guardian is legally a 'temporary parent'.[10] The intermediate quality of his authority is particularly pronounced when the ward is female, for in this case the guardian occupies the space between father and husband. Taking over his ward's protection where her father left off and consigning her eventually to the permanent guardianship of her husband, the guardian is neither the first influence on his ward nor the last. Even the lessons with which he educates the ward, like those with which the eighteenth-century didactic author edifies the reader, convey ideas that her father and husband, if they are good men, would endorse: material oft thought, or at least apt to win acclaim and conviction once well expressed. Like the didactic author, the guardian is duty-bound to act as deputy to the father whose authority precedes his own and to the husband whose authority follows it.

What makes Sir Charles especially interesting as a figure for his author – and complicates his charm for later imitators – is his transcendence of this requirement. True to the guardian role, Sir Charles is an educator and 'great friend to the married state' who acts as 'matrimony-promoter' for his wards and thereby sways them as his author avowedly wished to sway his public.[11] But Sir Charles's supreme and permanent guardianship also escapes the very limitations that help to make guardianship a tactful metaphor for the didactic author's relation with the reader. In Richardson's hands, the guardian metaphor becomes a means of extending to readers the unlimited authority that the novelist commands over his characters, for none of the customary restrictions on guardians can hinder the exercise of Sir Charles Grandison's influence. Instead of seeming an inferior replacement for the father and a pale preview of the husband, Sir Charles is wiser than any parent, more beloved than any spouse. This guardian is 'more than a father', not less than one, even to his grizzled uncle Lord W., and each of his main female wards proves destined for a marriage that will perpetuate rather than replace his guardianship.[12] Sir Charles marries one of them himself and consents to match the other with a man who imitates and replicates Sir Charles. As I will show, *Grandison* charismatically reverses the direction of deputation ordinarily associated with guardianship. In the allegory of Richardson's intended effect upon the reader that Sir Charles's impact upon his wards supplies, the guardian-like author does not act as the representative and subordinate of the good husband whom he teaches his female reader to select but rather conscripts that reader's husband into service as his own delegate. The first part of this essay describes how the male beneficiaries of Richardson's matchmaking efforts for readers come to seem mere phantoms of Richardson's avatar, Sir Charles Grandison; the second part argues that through the ghostly guardian John Jarndyce, Dickens takes up rather uneasily Richardson's match-making, marriage-haunting strategy.

* * *

Sir Charles Grandison foregrounds guardianship by giving the orphaned Harriet Byron a complicated status as ward. Harriet is initially over-supplied with guardians, for she counts among her protectors her grandmother, Mrs Shirley; her childless aunt and uncle Selby; her godfather, Mr Deane; and the de facto guardians, Mr and Mrs Reeves, her hosts in London. Soon she picks up a further not-quite-parent in Sir Rowland Meredith, who courts her on behalf of his nephew and whom she lets down easily, in one of the affective highpoints of the first volume, by offering him gratis, as it were, the father-like relation to her that he would have enjoyed had she consented to marry his heir. This excess of parent-surrogates ends up contributing to the reader's sense that Harriet is fundamentally unprotected, in urgent need of that ultimate guardian, a husband. Her vulnerability is partly a consequence of her surpassing virtue: suitors flock to her, and so much confidence does her wisdom inspire that her official guardians have decided to leave the choice of a husband entirely to herself, a privilege that exposes her to manifold embarrassments and importunities.[13] In her temporary London residence, Harriet is also physically unshielded, for Mr Reeves, good-natured and perhaps ambitious, is more bent on conciliating her suitors than on defending her from them. Mr Reeves thus neglects to prevent one suitor, Mr Greville, from leaving teeth-marks in her hand while kissing it and another, Sir Hargrave Pollfexen, from abducting Harriet as she exits a masquerade party. Harriet's fruitless pleas for help from Sir Hargrave's accomplices emphasize her unprotected state and set in high relief Harriet's efficient rescue by Sir Charles Grandison, who enters the novel in the role of the guardian that Harriet requires.

Sir Charles's status as a superior successor to Harriet's previous guardians is evident long before he ratifies it by marrying her. Having wrested Harriet from Sir Hargrave's clutches by means of athletic prowess that Harriet's middle-aged and elderly guardians cannot rival, Sir Charles restores Harriet to the Reeves household with an explicit declaration of his present and future guardian role, addressing Mr Reeves with an allusion to '*our* lovely ward' and courteously adding, 'You see, Sir, that I join myself with you in the honour of that agreeable relation'.[14] Sir Charles's guardianship of Harriet gains further emphasis when the penitent but still hopeful Sir Hargrave poses to Sir Charles his questions concerning Harriet's marital intentions, thereby acknowledging Sir Charles not just as Harriet's physical protector but also as her marriage broker. Of course, Sir Hargrave's hopes are unavailing, for the same qualities that render Sir Charles the best possible guardian for Harriet also make him, the novel repeatedly insists, the best possible choice of husband. Any husband is after all his wife's guardian, 'her guide and protector through Life', as Harriet's grandmother puts it.[15]

While Harriet, if she marries, will end up with one sole guardian, Sir Charles's capacious guardianship, charged as it is with conveying Richardson's care for his readers, is not easily imagined as encompassing only one ward. Sir Charles collects wards wherever he goes, as a mark of his good deeds. Already established as the guardian of his sister Charlotte, who calls him 'A father and a brother in one!',[16] he soon becomes an honorary guardian to Harriet's treacherous servant William Wilson, who receives from Sir Charles 'a deliverance ... of soul as well as body',[17] and to the three young Danby siblings, whose uncle has left Sir Charles the executor and main beneficiary of a legacy that Sir Charles carefully restores to them. In order to determine how best to invest the money he plans to give her, Sir Charles asks 'my dear Miss Danby', whom he has just met, after the state of her heart – and thereby claims the guardian's marriage-advising prerogative.[18] As his good deeds continue to unfold, Sir Charles acquires further wards, brokers further marriages, and practises a flexibly expanding guardianship that ever more conspicuously resembles Richardson's authorship. To exert his beneficent influence upon the world, Sir Charles 'employ[s]' an author's talents, namely 'invention, forecast, and contrivance', and takes on the Richardsonian task of finding answers to casuistical dilemmas.[19] In the Danby case, for example, Sir Charles determines which should take precedence, the expressed will of a testator or the claims of consanguinity. The novel's education for the male reader in how to become a good man and consequently, it insists, a man maximally attractive to the opposite sex proves a lesson in becoming a good guardian and a good author.

As for the female reader, Richardson conveys his marital plans for her not through the romantically successful Harriet Byron but rather through Sir Charles's official ward Emily Jervois, with her doomed infatuation.[20] The teenage Emily loves Sir Charles for the same reason that readers do: because loving him is the only possible reaction to witnessing or reading of his goodness.[21] As Richardson hoped his readers would, Emily soaks up Sir Charles's precepts and examples; her love makes her teachable. Like Richardson's female readers, Emily cannot marry the man she prefers, but she can marry one of those men who have 'form[ed] themselves by *his* example'.[22] The suitor whom Emily eventually favours is Sir Edward Beauchamp, who has been profiting from Sir Charles's 'blazing' example, principally by reading Sir Charles's letters, ever since meeting him.[23] A figure, clearly, for the instructed male reader, Sir Edward is so like the great original as to be designated 'a second Sir Charles Grandison'.[24] Through the budding courtship of Emily and Sir Edward, *Grandison* proposes that its readers fall in love with Sir Charles, remake themselves according to his example and specifications, and then extend their love for him to other, similarly influenced readers of Richardson.[25]

As Jocelyn Harris emphasizes, it is far from clear that a woman who has once loved Sir Charles can ever fully content herself with another man, but the circumstance that no replica can possibly live up to the original is an element of the plan.[26] What Emily likes about Sir Edward is his connection to Sir Charles; there is never any question of Sir Edward *replacing* Sir Charles in Emily's affection. First asked what she thinks of not-yet-titled Beauchamp, Emily responds, 'Next to my guardian, I think Mr. Beauchamp is a very agreeable man', then protests, 'Well, but enough of Mr. Beauchamp. My guardian! my gracious, my kind, my indulgent guardian! who, that thinks of him, can praise any-body else?'[27] The happy evolution that occurs over the next three volumes is that Emily stops insisting that her love for Sir Charles excludes praise for his friend and finds instead that her love for Sir Charles can inspire and find expression in her liking for Sir Edward. We get a sense of how the courtship will go when, at the wedding of Harriet and Sir Charles, Sir Edward leads Emily out of the church: 'She seemed pleased, and happy; for he whispered to her, all the way, praises of her Guardian'.[28] At the end of the novel, when Emily asks Harriet's advice about whether to encourage Sir Edward's attentions, there is still no doubt which man Emily prefers: 'Next to my guardian, I think him the most agreeable of men'. Now at last, however, Emily can acknowledge, 'I think it is a right thing for young women to marry when young men are so desirous to copy Sir Charles Grandison'.[29] Once suitably married, Emily and the female reader are to continue adoring Sir Charles and to love in their husbands the qualities that reflect and represent Sir Charles, just as, in Mary Astell's vision of a good marriage, the wife loves in her husband those 'amiable Qualities, the Image of the Deity impress'd upon a generous and godlike Mind', which, 'in imitation of that glorious Pattern it endeavours to copy after, expands and diffuses it self to its utmost Capacity in doing Good'.[30] Taught to eschew possessiveness by Sir Edward's complacency and Harriet's embrace of Sir Charles's first love, Clementina, in a symbolic three-way marriage,[31] husband and wife are to adulate and emulate the paragon jointly. Instead of superseding Sir Charles by establishing a new mode of guardianship, the husband is to carry out the work of protection and guidance begun during his wife's perusal of *Grandison*: he is deputy to Sir Charles and, beyond him, Richardson. The marriages to which Richardson would consign Emily and his readers are belated shadows of the original relation of guardianship they bring to symbolic but ever incomplete fulfilment.

Although, as we shall see, Richardson's blithe relegation of the husbands of his female readers to a secondary place in their wives' affections was not a precedent that Dickens could comfortably follow, in other respects *Bleak House* closely tracks *Grandison*'s model of literary mediation. Like *Grandison*, *Bleak House* makes guardianship its central metaphor for authorship. And like *Grandison*, *Bleak House* would deliver its characters and readers to marriages that imitate a guardian/ward union that never was. By claiming the female reader as his ward and envisioning her husband as his deputy, Dickens echoes Richardson's proposal for extending the author's control over the fictional world into the real world.

* * *

Like Richardson before him, Dickens was an innovator when it came to creating community among readers whom he sometimes imagined as his wards. Richardson developed a new 'coterie public', as David A. Brewer has called it, by soliciting advice in a voluminous correspondence that shared the form and canvassed the topics of his epistolary novels.[32] Dickens, in turn, elevated the status of serial fiction, tried the experiment of reissuing his old work in the Cheap Edition, and embarked upon his unprecedentedly large-scale public reading project with a reference to 'that peculiar relation (personally affectionate, and like no other man's) which subsists between me and the public'.[33] To be sure, Richardson's didactic concerns seem remote from those of Dickens, to stand opposed to them indeed as private to public: while Richardson, conspicuously guardian-like, teaches young people how to behave and whom to marry, Dickens directs his energies to 'penal and legal reform, sanitation and public health'.[34] Yet the problems, both public and private, that *Bleak House* addresses are all ones that – it suggests – a proper guardianship could solve. The novel's emblem of everything wrong with the English status quo is Jo the crossing-sweeper, a child without a guardian. Jo grows up in isolation, deprived of the benefits of civilization and devolving, like the Wild Boy of Aveyron, into an animal, despite the fact that he lives surrounded by people in a bustling city. Jo's luckier counterpart is another victim of radical neglect, Esther Summerson,[35] whose childhood, defining for the self-abnegating voice with which she narrates her chapters of the novel, is chilled by the unloving guardianship of her aunt Miss Barbary. Both Jo and Esther orbit the special target of *Bleak House*'s zeal for reform, the Court of Chancery, an institution charged with acting as guardian to widows and orphans, with transmitting inheritances, and with appointing flesh-and-blood guardians to minors.[36] Tom-all-Alone's, the noxious slum where Jo picks up the disease that before killing him infects Esther and wrecks the beauty of her face, is a property tied up 'in Chancery' and therefore sponsored – and guarded – by no one.[37]

Bleak House's opening description of the penetrating, blighting London fog, emblem of the Court of Chancery and its most perplexing suit, Jarndyce and Jarndyce, gives us our initial glimpse of guardianship-gone-wrong. In the topsy-turvy system ruled by Chancery's Lord High Chancellor from his position 'at the very heart of the fog', it is the wards who give shelter to their decrepit and powerless guardians: 'Fog in the eyes and throats of ancient Greenwich pensioners, wheezing by the firesides of their wards', chants the third-person narrator.[38] The suit of Jarndyce and Jarndyce resembles the fog in its ability to reach – and harm – multitudes. Exactly 'How many people … Jarndyce and Jarndyce has stretched forth its unwholesome hand to spoil and corrupt, would be a very wide question'. From master to copying clerk, 'no man's nature has been made the better by it', for Jarndyce and Jarndyce is one of those 'influences that can never come to good'. Prompting 'evasion, procrastination, spoliation … [s]hirking and sharking', it causes solicitors to lapse 'into a habit of vaguely promising themselves that they will look into that outstanding little matter … when Jarndyce and Jarndyce shall be got out of the office'.[39] Meanwhile, the '[f]air wards of the court' at various times associated with Jarndyce and Jarndyce 'have faded into mothers and grandmothers' before anything in the case has been decided.[40]

This bad guardianship that blights rather than edifies serves to define by opposition the novel's pedagogical aims. Indeed, Jarndyce and Jarndyce appears as the evil twin of the authorial project that Dickens had vowed to undertake in the famous statement, 'A Preliminary Word', that opened the first number of *Household Words*. There, seeking to be 'admitted into many homes with affection and confidence' in a journal whose title evokes household gods or guardians of the hearth, Dickens promises to avoid just the deleterious effects that Jarndyce and Jarndyce fosters as it creeps fog-like from house to house.[41] The 'receiver in the cause' of Jarndyce and Jarndyce 'has acquired' from it 'a distrust of his own mother, and a contempt for his own kind' and even 'those who have contemplated' Jarndyce and Jarndyce from afar 'have been insensibly tempted into a loose way of letting bad things alone to take their own bad course, and a loose belief that if the world go wrong, it was, in some off-hand manner, never meant to go right'.[42] But Dickens would promote faith in humanity and its development, gratitude for the reader's place in that enterprise, and persistence: 'We seek to bring into innumerable homes, from the stirring world around us, the knowledge of many social wonders, good and evil, that are not calculated to render any of us less ardently persevering in ourselves, less tolerant of one another, less faithful in the progress of mankind, less thankful for the privilege of living in this summer-dawn of time'.[43] While to be touched by that 'grim old guardian' the Court of Chancery as it pursues its representative case is to become dithering, suspicious, self-loathing, ungrateful, and hopeless, Dickens would counteract these qualities.[44]

The character in *Bleak House* who most obviously advances the work of the author by resisting the bad influence of Chancery is the good guardian John Jarndyce, who recalls Sir Charles Grandison in manifold ways.

Himself an unwilling party to the Jarndyce and Jarndyce suit, John Jarndyce takes responsibility not just for Esther Summersun and his Chancery-appointed wards Ada Clare and Richard Carstone, but also for the welfare of the Skimpole family, Miss Flite, the Neckett family, and Allan Woodcourt. Jarndyce's guardianship is as encompassing as Sir Charles's: nearly everyone who comes into contact with him seems eventually to become his ward. His financial resources never drained, Jarndyce, like Sir Charles, is actively charitable without being professionally employed. Both paragons of male virtue are described in terms suggesting halos, as shining, radiant with benignity, and bright, especially when they are doing good. Like those of Sir Charles Grandison, Jarndyce's good deeds are associated with authoring. Unveiling the first of these, Jarndyce's lawyer Conversation Kenge tells Esther that her new guardian has offered to place her in a school 'where she shall be eminently qualified to discharge her duty in that station of life to which it has pleased—shall I say Providence?—to call her'.[45] Kenge's words call attention to the novel's alignment between God, Jarndyce, and Dickens himself, those joint deciders of Esther's station. Yet the author-like guardian-figures of Dickens and Richardson are also linked through the feminine voices of those who narrate about them. The primary describer is in each case a ward-figure who, in praising, admiring, and often indeed, for all Harriet Byron's vaunted 'frankness', withholding a full account of her reactions to him, seems determined not to let any scrap of her guardian's goodness go uncelebrated.[46] As witnesses, Harriet Byron and Esther Summerson are remarkably similar – fluent but lapsing, through modesty, into omissions and distortions; often preoccupied with the sweetness and beauty of a younger woman companion, Emily in Harriet's case, Ada in Esther's, whom their guardian has appointed them, in turn, to guard; able to register obliquely the blind-spots as well as the virtues of their guardian; and apt to confess their own heavy burden of obligation to him, their crippling gratitude. Indeed, we could think of the very form of *Bleak House*, with its allotment of a 'portion' of its pages to Esther's first-person narration, as an homage to Richardson, who gave a large share of his final novel to Harriet Byron and who, unlike Dickens, habitually wrote in the voice of a woman.[47]

While as a narrator Esther resembles Harriet Byron, Esther's love story resembles that of another ward of Grandison, Emily Jervois. After disease has scarred her face and revelations concerning her illegitimacy have shaken her, Esther receives and sorrowfully accepts a marriage proposal from Jarndyce. Only now, while taking in this long-drawn-out transaction, does the first-time reader understand that Esther has been wishing to marry the young doctor, Allan Woodcourt, who is away at sea trying to make his fortune. When Woodcourt in due course returns, finds a steady source of income in Yorkshire, and proposes marriage to Esther, she turns him down, tearfully loyal to her guardian, and enters on a plan with Jarndyce to 'give Bleak House its mistress' in a month.[48] She has nearly finished her wedding preparations when Jarndyce summons her to meet him in Yorkshire, greets her with his 'genial face again at its brightest and best',[49] and explains that he has bought a house for Woodcourt and wishes her to help him decorate it. The domicile they tour the next day is a 'rustic cottage of doll's rooms' in which the flowerbeds, the wallpaper, the colours and disposition of appurtenances all replicate '*my* little tastes and fancies, *my* little methods' as she has expressed them in the domestic arrangements at Bleak House.[50] It is after Esther has begun worrying that these physical reminders of her may give Woodcourt pain that Jarndyce reveals that the name of this house, too, is Bleak House, that this little house is the one she is to be mistress of, and that he intends to bestow the cottage and herself upon Woodcourt, who suddenly appears in person. In Esther's case as in that of Richardson's Emily Jervois, the ward who begins romantically attached to the guardian ends up instead with a man whom the guardian endorses.

In Dickens's novel as in Richardson's, the ward's marriage serves not to terminate the guardian's influence but to memorialize and perpetuate it. Jarndyce has a hand in every aspect of Esther's nuptials. It is Jarndyce who has thrown Esther and Woodcourt recently together, by insisting that Woodcourt be consulted as a second medical opinion for Esther's friend, Caddy Turveydrop; it is Jarndyce who has found Woodcourt the position in Yorkshire that makes his marriage financially possible; and it is Jarndyce who has reconciled Woodcourt's mother to accepting Esther as a daughter-in-law. It is on Jarndyce's sufferance that Woodcourt obtains Esther's hand, and the containers that hold her remain marked by the preferences of her guardian. Not only does the couple's new establishment replicate the household that Esther once organized with Jarndyce's convenience and pleasure in view, but also it has been in the expectation of marrying Jarndyce that Esther has chosen her trousseau: 'Regulating my purchases by my guardian's taste, which I knew very well of course, I arranged my wardrobe to please him, and hoped I should be highly successful'.[51]

If Esther's new home is a miniature version of her guardian's, her husband, a man until now nearly without qualities despite his reported stint of heroism during a shipwreck, becomes from this point forward a younger imitation of Esther's guardian. Playing Sir Edward Beauchamp to Jarndyce's Sir Charles Grandison, Woodcourt has already displayed during the scene of his unsuccessful marriage proposal a fervent readiness to join his beloved in reverential praise of her guardian. As the novel draws to a close, we find that Woodcourt, like Jarndyce, calls Esther 'little woman', and Woodcourt's professional benefactions elicit from Esther the same tone of elegiac tribute as Jarndyce's amateur ones do.[52] Alexander Welsh has observed that Woodcourt does have one characteristic from the beginning – he tends to show up suddenly just when people are about to die: Nemo, Lady Dedlock, and Jo.[53] This pattern contributes to our feeling that when Woodcourt abruptly materializes at the new Bleak House after Jarndyce's *éclaircissement*, Jarndyce, renouncing Esther, dies – but only to retain Esther by possessing or haunting Woodcourt with his own spirit. Similarly, in the novel by Dickens preceding *Bleak House*, Dora bequeaths her husband David Copperfield to Agnes Wickfield just before dying. Dickens no doubt had this scene in mind, for Jarndyce, turning over Esther to Woodcourt, speaks as if he were giving up not a fiancée but an established spouse to whom Woodcourt will serve as second husband: 'take from me, a willing gift, the best wife that ever a man had'.[54] Near the end of the novel, Esther is moved to some Richardsonian writing-to-the-moment by the thought of her guardian, who again sounds deceased: 'when I write of him, my tears will have their way'.[55]

At other moments, it is the young people whom the end of the novel seems to condemn to death. Woodcourt in particular seems erased both as a husband to Esther and as her final guardian by the fact that Esther continues to call Jarndyce 'guardian' and always sits, when he visits, in the 'old chair at his side' where her engagement with Jarndyce first placed her.[56] Woodcourt, never very fully embodied, seems especially spirit-like now, for his children with Esther call Jarndyce 'guardian' as well, just as if their father were dead.[57] Likewise denominating Jarndyce 'guardian' at the very end of the novel is the child of Ada and Richard Carstone.[58] Richard's intervening death scene gives a posthumous look to everyone at the new Bleak House. In that scene, Jarndyce and Woodcourt fuse: Jarndyce adopts the latter's characteristic by appearing suddenly in the sick room, and the dying Richard says that Woodcourt has been a 'guardian-angel' to himself and Ada, those wards of Jarndyce.[59] Richard addresses Jarndyce with Sir Charles Grandison's epithet, 'you are a good man, you are a good man',[60] a phrase that tolls throughout the rest of the novel, and praises Jarndyce for having given Esther and Woodcourt their new home. Richard's last wish is to visit the new Bleak House, where he imagines waking from an erring dream in 'that pleasant country where the old times are': 'It will be like coming to the old Bleak House again', he says.[61] Of course, instead of journeying to Esther's new home, Richard journeys to '[t]he world that sets this right',[62] as if the new Bleak House and all its inhabitants were the old Bleak House transposed in the afterlife.

Between the old house and the new is a threshold not just between life and death but also between fiction and the facts it hopes to influence, the world of the novel and the world of the reader. The new Bleak House, recalling Grandison Hall, is both heaven's corrected version of the world and the correction that will result on earth after the novel's recommended reforms have been implemented, its lessons having taken effect. As Richardson did, Dickens imagines the readers upon whom his novel has the maximum happy effect as a married pair – a pair who owe their marriage to the ostensible rupture of a prior bond between the wife and her guardian. At the end of the novel, Jarndyce is on one level a guardian of the hearth: welcomed into the home as Dickens wished *Household Words* to be, presiding over and blessing it, a male angel of the house. But Jarndyce is also Esther's husband, embodied wrinkle-free as Woodcourt in the world that sets this one right. And meanwhile, the ménage at the new Bleak House is a 'simultaneous remarriage', to borrow a term from Maia McAleavey: what seems like a succession of spouses is in fact experienced, blissfully, as a bigamous simultaneity of partners.[63] In McAleavey's reading of *David Copperfield* (1849–50), 'David's marriage to Agnes unifies the past and future, refining rather than erasing Dora in a perfect (re)union'.[64] So does Esther's marriage to Woodcourt include Jarndyce. As in the case of Emily's marriage to Beauchamp, a union designed to include Sir Charles the Richardson surrogate, this marriage invites readers to include the author in their marriage: Dickens is to be both the matchmaker and the model whom the husband replicates.

Jarndyce is never more author-like than when, fulfilling the matchmaking part of the guardian's role, he presents his gift of the new Bleak House to Esther and Woodcourt as Dickens gears up to present *his* completed gift of the same name to his reader. Esther the character (as opposed to Esther who narrates these events seven years later) and the reader of *Bleak House* stand in the same position: both are treated to a shock when Jarndyce makes his stagey revelation. Nor is Woodcourt privy to Jarndyce's intention until a day before Esther is, for, as Jarndyce says, 'these surprises were my great reward, and I was too miserly to part with a scrap of it'.[65] Jarndyce declines to tell Esther *when* exactly he began to doubt the wisdom of his own marriage proposal, but it is clear that he has planned to give

Esther to Woodcourt almost from the beginning of the betrothal, for he acknowledges that Woodcourt's return from sea, which takes place in the chapter following the proposal, removed all doubt. Since that time, Jarndyce also reveals, he has been stage-managing everything that has occurred between Esther and Woodcourt, who now appear not just as readers but also as characters to Jarndyce's author. Working with the donné of her engagement with him, Jarndyce has set up dramas for Esther to star in, rightly confident that Esther would play the role scripted for her. It was in order that she might watch Esther and be convinced of Esther's worth that Jarndyce invited Woodcourt's mother for an extended visit at Bleak House, as he now acknowledges: 'my ward loves your son', Jarndyce told old Mrs Woodcourt, 'but will sacrifice her love to a sense of duty and affection, and will sacrifice it so completely, so entirely, so religiously, that you should never suspect it, though you watched her night and day'.[66] It was likewise with Jarndyce's consent and cooperation, Esther now learns, that Woodcourt proposed to Esther – and received a refusal that carried out Jarndyce's plan and prediction. Like Richardson's, Dickens's ward/reader is so well taught by the guardian that she blurs the line between reader and character, and her marriage will serve to extend the guardian's influence upon her through the rest of her life.

But Jarndyce, unlike Sir Charles Grandison, is no one's chosen romantic partner. While Emily Jervois prefers her guardian to her husband and marries that husband for her guardian's sake, Esther prefers her husband to her guardian and merely turns down her eventual husband's proposal for her guardian's sake. Esther is Jarndyce's to pass along to his delegate not because she loves her guardian but because she has promised herself to him. Ordinarily one would ascribe no very honourable intentions to the man who stayed engaged to a woman 'for months on months' while intending to break off with her, but Jarndyce, far from taking any overt sexual advantage of his position, rigorously retains his old, 'protecting manner' to his ward.[67] Jarndyce comes to seem as much a figure of chastity as that earlier adaptation of Sir Charles Grandison, Watkins Tottle.

The dramatic highpoint of the sketch by Boz can suggest how much closer to Richardson Dickens had moved in the nearly two decades separating it from *Bleak House*. At the end of an interview in which Watkins, having summoned the courage to court a lady on 'the Richardsonian principle', believes that he has successfully engaged himself to be married, the lady asks him to carry a letter from her to a clergyman of their mutual acquaintance.[68] Watkins agrees, joyful at the thought that the letter will set an early date for his and the lady's wedding, only to find

that through the letter the lady has in fact clinched a match between herself
and the clergyman. In this early story, to court on the Richardsonian
principle is not just to adopt a modest obliquity of speech but also to
become the go-between for another at the expense of one's own romantic
chances. In *Bleak House*, Dickens is again interested in what we could call a
Richardsonian principle of matchmaking via courtship, but here Dickens
is far truer to *Grandison*, where the act of matchmaking extends the sphere
of the matchmaker's erotic and pedagogical influence. Despite all the
renunciations implied by Jarndyce's manner and Dickens's decision to
deprive him of the glamour of Sir Charles, it is not finally at Jarndyce's
expense that Esther marries Woodcourt, for the marriage embraces
Jarndyce within it.

Still, the choice to tie Esther to Jarndyce by her promise rather than her
preference marks a significant difference from Dickens's predecessor.
Richardson could imagine no better pedagogical tool than erotic love,
and he boldly demanded it for his surrogates. Dickens, by contrast,
pointedly refrains from claiming his reader's love when he lingers on
Esther's failure to fall in love with Jarndyce. To be sure, the readerly love
that Dickens abjures with one hand he requests with the other, when his
author-figure Jarndyce proposes marriage to his reader-figure Esther. But
as I will suggest, so discomfiting does Dickens find this proposal that he
uses it to align Jarndyce, albeit temporarily, with the guardianship-gone-
wrong that *Bleak House* aims to redress and replace. While Richardson
barely disguises his wish that his representative Sir Charles could marry
all the single ladies and thereby give them the fullest possible dose of
Grandisonian excellence, Dickens evidently regards the idea of an untrian-
gulated erotic relation between author and reader as taboo.

The elaborate rituals of deferral and mediation through which Jarndyce
asks for Esther's hand betray his fear that the proposal, far from bringing
his guardianship of Esther to glorious fruition, as Sir Charles's proposal
to Harriet may be said to do, risks appearing to bring it to an end. His
anxiety is justified. Having announced 'You have wrought changes in me,
little woman, since the winter day in the stage coach', Jarndyce inconse-
quently demands to be assured of Esther's conviction 'that nothing can
change me as you know me', before he will open via letter the subject she
has already intuited from his face. If after a week Esther remains 'quite
certain' of Jarndyce's immutability, then may she send her maid Charley
for the letter.[69] The letter, when it comes, insists that Esther 'would gain
nothing by such a marriage, and lose nothing by rejecting it; for no new
relation could enhance the tenderness in which he held me', but it does

acknowledge one change their marriage would make: although Jarndyce will keep his old manner and Esther will continue to call him 'guardian' whatever her answer, the marriage would 'give him the best right he could have to be my protector'. With this rhetorical alignment of husband with guardian, Jarndyce protests (too much) that he will continue to be Esther's guardian whatever the event. But in presenting the projected marriage as the highest form of guardianship, he misses the mark. The letter, Esther observes, was 'written throughout with a justice and a dignity, as if he were indeed my responsible guardian, impartially representing the proposal of a friend against whom in his integrity he stated the full case'.[70] Esther's 'as if' registers the feeling that in their current, unmarried relation, Jarndyce is *no longer* her guardian.

The danger that Jarndyce's proposal may deprive Esther of the guardian with whom she has so gratefully taken refuge is also a threat to the legitimacy of the novel's didactic project, as we see when Charley delivers the proposal letter. The space that separates guardian from suitor proves to be a labyrinth that, in the syntax of its description, recalls the complex architecture of the house where Esther's mother Lady Dedlock received the document that causes her downfall. Much as Charley, to bring Esther the letter from Jarndyce, 'went up the stairs, and down the stairs, and along the passages – the zig-zag way about the old-fashioned house seemed very long in my listening ears that night – and so came back, along the passages, and down the stairs, and up the stairs, and brought the letter',[71] the villainous lawyer Tulkinghorn, 'solicitor of the High Court of Chancery',[72] delivers a 'few fresh affidavits'[73] about the Jarndyce and Jarndyce case to Lady Dedlock thus: 'Across the hall, and up the stairs, and along the passages, and through the rooms, which are very brilliant in the season and very dismal out of it – Fairy-land to visit, but a desert to live in – the old gentleman is conducted, by a Mercury in powder, to my Lady's presence'.[74] The progress through one house of Jarndyce's marriage proposal resembles the progress through another house of the documents that surprise Lady Dedlock into betraying herself to the man who, while acting nominally as the delegate of her husband, will torment and destroy her.[75] Both journeys resemble the progress of the fog, emblem of that bad guardian, Chancery, and its emblematic case, as it makes its way through the maze-like streets of London. In short, John Jarndyce's suit is disturbingly like the Jarndyce and Jarndyce suit.

Although the intimations of evil guardianship attaching to Jarndyce's proposal yield to a closing celebration of the novel's good guardianship, they give an ominous cast to the reader's figurative wardship. Jarndyce rehabilitates his engagement with Esther by using it to match her with his deputy, but one wonders why the novel's mechanism for extending its benevolent guardianship through the reader's lifetime should be imagined as a source of so much pain. Esther experiences her engagement to Jarndyce as one more calamity in the series beginning with her illness. Not only does it threaten the stability of her home, but also it alerts her to the idea that in Jarndyce's opinion, at least, she has no chance of attracting a proposal from anyone else. As the engagement continues, Jarndyce's very abstentions as a lover put Esther in a role detrimental to her modesty: that of sexual aggressor, whose physical overtures, meant to demonstrate her willingness to marry Jarndyce, go disregarded. The passion for Sir Charles that allows that other ward, Emily Jervois, to show readers how to marry a ghost of the guardian causes pain similarly acute. Consumed with unrequited love she does not recognize and jealousy she cannot avow, shamed, once she does understand her feelings, by her adulterous wishes, Emily, like Esther, is a model of suffering. To be a ward of the novelist is not so safe a position after all. Before doing readers the favour of embracing them in a guardianship that co-opts their love lives, *Sir Charles Grandison* and *Bleak House* may exact, they give warning, a high price.[76]

Notes

1 'A Passage in the Life of Mr. Watkins Tottle', *The Works of Charles Dickens*, National Library Edn, 20 vols. (New York: Bigelow, Brown and Co., 1930), vol. 1, part 2, p. 126. According to Nicolas Bentley, Michael Slater, and Nina Burgis, *The Dickens Index* (Oxford University Press, 1988), p. 217, 'Mr. Watkins Tottle' contains the only references to *Sir Charles Grandison* or Richardson recorded in Dickens's published writings. To be sure, Watkins Tottle bears less resemblance to Sir Charles than to the Samuel Richardson of nineteenth-century caricature, the 'concupiscent' 'milksop', to quote famous descriptions by Samuel Taylor Coleridge, *Anima Poetae*, ed. Ernest Hartley Coleridge (London: Heinemann, 1895), p. 166, and William Makepeace Thackeray, *Thackeray's Lectures: The English Humorists. The Four Georges* (New York: Harper and Brothers, 1867), p. 218.

2 On some of the British novels that reprised *Grandison*'s characters and situations, see Gerard A. Barker, *Grandison's Heirs: The Paragon's Progress in the Late Eighteenth-Century English Novel* (Newark: University of Delaware Press, 1985), and Isobel Grundy, '"A novel in a series of letters by a lady": Richardson and some Richardsonian Novels', in *Samuel Richardson: Tercentenary Essays*, eds. Margaret Anne Doody and Peter Sabor (Cambridge University Press, 1989), pp. 223–36. Several late eighteenth-century abridgements of *Grandison* rendered the novel's plot and characters in third-person narrative. An adaptation that borrowed characters but not plot was *Young Grandison* (London: Joseph Johnson, 1790), Mary Wollstonecraft's revision of John Hall's translation from

the Dutch of a novel for children by Maria de Cambon. Many scholars ascribe to Jane Austen a droll nutshell-version of *Grandison* in the form of a play.

3 Samuel Richardson, *The History of Sir Charles Grandison* (1753–54), ed. Jocelyn Harris, 3 vols. (Oxford University Press, 1972), vol. 3, p. 462.

4 On Austen's allusions to *Grandison* in 'Jack and Alice' (c.1790) and other pieces of juvenilia, see Jocelyn Harris, *Jane Austen's Art of Memory* (Cambridge University Press, 1989), pp. 228–38. This book carefully uncovers *Grandison*'s presence in several Austen novels.

5 On guardians as romantic leads and the fictional mentor-lover generally, see Jane Spencer, *The Rise of the Woman Novelist: From Aphra Behn to Jane Austen* (Oxford: Blackwell, 1986), pp. 140–80, and Eleanor Wikborg, *The Lover as Father-Figure in Eighteenth-Century Women's Fiction* (Gainesville: University Press of Florida, 2002), pp. 20–51. On certain novelists as mentor-lovers to their readers, see Patricia Menon, *Austen, Eliot, Charlotte Brontë and the Mentor-Lover* (Basingstoke: Palgrave Macmillan, 2003).

6 On *Mansfield Park*'s adaptations of *Grandison*, see Harris, *Jane Austen's Art of Memory*, pp. 130–68. For the most part, Harris finds Sir Charles not in the guardian figure Sir Thomas Bertram but rather in his son Edmund.

7 William Blackstone makes this division explicit: 'THE guardian with us performs the office both of the *tutor* and *curator* of the Roman laws; the former of which had the charge of the maintenance and education of the minor, the latter the care of his fortune', *Commentaries on the Laws of England, in Four Books* (1765–69), ed. Edward Christian, 12th edn (London: A. Strahan and W. Woodfall, 1793), p. 460.

8 Samuel Richardson, *Pamela; or, Virtue Rewarded* (1740), eds. Thomas Keymer and Alice Wakely (Oxford University Press, 2001), p. 1.

9 Richardson, *Pamela*, p. 508.

10 Mario Ortiz-Robles, 'Dickens Performs Dickens', *English Literary History*, 78:2 (2011), 457–78 (457); Blackstone, *Commentaries*, p. 460.

11 Richardson, *Grandison*, vol. 1, p. 290; vol. 2, p. 323.

12 Richardson, *Grandison*, vol. 2, p. 38.

13 Betty A. Schellenberg makes similar points in *The Conversational Circle: Rereading the English Novel, 1740–1775* (Lexington: University Press of Kentucky, 1996), pp. 55–56.

14 Richardson, *Grandison*, vol. 1, p. 169.

15 Richardson, *Grandison*, vol. 3, p. 397.

16 Richardson, *Grandison*, vol. 1, p. 138.

17 Richardson, *Grandison*, vol. 1, p. 176.

18 Richardson, *Grandison*, vol. 1, p. 452.

19 Richardson, *Grandison*, vol. 1, p. 295.

20 An illuminating discussion of Richardson's use of *Grandison* to 'tell men what to be if they wish to marry heroines' appears in Jocelyn Harris, *Samuel Richardson* (Cambridge University Press, 1987), p. 135.

21 Harriet Byron's various correspondents, privy to exactly the same descriptions of Sir Charles as Richardson's readers, set the example when they confess 'That

we every one of us are in love ourselves with this fine young gentleman':
Richardson, *Grandison*, vol. 1, p. 212.

22 Richardson, *Grandison*, vol. 3, p. 396.

23 Richardson, *Grandison*, vol. 1, p. 373.

24 Richardson, *Grandison*, vol. 1, p. 464.

25 I have elsewhere argued that Jane Austen took up this Grandisonian match-
    making project in *Emma* (1815) and that Austen's reception today fulfils
    Richardson's most ambitious ideas about the roles an author could play for a
    readership: Sarah Raff, *Jane Austen's Erotic Advice* (New York: Oxford Univer-
    sity Press, 2014), pp. 61–99.

26 In suggesting that Beauchamp's inadequacy is part of the novel's 'plan', I differ
    from Harris, who finds the introduction of Beauchamp 'an admission of
    defeat' on Richardson's part: *Samuel Richardson*, p. 153.

27 Richardson, *Grandison*, vol. 2, p. 420.

28 Richardson, *Grandison*, vol. 3, p, 229.

29 Richardson, *Grandison*, vol. 3, p. 443.

30 Mary Astell, *Some Reflections on Marriage*, 4th edn (1730), quoted in Harris,
    Samuel Richardson, p. 149.

31 On the ratification of this symbolic three-way union in marriage rituals at
    Grandison Hall, see David Macey, '"Business for the Lovers of Business":
    Sir Charles Grandison, Hardwicke's Marriage Act and the Specter of Bigamy',
    Philological Quarterly, 84:3 (2005): 333–55 (343–44). For an explanation of
    Sir Charles's 'achieve[ment]' of 'a kind of polygamy, a division of labour in
    which the orphan Harriet supplies biological offspring and Clementina affine
    "friends"', see Leah Price, 'The Executor's Hand in *Sir Charles Grandison*',
    Eighteenth-Century Fiction, 8:3 (1996), 331–42 (336).

32 David A. Brewer, *The Afterlife of Character, 1726–1825* (Philadelphia: Univer-
    sity of Pennsylvania Press, 2005), p. 141. On Richardson's request that his
    correspondents write material for *Grandison*, see Thomas Keymer (published
    as Tom Keymer), *Richardson's 'Clarissa' and the Eighteenth-Century Reader*
    (Cambridge University Press, 1992), pp. 75–76.

33 Charles Dickens, *The Letters of Charles Dickens*, eds. Madeline House, Graham
    Storey, et al., 12 vols. (Oxford: Clarendon Press, 1965–2002), vol. 8, p. 539.
    John Butt and Kathleen Tillotson discuss Dickens's 'transform[ation] in
    public estimation' of the 'shilling number' and 'love-affair with his reading
    public': *Dickens at Work* (London: Methuen, 1957), pp. 63, 75. For a more
    recent discussion of that love-affair, see Ivan Kreilkamp, *Voice and the Victorian
    Storyteller* (Cambridge University Press, 2005), p. 109. On the Cheap Edition,
    see John M. Picker, *Victorian Soundscapes* (New York: Oxford University
    Press, 2003), pp. 34–35.

34 I quote Grahame Smith's list of the 'dominating passions of [Dickens's]
    political life': 'The Life and Times of Charles Dickens', in *The Cambridge
    Companion to Charles Dickens*, ed. John O. Jordan (Cambridge University
    Press, 2001), pp. 1–15 (12). Schellenberg discusses 'the intermediate range
    between the public and the retired' of Sir Charles's sphere of influence:
    Conversational Circle, p. 58.

35 Alexander Welsh connects Jo with Esther through the former's broom and the latter's so-called housekeeping: *Dickens Redressed: The Art of 'Bleak House' and 'Hard Times'* (New Haven: Yale University Press, 2000), p. 30.

36 The Lord Chancellor who presides in the Court of Chancery 'is, by right derived from the crown, the general and supreme guardian of all infants, as well as idiots and lunatics; that is, of all such persons as have not discretion enough to manage their own concerns': Blackstone, *Commentaries*, p. 463.

37 Charles Dickens, *Bleak House* (1852–53), ed. Nicola Bradbury (London: Penguin, 1996), p. 257. Welsh points out that, in the case of Tom-all-Alone's, 'the law's delay and costs have effectively destroyed responsible private ownership': *Dickens Redressed*, p. 104.

38 Dickens, *Bleak House*, p. 13.

39 Dickens, *Bleak House*, p. 17.

40 Dickens, *Bleak House*, p. 16.

41 Charles Dickens, 'A Preliminary Word', *Household Words*, 30 March 1850, p. 1.

42 Dickens, *Bleak House*, pp. 17, 18.

43 Dickens, 'Preliminary Word', p. 1.

44 Dickens, *Bleak House*, p. 215.

45 Dickens, *Bleak House*, p. 35.

46 Richardson, *Grandison*, vol. 1, p. 38.

47 Dickens, *Bleak House*, p. 27.

48 Dickens, *Bleak House*, p. 943.

49 Dickens, *Bleak House*, p. 961.

50 Dickens, *Bleak House*, pp. 962, 963.

51 Dickens, *Bleak House*, p. 959.

52 Dickens, *Bleak House*, p. 989.

53 Welsh, *Dickens Redressed*, pp. 32–33.

54 Dickens, *Bleak House*, p. 966. These scenes of bequest present Dora and Jarndyce as author-figures, for each gives a gift that shares the name of the novel that Dickens is about to present, completed, to the public: Dora gives David Copperfield, and Jarndyce gives not just Esther but Bleak House as well.

55 Dickens, *Bleak House*, p. 987.

56 Dickens, *Bleak House*, pp. 987, 988.

57 Dickens, *Bleak House*, p. 986.

58 Dickens, *Bleak House*, p. 986.

59 Dickens, *Bleak House*, p. 977.

60 Dickens, *Bleak House*, p. 977.

61 Dickens, *Bleak House*, pp. 979, 978. On other Victorian writing that 'imagines heaven as a perfected repetition of the home', see Maia McAleavey, 'Soul-Mates: *David Copperfield*'s Angelic Bigamy', *Victorian Studies*, 52:2 (2010), 191–218 (195).

62 Dickens, *Bleak House*, p. 979.

63 McAleavey, 'Soul-Mates', p. 194.

64 McAleavey, 'Soul-Mates', p. 201.

65 Dickens, *Bleak House*, p. 965.
66 Dickens, *Bleak House*, p. 965.
67 Dickens, *Bleak House*, p. 965.
68 *The Works of Charles Dickens*, p. 168.
69 Dickens, *Bleak House*, p. 689.
70 Dickens, *Bleak House*, p. 691.
71 Dickens, *Bleak House*, p. 690.
72 Dickens, *Bleak House*, p. 23.
73 Dickens, *Bleak House*, p. 26.
74 Dickens, *Bleak House*, p. 23. On Lady Dedlock's reaction to the documents, see Hilary M. Schor, *Curious Subjects: Women and the Trials of Realism* (New York: Oxford University Press, 2013), pp. 133–62.
75 Jarndyce may not deliberately torture Esther as Tulkinghorn tortures her mother, but he does toy with Woodcourt, who is not only set up for rejection but also required to tell Jarndyce 'all that passed' during the unsuccessful marriage proposal: Dickens, *Bleak House*, p. 965. A strong competitive animus drives those schemes in which the proof of Esther's value is the invisibility of her love for Jarndyce's rival.
76 I thank Nicholas Seager, Daniel Cook, Jocelyn Harris, and Hilary M. Schor for their helpful comments on an earlier version of this essay.

CHAPTER 5

The Novel's Afterlife in the Newspaper, 1712–1750

Nicholas Seager

> At last having perfectly recovered
> the effects of her first unhappy passion,
> she seemed to have vowed a state of per:
> petual chastity. She was long deaf to
> all the sufferings of her lovers, till one
> day at a neighbouring fair, the Rheto-
> rick of John the hostler, with a new
> to be continued

The reader of *Joseph Andrews* (1742) in the farthing half-sheet *All Alive and Merry; or, The London Daily Post* who reached this point on 20 April 1743 had to wait a day to discover that it is John the hostler's 'new Straw Hat, and a Pint of Wine' that contribute to Betty the Chambermaid's (second) fall from virtue.[1] Hopefully the joke was not ruined by the interruption. This instalment straddles Chapters 15 and 16 of the serialization, corresponding to Chapters 16 and 17 in Book One of the original *Joseph Andrews*. If not a misnumbering, it may be that Fielding's meta-narrative first chapter was omitted; however, this is the only extant issue of *All Alive and Merry* to contain the serialization of *Joseph Andrews*. Fielding's novel is cramped into the middle column of three on the front page (the format of the last paragraph is replicated in the epigraph above). To its right is foreign news, lifted from the previous day's *Daily Advertiser*. To its left is another serial, *Memoirs of an Unfortunate Young Nobleman*, Haywood's fictionalized account of James Annesley's life. Annesley, aiming to be recognized as the legitimate Earl of Anglesey after having been tricked into slavery by his usurper uncle, was a *cause célèbre* occupying many column inches in the early 1740s; extracts of Haywood's version were also serialized in *The Gentleman's Magazine* in 1743. Like *Joseph Andrews*, it is the story of a virtuous and chaste youth whose lowly station belies his true nobility, making these apt companion pieces in *All Alive and Merry*.

This essay charts newspaper reprints of fiction in the early eighteenth century, demonstrating that fiction in this form reached many new readers, helping to shape formal expectations for fiction and providing reading experiences that have been lost to our understanding of early eighteenth-century fiction: in newspapers, novels underwent textual alterations, were set alongside paratexts, and were parcelled up for serial delivery.

I

Eighteenth-century novels have afterlives in several senses, including the persistence of their conventions and techniques into fiction of later periods and their adaptation into different genres and media. The *textual* afterlives of novels, their republication, in full or in part, in new formats (chapbooks, anthologies, series) and with alterations falling short of creative appropriation (abridgement, excerption, editing) have proven fertile grounds for explorations of the ways in which the early novel was reproduced and disseminated. Essays in this collection by Leah Orr and M-C. Newbould address chapbooks, abridgements, and anthologies. But an overlooked aspect to the afterlives of fiction in the early century is their being reprinted in London and provincial newspapers, a practice that flourished between around 1712 and 1750. Serialization of fiction remains strongly associated with the nineteenth century, bound up with constructions of the Victorian outlook, a culture allegedly attuned to deferred gratification – in economics, religion, sex, and light reading.[2] However, several modes of parts-publication existed during the long eighteenth century, and among the earliest was the newspaper reprint.

The practice of reprinting fiction in newspapers reflected and enhanced the novel's growing appeal, as newspapers helped to widen and democratize the readership for fiction. Novels in newspapers tailed off by the 1750s. By then, literary magazines for new and reprinted fiction had emerged.[3] Novels began to be written expressly for serialization: among the earliest were Tobias Smollett's *Launcelot Greaves* in *The British Magazine* (January 1760 to December 1761) and Charlotte Lennox's *History of Harriot and Sophia* in *The Lady's Museum* (March 1760 to January 1761). Multivolume publication could be another form of serialization, as original readers of fiction from *The Turkish Spy* (1684–97) to *Tristram Shandy* (1759–67) could attest. And the taste for continuation rather than closure, which resulted in sequels and other imitations and iterations, replicates this experience of additive, open-ended fiction. Following the end of perpetual copyright in 1774, large-scale, incrementally published anthologies like James Harrison's *Novelist's Magazine* (1779–89) and the books-in-parts industry supplied the market with reprinted fiction in affordable parts before the transformation of serial fiction – as an art and a commercial enterprise – by *The Pickwick Papers* (1836–37). Long before then, novels were repackaged in weekly, thrice-weekly and daily news outlets, sharing pages with news, advertisements, and each other. Many of the earliest readers of eighteenth-century fiction consumed it not in a volume, but in short injections with enforced breaks, these often coming mid-chapter, mid-paragraph, even mid-sentence (as with *Joseph Andrews* in *All Alive and Merry*). The novels' texts underwent transformation, including abridgement, emendation, truncation, and continuation. Classic staples like *Don Quixote* (1605–15) and the *Arabian Nights' Entertainment* (first published in English in 1706) were serialized in newspapers, as were less illustrious foreign fictions in translation, but the major British novels of the period received this treatment, from *Love in Excess* (1719–20), *Moll Flanders* (1722), and *Gulliver's Travels* (1726) to *Pamela* (1740), *Joseph Andrews*, and *Roderick Random* (1748).

Newspaper serialization had consequences not just for the way fiction was distributed and consumed, but also for its formal shape. J. Paul Hunter observes that eighteenth-century fictions are 'additive' and 'resistant to closure in the generally accepted sense'.[4] Hence, they were well-suited to incremental publication. Serial fiction works by stimulating without fully satisfying desire, impelling the reader repeatedly to return and inviting them to project narrative time and space that is not tangible (unlike the heft in one's right hand when reading a book).[5] For the newspaper, each issue of which was otherwise basically self-contained, serialization of literary works provided continuity which could ensure repeated custom in an increasingly competitive industry; it implanted fiction in the routine of regular reading. Stuart Sherman argues that technological developments in chronometry in the early eighteenth century produced new serial prose forms, so readers were becoming attuned to accretive delivery and new narrative modes matched a new temporal sense.[6] The compatibility of newspaper and novel reading supports this claim. Ian Watt claims that newspapers and novels 'encourage a rapid, inattentive, almost unconscious kind of reading habit'.[7] And Hunter discusses 'the commitment to contemporaneity' in evidence in the new taste for newspapers and novels, a 'sense of urgency about present time and current concerns'.[8] The novel's afterlife in the newspaper, then, was enabled by a demand for affordable and exciting stories; readers were comfortable with fragmentary, periodic modes of reading and with episodic, additive, and disposable forms of narrative. Furthermore, fiction, like the other content of newspapers, could potentially tell them things about the world they inhabited.

Serialization establishes routine, and its disruption can be upsetting. A letter in *Parker's London News* in 1724 complains to the proprietor George Parker about the omission, in consecutive numbers, of the *Arabian Nights*:

> You have very much disoblig'd me and a great many more of the Fair (or at least weaker) Sex, by your indirect Practices of late; in postponing the History of the Royal Lovers, for an Account of the Commitment of a Parcel of Goal-Birds to the Marshalsea (as you did the other Day) but which is still worse (when this Morning we were big with Expectation of hearing how *Prince* what d'ye call him recover'd his Talisman, and all Things were in a fair Way to be set right again) to fob us off with the Epitaph of an old Man of Fourscore, tho' he had been Lord Mayor . . .: Pray let us have no more of these Irregularities for the future, nor our diverting History interrupted by grave Trifles or dismal Ditties; as you value the Displeasure of us, who are your constant Readers and Admirers, while you write Things to please us.

The letter, signed '*Philo Romance*', ends with a threat to refer the matter to parliament if the prioritization of news over fiction continues, prompting Parker to '*promise the Continuance of the Arabian Nights Adventures, without Interruption, unless some unforeseen and more momentous Occurences, necessary to be timely publish'd, shall be sent us*'.[9] The letter illustrates the gendered discourse on the consumption of fiction, pointing to an anxiety on the newspaper's part about the mingling of discourses, the functional, factual, and masculine against the frivolous, fictional, and feminine. Though the letter satirizes women's debilitating dependence on romance, it also points to the anticipation ('this Morning we were big with Expectation') experienced by readers of serials. Thomas Keymer notes that this serialization of the *Arabian Nights*, a story of a thousand and one nights, when extended over three years and 445 instalments, approximately matched the time it took to read the narrative to the time that passed within it. He observes that 'the work's framing situation (in which a narrator staves off execution by repeatedly deferring narrative closure) catches to perfection the characteristic elasticity of serial writing, as well as the hovering threat of sudden curtailment'.[10] This hovering threat was realized in Parker's suspension of the *Arabian Nights*, and readers were unhappy. Parker required another prompt two years later when he interrupted another serial: 'Being requested by some of my Readers to continue the *Chinese Tales*, I have therefore (to oblige those Persons) inserted them again . . . and hope they will give a diverting Pleasure and Satisfaction to every Purchaser of my Paper'.[11] Readers' demands evidently proved hard to ignore.

Readers of novels serialized in newspapers are again cast as enthusiastic but credulous consumers in the famous anecdote of provincial villagers ringing church bells as 'news' of Pamela's marriage reached them via the newspaper serialization in *Robinson Crusoe's London Daily Evening Post* (1741–42).[12] The epistolary *Pamela* was well-suited to serialization, its 'allegiance to periodic, even diurnal pulse' creating 'serial-like present-tense excitements', whereby readers are left on tenterhooks from letter to letter, from crisis to lull, only ever knowing as much as the narrator and awaiting a new instalment.[13] Hester Thrale is the earliest source for the following anecdote about provincial readers' reactions:

> When [. . .] Pamela first came out, some Extracts got into the public Papers, and used by that means to find their way down as far as Preston in Lancashire where my Aunt who told me the Story then resided: One Morning as She rose the Bells were set o' ringing & the Flag was observed to fly from the Great Steeple; She rung her Bell & enquired the Reason of these Rejoycings when her Maid came in bursting with Joy, and said why Madam poor Pamela's married at last; the News came down to us in this Mornings Paper.[14]

The story should be treated with scepticism – it was first offered, second-hand, almost forty years after *Pamela*'s publication, and thereafter adapted for other provincial locales.[15] But there is surely a truth in anecdotes about readers' immersion in their serial stories, which results in disappointment when an instalment is missed or in elation following a revelation, and the communal aspect of this response qualifies current critical emphases on novel reading as private and secluded. Additive stories proved addictive, and communities of readers were developing.

II

Newspapers began to publish literary matter – including not just fiction, but also history, geography, and much more – largely as a result of legal and economic developments.[16] The pressure of competition after the lapse of the Licensing Act in 1695 occasioned an expansion of the London trade and the inauguration of the provincial one, leading newspapers increasingly to diversify and pursue variant readerships by aiming to entertain as well as inform readers.[17] As a consequence of the Stamp Act (1712), newspapers began to serialize literary material. The Stamp Act imposed a duty of a half-penny for every half sheet *per copy sold* on single– and half–sheet newspapers, prompting doubts about whether the industry could sustain this level of taxation. Swift predicted that 'Grubstreet has but ten days to live, then an Act of Parlmt takes place, that ruins it, by taxing every half sheet at a halfpenny', and Addison expected that the periodical press would be crushed 'under the Weight of a Stamp'.[18] Such predictions proved unfounded because the Act negligently defined a newspaper not in terms of its content or its periodic publication, but rather by its size, or more precisely by the quantity of paper it used. It became economical for newspapers to expand to one-and-a-half sheets, six pages in length, thus qualifying as pamphlets and incurring a lesser level of taxation, just two shillings per sheet in a single copy, regardless of the number of copies printed (also avoiding the one shilling tax on advertisements). With more space to fill after 1712, an issue compounded by the fact that war reports were drying up, some newspapers opted to incorporate 'literary' material. That this often continued after 1725, when the loophole was closed and the physical size of newspapers shrunk, indicates that readers by then expected both profit and pleasure from their periodical reading. A letter to the *Gloucester Journal* in 1723 said that readers 'are very desirous of seeing more frequently inserted in your Paper some pleasant Amusements in Prose or Verse'; serializations of *Shalum and Hilpa*, an oriental narrative derived from *The Spectator*, and Haywood's *Bath Intrigues* duly followed in 1724.[19] Andrew Brice in Exeter who serialized Defoe's *Captain Singleton* and parts of the *General History of the Pyrates* (1724–28) wrote in his *Post-Master* in 1729 that 'Many of our Customers have expressed some Uneasiness at the so long Discontinuance of the Entertainment wont to fill the Frontispiece of our Paper, for the sake of which principally they took it in'.[20] Literary entertainment took a prominent place, generally on the first page; it ensured sales, and its omission was sometimes met with dissatisfaction on the part of an increasingly vocal reading public.

The *British Mercury*, published by the Sun Fire Insurance Company and issued to customers with their policy at a supplementary charge of 6d., unsuccessfully appealed against having to pay the stamp duty on the basis that they made no 'Profit or Advantage of the said paper other than carrying on the said Insurance from Fire'.[21] It was among the earliest to take advantage of the legal loophole by expanding to 'pamphlet' size, going from a thrice-weekly half-sheet to a weekly sheet-and-a-half paper. And thereafter it offered serials. From October to December 1712, it published a tale purportedly derived from the '*Eastern* Nations, who are the first Inventors of all Romances' called *A Voyage Into Another World*, which '*being altogether new, may perhaps be acceptable to all Lovers of* Novelty'.[22] The *British Mercury* initiated a practice that continued for the next forty-odd years of including fiction in a newspaper. It published the fictional *A Letter from Madrid* from December 1712 to January 1713 and then from July to September 1714 an unacknowledged translation of the Spanish picaresque novel, *Varia fortuna del soldado Pindaro* (1626), by

Gonzalo de Céspedes y Meneses, retitled *The Rover* in the *Mercury*. *The Rover* followed a lengthy serialization of a historical work, occasioning the editor's apology for its longevity and promise that henceforth '*Our Method therefore shall be to treat of such Things as may be contain'd in a few* Mercuries, *and so to pass from one to another, sometimes treating of what is mostly diverting, and then again of what is more solid and entertaining*'. As well as the emphasis on variety, the discourse of commingled pleasure and profit became common in the novel's afterlife in the newspaper; newspapers could justify to themselves including fiction if they could present it as edifying. *The Rover* is mendaciously introduced in this way: '*The following Account of the surprizing Adventures of a Gentleman now living, and written by himself, it is hop'd may be acceptable, as being extraordinary entertaining, and full of Variety*'.[23] But the *Mercury* quickly experienced its readers' capriciousness. In 1715, the paper observed that '*There are solid Readers, who read for Information; and there are others more Mercurial, who value not a Book any farther, than for the Diversion and Amusement it affords*'. After surveying the variable reception of the historical, geographical, and fictional works hitherto included, the proprietor announces:

> It is intended now to find such Subjects, as may be short and pleasing; so that by constant Change, something may touch every different Genius. Whosoever then, in reading does not sometimes find his Account, that is, the Satisfaction he expected, is desir'd not to be too rash in condemning that which perhaps may be pleasing to another; but to let a Week or two pass with Patience, when perhaps he may meet with Matter more suitable to his Palate.[24]

Newspapers commonly adopted a solicitous manner when commenting on their literary material, stating that they aimed to entertain, and often indicating that continuation will depend on the readership's approbation. Many serializations were curtailed, presumably because they were failing with readers. Relying on regular sales, newspapers were at the mercy of their customers; readers might have expected to get whatever was available to some extent with the news, which was beyond the paper's control, but when reading fiction and history their discernment and predilections carried weight. The increasing popularity of fiction in this period is partly due to its suitability to entertain readers of periodicals looking for lighter fare than political and business news.

Newspaper serialization made financial sense for readers too. It provided those who could not customarily afford to purchase a book the opportunity to read fiction because it spread the cost, combined demands on their purses, and lent itself to shared reading to a greater extent than the 'private' volume.[25] *Gulliver's Travels* furnishes an important example. Published in two volumes in October 1726, it retailed for a whopping 8s. 6d. Even the first abridgement, which came out in February 1727, printed by Samuel Richardson, set readers back 3s.[26] By then, however, two rival serializations in penny papers were under way. In his *Penny London Post* on 25 November 1726, Thomas Read announced that his current serialization of *Don Quixote* would be suspended and *Gulliver's Travels* would replace it: 'That those who have not the Convenience of reading [the *Travels*] at the Price they are now sold, may not be debarr'd so delightful an Entertainment, we shall begin them in this Paper in the Manner following, and continue them till the whole is finished'. Readers were persuaded they were getting, in full and at a discount, a narrative that was the talk of the town, the *Travels* having 'bore so considerable a Share in almost every Conversation both in Town and Country'.[27] George Parker's rival serialization in *Parker's Penny Post* started three days after Read's, occupying 145 instalments of his thrice-weekly paper for the succeeding year.[28] Like Read, Parker appealed to his customers' pockets: 'The Travels of Capt. Gulliver ... having for their Variety of Wit and pleasant Diversion, become the general Entertainment of Town and Country, we will insert here in small Parcels, to oblige our Customers, who are otherwise, not capable of reading them at the Price they are sold'.[29] A reader who accessed *Gulliver* in *Parker's Penny Post* would have spent just over 12s in total, rather more than the book cost, but never more than a penny at a time, and would have had Gulliver's voyages unfold over the span of almost an entire year, a timespan comparable to serializations of Defoe's novels but greatly exceeding *The British Mercury's* tentative efforts and indicating an increasing appetite for longer works. Readers would not have been able to make this financial calculation, as they would not have known for how long such a serialization was to run.

Both *Parker's Penny Post* and the *Penny London Post* captured readers by overlapping serializations, so that patrons were (hopefully) already hooked on something new when a story came to a close. Back-issues were generally available for latecomers. In Read's paper, *Don Quixote* before its curtailment shared space not just with Thomas Salmon's *Modern History: or, The Present State of all Nations*, but also with fiction like Penelope Aubin's *Lady Lucy* (1726) and the anonymous Restoration novel, *Cynthia* (1687), the latter eventually cut off in mid-story. Parker similarly lined up a new serial before the present one was finished. Towards the end of the *Arabian Nights*, he announced the inauguration of Cervantes's *Exemplary Novels* (1613): '*The* Arabian *Nights Entertainments drawing towards an End, and being willing to divert our Readers to the utmost of our Power, we present them with the following Volumes of* Exemplary Novels ... *not doubting but they will be as kindly receiv'd by the Readers, as the Arabian Tales*'.[30] By the time the Cervantes had run its course (two and a half of the *Exemplary Novels* were included before it was arrested without notice), Thomas-Simon Gueulette's *Chinese Tales* (1723) was under way. Like the *Arabian Nights* and *Exemplary Novels*, the *Chinese Tales* is a series of shorter fictions with a framing device, making it particularly suited to serialization, as its stories are relatively short and self-contained, and periodic restarts occur when a new tale begins – a feature shared with *Gulliver's Travels*. Other titles that joined *Gulliver* in *Parker's Penny Post* were Countess d'Aulnoy's *Relation of a Voyage to Spain* (1690–91), *The Four Years Voyage of Captain George Roberts* (1726), and *Cynthia* again, rebranded here *The Unfortunate Lovers, A Novel*. There is a preference for travel fiction, as well as for framed narratives; the appeal is broad, including colonial adventure, continental travel, fantasy, and romance. Readers likely thought they were getting value and variety.

III

Robinson Crusoe undoubtedly stimulated the market for serialized fiction. First published on 25 April 1719, it cost 5s. Charles Gildon sneered that 'there's not an old Woman that can go to the Price of it, but buys thy Life and Adventures, and leaves it as a Legacy, with the *Pilgrims Progress*, the *Practice of Piety*, and *God's Revenge against Murther*, to her Posterity'.[31] Though he derides Defoe's populism, grouping *Crusoe* with the bestsellers of nonconformity, Gildon acknowledges the price was beyond many ordinary readers, who depended on chapbooks, abridgements, and serializations. *Crusoe* was the first major English novel to be serialized in a newspaper, appearing in abridged form in *The Original London Post; or, Heathcot's Intelligence*, starting 7 October 1719. When the first part ended, the paper moved immediately on to Crusoe's *Farther Adventures*, published the previous August, bridging the two parts with a *nota bene* acknowledging customers' desires for entertainment, and indicating a variegated and stratified readership for Defoe's novel:

> *Having thus passed through the First Part of the Life and surprizing Adventures of the famous* Robinson Crusoe, *as we hope, to the entire Satisfaction of our Readers; we have Reason to believe, that the Second Part (with which our next Post shall begin) will be equally as diverting; being full of many uncommon and Amazing Adventures as the First. Both which Volumes (very fit for the Closet or Library of Persons of Fashion) are sold by Mr.* Taylor, *a Bookseller, at the Ship in Pater-noster Row, near St.* Paul's *Church-yard.*[32]

Whereas the purchasers of the books waited four months between volumes, the *Post*'s readers pressed straight on. The paper omits the *Farther Adventures* preface, which is fairly standard practice for newspaper serials. This means that Defoe's criticism of piracy, directed at Thomas Cox's unauthorized abridgement, is not included. But before we reflect on the aptness of this omission, it should be acknowledged that the serialization is not a piracy by our understanding of the term. A piracy that directs its readers to purchase the 'authentic' original would be rather strange; it may be evidence that Heathcot and William Taylor, *Crusoe*'s publisher, had come to an agreement: the serialization may have been a way to promote the book after the first burst in sales had tailed off.[33] There is neither any record of a lawsuit by Taylor against Heathcot nor public announcement decrying his serial reprint, as there were against Cox, whose book may have harmed Taylor's sales, unlike Heathcot's newspaper, which may have helped them. Defoe's objection was that the religious reflections had been jettisoned, leaving just the story, a charge true of Cox's abridgement, less so of the *Original London Post*'s version, making it altogether less offensive.

Whether or not there was an agreement between Heathcot and Taylor, there is little that a copyright holder could do about newspapers printing extracts. The Copyright Act (1710) proscribed piracy of books, but not condensations or partial copies, or even periodical writing in general.[34] Excerpts and abridgements were not restricted until a concept of fair abridgement gradually emerged in mid-century. Abstracting and translating were the essence of what the newsmen did to the history and fiction they printed serially, and these fell without the protections afforded by copyright law. Only in 1739 did Lord Hardwicke grant injunctions barring further publication after he concluded that a magazine intended to publish an entire book serially, but similar cases broke down.[35] Richardson was famously litigious about his authorial rights, but the serialization of *Pamela* in *Robinson Crusoe's London Daily Evening Post* carried on for eighteen months. In 1761, Robert Dodsley sued James Kinnersley over the abridged parts of Johnson's *Rasselas* (1759) issued in Kinnersley's *Grand Magazine of Magazines* in April and May 1759. The plaintiff's objection, reminiscent of Defoe's attack on Cox, was that the reprint damaged the original because it omitted the moral reflections, leaving only the plot. Sir Thomas Clarke, presiding, ruled in favour of the defendant, concluding that 'a fair abridgement' is 'not a piracy', and that the abstract in the magazine 'may serve the end of an advertisement'.[36] Nevertheless the tide was turning towards greater legal protections against serial reprints.

At the end of *Crusoe*'s run in Heathcot's paper, the editorial voice again intervenes with a puff for all three parts, supporting the supposition that, as Clarke put it forty years later, such snippets would serve to advertise the book:

> *Having finished the Life and surprizing Adventures of the famous ROBINSON CRUSOE (excepting a Third Volume, which containing excellent Meditations, and other divine Subjects, we thin[k] not proper to be inserted in a Publick Paper, but recommend it as a Book highly useful in all Christian Families, especially those who have the two other Volumes, and is to be had of Mr. TAYLOR, at the SHIP in PATER-NOSTER ROW) we hope, to our Readers' Satisfaction; we shall continue our Care to entertain and divert them.*[37]

The non-narrative *Serious Reflections* is praised but deemed unsuitable for the paper's purposes, adventure books being fit for 'a Public Paper', religious meditations for more private perusal. But a part of *Serious Reflections* was serialized by Brice in Exeter.[38] Among the more adventure-filled titles that *The Original London Post* subsequently used were Hearne's *The Lover's Week* and *The Female Deserters*, and Haywood's *The Fatal Secret; or Constancy in Distress*, both anonymized and the latter announced as having been 'Done from the French'.[39] In 1738, towards the end of its life, *The Original London Post* was serializing Francisco de Quevedo's *Los Sueños* (1627).[40]

As a general rule, unlike number books – parts-publication by which complete books were issued periodically, one gathering or more at a time forming a fascicule – newspaper reprints of fiction did not lend themselves to preservation and independent binding. Generally, they were disposable ephemera. Instalments varied in length and their placement in the paper was not always uniform, and the serial came alongside news and other content. Its ephemerality means that survival rates are poor: more novels than we know of were likely reprinted in newspapers. Nevertheless, one run of *The Original London Post* has survived precisely on account of the fiction. A bound volume in the British Library contains just the leaves on which *Robinson Crusoe* appears, which have been separated from the discarded remainder containing news. Every verso features 'To be continued'; every recto has the newspaper's masthead, featuring two woodcuts, depictions of town-criers calling 'London Post' and 'News from Spain', as well as 'The Life of *Robinson Crusoe* of *York*, Continued', the recurring header. On some pages news appears on the verso, mostly foreign affairs, usually occupying the bottom part of the page following *Crusoe*, but sometimes all of it, a reminder of the way in which readers would have advanced from fiction to news in their daily reading. But the periodical has in this instance been transformed by one user into a codex.

Similarly, the four surviving issues of the serialization of *Moll Flanders* in *The Kentish Post* (1722) have been separated from the news sections and have an 'improvised stabbed binding', which may indicate that the intention was to keep them together and bind them when the run was completed.[41] Catch words for both serializations catch not with the following physical page of news, but with the next instalment of the story. Along with this material evidence that readers collected instalments for separate binding, a reader's letter in the Exeter *Post-Man* commends a recent serialization but bemoans its cessation: 'I carefully collected and preserved every Paper', the correspondent says, so as to 'bind them in a Volume; when in the midst of all you broke abruptly off'.[42] Another tactic newspapers adopted was to issue a serialization as a detachable supplement (on unstamped paper), with independent pagination and a title page at the end of the run. A serialization of Defoe's *A New Voyage Round the World* (1725) in forty-four parts was issued as supplementary sheets to the *Chester Weekly Journal*.[43] In this fashion were produced, in 1736 alone, Aphra Behn's *Love-Letters between a Nobleman and his Sister* (1684–87) in *The Oxford Journal: Or The Tradesman's Intelligencer*; the same author's *Oroonoko* (1688) in *The Oxford Magazine: Or Family Companion*; and *Robinson Crusoe* in *Walker's Half-Penny London Spy*, a paper which had portions of Ned Ward's *The London Spy* (itself originally published serially over eighteen months in 1698–99) on its first page, but which offered *Crusoe* 'printed distinct, so as to be bound up in a neat Volume'.[44] The tendency is towards parts-publication allowing for preservation, though the more ephemeral mode persisted into mid-century when *Roderick Random* appeared in *The Sussex Weekly Advertiser* (1748–49), *The Cambridge Journal* serialized a succession of narratives, including Hearne and Aubin, from 1749–52, and Voltaire's *Zadig* appeared in *The Leedes Intelligencer* (1754).

IV

Compared to the more familiar volume form, novels in newspapers represent fluid and contingent texts. Temporary interruption, variable instalment lengths, and columnar layout affect the reading experience but not the verbal form. However, the most common substantial editorial acts are abridgement and curtailment; rarer is continuation. Abridgement was common, but certainly not universal. *Gulliver* remained intact aside from some light editorial work to help the flow between instalments. The abridgement of *Crusoe* in *The Original London Post* seems to be original, unlike the one in *All Alive and Merry*.[45] In the event, *Crusoe* lasted just a few days in *All Alive and Merry*, starting on 8 December 1740 (when the paper was also serializing Defoe's *Tour*), but ending with this announcement three days later: 'The Life of Robinson Crusoe not being so well receiv'd by our Customers as we imagin'd it would, we shall instead thereof insert the following History of the Turks, which cannot but be acceptable to the Publick'.[46] Aaron Hill's *Present State of the Ottoman Empire* (1709) took Crusoe's place. Textual instability was the norm. *Captain Singleton* was subject to a different kind of condensation when serialized in the *Post-Master*. Nine months in, the novel is interrupted: '*Not to be tiresome to our Readers, it is thought proper to pass over a few Paragraphs of the Original of this Account, nothing very material occurring therein*'. Then proceeds a one-paragraph summary of the next twenty-five paragraphs' action, before the novel resumes to its conclusion.[47] Haywood's *Love in Excess* was revived from September 1741 to January 1742 in *The London Morning Advertiser*, a paper issued gratis to subscribers to William Rayner's Family Bible (a curious way to procure amatory fiction). Its thrice-weekly, four-month duration is quicker than the original publication of Haywood's debut in three volumes (January 1719, June 1719, February 1720). William B. Warner argues that seriality is intrinsic to the form as well as publication strategy of Haywood's amatory fiction, following the accretive and tantalizing delivery and structure of Behn's *Love-Letters* (1684–87) and Manley's *New Atalantis* (1709) in providing a succession of amorous trysts to secure 'a potentially endless repetition on the market'.[48] Again, then, Haywood's formal choices enabled her fiction to be taken up by the newspapers, but rather than 'potentially endless', the newspaper version is prematurely ended, near the end of Volume 3, leaving several ends untied. It closes immediately after the rejected Violetta writes to Count D'Elmont recommending the page, Fidelio, 'a Youth, who seemed to be about 13 or 14 Years of Age' and whose 'uncommon Beauty and Modesty' make such an impression on D'Elmont. Violetta signs off her letter: 'P.S. May Health Safety and Prosperity attend you in your Journey, and the Happiness you wish for, crown the End' – which is followed by 'The End'.[49] In the omitted remainder, not only is D'Elmont reunited with Melliora, but also Fidelio is revealed as Violetta herself, who dies of a broken heart just as the three weddings that close the novel are concluded. Were readers resistant to closure or becoming conversant with stories that could close without resolution as we have come to understand it?

One struggles to imagine any of Moll Flanders's five marriages being greeted with church bells as was Pamela's, but when it was serialized in

Read's *London Post* (March 1722 to March 1723), it proved popular enough to warrant being extended beyond where Defoe finished.[50] The narrative takes in Moll's further adventures in Ireland, emphasizing the sincerity of her repentance and naming her as Elizabeth Atkins, an identification still current fifty years later when Francis Noble published *The History of Lætitia Atkins, Vulgarly Called Moll Flanders* (1776). The version in *The London Post* even switches to the third person to report Moll's death, bringing the story 'up to the moment' in 1722, and offers an elegy on her life composed by the wits at Trinity College, Dublin. This is a rare example of a newspaper generating fresh material for its serial, suggesting that a more definitive closure was desired. The new material in *The London Post* mostly matches the new ending to the abridgement that Read published as a book just as the serialization was coming to a close. Read even advertised his *Life and Actions of Moll Flanders* (1723), divided into nine chapters and '*Adorn'd with Cuts suitable to each Chapter*', alongside the serial in the newspaper.[51] In Read's appropriations of *Moll Flanders*, the reformation of 'serial subjectivity' by a model of unified, bourgeois identity, identified by Mary-Jo Kietzman, is more strongly enforced with an ending that redeems and even lionizes Moll.[52] This novel's depiction of iterative self-fashioning in response to shifting circumstance is again conducive to newspaper serialization, and the novel's immersion in realistic, everyday life makes it resonate with some of the other material in the paper.

In *The London Post*, *Moll Flanders* shared space with news reports and advertisements that influenced its reception. Paula Backscheider, situating *Moll* in a milieu of the popular reportage of crime, aptly suggests that 'Defoe converted the "characters" of the back pages of periodicals into heroes and heroines'.[53] Equally, a couple of newspapers, in London and Canterbury, converted Defoe's character into a front-page celebrity. To the terse, factual, and condemnatory records of shoplifters and pickpockets one encounters in the newspapers, Defoe gave a central personality, subsisting in and developing through time, capable of reflecting on the nature of crime and punishment, and encouraging the reader's deeper pondering of the 'crime wave' of the early 1720s. One paragraph of news that comes alongside an early part of *Moll Flanders* informs readers that: 'Last Week a poor Girl, about Eight Years of Age, was Arrested at Ratcliff for Seven Shillings due for Schooling, and carried to Whitechappel Prison, a Place famous for burying People alive for Trifles'.[54] It is a rare moment of subversive commentary on the legal system in the paper, but it tallies with the early part of Moll's narrative, when she states that her mother was 'convicted of Felony for a certain petty Theft, scarce worth naming'.[55] For the most part, *Moll Flanders* interacts with its 'cellmates' in the *London Post* by way of sharp contrast. Newspaper advertisements, for instance, give us not just a generalized cultural context, but a specific reading context for the poorest consumers of Defoe's novel. One paper, after a great deal of routine crime reportage, has an advertisement for *A Full, True, and Impartial Account of all the Robberies committed in City, Town, and Country, for some Years Past* and other crime literature; there is also an advertisement for the fourth edition of *Whipping Tom; or a Rod for a Proud Lady*, a publication advocating spousal abuse, which chillingly promises 'to touch the Fair Sex to the quick'.[56] This is the milieu in which readers would have encountered Moll's marital and criminal adventures, throwing into relief the ethical complexity in these matters cultivated in Defoe's narrative. As well as book advertisements, there are curious personal notices. One announces the elopement from her husband of Elizabeth Ibyem; she was cohabiting with another man, so her husband was notifying people, as many deserted husbands did, that he would pay nothing given her on credit. As this appears in the paper, Moll is reflecting on the ways in which marriage is financially stacked against women; she will later cohabit with a man in the predicament of having been deserted – he has 'a Wife and no Wife'.[57] Some weeks later, the paper offers the facetious, anti-semitic story of a Jewish wife who, to punish her husband for abusively calling her a whore, makes herself one by sleeping with a neighbour. Meanwhile Moll – herself 'Twelve Year a Whore' – is wrestling with her conscience in the matter of her 'avowed Incest and Whoredom' with her half-brother, which she considers 'the worst form of Whoredom', and upon her return to England and her liaison with a married banker she 'exchange[s] the Place of Friend for that unmusical harsh-sounding Title of WHORE'.[58] Further on in the paper, there are stories of women being tried and executed for murdering their children, something that preys on the mind of Moll, herself a negligent mother who fantasizes about killing a child; and when Moll embarks on her career as a thief, reports of criminal trials, transportations, and executions are rife in the newspaper. I am not suggesting that the *London Post*'s serialization of *Moll Flanders* was in any way steering their news content, but there is a high degree of consonance, making *Moll* seem like material well-suited to an informative newspaper. Yet the closed, categorical, morally normative, or facetious treatment of crime and marital plights in the news coverage contrasts with the ethical complexity attained in *Moll Flanders*. Recovering these reading conditions – *Moll Flanders* alongside crime reports and misogynistic stories presented as news and

Joseph Andrews with another story of discovered parentage – adds to our appreciation of the cultural work the novel performed and its capacity to engage social questions readers encountered, perhaps in more closed and simplistic form, every day.

Publication modes, in general, help to shape formal choices. When Defoe wrote *Moll Flanders* and *Colonel Jack* in 1721–22, he was likely aware that *Robinson Crusoe, Farther Adventures*, and *Captain Singleton* had reached many readers in serial form. The association between journalistic writing and early fiction is well established: Defoe owes his circumstantial realism and his choice of subjects (criminal, colonial, marital, and military action) to the regular fare of topical publications.[59] But perhaps also the episodic structure of his later novels, including *Moll Flanders, Colonel Jack* (1722), *Roxana* (1724), and *A New Voyage Round the World*, are at some level purposely suited to serial publication, or at least the kinds of rapid, episodic reading habits periodical forms fostered. These are rather rambling novels that advance from incident to incident, taking a central protagonist through various walks of life, eschewing tight plotting, capitalizing on readers' interest in 'news', and embracing an improvisatory progression that emphasizes the hero or heroine repeatedly taking stock and embarking on new scenes of life that throw up recurrent dilemmas, but mainly with an ethical attention to the immediate problem. In the preface to *Moll Flanders*, as Kate Loveman observes, Defoe fragments the narrative into smaller and smaller 'Parts', and anticipates it being 'dispatch'd', read promptly and discarded.[60] Though *Colonel Jack* to our knowledge did not make it into a newspaper, Erasmus Darwin, complaining that it is 'told rather diffusely', said that it might suit a 'magazine, or a newspaper, if it was curtailed, or publish'd in parts'.[61] And though *Roxana* also did not appear in a newspaper, there were three number-book editions in the 1740s, by which readers would have received a fixed amount of the narrative on a regular basis.[62] Ian Watt declared that 'Defoe's forte was the brilliant episode' and argued that *Moll Flanders* consists of 'over a hundred realised scenes whose average length is less than two pages, and an equally large number of passages containing rapid and often perfunctory connective synopses'.[63] The eighteenth-century reader seems to have appreciated bursts of narrative intensity followed by reflective calm, and *Moll Flanders* suits that rhythm. The parcelling of instalments in the *London Post* moreover shows signs of care, its cadences falling into line with the serial structure of Defoe's novel. For example, number 53 contains seven paragraphs, the first starting 'WITH this Stock I had the World to begin again', giving at the outset a sense of narrative renewal, the end of one episode and the commencement of another. In this instalment, Moll proceeds to outline her precarity upon her return from America, describing herself as 'a loose unguided Creature', ruminating on the way in which an unattached and friendless woman is 'just like a Bag of Money, or a Jewel dropt on the Highway, which is a Prey to the next Comer'. But she fraudulently passes for a 'great Fortune' and ultimately agrees to remove to the country 'where I shou'd be plac'd to my content'.[64] As well as this kind of cohesion within instalments, the newspaper was able to generate considerable tension between instalments by intelligently parcelling the narrative. Number 79 sees Moll shortly after her first theft. 'I WENT out now by Day-light', she begins, 'and wandred about I knew not whether, and in search of I knew not what'. Her theft of a necklace from an untended child marks her 'second Sally into the World', and her carefully calculated getaway through the intricate streets belies her statement about being directionless and contrasts with the more haphazard, breathless escape from her first theft from the apothecary's shop. Moll relates a couple more opportunistic thefts, imputing her 'good Success' to her 'good Luck', but leaves the reader, at the end of this instalment, with her 'dread that some mischief would befall me', as Moll eyes a pair of valuable rings on a 'Window-board'.[65] A reader would have been left with a sense of an impending misfortune as the story is suspended here, as well as feeling that Moll's behaviour is recursive and her destiny imbued with the fate represented by the parallel reports of executions for paltry thefts. But there is a satisfying unity to the instalment. The crime reports with which Moll shared page space were closed affairs, generally reporting the felon's fate in the same breath as his or her crime. By reading *Moll Flanders* alongside these articles, sliced up in ways that I have suggested had particularly engaging narrative effects, readers experienced the *making* of a criminal, not merely the sentencing or punishment of one, and the suspension of moral judgement that is one of this narrative's significant artistic advances was realized through the actual suspension of the story, encouraging reflection at length.

V

The serialization of fiction in early newspapers was a relatively short-lived phenomenon. After tentative beginnings following 1712, the success of *Robinson Crusoe* spurred the first burst in the 1720s, which rode the challenge of the amendment to the Stamp Act and culminated with *Gulliver's Travels*. *Pamela* seems to have fuelled a second flurry in the

1740s, when responses like *Anti-Pamela* and *Joseph Andrews* appeared in newspapers, and older novels were revived. Low survival rates mean that it is hard to gauge the extent of this practice, but we know that a relatively small number of newspapers serialized fiction, and that fiction was only a fraction of the 'literary' material they used to supplement news. Though short-lived in duration and modest in quantity, this stage of the history of serialized fiction is important. The novels that received this treatment are landmarks of the emergent form. The two genres, novel and newspaper, in their infancy were finding their feet and provided support for one another. The newspapers that did serialize fiction often did so in a sustained way, showing some sense of developing tastes. The reach of these titles was significant: our knowledge of print runs is limited, but they were affordable for less affluent readers, several people could read one issue, and numerous people may have advanced from the newspaper serial to the book. We see here evidence for a reading public hungry for fiction. And finally readers' expectations of prose fiction were in flux; its formal shape was to some extent being worked out both in relation to the dynamic of reading incrementally yet extensively, which proved so important to the major mid-century fictions, *Clarissa* (1747–48) and *Tristram Shandy*.[66]

However, newspapers were becoming more standardized by the middle of the century; the industry was more regulated and copyright issues were less hazy, so they were less likely to recycle bestselling novels. Readers could buy novels as number-books, and miscellanies and magazines provided specialized outlets, so other serial modes for fiction displaced the newspaper. A sign of the rupture between newspapers and fiction is indicated by an issue of *The Ipswich Journal* from 1752, in which the editor announces:

> The following is a Chapter in AMELIA, *a Novel lately publish'd by* H. Fielding, *Esq; in four Pocket Volumes. We make no Doubt, but such of our Readers as have not seen it before, will be glad we happen to fall short of News, at a Time when we can fill up this Page so much more agreeably; though those who have had the Pleasure of reading this entertaining Work, may think we are not giving the most advantageous Specimen of it. But what principally induces us to make choice of this Chapter, is, that the Subject is most suitable to the Design of a News Paper, and that it scarce requires any Knowledge of the preceding Parts to explain it.*[67]

The chapter provided is 'Matters Political' (Book XI, Chapter II), Dr. Harrison's debate with a nobleman whom he hopes to interest in Booth's affairs, regarding those who get on by the strengths of their connections or their abilities. The sentiments about good rulership and political virtue in this illustrative vignette make it suitable for a newspaper, the editor reasons. Its inclusion is further justified by the shortage of news and the fact that it stands apart from the narrative. Ironically Fielding had contrasted the novelist's art in delineating a story with the efforts of 'the painful and voluminous historian' and the 'newspaper, which consists of just the same number of words, whether there be any news in it or not'.[68] Both cases attest to a sense of the difference between newspapers and novels. Stand-alone essays from mid-century periodicals like *The Female Spectator* and *The Adventurer*, especially those with something like a story, continued to be reprinted in newspapers after their use of longer fiction ended, sometimes extending over two or three issues.[69] But newspapers were increasingly homogeneous, devoted to factual content. And novels were gaining an increasing cultural presence – more were being written, sales were higher, they were regularly reviewed and digested in magazines, and they had more variegated systems of distribution, from magazines and anthologies to circulating libraries.

Notes

1 *All Alive and Merry*, 20 April [1743]; Henry Fielding, *The History of the Adventures of Joseph Andrews*, 2 vols. (London: A. Millar, 1742), vol. 1, p. 127.
2 Linda K. Hughes and Michael Lund, *The Victorian Serial* (Charlottesville: University of Virginia Press, 1991), pp. 1–14.
3 Robert D. Mayo, *The English Novel in the Magazines, 1740–1815* (Evanston: Northwestern University Press, 1962); see pp. 57–64 for a brief treatment of newspaper fiction.
4 J. Paul Hunter, 'Serious Reflections on Farther Adventures: Resistances to Closure in Eighteenth-Century English Novels', in *Augustan Subjects: Essays in Honor of Martin C. Battestin*, ed. Albert J. Rivero (Newark: University of Delaware Press, 1997), pp. 276–94 (278).
5 Benedict Anderson claims that novels and newspapers foster a sense of time necessary for the imagined community of nationalism, both a sense of else-where-but-meanwhile and of an open-ended future: *Imagined Communities: Reflections on the Origin and Spread of Nationalism* (1983; London: Verso, 1991).
6 Stuart Sherman, *Telling Time: Clocks, Diaries, and English Diurnal Form, 1660–1785* (University of Chicago Press, 1996).
7 Ian Watt, *The Rise of the Novel: Studies in Defoe, Richardson and Fielding* (London: Chatto and Windus, 1957), p. 49.
8 J. Paul Hunter, *Before Novels: The Cultural Contexts of Eighteenth-Century English Fiction* (New York: W. W. Norton, 1990), pp. 167–94.
9 *Parker's London News*, no. 840, 10 April 1724.
10 Thomas Keymer, *Sterne, the Moderns, and the Novel* (Oxford University Press, 2002), p. 124.

11 *Parker's Penny Post*, no. 121, 7 February 1726. The work in question is a translation of Thomas Simon Gueullette's *Les Aventures merveilleuses du mandarin Fum-Hoam, contes chinois* (1723).

12 *Robinson Crusoe's London Daily Evening Post*, 20 May 1741, 20 September 1742 (the only extant issues containing *Pamela*); Thomas Keymer and Peter Sabor, '*Pamela*' *in the Marketplace: Literary Controversy and Print Culture in Eighteenth-Century Britain and Ireland* (Cambridge University Press, 2005), pp. 39–40.

13 Stuart Sherman, '"My Contemporaries the Novelists": Isaac Bickerstaffe, Uncle Toby, and the Play of Pulse and Sprawl', *Novel*, 43:1 (2010), 107–15 (108); Ian Donaldson, 'Fielding, Richardson, and the Ends of the Novel', *Essays in Criticism*, 32:1 (1982), 26–47 (33). Mary Kingman produced a serial piracy of *Pamela* in 1741.

14 Hester Thrale, *Thraliana*, ed. Katharine C. Balderston, 2nd edn (Oxford: Clarendon Press, 1951), p. 145.

15 Kate Loveman, *Reading Fictions, 1660–1740: Deception in English Literary and Political Culture* (Aldershot: Ashgate, 2008), p. 184.

16 R. M. Wiles has described newspaper fiction at greatest length: *Serial Publication in England before 1750* (Cambridge University Press, 1957), pp. 25–60; *Freshest Advices: Early Provincial Newspapers in England* (Columbus: Ohio State University Press, 1965), pp. 303–38.

17 Michael Harris, *London Newspapers in the Age of Walpole* (Rutherford: Fairleigh-Dickinson University Press, 1987), p. 178. On provincial newspapers, see G. A. Cranfield, *The Development of the Provincial Press, 1700–1760* (Oxford: Clarendon Press, 1962).

18 Jonathan Swift, *Journal to Stella*, ed. Abigail Williams, The Cambridge Edition of the Works of Jonathan Swift (Cambridge University Press, 2013), p. 441; Joseph Addison, *The Spectator*, ed. Donald F. Bond, 5 vols. (Oxford: Clarendon Press, 1965), vol. 4, p. 63.

19 *Gloucester Journal*, no. 80, 14 October 1723.

20 *The Post-Master; or the Loyal Mercury*, no. 200, 7 February 1729.

21 Natasha Glaisyer, *The Culture of Commerce in England, 1660–1720* (London: Boydell and Brewer), p. 164.

22 *The British Mercury*, nos. 381–87, 22 October to 3 December 1712.

23 *The British Mercury*, no. 471, 7–14 July 1714.

24 *The British Weekly Mercury*, no. 519, 4–11 June 1715.

25 The Swiss visitor César de Saussure wrote in 1726, 'I have often seen shoe-blacks and other persons of that class club together to purchase a farthing paper': quoted in Hunter, *Before Novels*, p. 174.

26 Jonathan Swift, *Travels into Several Remote Nations of the World . . . Faithfully Abridged* (London: J. Stone and R. King, 1727).

27 *Penny London Post*, no. 251 [252], 25 November 1726.

28 *Parker's Penny Post*, nos. 246–390 (28 November 1726 to 3 November 1727); Nicholas Seager, '*Gulliver's Travels* Serialized and Continued', in *Reading Swift: Papers from the Sixth Münster Symposium on Jonathan Swift*, eds. Kirsten Juhas et al. (Munich: Wilhelm Fink, 2013), pp. 543–62.

29 *Parker's Penny Post*, no. 246, 28 November 1726.

30 *Parker's Penny Post*, no. 48, 16 August 1725.

31 Charles Gildon, *The Life and Strange Surprizing Adventures of Mr. D– de F–* (London: J. Roberts, 1719), pp. ix–x.

32 *The Original London Post; or, Heathcot's Intelligence*, no. 202, 30 March 1720.

33 Henry C. Hutchins, '*Robinson Crusoe' and Its Printing, 1719–1731* (New York: Columbia University Press, 1925), p. 162.

34 Ronan Deazley, 'The Statute of Anne and the Great Abridgement Swindle', *Houston Law Review*, 47:4 (2010–11), 793–818; Will Slauter, 'Upright Piracy: Understanding the Lack of Copyright for Journalism in Eighteenth-Century Britain', *Book History*, 16 (2013), 34–61.

35 Simon Stern, 'Copyright, Originality, and the Public Domain in Eighteenth-Century England', in *Originality and Intellectual Property in the French and English Enlightenment*, ed. Reginald McGinnis (London: Routledge, 2008), pp. 69–101.

36 Samuel Johnson, *Rasselas and Other Tales*, ed. Gwin J. Kolb, The Yale Edition of the Works of Samuel Johnson (New Haven: Yale University Press, 1990), pp. 251–53.

37 *The Original London Post; or, Heathcot's Intelligence*, no. 289, 19 October 1720.

38 *The Post-Master, or, the Loyal Mercury*, nos. 108–12, 24 August to 14 September 1722.

39 *The Original London Post; or, Heathcote's* [sic] *Intelligence*, nos. 816–61.

40 Starting *The Original London Post; or, Heathcote's Intelligence*, no. 4, 24 July 1738.

41 David J. Shaw, 'Serialization of *Moll Flanders* in *The London Post* and *The Kentish Post*, 1722', *The Library*, 7th series, 8:2 (2007), 182–92.

42 *The Post-Master; or, The Loyal Mercury*, no. 15, 4 November 1720.

43 Defoe, *A New Voyage Round the World* (Chester: W. Cooke, 1725?).

44 Wiles, *Serial Publication*, p. 69.

45 This used *The Wonderful Life, and Most Surprizing Adventures of Robinson Crusoe* (London: A. Bettesworth et al., 1737).

46 *All Alive and Merry*, 11 December [1740], quoted in Wiles, *Serial Publication*, p. 48.

47 *The Post-Master; or, The Loyal Mercury*, no. 55, 11 August 1721.

48 William B. Warner, *Licensing Entertainment: The Elevation of Novel Reading in Britain, 1684–1750* (Berkeley: University of California Press, 1998), p. 116.

49 *The Generous London Morning Advertiser*, no. 985, 6 January 1742.

50 *The London Post, The Freshest Advices and Most Remarkable Occurrences at Home and Abroad*, nos. 19–152, 11–14 May 1722 to 18–20 March 1723. *Moll* likely started in March 1722.

51 *London Post*, no. 145, 4–6 March 1723.

52 Mary-Jo Kietzman, 'Defoe Masters the Serial Subject', *English Literary History*, 66:3 (1999), 677–705.

53 Paula R. Backscheider, *Daniel Defoe: Ambition and Innovation* (Lexington: University Press of Kentucky, 1986), p. 162.

54 *London Post*, no. 19, 11–14 May 1722.

55 Daniel Defoe, *The Fortunes and Misfortunes of the Famous Moll Flanders* (London: W. Chetwood and T. Edling, 1721 [for 1722]), p. 2.

56 *London Post*, no. 33, 13–15 June 1722.

57 Defoe, *Moll Flanders*, p. 162.

58 Defoe, *Moll Flanders*, pp. 104, 105, 139.

59 Lennard Davis, *Factual Fictions: The Origins of the English Novel* (New York: Columbia University Press, 1983).

60 Kate Loveman, '"A Life of Continu'd Variety": Crime, Readers, and the Structure of Defoe's *Moll Flanders*', *Eighteenth-Century Fiction*, 26:1 (2013), 1–32.

61 Quoted in Gabriel Cervantes, 'Episodic or Novelistic?: Law in the Atlantic and the Form of Defoe's *Colonel Jack*', *Eighteenth-Century Fiction*, 24:2 (2011–12), 247–77 (258–59).

62 Nicholas Seager, 'The 1740 *Roxana*: Defoe, Haywood, Richardson, and Domestic Fiction', *Philological Quarterly*, 89:1–2 (2009), 103–26 (106).

63 Watt, *Rise of the Novel*, pp. 100, 130.

64 Defoe, *Moll Flanders*, pp. 153–56.

65 Defoe, *Moll Flanders*, p. 237.

66 On Richardson's and Sterne's employments of serialization, see Tom Keymer, 'Reading Time in Serial Fiction before Dickens', *Yearbook of English Studies*, 30 (2000), 34–45.

67 *The Ipswich Journal*, no. 673, 4 January 1752.

68 Henry Fielding, *The History of Tom Jones* (1749), ed. R. P. C. Mutter (1966; Harmondsworth: Penguin, 1985), p. 59.

69 Newspapers began to serialize fiction again in the 1850s: Graham Law, *Serializing Fiction in the Victorian Press* (Basingstoke: Palgrave, 2000).

CHAPTER 6

Wit and Humour for the Heart of Sensibility: The Beauties of Fielding and Sterne

M-C. Newbould

Writing in 1822, Samuel Taylor Coleridge attacked the type of literary anthology that had proved so popular in preceding decades:

> 'Beauties' in general are objectionable works injurious to the original Author, as disorganizing his productions – pulling to pieces the well-wrought *Crown* of his glory to pick out the shining stone – and injurious to the Reader, by indulging the taste for unconnected & for that reason unretained single Thoughts.[1]

As Daniel S. Malachuk suggests, however, Coleridge proceeds to outline the potential benefits of such a 'disorganized' way of presenting an author's 'productions', as readers are encouraged to reorganize material independently and so to exercise judgement: 'In themselves objectionable, selections or "beauties" arranged according to a "principle" of "sequency" will not corrupt the reader but prompt him into connected and worthwhile reflection'.[2] Coleridge's value-laden language indicates how the aesthetic qualities of an author's 'well-wrought *Crown*' meet commercial interests at the hands of those who strip its finest gems. His comments on how books were marketed, bought, and read reflect on how literary anthologies contributed to bookselling practices towards the end of the previous century.

The highly successful series published by George Kearsley under the banner '*Beauties of . . .*' played a significant part in shaping these trends from the 1780s onwards: it provides a focal point for addressing which authors were selected, what was chosen to represent their work, and how it was edited. Kearsley operated through a team of editors; his main compiler, W.H., was perhaps William Cooke, but most likely William Holland.[3] The nature and arrangement of these editors' selections from a variety of authors – including Pope, Swift, Johnson, Goldsmith, Fielding, and Sterne – was motivated by the mixture of commercial interest and didactic aims belonging to a series that sought to instruct by pleasurable precept. Kearsley's choice and treatment of Fielding and Sterne captures these varying impulses, as well as the combined drawbacks and possible benefits of literary anthologies signalled by Coleridge.

Whilst Fielding and Sterne were often compared as writers of 'humour', 'wit', and 'genius', Kearsley needed to negotiate the reputation and earlier critical reception of both authors, which potentially threatened any moralizing project: Sterne's association with bawdry was longstanding, while Fielding's plays and novels abounded with passages that might waylay the reader from the smooth path towards moral instruction. Kearsley's editorial practices confronted these challenges in variously inventive ways. However, there are also important differences in how these two authors were anthologized. Compared with Fielding, Sterne gained a more significant presence in Kearsley's *Beauties* series and in similar collections; was his writing really considered more suitable for such instructive enterprises? The quantitative evidence can partly be explained by situating these anthologies within the broader context of changeable reading tastes in this period. Kearsley was publishing in an age when the 'heart of sensibility' might profitably be moved by those passages of an author's works that provoke moral reflection through sympathetic engagement.[4] Extracts demonstrating sensibility were more easily found in Sterne's works than in Fielding's; as long as they were diligently pruned, they were well equipped to provide an edifying reading experience. By the early 1800s Sterne, more so than Fielding, was a confirmed classic of the anthology genre.

* * *

The term 'beauties' carries both a generic and an aesthetic function when used to describe a species of anthology that exerted an increasing appeal for booksellers and readers alike throughout the eighteenth century.[5] These collections assembled the most 'beautiful' extracts taken from a well-known author's work from a range of genres, including poetry, prose, and drama. *The Beauties of the English Stage* – the first publication to use the title – appeared in 1737; *The Beauties of Shakespear*, edited by William Dodd, was initially published in 1752 and proved so successful that others were quick to join in: Kearsley's version (with a different selection to Dodd's) entered its fifth edition in 1791.[6] In some anthologies, a literary-critical function sat alongside that of purely providing pleasure: 'faults' as well as beauties were sometimes exposed to view and to corrective commentary.[7]

The term 'beauties' also appeared in titles other than those belonging to literary anthologies: it could refer to a more directly visual type of experience. Numerous topographical and travel books applied it to the 'beauties of Stowe' or even of England itself. Philip Luckombe's 1757 *Beauties of England* described itself 'as a travelling pocket companion' designed to 'point out whatever merits the Attention of the English Traveller, or the Observation of the Foreigner'.[8] Yet the deictic function benefiting the tourist who carried the volume around in his or her pocket the better to see what it may 'point out' was partly subordinate to its potential both to entertain and instruct the armchair traveller: simply leafing through the book's pages allowed readers mentally to pursue a tour that beautified the places described, but also improved those who read about them. Although the guidebook nature of these 'beauties' and their distant literary anthology cousins is ostensibly identifiable only by the shared moniker, the 'beauties' of literature and of geography alike hold the potential not only to delight but to inform and instruct. By selecting and rearranging the choicest parts of an author's work on both aesthetically pleasing and morally improving grounds, the compiler guides the reader towards an ultimately edifying, because enjoyable, experience.

Kearsley, then, was far from innovative in attaching the term 'beauties' to his series; indeed, Melvyn New suggests that he was not even the first to compile extracts of Sterne's writing in book-form, an honour accorded to William Enfield's guide to elocution, *The Speaker* (1774).[9] Nevertheless, his method of capitalizing on an increasingly popular genre marked him out as distinct from his predecessors and immediate competitors. Daniel Cook's comprehensive account of Kearsley's series describes the combined aesthetic, didactic, and commercial motivations underlying an enterprise trading with such 'bankable' wares.[10] These volumes' visual and material qualities contributed to their commercial viability: the anthologies' appeal to potential buyers was spurred by their increased availability in relatively cheap, compact, pocket-sized formats designed (like the beautifying travel guide) for perusal on the go as well as at home.[11] Yet Kearsley's volumes are typical of the genre in becoming ever more embellished with decorative features and illustrations designed to exert an even greater appeal to an increasingly literate readership spread across a broader social spectrum, including greater numbers of women.[12] Selections of this kind potentially attracted those perhaps less able to afford full-length works or less inclined to read them in their entirety: a reader's digest of an author's best bits provided an admirable service.

The anthology thus promised to make hitherto less accessible publications available to a more expansive field of appreciative readers.[13] However, the process of extraction and distillation inevitably limits any seemingly democratic impulse: the editor's selection from and alteration of an author's work, often according to clearly discernible agendas, inevitably determines the apparently enlightened reader's acquaintance with it. The paratextual material and internal evidence of Kearsley's volumes exemplify the series' stated editorial policy, as found in the advertisement to the first and second editions of *The Beauties of Fielding* (1782):

> Though these Selections are principally intended for the Use of Youth of both sexes, they will be found interesting and instructive to all readers without distinction; they will inform the understanding, and entertain the imagination.[14]

Taken as a whole, Kearsley's *Beauties* instil a sense of consistent uniformity in pursuing this purpose: they bring their chosen authors to an expanding readership but in streamlined form. For Cook, this coheres with the anthologies' tendency to homogenize authorial difference and in effect to make of writers and their works what the editor wills: 'Eighteenth-century Beauties mimicked the canon-forming strategies employed in the major anthologies of the day.'

Yet the neatness of Kearsley's project was bedevilled by the resistance that some of his authors posed to such uniformity. Passages of both Fielding and Sterne's fiction were subject to suspicion, and so required cautious treatment; they met with ruthless efficiency. As Cook observes:

> In place of the obscene *Tristram Shandy* [1759–67] and *Sentimental Journey* [1768], we have a fully sanitized, alphabetized handbook of Sterne's senti- ments on such topics as beauty, charity, and forgiveness. No brothels, adultery, nakedness, bawdy language, or even Tom Jones's many escapades, are to be found in *The Beauties of Fielding*.[15]

Reactions to Fielding's novels were characterized by outraged propriety on one side tempered with delight on the other. *Joseph Andrews* (1742) received little critical attention; although readers remained divided over the 'moral value' of Fielding's novel, its success and 'favourable response' can be judged by its rapid sale.[16] *Tom Jones* (1749) was even more popular, its final full appearance eagerly awaited; yet the negative reactions it provoked were more virulently opposed.[17] One enthusiast judged *Tom Jones* to be 'excellent . . . and abounding with strong and lively painting of characters', but Thomas Sherlock, Bishop of London, described Fielding's hero as 'a Male-Prostitute'.[18] Richardson, no doubt motivated by the continuing rivalry between the two authors, declared that 'Tom Jones is a dissolute book' and commended the French for having banned it.[19]

Choosing an author whose work had excited such contrary opinions for a series as clear in its aims as Kearsley's *Beauties* no doubt posed certain challenges. Perhaps earlier reactions to Fielding's provocative fiction had sufficiently calmed by the 1780s for him to prove useful for such an enterprise.[20] Yet while his works were clearly still enjoyed in their 'strong and lively' colours, and even experienced contemporaneous afterlife in other forms – a French operatic adaptation of *Tom Jones* appeared in 1782 – the editorial processes displayed in *The Beauties of Fielding* reinvigorated the assumption that this author needed careful management to earn his place in the series.[21]

As the volume's title indicates, *The Beauties of Fielding: Carefully Selected from the Works of that Eminent Writer. To which is added Some Account of his Life* (1782) makes 'careful' decisions not only about what it extracts from this author's wide-ranging publications – plays, essays, and novels – but also how it arranges them. The contents list presents a condensed argument for the taxonomic principles underlying the volume, and indeed the series as a whole, and its ultimately enriching aim. An approximately alphabetical string of memorably succinct vices and virtues, to be castigated or condoned in appropriate measure, ranges from 'Avarice', 'Anxiety' and 'Ambition' to 'Zeal'. Unlike, say, *The Beauties of Swift* (1782), passages in the Fielding volume follow the running order listed on the contents page so that readers can move directly from discovering the dangers of 'Ambition' to the reward that modesty justly receives, 'Admiration'. They could effectively consume an already pastiched text in whatever fashion they chose, being able to dip in and out at will. Although cover-to-cover perusal is possible, the dictionary-type feel to *The Beauties of Fielding* invites readers to 'rove from topic to topic' – a criticism which, as Cook suggests, contemporary reviewers levelled against anthologies in general for encouraging 'degenerative reading habits'.[22]

Most extracts from Fielding are barely longer than a paragraph – although 'Adultery' and 'Adversity' (among others) are indulged with fuller quotations – with each subject-heading usually exemplified by one, but sometimes multiple, publication(s). The source-text of each excerpt is identified at its close, perhaps to reassure the reader of editorial assiduity rather than to offer a means of accessing the fuller work, undesirable as that might be. The beauty of such a volume, after all, is that it helps the reader to avoid contamination with the 'dissolute' book at large. Kearsley's editor achieves this by diminishing any real sense that there are more substantial fictional works behind Fielding's choice maxims. Extracts from his novels and drama eliminate all narrative elements; dialogue between the novels' characters, for instance, is divested of identifiable speakers. The edges of each passage are smoothed over to ensure that it makes sense without knowledge of its fictional context.

'Adultery' is taken from a lengthy section of *Amelia* (1751) in which the principal characters discuss one of the novel's important themes – albeit treated by Fielding with subversive humour, according to Simon Dickie; in the *Beauties*, it is distilled into an uninterrupted passage of prose, without the distractions of character interaction, the better to convey its point.[23] Gone, too, is Fielding's irreverent aside: 'I am afraid the priesthood, are, in a great measure, answerable for the badness of [adultery]'.[24] Similarly, 'Ambition' is illustrated by a passage from *Tom Jones* warning how 'The great are deceived if they imagine they have appropriated ambition and vanity to themselves'.[25] The editor cuts the opening section of Fielding's paragraph describing how Molly Seagrim 'dressed herself out . . . with a new laced cap, and some other ornaments' before setting out to church, a display of vanity that sets the village women 'sneering, giggling, tittering, and laughing' and climaxes in a mock-heroic battle.[26]

Paulson and Lockwood note the damaging impact that abridgement exerted on appreciation of Fielding's work in France; as these excerpts suggest, the anthology arguably performs an even more devastating operation.[27] *The Beauties of Fielding* demonstrates the negative effects of the framing device deployed by anthologies of extracts in general: they select, remove, and re-present a fundamentally new text, not only in the alterations introduced to ensure sensible cohesion and a clearer moral, but also in the process of recontextualization. Rather than the fragment acting as metonym, the concept of what the 'whole' it represents might be is only ever partial and, furthermore, is denatured by being placed in an alien context. Although the advertisement to *The Beauties of Fielding* claims to 'entertain' the imagination, framing snapshots of the author's work in this way effectively constricts it.[28] Framing serves the anthology editor who is less interested in providing a representative sample of an author's work than a sampler of commonplaces.

The Beauties of Fielding therefore seems little invested in how this particular author might 'morally improve' a youthful readership; in fact, it is almost the reverse. The prefatory matter outlines several aspects of Fielding's history that apparently offer some context for the selections, but which in reality bear little direct correlation with them. Kearsley's biography is a truncated version of Arthur Murphy's contentious 'Essay on the Life and Genius of Henry Fielding, Esq.', which prefaces the *Works* published by Millar in 1762; by condensing this essay and its fallacies, the *Beauties'* editor caricatures the author in a way that mirrors the anthology's reductive representation of his oeuvre.[29] The prefatory life declares that Fielding's 'follies and intemperances' are excusable thanks to his other qualities: he was 'a satyrist of vice and evil in manners, yet a lover of mankind; an useful citizen, a polished and instructive wit'.[30] Such merits are invaluable in a volume that promotes its 'instructive' credentials, whilst they partly excuse Fielding's variable temperament and the consequently uneven nature of his work: he produced, 'almost extempore, a play, a farce, a pamphlet, or news paper'. This inconsistency is rendered admirable because it is allied to the equally erratic qualities of 'wit, mirth, and good humour' that reach their zenith in Fielding's novels, 'first in *Joseph Andrews*, and most completely in his *Tom Jones*'.[31] Just as the author's character can be neatly packaged so too can his writings, yet the prefatory life and selected extracts do not really correspond: the picture does not fit the frame, for this aphoristic sequence of stirring thoughts and invigorating principles is divested of the wit, mirth, and good humour that putatively characterize Fielding's novels. These might almost be the sonorous pronouncements of any maxim-spinning hack.

Banishing Sterne from any identifiable association with his works was arguably more difficult. His self-alignment with, variously, Tristram Shandy and Parson Yorick was a notoriously playful gambit designed to enhance his own celebrity.[32] For all that Fielding's fiction was considered autobiographical by some, he did not overtly promote such quixotic links.[33] Sterne's glib identification with his characters perhaps accounts for the fact that the first edition of *The Beauties of Sterne: Including all his Pathetic Tales, and Most Distinguished Observations on Life. Selected for the Heart of Sensibility* (1782) is almost unique in the series for not including a prefatory biography of its author.[34] After all, Sterne's authorial-fictional persona – part-flippant, part-whimsical – was hardly a reputable campaigner able to support the *Beauties'* manifesto. Furthermore, whilst some of Fielding's readers had complained of his novels' prostitution to bad taste and, worse, wayward morality, Sterne's early critics were even more inflammatory. The case of indelicacy was levelled against Sterne from the outset, with cries of 'immodest words' and 'want of decency' filling *Tristram Shandy*'s initial reviews, alongside more cheerful appraisals of this 'sensible–humorous–pathetick–humane–unaccountable!' performance.[35] How could Kearsley consider including such an author in his series, and why? The second question is more easily answered: that Sterne continued to be popular is evident by the publication of yet more new editions of *Tristram Shandy* and *A Sentimental Journey* around the time of the *Beauties'* appearance, not to mention spin-off publications and posthumous works. Being a bookseller whom one critic has called a 'skilled adventurer in the vogue for Sterneana', Kearsley could not afford to miss such an opportunity.[36] His editor therefore confronts head-on the chequered history of *The Beauties of Sterne*'s chosen subject to assert this volume's coherence with the series' advertised aims:

> The *chaste* part of the world complained so loudly of the obscenity which taints the writings of *Sterne*, (and, indeed, with some reason), that those readers under their immediate inspection were not suffered to penetrate beyond the title-page of his *Tristram Shandy*; – his *Sentimental Journey*, in some degree, escaped the general censure; though that is not entirely free of the fault complained of.[37]

No '*chaste*' reader would wish to 'penetrate' Sterne's equivocal matter or indeed risk encountering it by even opening *Tristram Shandy*.[38] Kearsley's editor has undertaken this dangerous enterprise on his reader's behalf, having ventured beyond *Tristram Shandy*'s title page(s) to cull 'the most distinguished passages on which the sun of Genius shines so resplendent'. Removing provocative innuendo such as Toby's notorious aposiopesis ('My sister, I dare say ... does not care to let a man come so near her****'), and introducing a healthy splicing of inspiring thoughts from Sterne's sermons and letters, offered easy editorial choices.[39] Yet W.H. needed to go beyond simply cutting any passages' naughty bits to make their proper parts more visible.

Kearsley's editor was, however, significantly helped in making Sterne fit into the series by the fact that initial responses to Sterne as Rabelaisian jester had rapidly become subsumed by an increased appreciation of the 'pathetic' and the 'humane' in his writing. *A Sentimental Journey* provided the prime exemplar, for all that various critics might agree with Cook's assessment that some early readers considered it 'obscene'.[40] *Tristram Shandy*'s serialized publication over eight years helped to promote this image too: in its later volumes, Sterne introduced passages more acutely attuned to a growing taste for writing in the sentimental manner. A belief that sensibility held the capacity for improvement through affective experience sanctioned Sterne's inclusion in Kearsley's series.[41]

Sterne, in fact, effectively self-anthologizes before W.H. even begins weeding out this author's undesirables so that passages touching the 'heart of sensibility' might flourish. In both novels he manipulates the already fragmentary nature of sentimental fiction – its broken dialogues punctured by affective aphasia; its choice vignettes displaying moving scenes of sympathetic intensity – by segmenting pathos into short episodes.[42] Readers interested in the pathetic tales of Le Fever and Maria could dwell on those passages and ignore *Tristram Shandy*'s more provocative sections. *A Sentimental Journey*'s tableaux could be viewed as discretely sentimental (or otherwise) as readers chose, depending on their perspective. His novels present numerous pictures ready to be 'framed' anew within the anthology, realizing Benedict's suggestion that by 'framing feeling' it condenses the intensity of sentimental affect into even shorter passages the better to exert moral effect.[43]

In this respect, the framing concept is not so readily applicable to *The Beauties of Fielding*: he could not be as comfortably classed as a 'sentimental' author capable of moving the 'heart of sensibility' as could Sterne.[44] Indeed, as Dickie argues, *Amelia*'s lukewarm reception was partly due to its perception as a failed attempt to write a 'sentimental novel' in the manner its author had so admired in *Clarissa* (1747–48): it betrays 'Fielding's discomfort with Richardsonian sentimentality – his uneasy alternation between compressed or perfunctory episodes of feeling and others that are so hyperbolic as to be ludicrous'.[45] Sterne and Richardson, indeed, were aligned as sentimental writers as frequently as Sterne and Fielding were as comic authors.[46] It is, therefore, perhaps surprising that Kearsley did not include a *Beauties of Richardson* in his series, especially given the author's renowned didacticism and anthologization elsewhere.[47]

The Beauties of Sterne's long title bears witness to its emphasis on the sentimental aspect of his work: his 'Pathetic Tales' will move the 'Heart of Sensibility', whilst his 'Most Distinguished Observations on Life' will usefully instruct it. The title page epigraph, taken from *A Sentimental Journey*, reappears in almost all editions of *The Beauties of Sterne* and appeals directly to its envisioned readership: 'Dear SENSIBILITY! source inexhausted of all that's precious in our joys, or costly in our sorrows!'[48] The principles of organization are also significant in shaping the reader's appreciation of this sentimentalized Sterne. Although the contents page similarly lists the moral to be gleaned from each extract (more or less) alphabetically, many headings identify a particular episode (such as *A Sentimental Journey*'s notoriously touching 'The Captive') rather than a precept; furthermore, the passages are not presented in consecutive order according to the contents list but are reorganized to create a narrative coherence of their own. This allows the editor to temper carefully the pace of what might potentially be an overload of sensibility:

> I intended to have arranged them alphabetically, till I found the stories of Le Fever, the *Monk*, and *Maria*, would be too closely connected for the *feeling reader*, and would wound the bosom of *sensibility* too deeply: I therefore placed them at a proper distance from each other.[49]

The editor thus pre-empts some readers' concerns that sensibility, and especially volumes that concentrate its '*feeling*' intensity in this way, may simply be too 'enervating' to achieve any instructive purpose, and may even lead the young, impressionable reader astray.[50]

However, many of those passages deemed most morally effective in Sterne, because so sentimentally affecting, are also riddled with his characteristic innuendo. The dense ambiguity of Sterne's prose called upon W.H. to exercise his editorial skills with the utmost artfulness, as his treatment of *Tristram Shandy*'s Le Fever episode demonstrates. This story tearmarks the characteristically sentimental style in which Sterne as 'sensible' author was perceived to excel and reappeared in countless magazines – themselves alternative 'anthologies' for such sentimentalized fragments.[51] It tells how *Tristram Shandy*'s sentimental heroes, Uncle Toby and Corporal Trim, offer their services to Le Fever, a decayed brother soldier; Toby adopts his orphaned son, whom he eventually proposes as the young Tristram's tutor.[52] Le Fever's death is a moment poised between devastating sympathetic power and ironic subversion in Sterne's text, as Michael Bell suggests, but the *Beauties*' version shades over ambiguity and highlights sensibility.[53] The passage is stripped of distractingly whimsical reflections and metanarrative comment, which might encourage a reader to imagine that this is the capricious story-in-the-making of that notorious philanderer with straightforward tale-telling, Tristram Shandy ('I am so impatient to return to my own story . . .').[54]

W.H.'s editorial excisions persist throughout *The Beauties of Sterne*, especially where passages from *Tristram Shandy* are concerned; whilst he partly preserves Sterne's more genial humour (Toby, Walter, and Slop still make their entertaining interruptions during the sermon on the 'Abuses of Conscience'), Sterne's comedy is 'chastened' through a dual process of editing and recontextualization.[55] Hence the perhaps surprising inclusion of Trim's story about his brother's marriage to the widow of a Jewish sausage-seller at Lisbon, rampant as it is with Rabelaisian mirth at the mere mention of a sausage in Sterne's text. The *Beauties* judiciously cuts out Trim's suggestive explanation of how Tom finally won his bride as it appears in *Tristram Shandy*:

> She made a feint however of defending herself, by snatching up a sausage:——
> Tom instantly laid hold of another——
> But seeing Tom's had more gristle in it——
> She signed the capitulation——and Tom sealed it; and there was an end of the matter.[56]

By trimming this passage and placing it after *Tristram Shandy*'s sermon scene, W.H. perhaps moderates the imagination's wilder ramblings upon this 'matter'. Potentially provocative scenes from *A Sentimental Journey* receive similar treatment: Le Fever's story is followed by 'The Pulse', in which Yorick measures the heartbeats of a Parisian glove-selling Grisset. For all the raciness that some detected in this scene, its positioning after the Le Fever tear-jerker reassures the *Beauties*' reader that the body's fibrous sensations operate in pure harmony for those attuned to 'dear sensibility' and brings its touching sympathy to beat at a moderated tempo. Whilst the text of *A Sentimental Journey* generally remains uncensored, its extracts are thus newly framed within the *Beauties* to ensure that the grey margins of ambiguity do not risk shading the 'sun of [Sterne's] Genius'; after all, his second novel 'is not entirely free of the fault complained of'.

* * *

Anthologies of extracts had their detractors before Coleridge, not least those who used the rhetoric of literary and monetary wealth in order to attack them; Edward Barry, for instance, claimed in 1794 that their 'wasteful habit of quotation from many of our admired English writers, [has] *impoverished* their richness and lessened their *consequence*'.[57] Nevertheless, the popularity of Kearsley's *Beauties* prompted future additions to the series, now expanded and altered, but also a host of imitative volumes that capitalized on their commercial success. Several discarded the single-author focus to offer a feast of literary titbits in multi-author collections that frequently included both Fielding and Sterne.

These authors had long been compared as excelling in 'wit' and 'humour', qualities which emerge in compilations of fabricated anecdotes about eminent men in which both authors appear, such as Robert Alves's *Sketches of a History of Literature* (1794).[58] Several literary anthologies align Fielding and Sterne on similar terms. One compendium of quotations, *The Flowers of Literature, or Treasury of Wit and Genius* (1782), promised to distil '*the Essence of the Beauties of Johnson, Swift, Fielding, Pope, Goldsmith, Hervey, Sterne, Watts, &c.*'[59] Kearsley's series is clearly the template. The *Flowers*' 'Adultery' passage, for instance, replicates the excisions from *Amelia* found in *The Beauties of Fielding*, whilst Sterne and Fielding both exemplify 'Beauty' with excerpts that are similarly recycled from Kearsley's volumes.[60] As Cook notes, critics were quick to detect the plagiarism; *The London Magazine*, for example, called this volume 'a most crude and ill-sorted selection from the beauties of various authors, published by

Kearsley'.[61] The volume's second title page nevertheless stakes its own claim for the value of such an enterprise:

> To the admirers of genius and literature and such as are desirous of preserving and perpetuating to posterity the remembrance of those writers who, for their great abilities, reflect honour on the British nation, namely, Johnson, Swift, Fielding, Sterne, Watts, Hervey, Goldsmith, Pope, &c. this selection from the beauties of these eminent men is most respectfully inscribed by the editor.[62]

The mention of 'genius' here reinforces its use in the title, where it is coupled with 'wit'; as these are peculiarly 'British' traits, those authors possessing them — even, it seems, those that hail from Ireland — are deposited in a national 'Treasury' that can rightfully be plundered by an editor for his readers' benefit. This compiler thereby exploits existing ideas about how 'Native Genius' is characterized by eccentric and 'original' humour.[63]

The Flowers of Literature makes a perhaps unwitting contribution to the notion that humour is an admirable, eccentrically British form of genius which pervades Kearsley's subsequent editions of *The Beauties of Sterne*. Whilst *The Beauties of Fielding* was published just twice in identical editions in 1782, Kearsley's Sterne volume entered its thirteenth in 1799. Its longevity suggests that anthologizing Sterne's prose remained commercially viable rather than a declining interest in the earlier author; after all, 1799 also saw the appearance of Newbery's edition of *Joseph Andrews*.[64] Yet Kearsley's editor introduces alterations to new volumes of Sternean extracts that reveal him gradually yielding to this author's refusal to fit the *Beauties'* homogenizing intentions, but also to changing perceptions of both man and work. As Cook suggests, 'Sterne is unique in the series: the new issues of the *Beauties* pay increasing homage to his standing as a modern classic.'[65] The appearance of multi-volume collections of his publications – such as William Strahan's ten-volume *Works* (1780), the source for Kearsley's extracts – reflects this rising stature.[66]

The Beauties of Sterne remained unchanged until the third edition (1782); its Advertisement declares that, in 'gratitude' to his admiring public, the editor 'has added . . . above forty pages of new matter' – mostly extracts from the *Sermons*, a few from the letters, and one or two from Sterne's fiction.[67] The volume also includes a head-and-shoulders engraving after Reynolds's well-known portrait of Sterne, putting the third edition of his *Beauties* on a par with the first *Beauties of Fielding*, whose 'Life' is complemented by an engraving of Hogarth's sketch of the author.[68] The fourth edition of *The Beauties of Sterne* (1782) offers the author's 'Life' for the first time, bringing it in line not only with *The Beauties of Fielding* but also with most other volumes in the series.[69] The text is an edited version of Sterne's 'Memoirs', first made public in Lydia Medalle's heavily edited version of her father's correspondence (1775).[70] This publication competed with many others that capitalized on Sterne's fame following his death in 1768. It also provided Kearsley's fourth edition with the source for a few eulogistic verses appended to its 'Life' of Sterne, a feature that similarly enriched *The Beauties of Goldsmith* (1782).[71] They include Garrick's 'Epitaph', which in praising Sterne's 'genius, wit, and humour' confirms his growing claim to possess those qualities that earn him a place in the national literary treasury.[72]

By the eighth edition of *The Beauties of Sterne* (1785), the beloved 'Yorick' praised in poetic eulogies seemed to have reached a level of sanctification that permitted more contentious parts of his corpus to enter the anthology. *The Beauties of Sterne* begins to become a new body of work altogether. 'Additions to this Eighth Edition' include 'The History of a Watch Coat', now known as *A Political Romance* – Sterne's scurrilous satire upon local Yorkshire politics, suppressed shortly after its publication in 1759.[73] That this facetious piece should be included in a volume dedicated to touching the heart of sensibility suggests Sterne's increasing acceptance as a writer whose variable output results from an eccentric originality belonging to genius. Although Murphy had earlier identified similar qualities in Fielding, they are not reflected in anthologies collecting his extracts; with those dedicated to Sterne, they become an indelible feature.

The tenth edition of *The Beauties of Sterne* (1787) promotes this assessment of Sterne as an idiosyncratic genius most energetically, as the addition of '*Humorous Descriptions*' to the volume's title suggests.[74] The editor, who now changes from 'W.H.' to 'A.F.', indicates in a new preface the need to adopt an alternative approach to Sterne, which has emerged in the space of just five years: 'those objections which at first might have been supposed to exist' about 'the propriety of such a work' have now dissipated.[75] Rather than suggesting a slippage towards impropriety, A.F. hints instead that attitudes towards Sterne's 'humour' have sufficiently altered for his work to be read in a new light:

> It has been a matter of much general complaint, that the selections hitherto made were of rather too confined a cast, – and that, contrary to the original, the *utile* and the *dulce*, were not sufficiently blended, or in equal quantities. . . . [I]t dragg'd on rather too serious a system of grave morality, unmix'd with those sprightlier sallies of fancy, which the great Original knew so judiciously and equally to scatter in our way.[76]

'The reader' – no longer just the 'more juvenile' but now that of 'riper years' too – 'whether of a grave or gay complexion, will find an equal attention paid him'; he (or she) must be allowed to exercise judgement to appreciate the 'morality' and the entertainment of this volume alike. The preface lists those 'humorous' passages now deemed suitable for inclusion – 'Mr. Shandy's Beds of Justice—Dr. Slop and Susannah—Parson Yorick's Horse—' – but stresses that frivolity alone does not hold sway: the volume also includes a whole sermon, 'The Case of Elijah and the Widow of Zarephath Considered', that 'most excellent discourse upon Charity'.

The organization of chosen extracts is also significantly different in this tenth edition. Now the volume opens with Tristram Shandy's famous declaration of his narratorial method and supposed interaction with his readers: 'Writing, when properly managed, (as you may be sure I think mine is) is but a different name for conversation'.[77] The editor thus confirms the increasingly valuable emphasis on Sterne's perceived eccentricity, as displayed in his 'humorous' novels, and in his own letters: Shandean wit – 'When a man's brains are as dry as a squeez'd Orange ——' – mingles with Yorick-style (good-humoured) pathos, such as in Sterne's compassionate exchange with Ignatius Sancho.[78] The combination of wit and pathos is further reinforced by this edition's illustrations – The Death of Le Fever; Trim's oration on mortality in the kitchen – a new feature of Kearsley's *Beauties* that testifies to these anthologies' saleability on the grounds of aesthetic pleasure as much as instructive potential.

Illustrations continue to be a significant feature of new *Beauties of Sterne*; as Peter de Voogd suggests, they contribute to the recirculation of the same 'memorable scenes' found in book illustrations of Sterne in this period.[79] The frontispiece to the twelfth (1793) and thirteenth editions (1799) juxtaposes Reynolds's portrait of Sterne in clerical robes, Hogarth's illustration of *Tristram Shandy*'s sermon-reading scene, and two satyrs' masks.[80] The title to the twelfth edition indicates its significant leap from sentiment towards greater, albeit appropriate, humour: for the first time, Kearsley cuts out the 'Heart of Sensibility'. Similar movements are evident in comparable anthologies produced by other booksellers. Sharpe's 1810 *Beauties of Sterne* excludes both the 'Heart of Sensibility' from its title and the epigraph in which Yorick addresses 'Dear SENSIBILITY', which had stamped the title pages of all previous *Beauties of Sterne*.[81] Thomas Tegg's 1809 *Beauties of Sterne*, meanwhile, offers a selection of 'Humorous and Descriptive Tales, Letters, &c. &c.', and includes illustrations by Thomas Rowlandson that depict comic and pathetic moments alike.[82]

New volumes collecting both Sterne's and Fielding's extracts continued to appear not only in Britain but also in America.[83] Yet for all their success, these publications still encountered some scorn, especially when pitted against more authoritative-seeming, multi-volume collections of an author's works. In his Advertisement to the 1806 *Works of Fielding*, Alexander Chalmers distinguishes this imposing enterprise from the anthology of extracts: he draws attention to a new addition to the corpus, '"The Essay on Nothing," originally published by Fielding, and often since reprinted in various miscellaneous collections, but hitherto not admitted into his Works'.[84] Chalmers's comment chimes with an increasing emphasis on literary-critical appreciation of an author's writings that the anthology of extracts potentially jeopardizes: his work must be viewed in its entirety the better to evaluate its 'beauties and faults' alike.

Nevertheless, the literary anthologies attempted to repel such attacks by promoting their value as both morally instructive and, increasingly, informative tools for discovering a famous author's work. The Advertisement to Sharpe's 1810 *Beauties of Sterne* reaffirms 'the utility of selections of this kind'; the language of value, economic and literary alike, is entwined in the Advertisement's claim that 'time has been allowed to give the stamp of currency' to the 'ore' of Sterne's writing, whose 'fortune' it has been to continue basking in 'the sunshine of popularity'.[85] The volume's 'utility' is reinforced by Sharpe's attempts to taxonomize his selections the better to direct the reader's appreciation of this author's 'beauties': he innovatively classes his chosen extracts into four different 'types': 'Pathetic Pieces', 'Humorous Pieces', Observations on Life', and 'Selections from Mr. Sterne's Sermons'.

Sharpe's volume is indicative of a growing trend in a critical appreciation of Sterne that Fielding's work did not comparatively receive and the anthology's role in shaping it. The preface to Walker's 1811 *Beauties* posits 'LAWRENCE STERNE' [*sic*] as 'the author of this original and entertaining miscellany'.[86] The anthology sells itself as a work in its own right, an important repository of the famed Sternean 'style and manner'.[87] The pernicious effects of framing are thus gilded over by a claim to offer both writer and readers a service: the anthology provides a worthwhile route into this well-known author's wider oeuvre.

Yet Fielding continued to be admired well into the nineteenth century as a virtuoso author, drawing praise from commentators from Walter Scott to Thackeray, albeit jollified by the former into 'that astonishing genius . . . Harry Fielding'.[88] Sterne fared less well; his formerly admired 'outré' genius was now 'posture-making', his sensibility sickening – 'I don't value or respect much the cheap dribble of those fountains', writes Thackeray of Yorick's tears.[89] Nevertheless, by 1905 an edition of *The Beauties of Sterne* enthusiastically declared that 'one of the most charming authors in the English language' had secured his rightful position in the nation's pantheon of treasured authors: 'Laurence Sterne is a classic of English prose fiction', even likened to 'the creator of Falstaff'.[90] It is the 'unaccountable' Sterne, rather than Fielding, who is made more accountable by the processes of anthologization in which such volumes initially resist, then yield to accommodating, the seemingly conflicting qualities of this author's writing.[91] *The Beauties of Sterne* seemed to have earned him a place alongside the national poet whose own *Beauties* had originally sown the seeds for the flourishing enthusiasm these anthologies enjoyed in their late eighteenth-century heyday.

Notes

1 Samuel Taylor Coleridge to John Murray, 18 January 1822, *Collected Letters of Samuel Taylor Coleridge*, ed. Earl Leslie Griggs, 6 vols. (Oxford: Clarendon Press, 1956–71), vol. 5, pp. 197–200 (200).
2 Daniel S. Malachuk, 'Coleridge's Republicanism and the Aphorism in *Aids to Reflection*', *Studies in Romanticism*, 39:3 (2000), 397–417 (408).
3 Daniel Cook, 'Authors Unformed: Reading "Beauties" in the Eighteenth Century', *Philological Quarterly*, 89:2–3 (2010), 283–309 (291). Thomas Keymer identifies William Holland as the figure behind this 'enterprising compilation': '*A Sentimental Journey* and the Failure of Feeling', in *The Cambridge Companion to Laurence Sterne*, ed. Thomas Keymer (Cambridge University Press, 2009), pp. 79–94 (79–80; 93, n.1).
4 Barbara M. Benedict, *Framing Feeling: Sentiment and Style in English Prose Fiction, 1745–1800* (New York: AMS Press, 1994), pp. 1–3.
5 Barbara M. Benedict, *Making the Modern Reader: Cultural Mediation in Early Modern Literary Anthologies* (Princeton University Press, 1996), pp. 12–13, 25.
6 *The Beauties of Shakespeare*, 5th edn (London: C. and G. Kearsley, [1791?]).
7 Cook, 'Authors Unformed', p. 285.
8 Philip Luckombe, *The Beauties of England* (London: L. Davis and C. Reymers, [1757]).
9 Melvyn New, 'Scholia', *The Scriblerian and the Kit-Cats*, 45:2 (2013), 292.
10 Cook, 'Authors Unformed', pp. 283, 289–92.
11 Benedict, *Framing Feeling*, p. 162.
12 As Benedict observes, because it is uncertain who was literate in this period it is difficult to ascertain the anthologies' target audience: *Modern Reader*, pp. 26–27.
13 Benedict, *Modern Reader*, p. 29.
14 *The Beauties of Fielding: Carefully Selected from the Works of that Eminent Writer. To which is added Some Account of his Life* (London: G. Kearsley, 1782).

15 Cook, 'Authors Unformed', pp. 286, 290.

16 *Henry Fielding: The Critical Heritage*, eds. Ronald Paulson and Thomas Lockwood (1969; London and New York: Routledge, 2002), p. 7.

17 Martin C. Battestin and Ruthe R. Battestin, *Henry Fielding: A Life* (London and New York: Routledge, 1989), pp. 441, 452; Paulson and Lockwood, *Critical Heritage*, pp. 11–15; Donald Thomas, *Henry Fielding* (London: Weidenfeld and Nicolson, 1990), pp. 293–94.

18 Paulson and Lockwood, *Critical Heritage*, p. 144, pp. 235–37 (235).

19 Samuel Richardson to J. B. de Freval, 21 January 1750–51, in Paulson and Lockwood, *Critical Heritage*, p. 238.

20 Thomas, *Fielding*, p. 294.

21 Pierre-Jean-Baptiste Desforges, *Tom Jones à Londres: comédie en cinq actes, en vers* (Paris: Baudouin, 1782). Michael Burden's essay in this collection considers operatic adaptations of novels.

22 Cook, 'Authors Unformed', p. 286.

23 Simon Dickie, '*Amelia*, Sex, and Fielding's Woman Question', in *Henry Fielding (1707–54): Novelist, Playwright, Journalist, Magistrate; A Double Anniversary Tribute*, ed. Claude Rawson (Newark: University of Delaware Press, 2008), pp. 115–42 (135).

24 *Beauties of Fielding*, pp. 8–9; Henry Fielding, *The History of Amelia*, 2 vols. (London: Hutchinson, 1905), vol. 2, p. 117.

25 *Beauties of Fielding*, p. 3.

26 Henry Fielding, *The History of Tom Jones* (1749), ed. R. P. C. Mutter (1966; Harmondsworth: Penguin, 1985), pp. 139–40.

27 Paulson and Lockwood, *Critical Heritage*, p. 21.

28 Cook, 'Authors Unformed', p. 301. By contrast, for Elizabeth Wanning Harries fragments hold a spiritually affirmative, socially cohesive power: *The Unfinished Manner: Essays on the Fragment in the Later Eighteenth Century* (Charlottesville: University of Virginia Press, 1994), pp. 34–38.

29 Arthur Murphy, 'An Essay on the Life and Genius of Henry Fielding Esq.', in *The Works of Henry Fielding, Esq*, 4 vols. (London: A. Millar, 1762), vol. 1, pp. 5–49; Battestin and Battestin, *Life*, pp. 618–22; Paulson and Lockwood, *Critical Heritage*, p. 18.

30 *Beauties of Fielding*, p. xii.

31 *Beauties of Fielding*, pp. ix, v, x.

32 Ian Campbell Ross, *Laurence Sterne: A Life* (Oxford University Press, 2001), pp. 6–9.

33 Thomas, *Fielding*, p. 394; Battestin and Battestin, *Life*, p. 5.

34 *The Beauties of Sterne: Including all his Pathetic Tales, and Most Distinguished Observations on Life. Selected for the Heart of Sensibility* (London: T. Davies, J. Ridley, W. Flexney, J. Sewel, and G. Kearsley, 1782).

35 *Universal Magazine of Knowledge and Pleasure*, 26 (1760), 189–90; *The London Magazine*, 29 (February 1760), 111, quoted in *Laurence Sterne: The Critical Heritage*, ed. Alan B. Howes (London and New York: Routledge and Kegan Paul, 1974), p. 52.

36 *Sterne's Memoirs: A Hitherto Unrecorded Holograph now Brought to Light in Facsimile*, ed. Kenneth Monkman (Coxwold: The Laurence Sterne Trust, 1985), p. ix.

37 *Beauties of Sterne* (1782), p. vii.

38 Tristram Shandy illuminates his 'equivocal matter' with 'stars' (asterisks): Laurence Sterne, *The Life and Opinions of Tristram Shandy, Gentleman*, eds. Melvyn New and Joan New, The Florida Edition of the Works of Laurence Sterne, 9 vols. (Gainesville: University Press of Florida, 1978–2014), vol. 2, p. 558.

39 *Beauties of Sterne* (1782), pp. viii, 171–77; Sterne, *Tristram Shandy*, vol. 1, p. 115.

40 Cook, 'Authors Unformed', p. 290.

41 Stephen Ahern, *Affected Sensibilities: Romantic Excess and the Genealogy of the Novel, 1680–1810* (New York: AMS Press, 2007), pp. 20–22; Benedict, *Framing Feeling*, pp. 1–3, pp. 69–92.

42 Warren Oakley, *A Culture of Mimicry: Laurence Sterne, His Readers and the Art of Bodysnatching* (London: MHRA, 2010), pp. 4–5.

43 Benedict, *Framing Feeling*, pp. 1–10.

44 Paulson and Lockwood, *Critical Heritage*, pp. 8–9.

45 Dickie, '*Amelia*, Sex', p. 129. See also Battestin and Battestin, *Life*, pp. 441–42. See Paulson and Lockwood, *Critical Heritage*, p. 15, on *Amelia*; see pp. 19–20 on the comparison between Fielding and Richardson.

46 Robert D. Mayo, *The English Novel in the Magazines, 1740–1815* (Evanston: Northwestern University Press, 1962), pp. 347–48.

47 On anthologies of excerpts from Richardson's fiction, see Leah Price, *The Anthology and the Rise of the Novel: From Richardson to George Eliot* (Cambridge University Press, 2000).

48 Laurence Sterne, *A Sentimental Journey through France and Italy and Continuation of the Bramine's Journal: The Text and Notes*, eds. Melvyn New and W. G. Day, The Florida Edition of the Works of Laurence Sterne, 9 vols. (Gainesville: University Press of Florida, 1978–2014), vol. 6, p. 155. The *Beauties'* epigraph adds the capitalization.

49 *Beauties of Sterne* (1782), p. viii.

50 Elizabeth Sibthorpe Pinchard, *Dramatic Dialogues, for the Use of Young Persons*, 2 vols. (London: E. Newbery, 1792), vol. 1, p. 53. See M–C. Newbould, *Adaptations of Laurence Sterne's Fiction: Sterneana, 1760–1840* (Farnham: Ashgate, 2013), pp. 97–103.

51 Mayo, *English Novel*, pp. 337, 345–46; John Mullan, *Sentiment and Sociability: The Language of Feeling in the Eighteenth Century* (1988; Oxford: Clarendon Press, 1997), p. 154.

52 Sterne, *Tristram Shandy*, vol. 2, pp. 499–520.

53 Michael Bell, *Sentimentalism, Ethics and the Culture of Feeling* (Basingstoke: Palgrave Macmillan, 2000), pp. 67–73.

54 Sterne, *Tristram Shandy*, vol. 2, p. 513.

55 *Beauties of Sterne* (1782), pp. 43–72.

56 Sterne, *Tristram Shandy*, vol. 2, pp. 751–52.

57 Edward Barry, *Familiar Letters on a Variety of Subjects, Addressed to a Friend* (London: Payne and Parsons, 1794), pp. 25–27.

58 Robert Alves, *Sketches of a History of Literature* (Edinburgh: Chapman, [1794]).

59 *The Flowers of Literature, or Treasury of Wit and Genius. Containing the Essence of the Beauties of Johnson, Swift, Fielding, Pope, Goldsmith, Hervey, Sterne, Watts, &c.* (London: J. Cooke, [1782]).

60 The passages are taken from Sterne's *Sermons* and Fielding's *Temple Beau*: *Flowers of Literature*, vol. 1, pp. 29–30.

61 Quoted in Cook, 'Authors Unformed', p. 292.

62 *The Flowers of Literature, or Treasury of Wit and Genius.*

63 William Temple, 'Of Poetry', in *Miscellanea*, 4th edn (London: Jacob Tonson, 1705), pp. 303–65 (307).

64 *The History and Adventures of Joseph Andrews, and his friend Mr. Abraham Adams. Abridged from the Works of H. Fielding, Esq.* (London: E. Newbery, 1799).

65 Cook, 'Authors Unformed', p. 298.

66 The Advertisement identifies the source. Other contemporary *Works* of Sterne include Wenman's *Entertaining Library* and Harrison's *Novelists Magazine* (both 1781).

67 *The Beauties of Sterne...*, 3rd edn (London: G. Kearsley, 1782), p. ix.

68 David Alexander, 'Sterne, the 18th-Century Print Market, and the Prints in Shandy Hall', *The Shandean*, 5 (1993), 110–24 (111).

69 *The Beauties of Sterne...*, 4th edn (London: G. Kearsley, 1782); Cook, 'Authors Unformed', pp. 291, 298–99.

70 *Letters of the Late Rev. Mr. Laurence Sterne, To his most intimate Friends*, 3 vols. (London: T. Becket, 1775). See Introduction to Laurence Sterne, *The Letters*, ed. Melvyn New and Peter de Voogd, The Florida Edition of the Works of Laurence Sterne, 8 vols. (Gainesville: University Press of Florida, 1978–2009), vol. 7, p. xlix; Monkman, *Sterne's Memoirs*, pp. vii–xvi; Arthur H. Cash, *Laurence Sterne: The Later Years* (London: Methuen, 1986), p. 351, n.63.

71 Cook, 'Authors Unformed', p. 289.

72 Richard Terry, *The Plagiarism Allegation in English Literature from Butler to Sterne* (Basingstoke: Palgrave Macmillan, 2010), pp. 166–68.

73 *The Beauties of Sterne...*, 8th edn (London: G. Kearsley, 1785); Arthur H. Cash, *Laurence Sterne: The Early and Middle Years* (London: Methuen, 1975), pp. 270–77.

74 *The Beauties of Sterne ... Enlarged and Ornamented with Plates, from Original Drawings*, 10th edn (London: G. Kearsley, 1787).

75 *Beauties of Sterne...*, 10th edn (1787), p. v.

76 *Beauties of Sterne...*, 10th edn (1787), pp. v–vi.

77 Sterne, *Tristram Shandy*, vol. 1, p. 125; *Beauties of Sterne*, 10th edn (1787), pp. 1–2.

78 *Beauties of Sterne...*, 10th edn (1787), pp. 2, 9–10.

79 Peter de Voogd, 'Sterne and Visual Culture', in *Cambridge Companion*, pp. 142–59 (149).

80 John Barlow after Joshua Reynolds, 'Lawrence Sterne, A.M.' [*sic*], engraving and etching, frontispiece, *The Beauties of Sterne: Including Many of his Letters*

and *Sermons, All his Pathetic Tales, Humorous Descriptions, and Most Distinguished Observations on Life*, 12th edn (London: C. and G. Kearsley, 1793), and 13th edn (London: G. Kearsley et al., 1799).

81 *The Beauties of Sterne: Containing all his Pathetic Tales, His Humorous Descriptions, His Moral Distinguished Observations on Life, and a Copious Selection from his Sermons* (London: J. Sharpe, 1810).

82 *The Beauties of Sterne: Comprising his Humorous and Descriptive Tales, Letters, &c. &c.; Embellished by Caricatures, by Rowlandson, from Original Drawings by Newton* (London: T. Tegg, 1809); David Alexander, *Richard Newton and English Caricature in the 1790s* (Manchester University Press, 1998), pp. 40–41, 122; M-C. Newbould, 'Character or Caricature?: Richard Newton's Illustrations of Laurence Sterne's *A Sentimental Journey*', *Word & Image*, 25:2 (2009), 115–28. The connection between Newton, Holland, and Rowlandson adds further interest to Keymer's identification of 'W.H.' as William Holland.

83 *The Beauties of Sterne* was published in Philadelphia (1789, 1790) and Boston (1793); *The Beauties of Fielding* was published in Philadelphia (1792) and Boston (1807).

84 *The Works of Henry Fielding Esq.*, 10 vols. (London: J. Johnson et al., 1806).

85 *Beauties of Sterne* (1810), 'Advertisement'.

86 *The Beauties of Sterne, with Some Account of his Life* (London: J. Walker and J. Harris, [1811]), p. ix.

87 *Beauties of Sterne* (1811), p. ix. See also Walter Scott, 'Prefatory Memoir to Sterne', in *The Novels of Sterne*, Ballantyne's Novelist's Library, 10 vols. (London: Hurst, Robinson, and Co., 1821–24), vol. 5, p. xxi.

88 Walter Scott, 'Prefatory Memoir to Fielding', in *The Novels of Henry Fielding, Esq.*, Ballantyne's Novelist's Library, 10 vols. (London: Hurst, Robinson, and Co., 1821–24), vol. 1, pp. 1–2; William Makepeace Thackeray, *The English Humourists of the Eighteenth Century: A Series of Lectures* (New York: Leypoldt and Holt, 1867), p. 250.

89 Thackeray, *English Humourists*, p. 274.

90 'An Appreciation of Laurence Sterne', facing title page, *The Beauties of Sterne* (London: The Library Press, [1905]).

91 Howes, *Critical Heritage*, p. 52.

CHAPTER 7

The Spectral Iamb: The Poetic Afterlives of the Late Eighteenth-Century Novel

Dahlia Porter

As Barbara Benedict has argued, eighteenth-century literature resembles a 'genre salad', a concoction of miscellaneous types tossed together to make a text.[1] Epitomized by the miscellany or collection of beauties (such as those discussed by M-C. Newbould in this collection), this dish was often held together by little more than the dressing of the leather binding, but its separate generic components sometimes coalesced into new, mixed forms. As J. Paul Hunter demonstrates, the eighteenth-century novel contained multitudes; an encyclopaedic form, it came into prominence by eating up other genres, incorporating them into itself.[2] G. Gabrielle Starr argues that traces of the novel's incorporation of poetic modes remain in its language of emotions and exploration of individual experience.[3] In this essay, I consider the more blatant reminders of the novel's generic mixture: poetry that was not digested into the fabric of fiction. By attending to how excerpted and original verse appeared in novels and subsequently circulated outside of the novel in the larger sphere of print, I argue that late eighteenth-century novelists maintained the formal integrity and distinction of verse within the novel to cultivate a specific kind of afterlife for fiction in anthologies, miscellanies, periodicals, and other novels.

Verse and prose appeared next to each other on the page throughout the eighteenth century in drama, essays, and various miscellaneous collections. While these forms co-existed in the spaces of print, there was no clear agreement about their relationship. This becomes particularly obvious in the context of the novel's consolidation as a genre. In the early and mid-eighteenth century, poetry might be used to define, legitimate, mock, or rewrite 'the novel' – or to do several of these things simultaneously. As David A. Brewer notes, the mock-pastorals and mock-heroic epistles produced by the Scriblerians from *Gulliver's Travels* (1726) act as surrogates for, and consequently displace, the novel – until they are reprinted as paratexts in succeeding editions of Swift's text.[4] Samuel Richardson and Henry Fielding practise a similar form of incorporation when they draw on the elite cultural cachet of poetry to bolster the reputation of the new prose genre. Beyond invoking poetry to define the novel generically – Fielding famously called *Joseph Andrews* (1742) a 'comic Epic-Poem in Prose' and labelled *Tom Jones* (1749) a 'Heroic, Historical, Prosaic Poem'[5] – both authors employ inset poems within the novel. The mechanics and effect of integrating verse varied: inserting two lines from Pope's *Essay on Criticism* (1711) in the opening pages of *Tom Jones* does not call on the same authority or work in the same way as Pamela's rewriting of Psalm 137 to chastise Mrs Jewkes. In both cases, however, the author sets the generic parameters of the novel by citing, quoting, rewriting, and commenting on excerpted verse.

These examples speak to the afterlife of poetry in the novel as much as to authors' attempts to situate the novel in relation to older, established literary forms. As the novel grew into prominence, it participated in redefining the relationship between poetry and prose. Ann Radcliffe, Charlotte Smith, John Thelwall, Matthew Lewis, Sydney Owenson, and many others writing in the final decades of the century employed excerpted verse as chapter mottos, but they also included original poems – often recited, written, or sung by one of the characters – specifically composed for inclusion in the novel. Borrowed poetic excerpts and original poems may function similarly within the borders of the novel: to convey a character's emotional state indirectly or to render intense feeling less melodramatically than was thought possible in prose. But original poetry was perceived by authors, reviewers, and readers as having a more intimate relationship to the novel in which it first appeared. Most reviews of Smith's *Emmeline, The Orphan of the Castle* (1788) and Lewis's *The Monk* (1796), for example, excerpt original poems, not passages of prose, as representative of the author's style. Furthermore, both Smith and Lewis mark poems as 'originally published in' the novel when they republish them in *Elegiac Sonnets* (1784) and *Tales of Wonder* (1801) respectively. Embedded poems encapsulate and reflect the novel as a whole, as Jerome McGann has suggested, a condition that allowed these poems to stand in for novels in the wider sphere of print.[6] In this essay, I use the term 'embedded' to describe original poems that were 'firmly fixed' in the 'surrounding mass' of novelistic prose when they were first published.[7] By tracing the various and tangled paths of embedded poems as they were republished in single-author collections, periodicals, reviews, anthologies, and various other media (on children's writing paper and advertisements, for example), this essay details how the late eighteenth-century novel was recirculated in print not primarily as prose fiction, but as excerpted verse.

As in earlier decades of the eighteenth century, embedding poems was a strategic practice in the 1790s: both authors and publishers recognized the value of compact, ready-made snippets for promoting novels through conventional reprinting practices and for directing how the novel would be represented in reviews. Littering novels with portable excerpts also had less immediate reverberations in the nineteenth-century afterlives of late eighteenth-century novels. As the popularity of gothic and sentimental novels faded and 1790s novels themselves saw fewer reprints, poems from these novels continued to circulate widely, sometimes with, but more often without, reference to the novel in which they originally appeared. Even so, the early novelistic publication context did not disappear. In many cases, excerpted poems neither displace nor replace the novel; instead, they serve as placeholders for an author's literary corpus and, more broadly, for outdated sub-genres of the novel itself. In what follows, I argue that attending to Romantic-era generic mixtures and the print recirculation of embedded original poems illuminates poetry's role in defining and per-petuating the cultural currency of the specific modes of Romantic-period fiction. Following the afterlives of embedded poems reveals an alternative view of the Victorian reception of Romantic authors, one that evolved with the shifting fates of literary genres across the long nineteenth century.

Poetry in 1790s Fiction

If poetry in the novel functioned to legitimate prose fiction in the mid-eighteenth century, critics have suggested this relationship changed in the final decades of the century. Leah Price, for example, argues that by including excerpted verse and original poems in her novels, Radcliffe 'turned narrative into a hook to hang anthology pieces on'; rather than defining the novel vis-à-vis elite poetic genres, her novels mimic the modular form of the anthology that burgeoned after the end of perpetual copyright in 1774.[8] For Price, excerptable poems interrupt narrative pro-gress, providing the occasion to differentiate between modes (lyric from narrative, style from plot, taste from curiosity).[9] Mary Favret also notes that inset and excerpted poems mark the difference between prose and verse. While Price argues that collectible poems render the narrative dispensable, Favret suggests that by merely repeating what has already been said in prose, poems announce *their* disposability and artificiality and, consequently, the realism of prose narrative.[10] The novel of the 1790s, Favret argues, displays poems as visual objects 'to make itself look good – that is, to sell itself as real, natural, well-grounded'.[11] Alternatively, Ingrid

Horrocks argues that the redundancy of the inset poem or excerpt in Radcliffe's *The Mysteries of Udolpho* (1794) is crucial for moving private feeling into a community of readers: 'rather than stealing *into* a character's reverie … quotations momentarily release the character *out* of his or her own reveries into the "visionary scenes of the poet"'.[12] For Horrocks, this release counters the trauma inflicted by the gothic plot and allows the heroine access to a communal past or landscape through the medium of poetry.[13] Ann Wierda Rowland reads the original poetry in Charlotte Smith's *Old Manor House* (1793) along similar lines: quoted poetry reveals that 'Orlando's interiority is, in fact, a communal construct crafted in a series of movements out into a shared social world'.[14]

As this representative sampling of critical positions indicates, arguments about poetry and the novel in the final decade of the eighteenth century fall into two broad camps: those that take poems as ready-made excerpts alien to the prose narrative that surrounds them and those that understand embedded poetry as integral to the novel's expression of subjective interiority and communal feeling. In general, the first critical position corresponds to an interest in the 'rise of the novel' (a phrase in Price's title; Favret's essay appeared in *Studies in the Novel*), while the second position correlates to a sustained interest in poetry (Rowland's essay appears in *The Cambridge Companion to British Romantic Poetry*; Horrock's subtitle is 'Re-membering Poetry in Radcliffe').[15] While giving primacy to a genre will, of necessity, colour our understanding of any composite form, all of these critics would likely agree with Rowland's assessment that novels with embedded poems stage how 'formal and social categories of Romantic literary genre took shape through persistent acts of both differentiation and appropriation'.[16] I would like to extend this insight by focusing on acts of recontextualization and recirculation – on what happens to inset poems both during and after they appear in novels.

As with poetry included in early eighteenth-century novels, embedded poems at the end of the century are not stable in their function across novels or even within one text. Perhaps the most obvious difference exists between original poetry and lines borrowed, with or without attribution, from other works. Radcliffe, Smith, Lewis, Thelwall, Walter Scott, and Owenson, among others, make extensive use of excerpts from poems and popular dramas in their novels; Shakespeare was a common choice, but selections run the gamut of sources from translations of Horace and lines from Tasso to ballads lifted from Thomas Percy's *Reliques of Ancient English Poetry* (1765). These excerpted lines often appear as chapter mottos that set the tone or foreshadow the plot twists of the ensuing chapter.

Beyond serving as epigraphs, lines of borrowed verse populate the text itself. For example, early in Owenson's *The Wild Irish Girl* (1806), the English hero Horatio quotes Milton's *Paradise Lost* (1667–74) to heighten his description of his Irish host; later, he and Glorvina – the wild Irish girl of the title – consolidate their shared tastes and blossoming love by exchanging Tasso's lines on violets and quoting William Collins's 'Ode to Evening' (1746).[17] Horrocks, Rowland, and others have suggested that quoted verse in novels allows the reader to participate in the emotional circuits connecting the characters by tapping into a shared cultural context. In Owenson's novel, inset poems initially substantiate national differences, but as the novel progresses, poetry's cosmopolitanism bridges English and Irish cultures, reinforcing the novel's ostensible support for the 1801 Act of Union.[18]

Original poems in novels can and do work in a similar fashion as excerpted verse, but they also introduce a different set of conditions. Again most obviously, original poems conflate a novel's author and its characters in ways that borrowed lines do not. Smith's practice of re-collecting the sonnets and other poems appearing first in her novels illustrates the consequences of this convergence. In Smith's *Emmeline*, the eponymous heroine's preferred suitor, Godolphin, recites 'To Night' at a crucial moment in the plot's development.[19] Crossing the English Channel on his return from France, Godolphin tells his 'embosom'd grief' directly 'to sullen surges, and the viewless wind'. His 'exhausted heart' is 'hopeless and resign'd' because he believes he has lost Emmeline to his rival Delamere. The poem ends with his hope that his sorrows will reach 'the ear of heaven' even though they are 'lost on earth'.[20] His final lament, however, is quickly exposed as precipitous: Emmeline and Mrs Stafford have overheard his lament, recognized his passion, and eventually restore him to hope.[21] While it is unclear whether Godolphin is quoting from memory or composing this effusion *extempore*, when the poem appears as Sonnet XXXIX in the fifth edition of Smith's *Elegiac Sonnets* in 1789, he is replaced by Smith herself.[22] With this reattribution, the meaning of the poem changes. Spoken in the voice of Charlotte Smith and framed by the autobiographical prefaces of *Elegiac Sonnets*, the sonnet reinforces rather than releases the speaker from a state of hopeless depression. Readers familiar with the novel would feel this divergence: while Godolphin's Channel-jumping restores him to happiness and love, Smith's own crossing (undertaken, like Mrs Stafford's, because her husband has fled to France to escape his creditors) produced only misery. Smith's misery, as readers of her sonnets well knew, was compounded by the ongoing legal battles over her children's inheritance. The reprinted sonnet thus heightens the disjunction between the author and the novel's heroine: if Emmeline's chance reunion with Godolphin through the sonnet predicts the return of her rightful inheritance as well as the eventual consummation of their love, no such happy resolution awaits the poet of *Elegiac Sonnets*. Telling her sorrows to heaven's – and the public's – supposedly sympathetic ear, Smith heightens the poem's pathos by drawing attention to her legal battle, which does in fact seem 'lost on earth'.

Smith's case may well be unique among novelists of the 1790s: no other woman author, not even the infamous Mary Robinson, made the conditions of her private life a prerequisite for reading her verse or novels in quite the same way. The confusion of author and character that adheres to original sonnets published in Smith's novels is less pronounced – or fundamentally different – in the work of her contemporaries. In Radcliffe's *The Romance of the Forest* (1791), for example, Adeline composes, repeats, overhears, and occasionally is forced to listen to poems of varying lengths and styles. In most cases, her imagination is struck by a particularly beautiful, romantic, or grand natural scene, which in turn activates her poetic sensibility. The embedded poem is preceded by reverie so profound it immobilizes her: at the summit of a 'wild eminence' she is 'seized with a kind of still rapture impossible to be expressed, and stood unconscious of the flight of time'.[23] In another passage, it is only once 'her senses were no longer absorbed in the contemplation of this grand scenery, and when its images floated on her memory, only, in softened colours' that she is able to repeat or compose lines of verse.[24] As Horrocks argues of *Udolpho*, original poems, like excerpted verse, may act to release the heroine from the gothic plot that engulfs her and give her access to a community beyond herself. But even as poetry in general draws Adeline out of herself, the original poems also establish her as an author who is not quite in control of her medium. Adeline is more likely to 'yield' to the poetic impulse than actively to pursue it. One could argue that this merely reiterates the heroine's lack of control in the gothic context, but her condition also parallels contemporary theories of how poetry should be composed – most pointedly the compositional theory put forward in Wordsworth's Preface to *Lyrical Ballads* (1800). Adeline recites and composes from 'emotions recollected in tranquillity'; poetry seems to arise from 'habits of mind' she has acquired by allowing 'influxes of feeling [to be] modified and directed by our thoughts'.[25] In this context, Adeline's sentiments are of less importance than her process; she appears as a surrogate for the author, a vehicle for Radcliffe's original poems who also articulates the author's compositional theory for readers of the novel.

Poetic Afterlives: Reviewed and Re-collected

If readers were pressed to make direct comparisons between Smith and her characters, it is because Smith was well known as the author of *Elegiac Sonnets* before she published her first novel in 1788. Poems, and particularly sonnets, appearing in Smith's novels thus announced their intertextuality, and reviewers explicitly commented on both her life and the original poems she inserted into her novels. All of the reviews of *Emmeline* mention Smith's poetry, and many of the reviews reprint at least one of the embedded sonnets. Rather than 'mutilate' the prose, the notice in *The Critical Review* for *Emmeline* chooses to excerpt 'To Night'; reviewers for *The Monthly Review* and *The European Magazine* excerpt 'Far on the sands, the low, retiring tide'; and Mary Wollstonecraft praises the poetical qualities of Smith's descriptions, which she claims cannot be 'separated from the woven web [of the prose] without injuring them'.[26] Smith's sonnets seem inserted to be excerpted, an invitation taken up by reviewers and excused by the wish to preserve the integrity of the prose. (It should be noted, however, that a number of reviews also excerpt long passages of prose, particularly sections that appear to comment on Smith's unhappy marriage and legal difficulties.[27]) The practice of excerpting poems in place of prose was not, however, limited to Smith: reviews of novels by Radcliffe, Lewis, and Thelwall all reprint embedded original poems. While Thelwall was an established poet when he published *The Peripatetic* (1793), Lewis and Radcliffe would not reprint poems from their novels until much later: Lewis republished original poems from *The Monk* in *Tales of Wonder* in 1801; Radcliffe collected poems from her novels in *The Poems of Mrs. Ann Radcliffe: Author of 'The Mysteries of Udolpho'* in 1816. Whether or not the author was an established poet did not condition reviewers' preference for excerpting original poetry.

Poetry, of course, was easy to extract from the fabric of prose, as the novels themselves amply demonstrated in their own borrowings. As Price argues, ease was not the only motivation reviewers had for excerpting verse: by drawing attention to the poetic 'beauties' in Radcliffe's novels – beauties that a 'reader, in eagerness of curiosity, should be tempted to pass over' – reviewers from Vicesimus Knox to Anna Laetitia Barbauld distinguished 'true lovers of poetry' from 'common readers' of prose.[28] As it had earlier in the century, poetry continued to carry the weight of cultural legitimacy, but 1790s reviewers of Radcliffe deployed this authority to denigrate novel readers. Beyond this, early reviews and early nineteenth-century commentary tend to assess the success of Radcliffe's prose with reference to poetry. For example, Walter Scott's 'Prefatory Memoir' to *The Novels of Mrs. Ann Radcliffe* (1824) praises *The Sicilian Romance* solely on the grounds that in it Radcliffe had been the first to 'introduce into her prose fictions a tone of fanciful description and impressive narrative, which had hitherto been exclusively applied to poetry'.[29] Radcliffe's novels, Scott argues, are rendered striking by descriptions of scenery that combine 'the eye of the painter, with the spirit of a poet', and her 'poetry partakes of the rich and beautiful colouring which distinguishes her prose composition, and has, perhaps, the same fault, of not being in every case quite precise in expressing the meaning of the author'.[30] In place of an opposition between prose and poetry, Radcliffe's practice of embedding original poetry in her novels provokes Scott to make comparative judgements that yoke the two together.

The same holds true in reviews of Lewis and Smith. Samuel Taylor Coleridge's 1797 review of *The Monk* explicitly elevates the embedded verse at the expense of Lewis's prose: while the novel manifests incongruity in characterization and impiety in subject, one 'exquisitely tender' poem, 'The Exile', will 'melt and delight the heart, when ghosts and hobgoblins shall be found only in the lumber-garret of the circulating library'.[31] While Coleridge's comparison divides terror-filled prose from tender verse, other reviews call on Lewis's embedded original poems to characterize his prose style. Citing the same poem as Coleridge, the *European Magazine and London Review* suggests the 'chief excellence of Mr. L.'s *prose* consists in this latter attribute [imagery] of the *muse*': even though the novel on the whole has 'neither *originality, morals,* nor *probability* to recommend it', scenes on which Lewis has bestowed care exhibit 'the truth of nature and the animation of genius' characteristic of his poetry.[32] Reviews and biographical notices of Smith likewise measure her prose and verse against each other. *The Critical Review*, for example, asserts that scenes in *Emmeline* 'are often drawn with great beauty', just as the 'fetters' imposed by the sonnet form 'add to [the] beauty' of the sentiment expressed. Like characters who are 'excellent copies of nature', Smith's original poems render an 'artificial species of poetry' both 'natural and pleasing'.[33] In all of these cases, reviewers deploy the poems embedded in the novel as an assessment metric: poems function as the yardstick by which to measure the successes and failures of the author's prose style, characterization, and rendering of 'scenes', as well to establish the direction of the novel's moral compass.

As this brief survey suggests, in the 1790s embedded original poetry constituted a very specific kind of afterlife for novels in the months and years directly following publication. Whatever function the verse served *in* the novel, in reviews and other forms of critical commentary it was deployed to evaluate the prose narrative in which it appeared. How the prose stood up to the verse was determined by several factors working in combination: the author's existing reputation as a poet or novelist, the sub-genre or mode of the novel, and the genre, form, and perceived 'excellences' of the embedded verse. Whereas Smith's early novel of manners was seen as consonant with her poetry, reviewers repeatedly drew attention to the tonal gap between Radcliffe and Lewis's gothic plots and the 'tender' lyrics they contained. Considering Horrocks's argument that poetry functions as the heroine's escape from the gothic, this divergence is not surprising. What is striking, however, is the extent to which embedded poems continue to signal their original publication context as they are reprinted and recirculated across the nineteenth century. Consonance between novel and poem did not ensure that the poem would continue to be associated with the novel when it was reprinted; indeed, in the case of Smith, it was quite the opposite. However, when a poem did continue its association with the novel in which it first appeared – as in the case of Radcliffe's 'Song of a Spirit' and Lewis's 'Alonzo the Brave and the Fair Imogene'– the poem would eventually stand in for and characterize the author's complete novelistic oeuvre.

I am drawing these conclusions from specific case studies detailed later. Since my claims rest on poem-specific surveys of republishing trends, a word on methodology will be useful here. Using a combination of date-constrained searches of books and periodicals available online and targeted research directed by criticism on reception, I tracked the nineteenth-century reprinting histories of poems by Smith, Radcliffe, and Lewis that were first published in *Emmeline, The Romance of the Forest,* and *The Monk,* respectively. In each case, I chose poems that were lauded and/or reprinted in contemporary reviews and that had relatively extensive republication histories. As this suggests, unlike recent studies that trace the influence of Romantic poetry or novels on prominent Victorian authors, my approach to reception history focuses on commercial practices of reprinting.[34] As Tom Mole has argued of Byron, the cultural impact of Romantic authors can be measured through mediated, commercialized products of the publishing industry – products defined by 'practices of citation and appropriation that distributed Byron's writings to a socially mixed and geographically dispersed audience'.[35] The same is true of poems by Radcliffe, Smith, and Lewis: by following the fate of specific poems, we open a different window onto the reception of both the author and their work more broadly, which for these authors includes their novels. While my results are necessarily limited by the scope of the digital archive and issues inherent in full text searches of scanned books, the research clearly establishes the extent to which specific poems constitute an afterlife for the novel in which they originally appeared.[36] Why a novel does or does not live on vicariously through a particular poem, and what kind of afterlife the poem creates for the novel, are substantively different questions, both of which I address later.

Of my three case studies, Smith and Radcliffe constitute clear antipodes: Smith's sonnets are quickly detached from her novels, while Radcliffe's poems tend to maintain a strong connection to their original publication context throughout their nineteenth-century republication history. This was not entirely unexpected: Smith promoted her poetry much more vigorously than her novels – as the illustrated subscription editions of *Elegiac Sonnets* attest – and the melancholy cast of her sonnets was often taken as a defining quality of her novels. Walter Scott's comments in his memoir of Smith indicate the conventional nineteenth-century assessment: having already noted the pleasing blend of melancholy and humour in Smith's 'To my Lyre' (which he reprints in full) and described her poetry as 'generally melancholy and sentimental', Scott proceeds to argue that a 'general tone of melancholy pervades her composition' of fictional narratives.[37] In the structure and development of his comments, Scott makes the novels' characteristic tone an outgrowth of Smith's poetry. To be fair, Scott also follows the same method in his criticism of Radcliffe's novels. In his memoir of Radcliffe, he quotes an 'address to Melancholy' as a 'specimen' of her poetic powers, upon which he levels the following criticism: 'the poetess is too much busied with external objects, too anxious to describe the outward accompaniments of melancholy, to write upon the feeling itself'. He goes on to argue that '[s]omething like this may be observed in Mrs. Radcliffe's romances, where our curiosity is too much interested about the evolution of the story, to permit our feelings to be acted upon by the distresses of the hero or heroine'.[38] In Scott's assessment, Smith enables her readers to feel melancholy whether she is writing poetry or prose, whereas Radcliffe has failed equally in both genres.

What happens when the poems are reprinted in other contexts does not entirely correlate with Scott's comparison. Early reprintings of Smith's 'To Night' in, for example, *The Gentleman's Magazine* and the *Town and Country Magazine*, in 1788 and 1789, specifically draw attention to Smith as the 'Author of *Emmeline*'.[39] When the poem is reprinted in the 1790s and the first decade of the nineteenth century, however, it is attributed to Smith, but the context of the novel has disappeared. We can account for this simply by noting that Smith incorporated 'To Night' and the other poems from *Emmeline* into the fifth edition of *Elegiac Sonnets*, published in 1789. In reprinting these sonnets, Smith explicitly directs the reader back to the novel by labelling the sequence 'From the Novel of Emmeline', a practice she continued for poems that appeared in her subsequent novels.[40] Anthologies that reprint 'To Night' eliminate this part of Smith's title and contextualize it among poems by other established authors. In Vicesimus Knox's *Extracts, elegant, instructive, and entertaining, in poetry* (1791), for example, 'To Night' appears in a sequence labelled 'Sonnets, by Smith', which is preceded by excerpts from Milton's *Lycidas* and followed by poems by Helen Maria Williams, William Shenstone, Richard Savage, William Collins, and Robert Burns.[41] In John Evans's *The Parnassian Garland; Or, Beauties of Modern Poetry* (1807), 'To Night' appears with poems by Samuel Taylor Coleridge, Samuel Rogers, and Robert Southey, as well as several by the translator and deacon John Langhorne and Alice Flowerdew, author of *Poems, on Moral and Religious Subjects* (1803).[42] In these explicitly educational collections of 'beauties' – Knox claims his collection is a 'vehicle for instruction' of young persons, and Evans announces his book is 'designed for the Use of Schools' – Smith's sonnets circulate as examples of elegant modern poetry without reference to their original publication context.[43]

By contrast, Radcliffe's reputation was primarily as a novelist, and even though her poems were employed to evaluate or denigrate her novels, the novels were central to the republication of her poems in magazines, anthologies, and collections. In the 1790s, reprintings of Radcliffe's 'Song of a Spirit' from *The Romance of the Forest* explicitly state that the poem has been excerpted from the novel.[44] In a twist that suggests the novel's popularity and wide readership, *The Gentleman's Magazine* for 1793 reprinted the poem but attributed it to the novel's heroine, Adeline.[45] More strikingly, references to the novel continue even after Radcliffe issued a free-standing collection of her verse in 1816. For example, in *Specimens of British Poetesses* (1825), the editor Alexander Dyce prefaces Radcliffe's entry with a note: 'Ann Radcliffe, Born 1764, died 1823. The well-known works of this lady are interspersed with pieces of poetry'.[46] Likewise, the editor of *The Female Poets of Great Britain* notes that Radcliffe's 'fame rests, as needs hardly to be said, upon her splendid but terrible novels *The Italian* and *The Mysteries of Udolpho*', but she was also 'a poetess of no mean pretensions. The pieces of verse interspersed in her various romances display the same peculiar powers which characterize her prose compositions'.[47] While Smith's entries in these same anthologies made brief, offhand mention of her novels, Radcliffe's novels actively defined her verse even as she was anthologized as a poet.

Even when no commentary was provided for reprinted poems, other forms of mediation suggest a reprinted poem's ongoing – or severed – relationship to the novel in which it initially appeared. In *The Poets of the Nineteenth Century* (1857), a series of Radcliffe's poems is preceded by an illustration showing a solitary figure looking over a river at a ruined castle by moonlight.[48] The engraving acts as a gothic set piece, connecting a 'wild romantic dream' where 'spectres raise the midnight chaunt' in the poem 'To Melancholy' to its original publication context in *The Mysteries of Udolpho*: in the novel, Emily sings the poem, accompanied by her lute, from behind a grated window in a ruined tower overlooking a lake.[49] The illustration even more directly represents a stanza in 'Song of a Spirit', also reprinted in the collection, where a 'lone wanderer' sees 'shadows dire that substance seem' in a 'ruin'd tower | Faintly shewn by moonlight gleam'; in *The Romance of the Forest*, this stanza in the poem foreshadows Adeline's encounters with shadowy forms during her narrow escape from the Marquis's chateau by moonlight.[50]

The selection of Smith's poems in the same collection is also prefaced by an illustration of a solitary figure beside a lake – but without the moon or the ruined castle and with the addition of a bird skimming the surface of the water. Despite the apparent similarity in the illustrations, they draw attention to concrete differences in the construction of each author's work and literary reputation.[51] The bird in the illustration of Smith's poems reflects the editor's choice to republish 'The Swallow' and 'The Departure of the Nightingale' along with a passage from 'Beachy Head' rife with references to birds and botany. But the 'lone wanderer' of the illustration comes from Sonnet XXXVI, a poem about being a poet. In the fifth edition of *Elegiac Sonnets*, this sonnet was accompanied by an illustration of 'sickening Fancy' throwing away her pencil while 'weary Hope reclines upon the tomb'. The poet longs for 'that tranquil shore | Where the pale spectre Care, pursues no more', but neither the illustration in *Elegiac Sonnets*, nor the one included in *The Poets of the Nineteenth Century* in 1857, admits the poem's explicitly gothic turn in the final lines. Rather, both emblematize the figure of the poet, and specifically a Romantic poet who trades in picturesque scenes and moulds descriptions of external nature to the poet's inward state.

The comparison I have drawn between Smith and Radcliffe indicates how specific poems like 'Song of a Spirit' constitute an afterlife for the novel in which they appeared. When this is the case, the novel tends to define the character of the poems regardless of the ostensible subject matter of the verse. (Smith's Sonnet XXXVI has as much gothic imagery as Radcliffe's 'Song'.) As this suggests, an author's literary reputation in their lifetime influenced whether or not the novel stuck to the poem through subsequent reprintings in educational miscellanies and anthologies of the 'most approved' poets, women poets, and so on. I have not yet accounted for reprintings in other types of collections, specifically those that collect a specific genre or are intended for educational uses other than teaching elocution. For example, Smith's 'To Night' appears in collections of sonnets, but also as an exercise in French and Spanish translation guides. I suspect this may be because of the cosmopolitanism and literary intertextuality of Smith's poems, but how and why her poems came to be used in these guides deserves further investigation. Radcliffe's 'Song of a Spirit' has a separate reprinting history in collections of songs, beginning with a shortened version that first appeared in *The poetry of various glees, songs, &c: as performed at the Harmonists* (1798). This modified version of the poem was subsequently reprinted in Thomas Park's revised edition of Joseph Ritson's *A Select Collection of English Songs, with their original airs* (1813), and again in *A Gallery of English and American Women Famous in Song* (1875). In 1885, it appeared once again in *Songs from the Novelists, from Elizabeth to Victoria*, edited by William Davenport Adam. In his Introduction to the volume, Adam rejects Scott's equivalence of Radcliffe's prose and verse but agrees with Barbauld's assessment that 'there are many elegant pieces of poetry interspersed through the volumes of Mrs. Radcliffe'. He goes on to lament that many of her poems remain 'hidden within the little-opened pages of *Romance of the Forest*. Mrs. Radcliffe, it may be recorded, published a volume of her verses. Alas! Who reads it now?'[52] While most collections of songs lose sight of the novel to focus on musical accompaniment, Adam follows the educational collections noted above by returning Radcliffe's poetry to its novelistic context: each poem includes a footnote that quotes the sentences directly preceding it in the novel. In doing so, Adam crystalizes the extent to which Radcliffe's original poetry had come to stand in for, and perhaps even displace, her novels in the second half of the nineteenth century. Radcliffe would always be remembered for having written in the outmoded and now little read subgenre of the gothic novel, even if what readers actually encountered in print were poems originally embedded in her fictions. The novel had become a footnote to its one-time poetic paratext.

Setting Smith against Radcliffe allows for a relatively tidy argument: authorial reputation – which might be collectively produced by the author, reviewers, editors, and publishers – combined with the novel's subgenre to determine whether a novel would have an afterlife through its embedded poetry. The case of Matthew Lewis's *The Monk* both reinforces and complicates this conclusion, particularly through reprintings of the ballad 'Alonzo the Brave and the Fair Imogene', which had a wider and longer republication history than any of the other poems I investigated for this essay (and quite possibly of any poem published in a novel in the 1790s). Like poems by Smith and Radcliffe, 'Alonzo the Brave' retained a strong connection to the novel in reviews and reprintings that followed its publication in 1796; like the novel proper, it also spawned an array of poetic parodies and imitations, as well as a melodrama, a burlesque, and even a ballet.[53] As with Smith's sonnets, soon after 'Alonzo the Brave' was reprinted in *Tales of Wonder* – a collection of original poems, imitations, and translations primarily by Lewis, Scott, and Southey that appeared under Lewis's name in 1801 – the poem occurs with poems by the cadre of Romantic poets involved in collecting, reprinting, and imitating German and Scottish folk ballads. In 1804, for example, 'Alonzo' was included in *Poems by Robert Southey, Lewis, and others, with the Life of Southey*; in *The Oddest of all Oddities*, 'Alonzo' is followed by Lewis's own parody of the poem from *Tales of Wonder*, 'Giles Jollop the Grave and Brown Sally Green'; in *Poetical Selections: Consisting of the Most Approved Pieces of Our Best Modern British Poets* (1811), Lewis's poem sets the stage for Southey's popular gothic ballad, 'Poor Mary, The Maid of the Inn'.[54] This coalition between Lewis, Southey, and Scott continued in 1820s reprints of the poem: *The Harp of Parnassus* reprints both 'Alonzo' and 'Mary' in a section titled 'Legendary Poetry', and the 1828 *Popular Ballads and Legendary Tales* groups 'Alonzo' with Lewis's 'Bonny Jane', Scott's 'Cadyow Castle', and Southey's 'Mary'.[55] In these collections, 'Alonzo' circulates as an example of a popular imitation of older ballads, not as part of *The Monk*.

Another reprinting trend for the poem developed in parallel to this one, which also erased the poem's original publication in Lewis's novel: like Smith's sonnets, Lewis's poems appeared in nineteenth-century educational miscellanies and elocutionary manuals. Beginning with its inclusion in Knox's *Elegant Extracts* in 1805 – where it was grouped with excerpts from Milton and Spenser, a selection of Smith's sonnets, and miscellaneous poems by Savage, Shenstone, Swift, Cowper, Goldsmith, Sir William Jones, Peter Pindar (a.k.a. John Wolcott), Thomas Campbell, and William Leslie Bowles in a section titled 'Sentimental, Lyrical and Ludicrous' – it was anthologized in *The Modern Speaker* in 1826, *The United States Speaker* in 1836, *Sam Weller's Budget of Recitations* in 1838, *The Theatrical Speaker* in 1840, *The General Reciter* in 1845, *Practical Elocution* in 1846, *The Reciter's Companion* in 1848, and *The New American Speaker* in 1851.[56] The poem is seldom attributed to Lewis in these elocutionary collections, but it is often subtitled 'A favorite Recitation', which indeed it was – so much so that it figured in scenes of recitation in novels published between 1813 and 1840.[57] In Catherine Cuthbertson's *Adelaide, or the Countercharm* (1813), for example, Lady Dinwood recites the poem in hopes that 'by her skillful management in emphasis, cadences, and fear-awakening starts and gestures' she would raise 'horror to its nervous susceptibility'.[58] The recitation fails to have the desired effect on her hearers, which is often the case in these scenes: the ballad's gothic content provokes horror in only the most feeble of characters, like 'poor little Miss Langrish' in Alicia Lefanu's *Strathallan* (1816).[59] As in Lefanu's novel, the poem is more often a trigger for the comedic exposure of a character's vanity, ignorance, or immorality. In *Strathallan*, Miss Mountain, a young Lady who considers herself 'a literary genius', exercises her skill at declamation by reciting 'the soul harrowing style of poetry she thought she excelled the most', a performance enhanced by her 'tall, bony form' and 'red rolling eye'.[60] As Lefanu's satire makes clear, a preference for 'Alonzo' signals a pedagogical failure, an argument made explicit in Mary White's *Beatrice; or, The Wycherly Family* (1824), where the narrator argues that the 'memory is the cabinet of the soul, and it should be filled with enlightening and precious things. But Lady Holt was quite satisfied if Beatrice said her arithmetical tables well, and repeated "Alonzo the Brave and the Fair Imogene" correctly and said "My name is Norval," suiting the word to the action, and the action to the word'.[61] Marked by its frequent inclusion in elocutionary textbooks, 'Alonzo the Brave' raises the spectre of the gothic novel only to have it subsumed into debates over female education. While Radcliffe's poems remained tied to her novels, the reprinting history of 'Alonzo' shows how a poem with explicitly gothic content that was published in a gothic novel became emblematic of an entirely different literary genre.

'Alonzo the Brave' continued to cameo in prose fiction throughout the 1840s and 1850s, making appearances in Harriet Gordon Smythies's *Cousin Geoffrey, the Old Bachelor* (1840), Cuthbertson's *Phoebe; Or, The Miller's*

Maid: A Romance of Deep Interest (1842), Jemima von Tautphoeus's *Quits* (1857), Charlotte Mary Yonge's *Dynevor Terrace, Or, The Clue of Life* (1857), and Charles Dickens's 'The Holly-Tree Inn' (1855) from the series *Household Words Christmas Stories*. In these novels and stories, the poem continues its association with education, and even more specifically, it signals the pretence to poetry's cultural capital assumed by upwardly mobile working- and lower middle-class characters like the rhyming miller's apprentice Tim Miggles in *Phoebe* or the laughable and dull Geraldine in *Cousin Geoffrey*.[62] While still pointing to the poem's popularity as a set recitation piece, a number of these later fictional citations also reinscribe the poem in its original publication in the gothic novel. In *Quits*, Arthur revisits his childhood nursery and finds well-worn copies of *The Mysteries of Udolpho* and *The Children of the Abbey* – a gothic novel by Regina Maria Roche published in 1796 – alongside Lewis's *Tales of Wonder*; the sight provokes a recitation of 'Alonzo the Brave', which had been 'fixed in his memory for life' by his nurse Ann Ducker.[63] The narrator of Dickens's 'The Holly-Tree Inn' similarly beguiles his time recalling the 'barbarous stories' told to him by his nurse, who had an 'authentic anecdote within her own experience, founded, I now believe, upon Raymond and Agnes or the Bleeding Nun'. Going over this section of *The Monk* in his mind makes him 'quite uncomfortable', and 'looking up at the darkness beyond the screen' he begins to study 'the wormy curtains creeping in and creeping out, like the worms in the ballad of Alonzo the brave and the fair Imogene'.[64] As in Cuthbertson's *The Hut and the Castle: A Romance* (1823) – which conflates Raymond's carriage ride with the bleeding nun with Imogene's forced descent into the grave with Alonzo – Dickens represents how prose and verse have become fused on memory's tablet.[65] Both stand in for the gothic terrors of a Victorian childhood filtered through voices of witch-like old nurses, but the poem's creeping worms – its language and anaphoric structure – stick in the mind, overwriting Lewis's prose. Gothic fiction of the 1790s continues to haunt the Victorian novel, but only as a spectral iamb (or, more accurately in the case of 'Alonzo', a spectral anapest).

Notes

1 Barbara Benedict, 'The Paradox of the Anthology: Collecting and *Différence* in Eighteenth-Century Britain', *New Literary History*, 34:2 (2003), 231–56 (231).
2 J. Paul Hunter, *Before Novels: The Cultural Contexts of Eighteenth-Century English Fiction* (New York: W. W. Norton, 1990).

3 G. Gabrielle Starr, *Lyric Generations: Poetry and the Novel in the Long Eighteenth Century* (Baltimore: Johns Hopkins University Press, 2004), pp. 6–13.

4 David A. Brewer, *The Afterlife of Character, 1726–1825* (Philadelphia: University of Pennsylvania Press, 2005), p. 35. Brewer argues that the surrogacy is enhanced by this incorporation of mock-epistle, but we might also read this as the novel subsuming its own outgrowths into the form of a paratext that exists to serve the novel's cause.

5 Henry Fielding, *The History of the Adventures of Joseph Andrews*, 2 vols. (London: A. Millar, 1742), vol. 1, p. v; Henry Fielding, *The History of Tom Jones*, 4 vols. (London: A. Millar, 1749), vol. 1, p. 153.

6 Jerome McGann, *Byron and Romanticism* (Cambridge University Press, 2002), p. 278.

7 'embed | imbed, v.', *Oxford English Dictionary Online*, www.oed.com/view/Entry/60835 (accessed 14 September 2014).

8 Leah Price, *The Anthology and the Rise of the Novel: From Richardson to George Eliot* (Cambridge University Press, 2000), p. 91.

9 Price, *Anthology*, p. 98.

10 Mary Favret, 'Telling Tales about Genre: Poetry in the Romantic Novel', *Studies in the Novel*, 26:2 (1994), 153–72.

11 Favret, 'Telling Tales', p. 166.

12 Ingrid Horrocks, '"Her ideas arranged themselves": Re-membering Poetry in Radcliffe', *Studies in Romanticism*, 47:4 (2008), 507–27 (517).

13 Horrocks, 'Re-membering', p. 520.

14 Ann Wierda Rowland, 'Romantic Poetry and the Romantic Novel', in *The Cambridge Companion to British Romantic Poetry*, eds. James Chandler and Maureen McLane (Cambridge University Press, 2008), pp. 117–35 (130).

15 Marshall Brown's 'Poetry and the Novel' is an exception to this rule. Brown emphasizes the generic mixture of the 'Romantic novel' and contends that poetry in Smith's *Old Manor House* functions to reveal that ungraspability of feeling, while also giving 'privileged access to the unplumbed and unthought'. By attending to poetry in Walter Scott's novels, Brown suggests that 'verse communicates not perfect knowledge but the limits of the knowable'; the mixture of forms in the 'Romantic novel' thus 'overlays disparate and imperfect explanatory frameworks': 'Poetry and the Novel', in *The Cambridge Companion to Fiction in the Romantic Period*, eds. Richard Maxwell and Katie Trumpener (Cambridge University Press, 2008), pp. 107–28 (113–15, 121–22).

16 Rowland, 'Romantic Poetry', p. 118.

17 Sydney Owenson, *The Wild Irish Girl, A National Tale* (1806), ed. Kathryn Kirkpatrick (Oxford University Press, 1999), p. 80.

18 I hesitate to say Owenson was unequivocal in her support. The gothic turn of the novel's concluding pages, in which two Englishmen, father and son, both stake a claim to Glorvina's hand, raises questions about the terms on which Ireland's political marriage to England was carried out.

19 Charlotte Smith, *Emmeline, The Orphan of the Castle* (1788), ed. Loraine Fletcher (Peterborough, Ont.: Broadview Press, 2003), p. 386.

20 Smith, *Emmeline*, p. 386.

21 Smith, *Emmeline*, pp. 385–87.

22 Charlotte Smith, *Elegiac Sonnets, with additional sonnets and other poems*, 5th edn (London: T. Cadell, 1789), p. 39.

23 Ann Radcliffe, *The Romance of the Forest* (1791), ed. Chloe Chard (Oxford University Press, 1999), p. 297.

24 Radcliffe, *Romance*, p. 282.

25 Samuel Taylor Coleridge and William Wordsworth, *Lyrical Ballads, and other poems* (1800), vol. 1, p. xiv, rpt. in *Lyrical Ballads, an electronic scholarly edition*, ed. Bruce Graver and Ron Tetreault, *Romantic Circles*, http://archive.rc.umd.edu/editions/LB/index.html (accessed 31 August 2014).

26 Reviews of *Emmeline*, rpt. in Smith, *Emmeline*, pp. 477–82.

27 See, for example, the review of *Emmeline* in *The Monthly Review*, which quotes Mrs Stafford's complaints about her dealings with lawyers and her unhappy marriage: *Monthly Review; or Literary Journal*, 79 (July–December 1788), 243–44.

28 Price, *Anthology*, p. 95.

29 Walter Scott, 'Prefatory Memoir', *The Works of Mrs. Ann Radcliffe*, Ballantyne's Novelist's Library, 10 vols. (London: Hurst, Robinson, and Co., 1821–24), vol. 10, p. iv.

30 Scott, 'Prefatory Memoir', vol. 10, pp. vi, xxxv.

31 *The Critical Review*, 19 (1797), 198.

32 *The European Magazine, and London Review*, 31 (January–June 1797), 112, 111.

33 *The Critical Review*, 65 (1788), 532.

34 For studies that focus on the reception of Romantic authors by Victorian authors, see Andrew Elfenbein, *Byron and the Victorians* (Cambridge University Press, 1995) and Stephen Gill, *Wordsworth and the Victorians* (Oxford University Press, 1998). Although primarily focused on prominent authors' reception of Wordsworth, Gill's study does include a chapter that examines how Victorian editions of Wordsworth were marketed via illustrations: Gill, *Wordsworth*, pp. 81–113. For studies that treat the posthumous afterlives of Romantic authors, see Sarah Wootton, *Consuming Keats: Nineteenth-Century Representations in Art and Culture* (Basingstoke: Palgrave Macmillan, 2006); and the essays by Lisa Vargo, Julie Crane, Andrew Bennett, and Sarah Wooton in *Romantic Echoes in the Victorian Era*, eds. Andrew Radford and Mark Sandy (Aldershot: Ashgate, 2008), pp. 15–66.

35 Tom Mole, 'Lord Byron and the End of Fame', *International Journal of Cultural Studies*, 11:3 (2008), 343–61 (351).

36 Full text searches of scanned books available through Google Books, Archive.org, the HathiTrust, and Eighteenth-Century Collections Online are limited by the quality of Optical Character Recognition (OCR) scanning and the number of scanned texts. As Ryan Cordell succinctly puts it, '"dirty" OCR forces more creative search techniques from scholars mining archives for specific treasure, and scholars must be content knowing their results will be incomplete': '"Taken Possession of": The Reprinting and Reauthorship of

Hawthorne's "Celestial Railroad" in the Antebellum Religious Press', *digital humanities quarterly*, 7:1 (2013), www.digitalhumanities.org/dhq/vol/7/1/000144/000144.html (accessed 28 August 2014). Cordell's work tracking republications of Hawthorn's 'Celestial Railroad' is one example of how collaboration between literary scholars and computer scientists can improve the reliability and scope of searches on OCR-scanned texts by using n-gram shingling. For a detailed description of this method, see David Smith, Ryan Cordell, and Elizabeth Maddock Dillon, 'Infectious Texts: Modeling Text Reuse in Nineteenth-Century Newspapers', *IEEE Workshop on Big Data and the Humanities*, 2013, www.viraltexts.org/infect-bighum-2013.pdf (accessed 9 September 2014).

37 Walter Scott, *Miscellaneous Prose Works*, 6 vols. (Boston: Wells and Lily, 1829), vol. 4, pp. 12, 33, 39.

38 Walter Scott, 'Prefatory Memoir', vol. 10, p. xxxviii.

39 *The Gentleman's Magazine*, 63 (1788), 335; 'Sonnet. By Mrs. Smith, Author of Emmeline', *The Town and Country Magazine*, 20 (1788), 382.

40 Charlotte Smith, *Elegiac Sonnets*, 5th edn, pp. 38–40.

41 *Extracts, elegant, instructive, and entertaining, in poetry*, ed. Vicesimus Knox, 2 vols. (London: Messrs. Rivingtons et al., 1791), vol. 2, p. 243.

42 *The Parnassian Garland; or, Beauties of Modern Poetry*, ed. John Evans (London: Albion Press, 1807), p. 146.

43 Knox, Preface, *Extracts*, n.p.; Evans, *Parnassian Garland*, t.p.

44 *The Lady's Magazine*, 23 (1792), 607–8; *The European Magazine, and London Review*, 22 (July–December 1792), 237; *The New-York Magazine*, 6 (1795), 696–97.

45 *The Gentleman's Magazine*, 68 (1798), 428. While less frequently than Smith's, Radcliffe's poems also found a place in collections like *The Poetical Commonplace Book: Consisting of an Original Selection of Standard and Fugitive Poetry* (1822), which included poems by Coleridge, Scott, Southey, Blair, Cowper, Gay, Procter, Lewis, Collins, Opie, Hemans, Bloomfield, and Shelley, among others.

46 *Specimens of British Poetesses*, ed. Alexander Dyce (London: T. Rodd, 1827), pp. 340–42.

47 *The Female Poets of Great Britain*, ed. Frederic Rowton ([1848]; Philadelphia: Carey and Hart, 1849), pp. 269–70.

48 *The Poets of the Nineteenth Century*, ed. Robert Aris Willmott (London: George Routledge and Co., 1857), p. 72.

49 Ann Radcliffe, *The Mysteries of Udolpho: A Romance; Interspersed with Some Pieces of Poetry*, 2nd edn, 4 vols. (London: G. G. and J. Robinson, 1794), vol. 4, p. 409.

50 Ann Radcliffe, *The Romance of the Forest, interspersed by some pieces of poetry*, 3 vols. (London: T. Hookham and J. Carpenter, 1791), vol. 2, p. 131.

51 Surveying the illustrations in this volume, it is clear that they were carefully paired with the poems: Hannah More's 'Florio and his Friend' follows a group portrait of young men of fashion in full eighteenth-century dress; Bowles's

'On the Rhine' is interrupted by an illustration of a small vessel sailing on a steep-banked river where 'castles, like prisons of despair, | Frown as we pass!'; and Bowles's 'Landing at Tynemouth' is preceded by an accurate depiction of Tynemouth at low tide: Willmott, *Poets of the Nineteenth Century*, pp. 78, 89, 97.

52 *Songs from the Novelists, from Elizabeth to Victoria*, ed. William Davenport Adam (London: Ward and Downey, 1885), p. xx.

53 For reviews of *The Monk* that mention or reprint 'Alonzo the Brave', see *The Monthly Review*, 23 (May–August 1797), 451 and *The Monthly Mirror*, 2 (October 1796), 324–28. For 1790s reprints of the poem that link it to the novel, see *The Lady's Magazine, or Entertaining Companion for the Fair Sex*, 27 (1796), 373–74; *Spirit of the Public Journals for 1797* (London: R. Phillips, 1798), pp. 199–201; *The Annual Register, Or, A View of the History, Politics, and Literature for the year 1797* (London: W. Otridge and Sons et al., 1800), pp. 445–47. For parodies, see Charles Few, *A Parody Upon the Poem of Alonzo the Brave and the Fair Imogene.* (London: Laurie and Whittle, 1799); *The Sporting Magazine, or Monthly Calendar*, 15 (February 1800), 270; Samuel Jackson Pratt, 'Parody on Alonzo the Brave', *Harvest-home*, 3 vols. (London: Richard Phillips, 1805), vol. 3, pp. 268–71; Egerton Smith, 'Reconciliation of St. George and Caroline', *The Melange: A Variety of Original Pieces in Prose and Verse* (Liverpool: Egerton Smith and Co., 1831), pp. 136–38; 'Alonzo the Brave and the Fair Imogene', *The Wide World Songster* (London: Music-Publishing Company, [1863]), pp. 8–11. For theatrical and musical adaptations, see *Monstrous Good Songs, Sentiments & Toasts ... to which are Added the Celebrated Spanish Ballad of Alonzo the Brave and the Fair Imogine, as Sung and Recited by G. Saville Carey ...* (London: R. Rusted and J. Parsons, 1798); Charles Louis Didelot, *Alonzo the Brave and The Fair Imogine: A Grand Ballet, in Three Acts.* (London: Bastie and Brettell, 1801); Henry M. Milner, *Alonzo the Brave and the Fair Imogene: Or, The Spectre Bride! A Legendary Romantic Melo-drama, in Two Acts* (London: John Duncombe, 1826); *Playbill of Humber-Street Theatre, 1827, Announcing Alonzo the Brave; Or, The Spectre Bride, A Pas Seul, The Force of Love. Or, The Doctor Outwitted, The Death of Nelson and The Warlock Etc.* (Hull: Thomas Topping, 1827); Francis Cowley Burnand, *A Tragical, Comical, Demoniacal, and Whatever-you-like-to-call-it Burlesque, Uniting in Its Construction the Romantic Pathos of the Well-known Ballad, 'Alonzo and Imogene', with the Thrilling Horrors of Goethe's Tragedy, 'Faust and Marguerite'* (Cambridge: W. Metcalfe, [1857?]).

54 *Poems by Robert Southey, Lewis, and others, with the Life of Southey* (Paris: Parsons and Galignani, 1804), p. 40–43; *The Oddest of all Oddities, being an Odd Book of all the Odd Sermons that have been Preached in the Fields* (London: S. Bailey, [1810?]), pp. 14–18; *Poetical Selections: Consisting of the Most Approved Pieces of Our Best Modern British Poets ...* (Birmingham: Thomson and Wrightson, 1811), pp. 120–26.

55 *The Harp of Parnassus: a New Selection of Classical English Poetry*, ed. John Fitzgerald Pennie (London: G. and W. B. Whittaker, 1822), pp. 306–12;

Popular Ballads and Legendary Tales, Selected from the Most Eminent Writers (Glasgow: Richard Griffin and Co., 1828), pp. 110–24.

56 *Elegant Extracts or Useful and Entertaining Pieces of Poetry*, ed. Vicesimus Knox (London: J. Johnson et al., 1805), pp. 310–11; *The Modern Speaker; Containing Selections from the Works of our most Approved Authors in Prose and Verse*, ed. Leman Thomas Rede (London: George Virtue, 1826), pp. 127–29; *The United States Speaker: A Copious Selection of Exercises in Elocution*, ed. John Epy Lovell (Charleston: S. Babcock and Co., 1836), pp. 323–25; *Sam Weller's Budget of Recitations* (London: J. Clements, 1838), pp. 73–74; *The Theatrical Speaker: A Selection of the Newest and Most Popular Recitations of the Present Day* (Paisley: Caldwell and Son, 1840), pp. 11–15; *The General Reciter; A Unique Selection of the Most Admired and Popular Readings and Recitations* (Halifax: William Milner, 1845), pp. 72–74; *Practical Elocution: Containing Illustrations of the Principles of Reading and Public Speaking*, ed. Samuel Niles Sweet (Troy: Merriam, Moore and Co., 1846), pp. 345–48; *The Reciter's Companion; Comprising the Most Popular Recitations, Comic Tales, Dramatic Readings and Queer Stories* (London: W. Strange, [1848?]), pp. 218–20; *The New American Speaker: A Collection of Oratorical and Dramatical Pieces*, ed. John Celivergos Zachos (New York: Collins and Brother, 1851), pp. 197–99.

57 *Sam Weller's Budget*, p. 73.

58 Catherine Cuthbertson, *Adelaide, or, the Countercharm: A Novel*, 5 vols. (London: G. and S. Robinson, and Cradock and Joy, 1813), vol. 4, pp. 187–88.

59 Alicia Lefanu, *Strathallan*, 2nd edn, 4 vols. (London: Sherwood, Neely, and Jones, 1816), vol. 1, pp. 193–94.

60 Lefanu, *Strathallan*, vol. 1, p. 194.

61 Mary White, *Beatrice; or, The Wycherly Family*, 4 vols. (London: A. K. Newman and Co., 1824), vol. 1, p. 24.

62 [Catherine Cuthbertson?], *Phoebe; or, The Miller's Maid: A Romance of Deep Interest* (London: E. Lloyd, 1842), p. 156; Harriet Gordon Smythies, *Cousin Geoffrey, the Old Bachelor: A Novel*, ed. Theodore Edward Hook, 3 vols. (London: Richard Bentley, 1840), vol. 1, pp. 223–24.

63 Jemima von Tautphoeus, *Quits: A Novel*, 2 vols. (Leipzig: Barnhard Tauchnitz, 1858), vol. 1, pp. 164–65.

64 Charles Dickens, 'The Holly-Tree Inn, being the extra Christmas Number of Household Words' (1855), *Household Words Christmas Stories, 1851–1858* (London: Ward, Lock and Tyler, [1870?]), pp. 4–5.

65 Catherine Cuthbertson, *The Hut and the Castle: A Romance*, 4 vols. (London: Hurst, Robinson and Co., 1823), vol. 2, p. 215.

CHAPTER 8

Rethinking Fictionality in the Eighteenth-Century Puppet Theatre

David A. Brewer

In recent years, following the pioneering work of Catherine Gallagher, a rough consensus has emerged that the mid-eighteenth century saw the advent of fictionality in something like its modern form. By this account, prior to, say, the 1740s, we have stories that purport to be true (what Nicholas Paige terms 'pseudofactual' narratives) and stories that are patently untrue, exercises in pure fantasy.[1] After then, we get tales that are true in broad mimetic or probabilistic terms, but that concern 'nobody in particular': that is, tales that are realistic, rather than real.[2] Notwithstanding Gallagher's own caveat that some stories 'asked the reader to switch back and forth between [the] referential and nonreferential', our general presumption has been that the beings who inhabit eighteenth-century narrative fall on one side or the other of this ontological divide.[3] Either they refer to actual persons, historic or contemporary, *or* they are wholly fictional (and so do not represent any specific individual, though they may exemplify a type). They are, to use the terms made famous by Gallagher, either Somebodies *or* Nobodies.

Despite the often exhilarating insights that this work has opened up (and it may well be the single most exciting development in novel theory of the past quarter century), we remain curiously unable to account for the ways in which the beings we encounter could apparently operate on multiple ontological planes at once. Yet even the most cursory dip into the history of reading in the period will yield examples of figures being regarded as both referential *and* fictional, Somebody *and* Nobody. For instance, neither category seems adequate to describe the blend of fictionality and reference

I am grateful to Kevin Bourque, John Chalmers, Daniel Cook, Darryl Domingo, Rob Hume, Tom Lockwood, Nush Powell, Nick Seager, Kathleen Wilson, Anne Wohlcke, and, as always, Rebecca Morton for their help and encouragement. I could not even have conceived of this essay, much less written it, without the provocation and support, over the past two decades, of Cathy Gallagher. What follows should be taken as a testament to how good her work is to think with, even when I want to push in a different direction.

we get in someone like Beau Didapper. Nor are they any better at capturing the peculiar mixture of typicality and singularity characteristic of, say, Roderick Random. And these are comparatively simple examples. Far more complicated cases abound, both in these specific texts (Joseph Andrews himself; Miss Williams) and in the age more generally. We have come to recognize how subtle and complex other aspects of eighteenth-century representational practice can be (think only of the slipperiness of mock-form); it seems high time for us to rethink our stock ways of talking about fictionality and reference.

One of the best ways in which to begin is to tease out the theory implicit in these practices, especially their more playful and self-reflexive varieties. This is not the programmatic theory announced in prefaces and dedications, much less formal aesthetic treatises, but rather a kind of vernacular theory (on the model of vernacular architecture): an only half-articulated and non-systematic, but nonetheless coherent way of doing things. As such, it is more a matter of patterns and tendencies than grand pronouncements, which can be frustrating for anyone seeking a straightforward manifesto of first principles. But such frustrations are more than made up for by how much closer to the proverbial ground this mode of enquiry can take us. Put simply, reconstructing vernacular theories of fictionality and reference allows us to better grasp how representation actually worked in the world – a goal which ought to be at the heart of any literary history worthy of the name.

Perhaps counterintuitively, one of the most provocative sources of such a theory lies not in the novelistic narratives that the term 'fiction' now conjures up, but rather in a realm that would seem far more of an antiquarian curiosity: the high-end puppet theatre of the mid-eighteenth century, particularly its productions of two scripts by Henry Fielding – *The Author's Farce* and *The Covent Garden Tragedy*. This might seem an unlikely avenue to pursue. Our stock associations with eighteenth-century puppets, such as they are, tend to involve travelling showmen and the great London fairs, which is to say supposedly 'low', 'popular', 'plebeian' entertainment: Bible stories and ballad narratives, punctuated by the casual violence of Punch and Joan – not the most promising territory to explore the emergence of the deep, 'round' subjectivity that still characterizes most of our accounts of the 'rise of the novel'. Yet an objection along these lines not only betrays a misunderstanding of eighteenth-century puppetry (which James Ralph termed one of 'the Standard *Entertainments* of the present Age'), but also highlights the source of our current dilemma: namely, the fact that we have taken a small subset of novelistic characters (those presented in a manner that encourages the illusion of individual subjectivity), pronounced them to be representative of fictional beings as a whole, and then regarded types, personifications, historical personages, and figures *à clef* as departures or fallings-off from that supposed norm.[4] Not surprisingly, then, the genres and media in which that particular kind of illusion was not the chief desideratum have been pushed to the side in our conceptions of fictionality (as has our ability to notice the referential in even the most seemingly self-contained kinds of novelistic fiction).[5]

However, the eighteenth century was far more willing to see the continuities between different forms and media. In *Jonathan Wild* (1743), for example, Fielding insists that, in puppet theatre, 'no one is ashamed . . . of helping on the *Drama*, calling the several Sticks . . . by the Names which the Master hath allotted to them. . . . The Truth is, they are in the same Situation with the Readers of *Romances*; who, though they know the whole to be one entire Fiction, nevertheless agree to be deceived; and . . . find Ease and Convenience in the Concurrence'.[6] Accordingly, I propose we set aside our default sense of fiction as first and foremost the domain of the so-called realist novel (with its apparent commitment to depth and interiority) and see where the affinities that Fielding points out might lead us.[7]

In order to do so, however, we first have to reconstruct the operations of the high-end puppet theatre, since any preconceptions we might have of puppetry as mere 'popular' entertainment are only likely to lead us astray. Beginning in the early eighteenth century, ambitious puppeteers erected permanent playhouses at the London fairs, giving them, on a smaller scale, most of the standard features of their counterparts at Covent Garden and Drury Lane. Their seating areas were divided into boxes, pit, and one or more galleries; there were curtains; there was at least the basic infrastructure for lighting, music, and moveable scenery.[8] And these theatres (and the fairs more generally) could attract a far broader social range than our current conceptions of them tend to allow: for example, the Prince and Princess of Wales took in a Southwark Fair puppet show in 1738 and 'express[ed] great Satisfaction'.[9] Around the same time, small buildings in the West End were retrofitted for year-round use by puppeteers and other non-patent theatre. In 1711–13, Martin Powell performed in the Little Piazza, Covent Garden, where he offered 'a Place Commodious and fit to receive the Nobility and Gentry of both Sexes'.[10] This sounds like puffery, but at least some of his patrons were, in fact, drawn from those ranks: Lord Bolingbroke (in whose lap the young Mary Granville, later Mrs Delany, sat), Catherine Hyde (the future Duchess of Queensbury),

Addison, and Steele. Similarly, in the spring of 1745, a Mr Russell staged a puppet show mocking Italian opera (to which 'several Persons of the first Quality' lent 'real Diamonds') at 'Mr. *Hickford's* Great Room, in *Brewer's-Street*', just south of Golden Square.[11] Three years later, a 'Madame *De La NASH*' (most likely Fielding in drag) 'fitted up in the most elegant Manner' 'her large BREAKFASTING-ROOM for the Nobility and Gentry in *Panton-street*, near the *Haymarket*, where she will sell the very best of TEA, COFFEE, CHOCOLATE, and JELLIES', while entertaining 'the Company Gratis with that Excellent ... Entertainment, called A PUPPET-SHEW' (charging for drinks and providing a play for free was a popular 1740s strategy for working around the Licensing Act).[12] At least according to the papers, the demand was such that 'a great many Persons of the politest Taste' attended even the rehearsals.[13] Moreover, as part of his courtship of Melinda, Roderick Random 'became acquainted with a good many people of fashion, and spent [his] time in the modish diversions of the town', including 'puppet-shews'.[14] Certainly the pricing at these productions, while not as high as what the patent theatres charged, was expensive enough to preclude a good chunk of the population from regularly attending: in 1738, Charlotte Charke was asking three shillings for the boxes, two for the pit, one for the 'Rail'd Gallery' and 6d for the 'Upper Gallery'.[15]

And it was not just the rooms and at least some portions of the audience that were, as the playbill for a puppet version of *Doctor Faustus* put it, 'fitted up in a genteel manner': the marionettes themselves were something to behold.[16] Charke, for example, 'spared for no Cost to make [their clothes] splendidly magnificent, and the Scenes were agreeable' to that standard. It cost her 'some Hundreds', but her show 'was allowed to be the most elegant that was ever exhibited'.[17] Similarly, Isaac Fawkes boasted that 'the clothes, scenes, and decorations' in his puppet version of 'the comical tragedy of *Tom Thumb*' were 'entirely new', while Thomas Yeates proclaimed his 'Large Operatical' puppets to be 'the richest ... Figures ever seen in England'.[18]

Even more striking, however, was the size of many of these puppets. Traditional fairground marionettes were '*Figures as large as Children two years old*' – that is, a little more than two feet tall.[19] The ones exhibited at most of the indoor theatres (and many of the more ambitious booths at the fairs), on the other hand, were 'Figures four Foot and a half high ... quite different from all Common Poppet-shows' – or even 'five Foot high'.[20] And while these measurements would suggest that they were only 'nearly as large as life', it is not clear that the missing inches registered as much of a

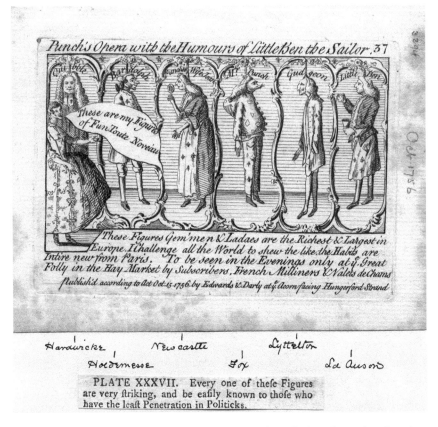

8.1 *Punch's Opera with the Humours of Little Ben the Sailor* (London: Edwards and
Darly, 1756)

difference.[21] In 1735, the Abbé Prévost reported to his Parisian readers
on 'une autre invention de l'art', an opera performed in London by
'Marionettes de grandeur humaine', while a mock-playbill for 'the Norfolk
Company of artificiall Commedians at ROBINS great Theatricall Booth
PALACE YARD' (that is, the Walpole administration) highlighted the
debut of 'a new sett of Puppets as big as the Life'.[22] Indeed, the only
depictions of these puppets that I have been able to discover show them as
on the same scale as their presenters and audience (figs. 8.1 and 8.2).[23]
As these images suggest, the bodies of the puppets (most likely made of
wax to reduce their weight) were supported from above by a rod, and their
operators had enough strings to control the marionettes' limbs, move

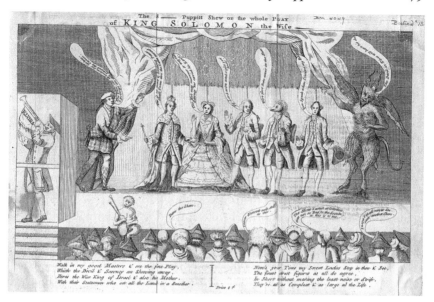

8.2   *The S—— Puppitt Shew or the whole Play of King Solomon the Wise*
(London: E. Sumpter, 1763)

their mouths, roll their eyes, and otherwise give them 'all the just motions and gestures of human life'.[24]

But what set the most interesting and ambitious puppets apart from their colleagues were their heads. All eighteenth-century marionettes have painted heads, either carved out of wood or cast in wax. Usually they are grotesque and in no danger of resembling a real person. At the high-end theatres, however, the heads would often be fashioned to look like celebrities (which may explain their suitability for the political satire of figs. 8.1 and 8.2). Pope reported to John Knight that the public was looking forward to seeing the coronation of George II 'again in a puppet-show, which is to recommend itself by another qualification, of having the exact portraits of the most conspicuous faces of our nobility in wax-work'.[25] Similarly, Charke 'bought Mezzotinto's of several eminent Persons, and had the Faces [of her puppets] carved from them'.[26] For example, 'the part of Hunter' in *The Beggar's Wedding* was played by 'Farinelli, taken from the Picture of that celebrated Singer'.[27] That is, the performer taking on the role of 'the reputed son' of '*Chaunter*, King of the Beggars' was a puppet carved to look like Farinelli, the castrato who so dominated Italian opera in the mid-1730s that 'it was said, in the Pit, after one of his Songs,

ONE GOD, ONE FARINELLI!'[28] And in the spring of 1748, Nash 'added' to her production of *Fair Rosamond* 'the Comical Execution of *Mr.* PUPPET FUT, *Esq; Grocer and Mimic*', suggesting that she had a puppet carved to look like Samuel Foote, who had been doing an impression of Fielding just around the corner.[29]

Perhaps the most intriguing evidence of puppets that resembled actual individuals, though, is to be found in the *Female Spectator's* account of 'that Puppet-Shew Project, which at present engrosses the Attention of some of our Nobility': a production being organized by 'the Ladies of the Beau-monde' to mock prominent Cits.[30] According to its promoter, 'not a Face in the City of any Note, but ... is to be taken off to the Life ...; and let me alone to mimic their Voices'.[31] The puppets were 'large' and apparently good likenesses of their referents: 'this is Alderman *Brawn*—as like as two P's,—mind his Treble Chin—his Pent-house Eyebrows, and his promontary Belly;—and this is Mrs. Puppet *Atlas*, ... a *Director's Wife*. You would swear 'twas she herself.—Lady *Betty* dressed the Alderman, and Lady *Charlotte*, the *Director's Wife*'.[32] Euphrosine, a member of the club responsible for the journal, 'proposes, by Way of Retort, to make a Party among her City-Friends, and have another of the same Nature presented at *Guildhall*', 'all the Persons and Places to be represented to the Life'.[33] Euphrosine's counter-production would involve several dozen quite specific-sounding puppets, such as 'Sir *Dubious Eitherway* in Petticoats, and a long Riding-Hood, skulking into a Hedge Tavern near *Charing-Cross*'.[34] The names here are the standard abstractions of comedy, but the terms on which the ladies' project is described make it clear that these marionettes stand in for actual persons: a mildly critical observer describes their play as an attempt 'to revive ... the old *Comedy*' – Aristophanic satire of particular individuals – 'in a *Puppet-Shew*'.[35] And the casual way in which the Female Spectator presumes her readers are already familiar with the scheme ('that Puppet-Shew Project ...') suggests that this show – or at least the plans for such a show – was the talk of the town in spring 1745.[36]

The last thing to consider before we turn back to the ways in which the high-end puppet theatre can serve as a sort of vernacular theory is the issue of repertory. Until the early eighteenth century, the stock plays of English puppetry (and fairground theatre more generally) were a hodgepodge of Bible stories, classical mythology, folk tales, and historical anecdotes. So, for example, at any given puppet show, one might encounter *Arden of Faversham*, *Bateman's Ghost*, *The Children in the Wood*, *The Creation of the World* (accompanied by *Noah's Flood* and *Dives and Lazarus*), *Friar Bacon and Friar Bungay*, *Jephtha's Rash Vow*, *Judith and Holofernes*, *Mother*

Shipton, Patient Grissel, St. George and the Dragon, The Siege of Troy, or *Whittington and his Cat*. What one would not find is much in the way of stories or figures less than a century old. There was no overlap between the puppet and live theatres in terms of scripts and very little in terms of subject matter (though both would occasionally offer stories from English history, such as *Jane Shore*). There is certainly nothing to suggest any real cross-fertilization beyond what we get in Jonson's *Bartholomew Fair*.

Starting in the early eighteenth century, however, the indoor puppet theatres and some of the more ambitious showmen at the fairs began to present plays from the live repertory, including *The Beggar's Opera*, Colley Cibber's *Damon and Phillida*, Henry Carey's *The Dragon of Wantley*, *Henry IV* (presumably Part 1), *Henry VIII*, Lewis Theobald's *Perseus and Andromeda, Richard III, The State of Innocence* (Dryden's opera based on *Paradise Lost*), and ballad opera versions of both *A Harlot's Progress* and *A Rake's Progress*.[37] The most popular crossover offerings, though, were by Fielding (*The Author's Farce, The Covent Garden Tragedy, The Mock Doctor, The Old Debauchees*, and *Tom Thumb*), and it is with an extended look at the first two that I would like to consider the ways in which the high-end puppet theatre can illuminate the relation between fictionality and reference.

As a show for live performers, *The Author's Farce* was the single most performed play of the 1729–30 season, with forty-two performances at the Little Theatre in the Haymarket. Thomas Lockwood estimates that 'even allowing for many repeat customers . . ., some 20,000 people would have seen' the play 'during its first run', including the Prince of Wales (twice) and the Earl of Egmont.[38] There were perhaps another fifty-four performances of just the third act at Tottenham Court Fair that summer,[39] sixteen performances of the whole thing at the Haymarket the following season, one more in 1732, followed by a moderately successful revival at Drury Lane in 1734 (six performances) and two unsuccessful attempts (at Covent Garden and the Haymarket) in 1748.

The Author's Farce is, of course, an odd hybrid in terms of form. Its first two acts are lightly satiric comedy about the inability of a playwright, Luckless, to get his tragedy staged. Without a theatrical performance, the booksellers have no interest in it, and without money from either the playhouses or the booksellers, Luckless cannot pay his rent and so must either submit to the advances of his termagant landlady or lose access to his true love, her daughter, Harriot. However, these two acts, which are engaging, but fairly conventional (indeed, Fielding was accused of 'steal[ing]' a scene from Farquhar's *Love in a Bottle*),[40] are followed by a

surreal and utterly delightful third act that purports to be the puppet show
to which Luckless resorts after his tragic ambitions have been dashed.
The latter, 'The Pleasures of the Town', is a ballad opera about suitors
competing for the hand of the Goddess of Nonsense, and as Luckless
explains, its 'Scene is laid on the other side of the River *Styx*, so all the
People of the Play are Ghosts'.[41] A number of these ghosts have names that
suggest they are 'personifications of ... various dramatic forms': '*Signior*
Opera, *Don* Tragedio', '*Sir* Farcical Comick', '*Monsieur* Pantomime'.[42]
And they perform in ways that highlight their typicality: Signior Opera
communicates only through song, while Don Tragedio speaks exclusively
in heroic couplets, and Monsieur Pantomime just '*Makes Signs*'.[43] Yet they
are also given attributes (probably augmented by additional 'visual burlesque') that seem to solicit the audience to see them as at least partial stand-
ins for particular individuals.[44] For example, Don Tragedio's fondness for
anadiplosis ('And, had not Hisses, Hisses me dismay'd, | By this, I'd write
Two-score, Two-score, by Jay'd') may invite identification of him as
Theobald, though the trope is similarly overused by Osborne Sydney
Wandesford.[45] To make things still more baroque, Sir Farcical Comick
has lines – most notably, 'Stap my Vitals' – that explicitly echo ones made
famous by Lord Foppington, the role in John Vanbrugh's *The Relapse* that
Cibber monopolized for decades.[46] At the same time, though, Sir Farcical
says and sings things that encourage the audience to identify him as Cibber
the playwright and Poet Laureate, without the mediation of a theatrical
role. To add yet another layer, in the live performances, the 'Persons in the
PUPPET-SHOW' were, in fact, persons: flesh and blood actors, or, as
Jack Pudding puts it in his busking for the show, 'living Figures – some of
them Six foot high' (the Tottenham Court production trumpeted this
innovation as 'No Wires, all alive').[47] And in case these complications upon
complications were not enough, the play closes with Punch's revelation
that he is the brother of Harriot and that their mother, Luckless's landlady,
is actually the Queen of Old Brentford. So a fellow puppet (playing
his own ghost): 1) has a human sister; 2) is the son of a character whose
existence we can infer from *The Rehearsal*, but who never actually appears
in that play; and 3) is about to acquire a brother-in-law, Luckless, who is
the newly crowned King of Bantam, a nominally real, but proverbially
fantastic place.

   Let us pause for a moment and reflect upon all the different types of
beings we are dealing with, before we even get to the question of what
puppet performance adds to all this. Consider the case of Sir Farcical
Comick (perhaps the most recognizable of Luckless's 'Figures'): a live

actor, Mr Davenport, is playing a puppet, who is playing the ghost of Sir Farcical, the very personification of Comedy, who nonetheless recalls Cibber, sometimes 'directly' in his capacity as playwright and Poet Laureate and sometimes via the role of Lord Foppington. And as a ghost played by a puppet played by a man, Sir Farcical is apparently operating on the same ontological level as the ghost of Punch, who has human relations that are, on one hand, a conjecture upon a fiction (the King of Old Brentford must have a Queen) and, on the other, quasi-legendary.

Nonetheless, starting in 1734, the situation grew even more complex, as the third act of *The Author's Farce*, 'The Pleasures of the Town', was once again staged as a stand-alone show, but this time starring 'the best dress'd and largest artificial Actors ever yet seen, with all the just Motions and Gestures of real life'.[48] This production was revived the following year at Welch Fair, with 'large Wax-Work Figures, being five Foot high', which had 'all the human Gestures of Life'.[49] Given how successful *The Author's Farce* had been just a few years earlier, I suspect that the puppets added yet another dimension for many audience members. So, in the case we have been considering, we would have a puppet recalling a live performer playing a puppet, who is playing the ghost of Sir Farcical Comick, a personification with a type-name, who nonetheless recalls Cibber, sometimes 'directly' and sometimes via Lord Foppington. But even without the memory of the live productions, we are still left with a puppet playing the ghost of Sir Farcical, who recalls Cibber, sometimes 'directly' and sometimes through his most celebrated role.

What interests me about the sheer dizzyingness of these layers is the way in which, for all their jokiness, they call into question many of our supposedly commonsensical ideas about character and personhood in the eighteenth century. If, just to stay with the most baroque scenario for a moment, we have a puppet recalling a live performer playing a puppet, then it becomes an issue just how important the distinction between the animate and the inanimate, or the human and the non-human, really is. Recent scholarship on 'it-narratives' has certainly troubled these distinctions, but generally in the name of critique. In such texts, the fact that a dog or a banknote or an article of clothing can occupy the narrative position typically held by a human character tends to be regarded as a problem: an index of the dehumanizing practices of various institutions. The puppet versions of 'The Pleasures of the Town', on the other hand, suggest that these distinctions are largely without a difference. If puppets and persons can play the same role (and the size, dress and 'just motions' of these puppets would aid in their comparability), then characters lose their presumptive humanity and 'its' are no longer deviations from a supposed norm.[50] Rather, the entire range of fictional and pseudofactual beings can be more readily seen for what it is: a system of various combinations of implied personhood and narrative function, each of which can be presented and encountered multiple ways, but whose 'life' is never going to be more than suppositional.[51]

If high-end puppet theatre blurs the line between persons and things in the realm of character, then similar questions arise regarding the utility of insisting upon the difference between the material and the immaterial, or the embodied and the disembodied. Such distinctions have been crucial to the ways in which we have come to think about our emotional investments in character: the self-possession inherent in embodiment supposedly obstructs readerly appropriation. Accordingly, it is easier to engage with immaterial beings, those who – quite literally – have no bodies.[52] But a wood or wax figure straddles this boundary. It is every bit as material as a human body (and the role it plays is every bit as immaterial as a novelistic character: theatrical parts, *qua* parts, are no more inherently embodied than the beings to be found in other media). But a puppet cannot be said to have any sort of self-possession. Indeed, advertisements would sometimes explicitly highlight the provenance of their marionettes: a 1740 production specified that 'Mr PUNCH's Celebrated Company of COMEDIANS' was *'formerly Mrs. Charke's, from the Theatre in the* Hay-Market'.[53] So does the body of a puppet (or its status as someone else's property) alter its audience's engagement with the character played by that puppet? The commercial success of both the live and puppet versions of 'The Pleasures of the Town' suggests that it certainly did not have to, especially since one of Signior Opera's airs apparently became 'the favourite Song', suitable for performance in other shows and perhaps at home.[54] This is not to say that there is no difference between embodiment, non-bodily materiality, and disembodied immateriality (after all, it is in *The Author's Farce* that we get the distinction between 'your Acting Plays, and your Reading Plays').[55] But those differences, apparently, do not always matter for the purposes of audience engagement, especially when, as here, the characters in question had a certain typicality. Put another way, the difference between the characters whose depths one could plumb and those who prompted more 'superficial' reactions does not ultimately stem from the different relations of print and theatre to embodiment, but rather from whether or not the character in question seemed like he had any interesting depths to begin with (no one worries about the inner life of a personification).

And if the same figure, Sir Farcical Comick, can be a personification with no counterpart in the real world, a transparent stand-in for Cibber, *and* a parody of Cibber's most famous role, then it becomes hard to sustain a clear, much less categorical, distinction between fictional and referential beings, especially if, as in much of the puppet theatre we have been investigating, the marionette in question was carved and dressed to look like Cibber.[56] Customarily, we would say that what an author writes under his own name is more 'in his own voice' than what an actor speaks on stage in a part scripted by someone else. Accordingly, there would seem to be one less layer to negotiate when Sir Comical is jauntily singing about his 'Paraphonalia' – a notorious misspelling of Cibber's from the preface to *The Provok'd Husband* – or referring to a 'Bone' that 'stuck . . . confoundedly in the Stomach of the Audience' (a line from that play that the pit objected to as a bawdy interpolation of Cibber's), than when he utters Lord Foppington's tag-line, 'stap my Vitals'.[57] Yet the structural equivalence between these passages – the way in which they all operate at the same level of representation (they are what a puppet recalling a person playing a puppet playing the ghost of Sir Farcical refers to) – suggests that this distinction may too be one without a difference, which is to say, Cibber's utterances 'in his own voice' may be no more 'his' than those in the voice of Lord Foppington as written by Vanbrugh. Or, conversely, what he says in character as the fop to end all fops is every bit as Cibberian as anything he might say offstage. The fictional and the real, the persona and the person, the Nobody and the Somebody, are thus all tangled up (both with one another and with Sir Farcical's status as the personification of a form), perpetually on the verge of collapsing into one another without ever fully doing so.

This is not a state of affairs that our current ways of thinking about fictionality and reference can comfortably accommodate. But eighteenth-century audiences, schooled as they were in the ways of burlesque and mock-form, were far more willing to dwell in the realm of simultaneity. And I suspect they were especially likely to do so when cued by the ostentatious play with other distinctions that puppet versions of the live repertory seemed to specialize in. That is, the sheer intricacy and fluidity of the relation between Somebodies and Nobodies was thrown into high relief when they were being personated by Wood (or Wax) Bodies.

A different, yet equally complex and provocative array of beings may be found in *The Covent Garden Tragedy*, which closed as a piece of live theatre after a single night, but became perhaps the most frequently produced play in the entire high-end puppet repertory.[58] The characters are, first and foremost, burlesques of the figures found in what Lockwood calls 'pseudo-classical tragedy'.[59] As such, they are pretty ostentatiously fictional, although their tragic counterparts still had whatever historicity attached to the likes of Andromache. Indeed, their names alone mark them out as stock theatrical types (Mother Punchbowl is, unsurprisingly, a bawd who likes her liquor). At the same time, though, setting the burlesque in a Covent Garden brothel repeatedly pushes what purports to be mere tragic convention towards something close to actual tragedy. For example, Stormandra's threat to have Captain Bilkum arrested for a £2 debt if he does not 'dy[e]' his 'Sword' with 'curs'd *Lovegirlo*'s Blood' is, on one level, a parody of scenes like the one in Ambrose Philips's *The Distrest Mother* in which Hermione, abandoned by Pyrrhus, emotionally blackmails Orestes into killing her faithless lover on his wedding day.[60] Yet the very specificity that would seem to be Exhibit A in the burlesque (the self-evident lowness of murdering someone to avoid being imprisoned over such a supposedly trifling sum) is also a reminder that within a short walk of the theatre (two or three minutes for the initial live version; less than fifteen for the puppet shows) lived thousands of people for whom a £2 debt could be catastrophic. This edges the literary typicality of a figure like Captain Bilkum over towards a social typicality, in which a willingness to commit violence to stave off precarity could appear anything but fictional. Indeed, it could go a step further and seem the actions of a Somebody: say, Captain Edward Braddock.[61] After all, the lovers in this triangle are denizens of a brothel that resembles several actual Covent Garden establishments (the play was once advertised under the title *King's Coffee-House*), and the porter, Leathersides, to whom the 'Nymphs' of the surrounding neighbourhood 'communicate' their 'Lodgings', so he can fetch them when they have clients, recalls 'Leathercoat', who held a similar position at the Rose Tavern – and who gained additional celebrity from his appearance, bringing in the platter for the posture woman, in plate three of *A Rake's Progress*.[62]

So these characters are (alternately or simultaneously) burlesques of specific figures from classicizing tragedy, literary types quite removed from actuality, social types that can be encountered nearby, and stand-ins for minor celebrities in the London sex trade (also just a few blocks away, but made famous throughout the realm by Hogarth). Any attempt to confine them to a single sort of being risks appearing as dopey as the would-be contributor to the *Grub Street Journal* whom Fielding ventrilo-quizes in the 'Prolegomena' to the printed playbook: 'what is intended by the Character of *Gallano*, is difficult to imagine. Either he is taken from Life, or he is not'.[63]

Once again, it is in the puppet performances that audiences could best perceive all these overlaps and slippages (and enjoy them, rather than simply be disoriented: hence the puppets' success in the wake of the live version's failure). Marionettes heighten the absurdity of the burlesque: say, by giving 'the Part of Mother Punch-Bowl' to 'Punch, being the first Time of his appearing in Petticoats', and then later closing the show with 'the Black Joke, danced by Punch in Petticoats' – tragic heroines do not generally appear in drag, much less sing about pubic hair they do not possess.[64] Puppets also emphasize the literary typicality of these characters: we get conventionalized, wooden performers for a conventionalized, wooden form. At the same time, though, they drive home the social and geographic specificity of this show (puppets are native to Covent Garden and the Haymarket in a way that Trojan prisoners are not). And, of course, these particular puppets looked like individuals who might plausibly be found in a neighbourhood brothel. We do not know which 'eminent Persons', other than Farinelli, Charke's figures resembled, but it is a good bet that one of them looked like Leathercoat and that Punch's petticoats somehow recalled the characteristic dress of 'Mother Bentley', the preeminent bawd of the late 1730s. Nash took this even further and cast puppets who resembled persons her audience might well have seen in other settings, including printed portraits (thereby broadening their recognizability and removing the potential embarrassment of explaining where the previous encounter had occurred): 'Mr. Puppet Fut' played Captain Bilkum, 'Mrs. Puppet Fillips' was Stormandra, and 'Miss Puppet Morrey' took on the role of Kissindra.[65] This is not to say that anyone would have thought Foote, Constantia Phillips, and Fanny Murray were actually performing in *The Covent Garden Tragedy*. Rather, as with 'The Pleasures of the Town', the presence of the puppets simply begs the question of how much difference there really was between wood or wax and flesh: quite a bit, perhaps, when it came to desire (then, as now, puppets are rather a specialty taste); perhaps not much when it came to the joys of gossip or the frisson of learning how the other half lives. And as with 'The Pleasures of the Town', the conceptual gymnastics involved could be dizzying, but they also seem to have been capable of yielding what a puff for Charke extravagantly, but not necessarily inaccurately, termed 'infinite Pleasure' and 'Humour' that 'even exceeds real Life'.[66]

Now obviously high-end puppet versions of Fielding's most metatheatrical plays are not typical of eighteenth-century representational practices in any straightforward statistical way. But I would like to propose that in their very eccentricity they can serve as something akin to what

Italian microhistorians have termed 'the normal exception': the seemingly oddball that nonetheless reveals a whole host of broader, often only half-articulated presumptions and desires.[67] That is, for all their zaniness, these shows have a profound grasp of just how many different sorts of beings might appear within a single text, how complexly intertwined fictionality and reference could be, and how much pleasure and insight could result from adding still further twists and layers to that intertwining. If we are ever going to be able to do justice to the complexities of our evidence, much less to the ways in which fictional, pseudofactual, and 'real' personages have actually worked in the world, we would do well to follow their lead.

Notes

1 Nicholas Paige, *Before Fiction: The Ancien Régime of the Novel* (Philadelphia: University of Pennsylvania Press, 2011), pp. 18–24.

2 Catherine Gallagher, *Nobody's Story: The Vanishing Acts of Women Writers in the Marketplace, 1670–1820* (Berkeley: University of California Press, 1994), p. 172. See too her 'The Rise of Fictionality', in *The Novel*, ed. Franco Moretti, 2 vols. (Princeton University Press, 2006), vol. 1, pp. 336–63.

3 Gallagher, *Nobody's Story*, p. 165.

4 [James Ralph], *The Touch-Stone: or, Historical, Critical, Political, Philosophical, and Theological Essays on the reigning Diversions of the Town* (London: [no publisher], 1728), p. 237.

5 For similar complaints, see Srinivas Aravamudan, *Enlightenment Orientalism: Resisting the Rise of the Novel* (University of Chicago Press, 2012), pp. 18–29; Janine Barchas, *Matters of Fact in Jane Austen: History, Location, and Celebrity* (Baltimore: Johns Hopkins University Press, 2012), pp. 1–26; and Simon Dickie, *Cruelty and Laughter: Forgotten Comic Literature and the Unsentimental Eighteenth Century* (University of Chicago Press, 2011), pp. 250–81.

6 *Miscellanies by Henry Fielding, Esq.* (1743), ed. Hugh Amory, 3 vols., The Wesleyan Edition of the Works of Henry Fielding (Middletown: Wesleyan University Press, 1972–97), vol. 3, p. 125.

7 I here part company with the only other attempt I know to yoke puppets and novelistic characters: Julie Park's *The Self and It: Novel Objects in Eighteenth-Century England* (Stanford University Press, 2010), pp. 161–85. Park contends that puppetry, like the novel, offers the simulacrum of a human voice (and so a kind of gendered subjectivity) without the presence of a human body. I am far less convinced that either form is primarily concerned with conjuring an illusion of selfhood (or at least one with any plumbable depths).

8 On fairground booths, see Sybil Marion Rosenfeld, *The Theatre of the London Fairs in the 18th Century* (Cambridge University Press, 1960), pp. 150–69 and George Speaight, 'Punch's Opera at Bartholomew Fair', *Theatre Notebook*, 7:4 (1953), 84–85.

9 *London Daily Post, and General Advertiser*, 12 September 1738.

10 *Daily Courant*, 24 February 1711.

11 Charlotte Charke, *A Narrative of the Life of Mrs. Charlotte Charke* (1755), ed. Robert Rehder (London: Pickering and Chatto, 1999), p. 93. Charke's audience at her own puppet show supposedly included a 'number of People of Quality, as well as Foreign Ministers': *London Daily Post, and General Advertiser*, 29 April 1738. For a description of her venue (used by several other puppeteers as well), see David Clay Jenkins, 'The James Street Theatre at the Old Tennis Court', *Theatre Notebook*, 23:4 (1969), 143–50.

12 *General Advertiser*, 30 March 1748. For an overview of Nash's career (and the likelihood of her being Fielding), see Martin C. Battestin, 'Fielding and "Master Punch" in Panton Street', *Philological Quarterly*, 45:1 (1966), 191–208. For the other men involved, see Thomas Lockwood, 'William Hatchett, *A Rehearsal of Kings* (1737), and the Panton Street Puppet Show (1748)', *Philological Quarterly*, 68:3 (1989), 315–23.

13 *General Advertiser*, 28 March 1748.

14 Tobias Smollett, *The Adventures of Roderick Random* (1748), ed. O M Brack, Jr, *The Works of Tobias Smollett* (Athens: University of Georgia Press, 2012), p. 258.

15 *London Daily Post, and General Advertiser*, 11 March 1738. The booths at the fairs were only slightly cheaper, typically '*2s. 6d.* for the boxes, *1s. 6d.* for the pit, *1s.* for the gallery and *6d.* for the upper gallery': Rosenfeld, *Theatre*, p. 158.

16 Playbill (c.1760), Bodleian Library, University of Oxford: John Johnson Collection: London Playbills Haymarket 1 (12).

17 Charke, *Narrative*, pp. 43–44.

18 1734 advertisement of Fawkes, quoted in Thomas Frost, *The Old Showmen and the Old London Fairs* (London: Tinsley Brothers, 1874), p. 123; *General Advertiser*, 24 August 1752.

19 Playbill (c.1700) of John Harris, reproduced in George Speaight, *The History of the English Puppet Theatre*, 2nd edn (Carbondale: Southern Illinois University Press, 1990), p. 151.

20 *Daily Post*, 9 February 1730; c.1727 clipping for 'FAWKES's Theatre' (Bodleian Library, University of Oxford: John Johnson Collection: London Play Places 5 [98]).

21 1737 advertisement of Yeates, ventriloquized in Frost, *Old Showmen*, p. 131.

22 [Abbé Prévost], *Le Pour et Contre, Ouvrage Periodique d'une Gout Nouveau*, 3 (1735), p. 256; BM Satires 2140.

23 Obviously, these are satirical prints with particular anti-ministerial agendas, and so cannot be automatically presumed to be reliable forms of evidence. But the size of the puppets does not appear to be part of the attack (indeed, the mockery might be more effective if the figures were more trifling). Accordingly, I suspect, these images can offer useful confirmation of the appearance of these marionettes.

24 1734 advertisement of Fawkes, quoted in Frost, *Old Showmen*, p. 123.

25 Pope to Knight, 24 November 1727, *The Correspondence of Alexander Pope*, ed. George Sherburn, 5 vols. (Oxford: Clarendon Press, 1956), vol. 2, pp. 62–63.

26 Charke, *Narrative*, p. 43. She may have done the same thing a few years later: the cast list for her *Tit for Tat; or, Comedy and Tragedy at War* (offered at 'Punch's Theatre') features a performer described as 'a small strutting Hero' [Garrick?] and others bearing names like 'Miss Shylock' [Maria Macklin?] and 'Mr. Scriblerus' [Pope?]: *London Daily Post, and General Advertiser*, 9 February 1743.

27 *London Daily Post*, 2 May 1738.

28 Charles Coffey, *The Beggar's Wedding. A New Opera*, 2nd edn (London: James and John Knapton, 1729), n.p.; *Prompter*, 37 (14 March 1735).

29 *General Advertiser*, 23 April 1748.

30 Eliza Haywood, *Female Spectator*, 12 (5 April 1745), in *The Female Spectator, Volumes 1 and 2*, eds. Kathryn King and Alexander Pettit, *Selected Works of Eliza Haywood* (London: Pickering and Chatto, 2001), pp. 422, 420.

31 Haywood, *Female Spectator*, p. 421.

32 Haywood, *Female Spectator*, p. 421.

33 Haywood, *Female Spectator*, pp. 422, 423.

34 Haywood, *Female Spectator*, p. 423.

35 Haywood, *Female Spectator*, p. 421.

36 Scholars have presumed that this entertainment was the one organized by Russell for which Charke 'was hired ... to move ... Punch': *Narrative*, p. 93. See, for example, Ros Ballaster, '"Heart-Easing Mirth": Charm in the Eighteenth Century', *Essays in Criticism*, 43:3 (2013), 249–74 (266); Haywood, *Female Spectator*, p. 469, n.7; and Jonathan Sadow, 'The Puppet Show Conundrum: Haywood and "The Fittest Entertainment for the Present Age"', *Digital Defoe: Studies in Defoe and his Contemporaries*, 5 (2013), 121–29. But Russell's production mocked Italian opera, does not seem to have anything to do with a rivalry between the Court and the City, and involved what Charke described as 'very small' 'Figures': *Narrative*, p. 96. For more on Russell's show, see David Hunter, 'Puppet Politics: Tobias Smollett, Charlotte Charke, and Theatrical Opposition to Handel', *Theatre Notebook*, 58:1 (2004), 7–17. It seems there were at least two satiric puppet shows sponsored by ladies and funded through subscription underway in March 1745.

37 Alas, no actual puppeteer seems to have taken up 'the fine and serious Part of the *Provok'd Husband*': Henry Fielding, *The History of Tom Jones, A Foundling* (1749), ed. Fredson Bowers, intro. Martin C. Battestin, 2 vols., The Wesleyan Edition of the Works of Henry Fielding (Middletown: Wesleyan University Press, 1975), vol. 2, p. 638.

38 Lockwood, private communication, 12 May 2014, correcting the '2,000' given in Henry Fielding, *Plays*, ed. Thomas Lockwood, 3 vols., The Wesleyan Edition of the Works of Henry Fielding (Oxford: Clarendon Press, 2004–11), vol. 1, p. 204. The total capacity of the theatre 'with comfort' was probably about 650, with 150 in the boxes, 200 in the pit, and 300 in the gallery: Robert D. Hume, *Henry Fielding and the London Theatre, 1728–1737* (Oxford: Clarendon Press, 1988), pp. 54–55, n.37. A third of the way into the run, the advertisements began to trumpet that 'the Boxes not being equal to the

great Demand for Places, ... Pit and Boxes will be put together' – that is, spaces in the pit were sold at the price of those in the boxes: five shillings, rather than three: *Daily Post*, 6 May 1730.

39 Richard Reynolds advertised performances at the fair over five days (and probably offered a sixth), starting at 1pm and ending at 10: *Daily Post*, 4 August 1730. Given the usual running time of forty-five or fifty minutes for a fairground droll (see Rosenfeld, *Theatre*, pp. 146–47), this probably meant that the shows were offered hourly.

40 *The Candidates for the Bays. A Poem. Written by Scriblerus Tertius* (London: A. Moore, 1730), p. 10.

41 Fielding, *Plays*, vol. 1, p. 258.

42 Peter Lewis, *Fielding's Burlesque Drama: Its Place in the Tradition* (Edinburgh University Press for the University of Durham, 1987), p. 95; Fielding, *Plays*, vol. 1, pp. 227–28.

43 Fielding, *Plays*, vol. 1, p. 263.

44 Lewis, *Fielding's Burlesque Drama*, p. 98.

45 Fielding, *Plays*, vol. 1, pp. 270, 270, n.2.

46 Fielding, *Plays*, vol. 1, p. 271.

47 Fielding, *Plays*, vol. 1, pp. 227, 252; *Daily Post*, 1 August 1730.

48 *Daily Advertiser*, 11 September 1734. Southwark Fair ran from 8 to 21 September, so if Yeates's performance schedule was like that of Reynolds's at Tottenham Court Fair four years earlier, there could have been 108 shows. Lockwood thinks 'there were undoubtedly many more puppet theatre performances than records indicate': Fielding, *Plays*, vol. 1, p. 197.

49 *Daily Advertiser*, 22 August 1735. The fair ran through 28 August that year and performances began '*every Day at Twelve o'Clock*'. Accordingly, there may have been sixty shows.

50 Jennifer L. Roberts argues that representation 'at actual size' 'involves a ... logic of substitution and transposition', rather than the 'abstraction' involved in scale, and so lends itself to the forms of evaluation we reserve for our own 'real corporeal space': *Transporting Visions: The Movement of Images in Early America* (Berkeley: University of California Press, 2014), p. 84.

51 My thinking here is indebted to some of Sandra Macpherson's unpublished work and to Alex Woloch, *The One vs. the Many: Minor Characters and the Space of the Protagonist* (Princeton University Press, 2003).

52 See Gallagher, *Nobody's Story*, pp. 167–74; Lisa Freeman, *Character's Theater: Genre and Identity on the Eighteenth-Century English Stage* (Philadelphia: University of Pennsylvania Press, 2002), pp. 16–19.

53 *London Daily Post, and General Advertiser*, 21 August 1740.

54 *Daily Post*, 18 September 1730. We have no direct evidence of how well the puppet versions of 'The Pleasures of the Town' were attended, but if Yeates offered nine or ten shows a day at the fairs, there could have been 168 performances in 1734–35. Booths like the ones used by Yeates were 'often of considerable size': one at Southwark Fair in 1717 could seat 'near 150 noblemen and gentlemen ... on the stage' alone: Rosenfeld, *Theatre*, p. 152; George Daniel,

Merrie England in the Olden Time, 2 vols. (London: Richard Bentley, 1842), vol. 1, p. 119, n.1.

55 Fielding, *Plays*, vol. 1, p. 237.

56 None of the advertisements for the puppet versions of 'The Pleasures of the Town' highlight any special carving or other distinguishing features (for instance, the oversize wig for which Lord Foppington was famous). But it is not clear that they would: after all, Charke modeled her figures after 'several eminent Persons', but the only one mentioned in her advertising is 'Farinelli'.

57 Fielding, *Plays*, vol. 1, pp. 282, 271, 277.

58 After its disastrous premiere at Drury Lane on 1 June 1732, *The Covent Garden Tragedy* was revived as a live show five times in 1734 at the Little Theatre in the Haymarket and once in 1735 at York Buildings. On the puppet stage, on the other hand, it was performed ten times in 1738 at the Old Tennis Court by Charke, seventeen times in 1739 at the same venue by a Mr Hill (probably using Charke's puppets), and eleven times in 1748 by Nash. There was also a 1742 production at Bartholomew Fair (which may have involved three dozen performances) that seems to have combined live actors with puppets: 'Punch's celebrated company of comical tragedians from the Hay' appeared alongside Charke and a Mr Page, both of whom were cross-dressed: John Genest, *Some Account of the English Stage, from the Restoration in 1660 to 1830*, 10 vols. (Bath: [no publisher], 1832), vol. 10, pp. 163–64.

59 Fielding, *Plays*, vol. 2, p. 343.

60 Fielding, *Plays*, vol. 2, p. 396; Lewis, *Fielding's Burlesque Drama*, p. 136.

61 See Horace Walpole to Horace Mann, 21 August 1755, The Yale Edition of Horace Walpole's Correspondence, ed. W. S. Lewis, 48 vols. (New Haven: Yale University Press, 1937–83), vol. 20, pp. 492–93.

62 *Daily Advertiser*, 29 March 1739; Fielding, *Plays*, vol. 2, pp. 380, 376, n.1.

63 Fielding, *Plays*, vol. 2, p. 368. This seems to be a jab at Prosaicus's report in the *Grub Street Journal* (8 June 1732) of how his companion, a would-be 'man of wit and pleasure', spent his time 'explaining . . . the secret history, the reality of the characters, and some personal scandal' (after which he 'very lovingly hurried into the Rose', trading lines from the play with 'a Lady of his acquaintance').

64 *London Daily Post, and General Advertiser*, 25 April 1738, 26 April 1738.

65 *General Advertiser*, 9 May 1748.

66 *London Daily Post, and General Advertiser*, 29 April 1738.

67 See Edward Muir, 'Introduction: Observing Trifles', in *Microhistory and the Lost Peoples of Europe*, eds. Edward Muir and Guido Ruggiero (Baltimore: Johns Hopkins University Press, 1991), pp. xiv–xxi.

CHAPTER 9

The Novel in the Musical Theatre: Pamela, Caleb Williams, Frankenstein, and Ivanhoe

Michael Burden

There is no doubt that English opera – as opposed to opera in England – lent itself to the adaptation of novels into opera. English audiences, while enjoying music, indeed almost refusing to attend a play in which it was not included, did not relish regular evenings of only sung tunes and recitative. Even the Opera House in London, devoted to singing all-sung works in Italian, was required to provide dancing and, as the eighteenth century wore on, a *ballet d'action* after the end of the main work to keep the subscriber audience entertained.[1] What audiences *did* admire and enjoy was opera with spoken dialogue, where the fantastical, ceremonial, and magical episodes could be accompanied by music, but in which the dialogue was spoken. These preferences were also reflected in the division of the repertory the Lord Chamberlain's licensing arrangements required between the English playhouses (the Theatres Royal of Covent Garden and Drury Lane and the illegitimate theatres[2]) on one hand, and the Opera House (the King's Theatre) on the other. The first group largely put on spoken plays with lots of songs and incidental music added; some short, all-sung works; other related entertainments; and a genre called 'English opera' that had spoken dialogue between the musical numbers. In contrast to this billing, the King's Theatre put on only all-sung foreign opera. The division of the London theatre world was, then, between products that were 'local' and home-grown and those that were 'foreign' and rarefied.

But this preference also allowed the retention of more of a novel's complexities in the English operatic adaptations for London than would otherwise have been the case, for the central activity in any adaptation for the stage, whatever the ultimate form, usually involved compression: a drastic reduction in the time frame of the action of the novel, frequently to the Aristotelian twenty-four hours, and an equally drastic reduction in the number of characters. What *was* retained, not surprisingly, were clearly recognizable incidents and a few emotions – Gilbert Austin's 'love and pity, joy and sorrow, terror and valour' – which could be satisfactorily represented in a musical work.[3] So far, so good. However, one of the challenges for the librettist in adapting a novel for an all-sung opera was to ensure that the work was slimmed down enough to allow also for the addition of new song texts and simplified enough to make it function satisfactorily in an all-sung context, the speed of recitative being many times slower than any spoken dialogue. And, as it happened, this was one of the reasons why London opera-goers – and German ones as well – preferred their operas to have spoken text.

There were three issues involved here. One was the aforementioned, straightforward, long-standing detestation of English audiences for all-sung recitative, possibly partly because it was a foreign import. A second was the fact that they regarded all-sung recitative as 'irrational' – one did not sing when one gave orders to a servant – and therefore something that should only be used to colour text at appropriate dramatic moments. And a third was that, as a nation that admired Shakespeare and an audience that thought of themselves as one for primarily spoken drama, they regarded the type of text that was suitable for recitative as inferior in every respect. They agreed with Georg Benda, who in commenting on Friederich Gotter's libretto for a version of Shakespeare's *Romeo and Juliet*, praised him for 'not weakening the plot of this touching work with common operatic language'.[4]

And so it was with the London stage lives of the four novels of the long eighteenth century considered in this chapter: Samuel Richardson's *Pamela* (1740), William Godwin's *Caleb Williams* (1794), Mary Shelley's *Frankenstein* (1818), and Walter Scott's *Ivanhoe* (1819). Whatever the individual reasons for their adaptation, each novel represents particular genres and themes that are important to the history of opera – sentimentality, politics, horror, and history – but in the resultant stage works,[5] each also represents different solutions to the problems of musical forms and text setting, including the use of spoken dialogue, all-sung recitative, melodrama, and ballad.

Adapting *Pamela*

Perhaps one of the greatest novel-turned-opera stories is that of Pamela Andrews, the virtuous heroine of Samuel Richardson's sentimental novel, *Pamela; or, Virtue Rewarded*, published in London in 1740; the Europe-wide response to its appearance turned it into a publishing and commercial phenomenon of immense proportions. Using the Pamela story, it was the playwright and librettist Carlo Goldoni who developed a new 'theatrical genre between comedy and tragedy' which is 'an entertainment fit for sensitive hearts', that is, sentimental comedy.[6] Goldoni's first reworking of the novel was an adaptation in 1750 into the play, *Pamela nubile*; his second take on the story was in an opera libretto of 1760 with the title *La Cecchina*. Set by the Barian composer Niccolò Piccini, this wildly popular opera was performed in centres across the continent, under the titles of *La buona figliuola*, *Cecchina zitella o La buona figliuola*, *La buona zitella*, *La buona figliuola puta*, *La baronessa riconosciuta*, *Cecchina nobile o La buona figliuola*, *Das gute Mädchen*, *The Accomplish'd Maid*, *Der fromme Pige*, and *La bonne fille*. The success was such that Goldoni developed a sequel called *La buona figliuola maritata*, a work also known as *La baronessa riconosciuta e maritata* and *La buona moglie*. Piccini also set *La buona figliuola maritata*, and both his operas were all-sung Italian pieces with arias and recitatives.

It took longer for English dramatists to recognize the novel's potential, and by the time Isaac Bickerstaffe came to write his 1765 libretto for his English version of the story, *The Maid of the Mill*, he could justly claim:

> THERE is scarce a language in Europe, in which there is not a play taken from our romance of Pamela; in Italian and French, particularly, several writers of the first eminence, have chosen it for the subject of different dramas.[7]

As it happens, *The Maid of the Mill* was representative not just of 'sentimental opera' but was also only the second example of a new English musical genre given the modern title 'pastiche opera' by Roger Fiske. He used it to refer not only to the *pasticcio*, but also to a genre in which there was a more elaborate re-working of the original material than one would expect to find in a London Italian opera *pasticcio*.[8] The genre used largely borrowed tunes, which were drawn from serious operas and other upmarket sources, and then given elaborate orchestrations. Unlike the Italian *La buona figliuola*, *The Maid of the Mill* had spoken dialogue: the need of London's theatregoers to have opera in their own language was therefore satisfied.

But no sooner had *The Maid of the Mill* been brought out than both *La buona figliuola* and *La buona figliuola maritata* were staged in the 1767–68 season at the King's Theatre. *La buona figliuola* played for twenty-eight performances, more than three times that of any other opera that season, while *La buona figliuola maritata* played for nine performances, equaling the next highest total, that for the *opera buffa*, *Gli extravaganti*. The opera-goer Horace Walpole commented:

> Nothing is so much in fashion as the *Buona Figliuola*. The second part [*La buona figliuola maritata*] was tried, but did not succeed half so well, and they have resumed the first part, which is crowded even behind the scenes.[9]

The wide appeal of the relatively new brand of sentimental opera represented by *La buona figliuola* meant that, in performing statistics at least, the opera overshadowed *opera seria*, the genre which had been the predominant force in Italian opera in London for over sixty years. After its premiere, *La buona figliuola* went on to be included in every London season before the end of the century, apart from that of 1784–85. Nevertheless, it did not outstrip the English *The Maid of the Mill* in popularity:

> Half past 5 went to the 5/-Gallery at the Opera House to see the comic opera 'La Buona Figliuola', altered by Goldoni; the music by Sig. Nic. Piccini, a Neapolitan Composer ... I can't say I was greatly entertained, tho' the music is very pleasing. There is something very absurd and truly characteristic of the present age in supporting a set of people at immense expence to perform plays in a language which very few here understand.[10]

Both the particular success of Bickerstaffe's opera and the more general rise of the cult of the sentimental on the London stage clearly relied in part on the popularity of Richardson's novel. But there was also an appropriate performing style to present the work convincingly to the public, and as it happened, performing styles on the London opera stage were as polarized as the division of repertory between the theatres; the English style, perceived as 'natural', 'simple', and 'agreeable', was understood in contrast to the more 'formal', 'artificial', and 'histrionic' style of the Italians. The lack of such artifice was a condition to which actors aspired:

> There is a girl who performs, without any exaggeration, infinitely superior to any thing ever seen on our stage. The action of our best players is only imitation; she alone is quite natural, without the least appearance of art, and various [*sic*] infinitely as the subject requires.[11]

This remark suggests the importance of appearances; the commentator does not claim naiveté or lack of training, but the importance of the 'imitation' being practised to such a degree that there is 'no appearance of art'. And ultimately this was carried through even to the costumes; in the great sweep of plates prepared for *Bell's British Theatre*, the only two characters to have the simple clothes of a country girl were Rosetta, played by Elizabeth Billington, in *Love in a Village* and Patty, played by Elizabeth Harpur, in *The Maid of the Mill*. Gone are the frills, feathers, and so on, and in their place the characters have plain and simple caps, loose drawn sleeves, and a petticoat hanging below the hem of the overskirt; furthermore, Rosetta is placed in an informal garden rather than a formal operatic context.[12]

As far as the plot is concerned, both Goldoni's and Bickerstaffe's stage versions use the central part of the novel as the basis for stories on similar themes. In Goldoni's case, the Marchese della Conchiglia (the Mr B. figure) is in love with Cecchina (the Pamela figure), a match to which his sister, the Marchesa Lucinda (the Lady Davers figure) objects. Her objections have an added dimension to those of Lady Davers: her lover, the Cavaliere Armidoro, will not marry her if her family name is stained in such a fashion. In Bickerstaffe's tale, Patty is the Pamela character, and Lord Aimworth is Mr B. The mill of the title is Patty's home, still occupied by her parents, while the amorous Parson Williams becomes a somewhat heavy-handed farmer called Giles. Both adaptations, however, modify the humble circumstances of Pamela's birth: Bickerstaffe provides middle class mill folk as her parents, while Goldoni provides a flight of fancy in elevating Cecchina's status to that of the daughter of a German baron. Both new endings address the original criticisms levelled by some, both in England and Italy, to whom it seemed 'to be an Encouragement to disproportionate Marriages; such as that mentioned by Sir Henry Sycamore of a Gentleman to his Cookmaid, or a Dutchess to her Footman'.[13] Goldoni felt that he 'would not have the Honour of a Family sacrificed to the Merit of Honour'.[14] Richardson's heroine, then, arrived on the operatic stage in both London and Rome, shorn of her low-born status, improved in class, and presented to audiences using a different performing style, which reflected the new genre of drama she represented.

Caleb Williams to The Iron Chest

In the *Pamela* operas, the London audiences met an encapsulation of a figure whom many of them knew and loved and to whom they could relate, but a character who was, nonetheless, a fantasy figure. In *The Iron Chest* they met Wilford – the Caleb Williams character of William Godwin's *Things as They Are; or, The Adventures of Caleb Williams*, a three-volume novel published in 1794 – and encountered what had become much-discussed political ideals presented as fiction. The novel, which in essence is a call to end the abuse of power by a tyrannical government, was Godwin's attempt to popularize the ideas of his treatise, *An Enquiry Concerning Political Justice and its Influence on Morals and Happiness*, published in 1793. *Caleb Williams*, which demonstrated that even when individuals are innocent of any crime, they can be destroyed by the very legal institutions that are supposed to protect them, was a commercial success but provoked extreme reactions to its themes, a response that Godwin must have both expected and desired.

The iron chest of the opera's title recalled the iron chest of the French Revolution, the *armoire de fer* that the locksmith François Gamain installed in the Tuileries Palace at the request of Louis XVI. The locksmith reported the presence of the safe to the Girondin Minister of the Interior, Jean-Marie Roland, who (without witnesses) opened it to discover documents that compromised bankers, Louis XVI's cabinet ministers, and other figures of the Revolution. Some of the documents were destroyed – Roland was accused of involvement here, and eventually resigned – but those that were not played a key role in the execution of the king.[15] In Godwin's novel, the chest contains evidence that the wealthy Ferdinando Falkland has murdered Squire Barnabas Tyrrel but has allowed two of his tenants, the Hawkins, father and son, to hang for the crime. Caleb Williams, secretary to Falkland, having discovered his employer at the iron chest, ultimately breaks it open, thereby precipitating his flight, pursuit, imprisonment, and escape, before he publicly accuses Falkland of the murders. Making an obvious political point, Godwin's novel was published on 12 May 1794, bookended by two of the extraordinary events of that year: William Pitt's government passed the Suspension of Habeas Corpus Act on 7 May, and its enactment on 16 May allowed the beginning of mass arrests of suspected radicals.[16] The conservative journal *The British Critic: A New Review* summed up one side of the reaction to the book's contents:

> This piece is a striking example of the evil use which may be made of considerable talents ... every gentleman is a hard-hearted assassin, or a prejudiced tyrant; every Judge is unjust, every Justice corrupt and blind.[17]

With such a reaction and such notoriety, to choose the work for the theatre was to make a political statement, and it can only have been disingenuous of the opera's author, George Colman the Younger, to claim that 'the stage now has no business with Politicks ... with which, many have told me, *Caleb Williams* teems'.[18] As one contemporary commentator implied,[19] it was not remotely credible that Colman was only interested in Godwin's 'book as a tale replete with interesting incident, ingenious in its arrangement, masterly in its delineation of character, and forcible in its language'.[20] In Colman's version, many of the key incidents remain. Edward Mortimer (Falkland) is guilty of the murder of his lover's uncle (Tyrrel) and has hidden the evidence of his crime in an iron chest. There it is discovered by Wilford (Williams), who cannot live in the house with such knowledge; he escapes from Mortimer's service, only to be captured by robbers, one of whom betrays him to Mortimer. However, Mortimer's brother establishes the truth, and Mortimer, taken ill, dies. The resultant text was a three-act dramatic piece, with music provided by Stephen Storace, which consisted of a bi-partite overture, four songs, and eight ensembles, including 'singing' finales to all three acts. However, much of the music was incidental to the plot, which caused some commentators to criticize it as superfluous.

The first performance was ill-received, and for the second, some cuts were made – the piece was 'discharged of its tedious and redundant contents', reduced from four hours to under two-and-a-half, and much improved[21] – and the work had performances throughout the early years of the nineteenth century. But whatever was done to the original text, this did not satisfy those writing in the press or those who came to examine the drama in a more considered fashion at a later date. One contemporary reviewer commented on Colman's effort:

> A writer, who understood *structure*, might have made of *Caleb Williams* a powerful play, which would never have delighted – A writer whose power is confined to dialogue, has produced scenes of declamation which weary, and of document which disgust.[22]

William Hazlitt, writing some years later, concurred, and suggested that the resultant drama was incoherent:

> The two plots (the serious and ludicrous) do not seem to be going on and gaining ground at the same time, but each part is intersected and crossed by the other, and has to set out again in the next scene, after being thwarted in the former one, like a person who has to begin a story over again in which he has been interrupted.[23]

The song texts fared little better:

> The Songs, considered as poetical compositions, are so truly contemptible, that we can scarcely persuade ourselves they are the productions of a man who can write so much better, and who is therefore the less excusable for writing ill.[24]

Storace's score, however, contains some of the best of his mature music,[25] and 'Five times by taper's light' was selected by the perspicacious Richard MacKenzie Bacon as an example that showed the 'strength and simplicity' of Storace's style.[26] But the music did not engage with the drama, and all in all, *The Iron Chest* was not to prove one of Colman's, or indeed Storace's, successes.

In the context of English opera, *The Iron Chest* does, however, provide an exemplar of not only the problems of adaptation but also the cross-currents of genre that, conceptually at least, plagued the London stage. On its appearance, the commentator in the *True Briton* remarked with some baldness:

> A *Play*, as it is now become *the fashion* to term a Serio-Comic Drama, interspersed with Songs under the title of *The Iron Chest*, was on Saturday evening produced at this Theatre.[27]

The notion that the term 'play' had become a catch-all term, one that could now include a 'Serio-Comic Drama, interspersed with Songs', was reminiscent of the illegitimate theatre:

> It is one of those jumbles of Tragedy, Comedy, and Opera, of which Colman Jun. was so fond, and which every friend of the legitimate Drama must reprobate.[28]

Here, Genest, writing in the early nineteenth century, undoubtedly had the burletta in mind, the form that Colman himself before the 1832 Select Committee on Dramatic Literature was to testify had no precise definition. He commented that it was one in which theatre managers, through the addition of music, converted straight plays into 'burlettas' to circumvent the restrictions on the performance of certain types of drama by theatres other than the patent houses.[29] Formally, then, *The Iron Chest* stood in no man's land, without even the assistance of the parameters of a defined musico-dramatic genre to aid its critical reception.

Colman's failure has the benefit of showing in practical (rather than theoretical) terms that the process of adaptation from novel to opera is not straightforward; by taking on a work with as clear an agenda as *Caleb Williams*, Colman the dramatist sank without a trace, as he interpreted the original novel without substituting a powerful dramatic shape of his own and allowed his characters to ramble through passages of dialogue. And, fatally for an English operatic adaptation, Storace did not provide music that supported the text or that had its own dramatic dynamic. Richard Brinsley Sheridan's comment on the fiasco was:

> To crown all, the theatre is out of order; our last new piece, the "Iron Chest," that should have been a golden one, is really iron.[30]

Frankenstein's Fate

What William Godwin made of *The Iron Chest* is anyone's guess; he certainly saw it on several occasions but appears to have left no recorded comments. Colman omitted to consult him or to ask him to the first night 'but seems to have made up for his impertinence by putting Godwin on the free list for the Haymarket'.[31] But Godwin did not reject the theatre as a further medium for exploitation, and when he heard of the adaptation of his daughter Mary Shelley's three-volume novel, *Frankenstein; or, the Modern Prometheus*, he wrote to her:

> It is a curious circumstance that a play is just announced, to be performed at the English Opera House in the Strand next Monday, entitled, Presumption, or the Fate of Frankenstein. I know not whether it will succeed. If it does, it will be some sort of feather in the cap of the author of the novel, a recommendation in your future negociations with booksellers.[32]

Those future 'negociations' resulted in the second edition of the novel, a two-volume version, which appeared in August 1823, made possible, in part, by the popularity of the new stage show. This was *Presumption; or, the Fate of Frankenstein* (*Frankenstein, a melodramatic opera in 3 acts*, in the Huntington Library Larpent play texts), which opened on 28 July 1823, adapted by Richard Brinsley Peake. Shelley's *Frankenstein* had been published anonymously in 1818 and, in its various stage and film adaptations, continues to hold a place in modern theatrical culture. When it appeared, a commentator in *Blackwood's Edinburgh Magazine* commented that:

> Here is one of the productions of the modern school in its highest style of caricature and exaggeration. It is formed on the Godwinian manner, and has all the faults, but many likewise of the beauties of that model. In dark and gloomy views of nature and of man, bordering too closely on impiety, – in the most outrageous improbability, – in sacrificing every thing to effect, – it even goes beyond its great prototype; but in return it possesses a similar power of fascination, something of the same mastery in harsh and savage delineations of passion, relieved in like manner by the gentler features of domestic and simple feelings.[33]

The novel did not, however, initially make much of a mark, one critic of the new *Presumption* show calling it 'Mrs Shelley's grand incoherence of a novel ... with a success as strange and mysterious as the being which brings it before us'. The author of the review continued to paint a picture of a bestselling penny dreadful, whose plot needed no further explanation for an audience whose members would have all read the book 'by stealth, by night, at some misshapen hour'.[34] As this review suggests, the critical response to the adaptation was likewise rather mixed: 'A drama more extraordinary in its plan, than remarkable in its execution ... we have not that taste for the monstrous which can enable us to enjoy it in the midst of the most startling absurdities', opined one commentator,[35] but a day later, the same newspaper declared 'whatever may be thought of *Frankenstein* as a novel ... the representation of this piece upon the stage is of astonishing, of enchanting interest'.[36] In the end, it held the stage through popular demand:

> The audience crowd to it; hiss it, hail it, shudder at it, loath it, dream of it, and come again to it. The piece has been damned by full houses night after night, but the moment that it is withdrawn, the public call it up again – and yearn to tremble once more before it.[37]

A 'trembling' and therefore engaged audience in the theatre was something most promoters desired. There were some outright objections to the material, such as the *Morning Post*'s distaste for the play's 'startling absurdities'.[38] Other protests declared the drama to be immoral – protests that may have arisen because the material, while in circulation in print, had not previously been played out on the public stage – and the performances were picketed.

As *The Theatrical Observer* remarked, the resultant drama 'deviates wildly' from Shelley's original, for in the adaptation:

> The hero, a perfect transcript from the German school, is an infatuated alchymist, who, as a punishment for his presumption in attempting to explore the dark secrets of nature, acquires the art of imparting life to inanimate matter, only to raise up a horrible monster that for ever after pursues and torments him.[39]

In fact, the central characters – Victor Frankenstein and the Creature – are essentially unchanged. Elizabeth, in the novel Frankenstein's love interest, is now his sister, about to marry his friend Clerval, while the newly introduced character of Agatha replaces Elizabeth. It is her murder, rather than that of Elizabeth, which sends Frankenstein after the Creature, and results in both their deaths in a snowy avalanche, an incident straight from the world of rescue opera. However, this avalanche is caused not by natural means, but by a pistol-shot discharged during the final conflict between Frankenstein and the Creature. Here, the protagonists, guilt-ridden creator and tormented created, are, through their own agency, buried in the rushing snow as the curtain falls. On this, one reviewer further wrote that Frankenstein is:

> sacrificed to the wrath of the Gods, by the fall of the avalanche, which not only executed poetical justice upon him, but also on the being that he had the presumptuous ingenuity to create.[40]

As *The Theatrical Observer* suggests, missing, or at least pushed into the background, is the reading of Shelley's novel as a critique of scientific enquiry, for in *Presumption* the Creature is not explicitly created with the use of electricity, but by the application of chemistry – 'Sir, he has as usual been fumi-fumi-fumigating all night at his chemistry'[41] – and Clerval believes him to be an alchemist.[42] In the new drama, Frankenstein is beginning to resemble the later topos of the mad scientist of independent means who spends time in his laboratory to the exclusion of all else. However, here his research is not driven by scientific enquiry,[43] but by a 'supernatural enthusiasm' in response to his unrequited love for Agatha.[44] The initial animation of the Creature – compared to statues that come to life in *Pygmalion* and *Don Giovanni*[45] – occurs offstage, and while entirely satisfactory from a dramatic point of view, so appals Frankenstein from the first that there is not time for any sympathy between Creature and creator.[46]

The original 1823 playbill for the English Opera House (which referred to the piece as a 'romance') and the press (which called it a 'peculiar romance' and 'a wild and wondrous romance'[47]) gave the composer's name as Mr Watson.[48] The music was enjoyed by the public, and seems to have been a new score, but either because it was in a style that was not *au courant* or was an identifiable re-arrangement of extant tunes, one commentator remarked that 'The scenery was old – and the music was taken out of the same *bin*'.[49] In one respect, though, Watson's music supported a fashionable dramatic technique which suited a work such as *Frankenstein*: melodrama. By the early nineteenth century, the term defined both spoken drama punctuated by, or spoken over, music and a genre that was particularly popular around the time of *Frankenstein*, 'in which romantic and frequently sensational happenings that follow certain conventions are carried through until at the end Good triumphs and Evil is frustrated'.[50] As it happens, *Frankenstein* clearly fits both these definitions, one of technique and one of genre, and, indeed, the commentator in *The London Magazine* called it 'A Melodrama'.[51] He went on to assert that the piece 'required certainly the finest powers of melodramatic acting, to make the extravagance commanding', a skill definitely required here by the actor, for the part of the Creature was mute:

> [The Monster] never speaks; – but his action and his looks are more than eloquent. The effect of music upon him is affecting and beautiful in the extreme. He looks gigantic – and so contrives his uncouth dress and hair as quite to warrant the belief that he is more than human. While he is on the stage, the audience *dare* not hiss.[52]

In this role, the actor Thomas Potter Cooke (representing it on the stage for the first time) was considered to have 'proved himself the very best pantomime

actor on the stage', whose 'melo-dramatic talent . . . was never more conspicuously displayed'.[53] The reviewer in *The Morning Chronicle* stated:

> It was for him to signify to the audience by mere dumb shew, the gradual
> waking of the faculties in a being of full corporeal strength, but in the
> infancy of mind, and he did so.[54]

There was no doubt that Cooke, who counted melodramatic parts among
his special skills, was a success in the role.

Presumption; or, the Fate of Frankenstein was only the first of many stage
adaptations of Shelley's work, adaptations that came in all sizes and genres;
among the myriad that followed, those for London included two more
by Peake, *Another Piece of Presumption* (1823) and *Frank-in-Steam; or,
The Modern Promise to Pay* (1823); two by Henry Milner, *Frankenstein;
or, The Demon of Switzerland* (1823) and *Frankenstein; or, The Man and the
Monster* (1826); *The Monster and Magician; or, The Fate of Frankenstein*
(1826) by John Kerr; and William and Robert Brough's *Frankenstein; or,
The Model Man* (1849).[55] As if this was not drama enough, in 1826 *Presumption* was re-staged on Thomas Potter Cooke's return from Paris, 'WITH AN
ENTIRELY NEW LAST SCENE, Conforming to the termination in the
original Story, representing *A SCHOONER IN A VIOLENT STORM*,
In which FRANKENSTEIN and THE MONSTER are destroyed'.[56] By
this stage, the audience probably had little interest in Shelley's original tale,
but every desire to see yet more spectacular scenery:

> The stage appears covered with waves, a vessel of considerable size is
> represented as in a dreadful sea-way, and the monster is seen with a torch
> plunging in the waves until he gains her side, when he rapidly mounts the
> deck, fires the canvas and cordage, and the conflagration being at the
> height, the curtain falls.[57]

Peake's *Presumption* also played a role in the history of opera in London
quite beyond that which any adaptation for an operatic entertainment
might have been expected to do; it helped to develop the public's taste for
wild and bizarre dramas, and in doing so, prepared the ground for the
arrival in 1826 of Carl Maria von Weber's *Der Freischütz*, a German opera
with spoken dialogue that took first Europe, and then London, by storm.

Walter Scott's *Ivanhoe*

But in parallel with the wilds of Scotland and Bohemia represented by
Frankenstein and *Der Freischütz*, the London audience also developed a
taste for chivalric and medieval history, most obviously seen in their

response to Walter Scott's *Ivanhoe*. Although *Ivanhoe* is set in England, one of the attractions of Scott's works for London and the Continent were his representations of Scotland, partly 'because it was understood to be a mysterious and wild (but attached and therefore dangerous) country, with customs only vaguely appreciated by those south of the border'.[58] In turn, Scott himself claimed continental influences on his work, suggesting that he had been 'German-mad';[59] coupled with this, he also had a particular interest in 'national identity, folk culture, and medieval literature'.[60] And although medievalism 'had grown up during the eighteenth century', it was Scott who 'created an imaginary Medieval world that most of his readers took for real',[61] and 'when the revival came, the whole educated world was ... conditioned to read its documents as Scott would have read them'.[62] And of Scott's medieval novels, it was *Ivanhoe* that was the most obviously popular.[63]

Ivanhoe was published on 18 December 1819; by the end of the next year, there had been five dramas on the subject staged in London: Samuel Beazley's *Ivanhoe; or, The Knight Templar* at Covent Garden; Thomas Dibdin's *Ivanhoe; or, The Jew's Daughter* at the Surrey; William Moncrieff's *Ivanhoe; or, The Jew of York* at the Royal Cobourg; George Soane's *The Hebrew* at Drury Lane; and the anonymous *Ivanhoe; or, The Saxon Chief,* which was staged at the Adelphi. Other operatic versions of the story were staged in 1824, 1826, 1827, 1828, and 1829 in cities as diverse as Venice, Paris, Bergamo, and Leipzig. This pattern exemplified the speed at which Scott's writings, once published, were taken up and adapted as stage works. And the appearance of numerous foreign language operas – such as the 1819 *La Donna del Lago* (based on *The Lady of the Lake*), set by Rossini; *Marie Stuart en Ecosse* (1823, based on *The Abbot*), set by François-Joseph Fétis; *Leicester; ou Le château de Kenilworth* (1823, based on *Kenilworth*), set by Daniel Auber; *La dame blanche* (1825, based on *Guy Mannering*), set by François-Adrien Boieldieu; *Lucia di Lammermoor* (1835, based on *The Bride of Lammermoor*), set by Donizetti; and *La jolie fille de Perth* (1867, based on *The Fair Maid of Perth*), set by Bizet – shows that this enthusiasm for such adaptations became a Continental phenomenon.

There was no question that the first of the *Ivanhoe* operas, Samuel Beazley's *Ivanhoe; or, The Knight Templar,* staged at Covent Garden from 2 March 1820, had action to go; there was 'some excellent new scenery and machinery, together with the most appalling conflagration', while 'nothing in point of scenic splendour or effect can excel the preceptory as arranged for holding a full convocation of *The Knight Templar*'.[64] Not for the first time, the fashionable pageantry and processions were the focus of attention for dramatists and audiences alike. But the same critic rather drily remarked of the adaptation that 'it will be seen that the dramatist has not suffered his genius to be cramped by too rigid adherence to the work from which the principal incidents of his Drama are derived'.[65] The twelfth-century context remained, but as elsewhere, there was a considerable diminution and conflation of the action. The drama starts after the novel's tournament at Ashby-de-la-Zouch, uses Rebecca's trial for witchcraft from later in the novel as climax to Act II, and makes her imprisonment by Baron Reginald Front-de-Boeuf the climax of Act III; the opera then ends with the 'conflagration', the burning of Front-de-Boeuf's Torquilstone Castle:

> The turret falls – A large blaze rises from the smouldering ruins – All assume attitudes of horror, Friar Tuck rushes on with Isaac – Rebecca throws herself in his arms and the curtain drops.[66]

In the adaptation, Ivanhoe's protagonist in the duel over Rebecca that takes place after the trial is Front-de-Boeuf rather than Brian de Bois-Guilbert, and the action moves smoothly to Rebecca's imprisonment in Torquilstone Castle and the subsequent storming of the fortress. The central, and perhaps surprising, alteration is the removal of both King Richard I and his brother Prince John, together with much of the dynastic conflict of the novel. Ivanhoe, back from the Crusades where he has been a henchman of Richard I (Richard Cœur de Lion) spends the opera disguised as a palmer – a Christian Pilgrim – and the revelation of his true identity seems to have been ineffective:

> This might have been made a very striking incident, if in the early part of the play any interest had been excited by Cœur de Lion; but as that is not attempted, the audience was not particularly delighted or surprised to find that it was a thing they have been looking on all the evening.[67]

What was striking, though, was Beazley's portrayal of Friar Tuck, Robin Hood, and his 'merry men' as a bunch of jovial outlaws, an interpretation that persists to this day.

The music of Ivanhoe was selected by William Kitchiner and arranged by John Parry, who also contributed some of his own compositions to the show. Much of it was drawn from Stephen Storace's works, and it included a number of ballads, the form that had become such a feature of London theatrical performances in this period; the operatic performances of the baritone Henry Phillips, for example, were characterized by his desire to have a ballad in each role he performed,[68] to the extent of squabbling with Maria Malibran over one particular ballad that he had learnt, but that she desired should be added to her role.[69] The form was composed in a number of stanzas, with the music repeated per stanza, and according to the instructions that appeared in 'Observations on Music' appended to the front of the published music to Beazley's *Ivanhoe*, it was regarded as the *chef-d'oeuvre* of difficulty:

> ... which, "when unadorned, is adorned the most," and, indeed will hardly admit of any ornament beyond an *appoggiatura*. This style of Song is less understood than any; and though apparently, from its simplicity, it is very easy, yet, to warble it with graceful expression requires a great deal of real judgement, and a most attentive consideration of every note and syllable, because it is an appeal to the heart. Decorated Ditties merely play about the ear, and seldom excite any sensation beyond.[70]

The ballad represented not simply folk traditions but was a genre that became a test of the skill and taste of the singers concerned. However, its abuses by performers became the focus of negative critical attention:

> At present in the musical pieces written for the English stage, the ballad holds a prominent position. It ought to hold *no place at all*. Its proper situation is the concert room and not the stage.[71]

The ballads were a playhouse phenomenon, and by 1838, the Opera House was rather smugly deemed, even at its worst, to have done better from an aesthetic point of view:

> Her Majesty's Theatre even at its lowest ebb has done something to show that better things may be heard than ballads characterised by coarse vulgarity on one hand, or unmeaning mawkish sentiment on the other.[72]

However, while it may have become a hackneyed musical intervention, for those adapting the works of Scott in the 1820s, the ballad could be harnessed in such a way as to represent themes of national identity on the London stage, and whether those tunes were real folk tunes or newly composed ones was neither here nor there.

Envoi

Essentially a private form with a private audience, the novel offered those writing operas the possibility of creating a new public work on a known text, one that would have its own followers. As the adaptation of *Ivanhoe* shows, vigorous intervention may take the author of the dramatic text far from the original novel but return to us a convincing, engaging, and dramatically satisfying theatrical piece, in which the deviation from the original troubled no one apart from those commentators who dealt with the work around the time of its premiere. But as the example of Colman and *The Iron Chest* suggests, the strength of the original could overwhelm the new object. In fact, Colman and Godwin neatly demonstrate a core aspect of this process; what is 'drama' is not necessarily 'theatre'. Colman the dramatist failed to translate a well-wrought novel into theatre, while Godwin the writer had to accept that he could not advance from theatrical criticism to convincing stage shows. From a musical standpoint, the scores of the operas discussed in detail in this chapter have, more or less, sunk without trace, with only Piccini's setting of *La buona figliuola* perhaps excepted. It would be foolish indeed to believe that the quality of the music for (say) *Presumption* is the sole reason for this circumstance, and the fact that it is Piccini's opera that is still known should give us pause: it is indicative of the modern privileging of all-sung opera over other operatic forms and types of musical theatre, a privileging usually portrayed as being in the pursuit of 'quality', but in fact representing a shrinking of dramatic horizons and a limiting of the theatrical imagination.

Notes

1 For an example of the problems the failure to provide dance caused the opera house on occasion, see Michael Burden, *Regina Mingotti: Diva and Impresario at the King's Theatre, London* (Farnham: Ashgate, 2013), p. 37.

2 For a study of this genre and context, see Jane Moody, *Illegitimate Theatre in London, 1770–1840* (Cambridge University Press, 2000).

3 Gilbert Austin, *Chironomia; or, A Treatise on Rhetorical Delivery* (London: T. Cadell and W. Davies, 1806), pp. 243ff.

4 Thomas Bauman, *North German Opera in the Age of Goethe* (Cambridge University Press, 1985), p. 125; Michael Burden, 'Shakespeare and Opera', in *Shakespeare in the Eighteenth Century*, eds. Fiona Ritchie and Peter Sabor (Cambridge University Press, 2012), pp. 204–24.

5 On novel-to-stage adaptation in the later part of the period, see Philip Cox, *Reading Adaptations: Novels and Verse Narratives on the Stage, 1790–1840* (Manchester University Press, 2000).

6 Carlo Goldoni, *Mémoirs*, II.iii, trans. Stefano Castelvecchi, in Castelvecchi, 'Sentimental Opera: The Emergence of a Genre, 1760–1790' (PhD diss., University of Chicago, 1996), pp. 17–18.

7 Isaac Bickerstaffe, *The Maid of the Mill* (London: Printed for J. Newbery et al., 1765), Preface, p. i.

8 See Roger Fiske, *English Theatre Music in the Eighteenth Century*, 2nd edn (Oxford: Clarendon Press, 1986), pp. 605–6, for the discussion of this genre and a listing of the numbers in *Love in a Village*.

9 Horace Walpole to Horace Mann, 13 February 1767, The Yale Edition of Horace Walpole's Correspondence, ed. W. S. Lewis, 48 vols. (New Haven: Yale University Press, 1937–83), vol. 22, p. 484.

10 24 February 1767: Sylas Neville, *The Diary of Sylas Neville 1767–1789*, ed. Basil Cozens-Hardy (London: Oxford University Press, 1950), pp. 4–5.

11 Thomas Harris to James Harris, 17 January 1754, in *Music and Theatre in Handel's World: The Family Papers of James Harris, 1732–1780*, eds. Donald Burrows and Rosemary Dunhill (Oxford University Press, 2002), p. 297.

12 See Michael Burden, 'The 18th-century English Novel as Opera: Sentimentality, *Pamela* and *The Maid of the Mill*', *Revue LISA/LISA e-journal*, 9:2 (2011), pp. 78–100, http://lisa.revues.org/4539 (accessed 27 June 2014).

13 *St. James's Chronicle or The British Evening Post*, 31 January 1765.

14 Charles (Carlo) Goldoni, *Pamela, commedia/Pamela, a comedy* (London: J. Norse, 1756), Preface, p. vii.

15 See Andrew Freeman, *The Compromising of Louis XVI: the* armoire de fer *and the French Revolution* (University of Exeter Press, 1989).

16 For one account of England during these years, see Jennifer Mori, *William Pitt and the French Revolution, 1785–1795* (New York: St Martin's Press, 1989).

17 *The British Critic: A New Review*, July 1794.

18 George Colman, *The Iron Chest* (London: W. Woodfall, 1796), To the Reader, p. xxi.

19 Anon., *Remarks on Mr. Colman's Preface, and also A Summary Comparison of the play of The Iron Chest with the novel of Caleb Williams* (London: Miller et al., 1796), Advertisement, p. iv.

20 Colman, *Iron Chest*, p. xxi.

21 *Whitehall Evening Post*, 19–22 March 1796.

22 *Oracle and Public Advertiser*, 14 March 1796.

23 William Hazlitt, *A View of the English Stage* (London: Robert Stobart, 1818), pp. 377–78.

24 *True Briton*, 14 March 1796.

25 Jane Girdham, *English Opera in Late Eighteenth-Century London: Stephen Storace at Drury Lane* (Oxford: Clarendon Press, 1997), p. 189.

26 Richard Mackenzie Bacon, 'The Operas of H. R. Bishop', *The Quarterly Musical Magazine and Review*, 1 (1818), 206.

27 *True Briton*, 14 March 1796.

28 John Genest, *Some Account of the English Stage from the Restoration in 1660 to 1830*, 10 vols. (Bath: H. E. Carrington, 1832), vol. 7, p. 233.

29 *Report from the select committee on dramatic literature with the minutes of evidence* (London: ordered by the House of Commons to be printed, 2 August 1832).

30 Richard Brinsley Sheridan, *The Dramatic Works of the Right Honourable Richard Brinsley Sheridan; with a memoir of his life by George Gabriel Sigmon* (London: Henry G. Bohn, 1842), p. 177.

31 David O'Shaughnessy, 'William Godwin and the Politics of Playgoing', in *The Oxford Handbook of the Georgian Theatre, 1737–1832*, eds. Julia Swindells and David Francis Taylor (Oxford University Press, 2014), pp. 514–31 (519).

32 William Godwin to Mary Shelley, 22 July 1823, Henry E. Huntington Library, US-HM 11634.

33 'Frankenstein; or, the Modern Prometheus', *Blackwood's Edinburgh Magazine*, 81 (1818), 251.

34 *The London Magazine*, 8 (1823), 322.

35 *The Morning Post*, 29 July 1823.

36 *The Morning Post*, 30 July 1823.

37 *The London Magazine*, 8 (1823), 322.

38 *The Morning Post*, 29 July 1823.

39 *The Theatrical Observer*, 29 July 1823.

40 *The Morning Chronicle*, 29 July 1823.

41 Richard Brinsley Peake, *Presumption; or, The Fate of Frankenstein*, in *Seven Gothic Dramas, 1789–1825*, ed. Jeffrey N. Cox (Athens: Ohio University Press, 1992), p. 388.

42 Peake, *Presumption*, p. 389.

43 Valdine Clemens, *The Return of the Repressed: Gothic Horror from 'The Castle of Otranto' to 'Alien'* (Albany: State University of New York Press, 1999), ch. 5.

44 Peake, *Presumption*, p. 401.

45 Louis James, 'Frankenstein's Monster in Two Traditions', in *Frankenstein, Creation and Monstrosity*, ed. Stephen Bann (London: Reaktion Books, 1994), pp. 77–94 (82–84).

46 *The Theatrical Examiner*, 3 August 1823.

47 *The Morning Chronicle*, 31 July 1823.

48 H. Philip Bolton, *Women Writers Dramatized: A Calendar of Performances from Narrative Works published in English to 1900* (London: Mansell, 2000), pp. 264ff; *Morning Post*, 29 July 1823.

49 *The London Magazine*, 8 (1823), 323.

50 Peter Branscombe, 'Melodrama', in *The New Grove Dictionary of Music and Musicians*, ed. Stanley Sadie, 2nd edn, 29 vols. (London: Macmillan, 2001), vol. 16, pp. 360–63.

51 *The London Magazine*, 8 (1823), 322.

52 *The London Magazine*, 8 (1823), 323.

53 *The London Magazine*, 8 (1823), 323.

54 *The Morning Chronicle*, 29 July 1823.

55 For a full list, and discussion of these versions, see Steven Earl Forry, *Hideous Progenies: Dramatizations of 'Frankenstein' from Mary Shelley to the Present* (Philadelphia: University of Pennsylvania Press, 1991), pp. 121–26.

56 See playbills for the English Opera House, for example, 1 September 1826.

57 *The Morning Post*, 10 July 1827.

58 Michael Burden, 'The Writing and Staging of Romantic Opera in Georgian England', in *The Oxford Handbook of the Georgian Theatre*, pp. 424–41 (433).

59 Scott to Mrs Hughes, 27 December 1827, *The Letters of Walter Scott*, eds. Herbert Grierson, Davidson Cook, and W. M. Parker, 12 vols. (London: John Constable, 1932–37), vol. 10, p. 331.

60 David Hewitt, 'Scott, Sir Walter (1771–1832)', *Oxford Dictionary of National Biography*, www.oxforddnb.com/view/article/24928 (accessed 27 June 2014).

61 Alice Chandler, 'Sir Walter Scott and the Medieval Revival', *Nineteenth-Century Fiction*, 19:4 (1965), 315–32 (315).

62 G. M. Young, 'Scott and the Historians', in *Sir Walter Scott Lectures, 1940–1948* (Edinburgh University Press, 1950), pp. 81–107 (88).

63 See Ann Rigney, *The Afterlives of Walter Scott: Memory on the Move* (Oxford University Press, 2012), chs. 3 and 4, for a broader discussion of the adaptations of *Ivanhoe* and their reception.

64 *The Morning Post*, 3 March 1820.

65 *The Morning Post*, 3 March 1820.

66 Samuel Beazley, *Ivanhoe; or, The Knight Templar* (London: J Bailey, 1820), p. 76.

67 *The Morning Post*, 3 March 1820.

68 *The Morning Post*, 3 March 1820; George Biddlecombe, *English Opera from 1834 to 1864* (New York: Garland, 1994), p. 38.

69 Henry Phillips, *Musical and Personal Recollections during Half a Century*, 2 vols. (London: C. J. Skeat, 1864), vol. 1, pp. 216–18.

70 'Observations on Music', preface to *Ivanhoe; or, the Knight Templar, written by S. Beazley. The music composed & selected chiefly from Storace's works by Dr. Kitchiner* (London: W. Smith, 1820), p. 3.

71 *Hints on the Italian Opera, in Italy, France, Germany and England* (London: John Nichols, 1839), in *London Opera Observed 1711–1844*, ed. Michael Burden, 5 vols. (London: Pickering and Chatto, 2013), vol. 5, p. 238.

72 *Hints on the Italian Opera*, p. 236.

CHAPTER 10

Gillray's Gulliver and the 1803 Invasion Scare

David Francis Taylor

We are almost too familiar with James Gillray's *The King of Brobdingnag and Gulliver* (fig. 10.1).[1] In a parodic reimagining of Part II, Chapter VI of *Gulliver's Travels* (1726), George III, dressed in military uniform, scrutinizes with his spyglass the diminutive, swaggering Napoleon stood on the palm of his outstretched right hand.[2] It is one of the most reproduced and recognizable political caricatures in British history, and it has come increasingly to be entwined in the cultural memory with the very text it adapts. Of course, the efficacy of this 1803 caricature lies in its simplicity – the juxtaposition of two profile figures, one small, one large, against a plain background – but the question of how it orients itself in relation both to *Gulliver's Travels* and to the broader history of this text's adaptation and political appropriation is more complex. In this essay, I read this print's reading of Swift. To do so is to understand both the significant ways in which *The King of Brobdingnag and Gulliver* departs from preceding graphic satirical uses of *Travels* and also the immediate and readily traceable cultural ripple effect of the caricature's conscription of Swift's book in the services of anti-Bonaparte propaganda.

Such propaganda was urgently produced following the collapse in May 1803 of the Treaty of Amiens, which had secured a fifteen-month peace between France and Britain. With the resumption of hostilities and widespread reports that Napoleon was mobilizing a huge fleet across the Channel, the country was gripped by fear of imminent invasion throughout the summer months especially. Along with broadsides, caricatures became an important print medium for the expression and consolidation of patriotism in response to this alarm, and it is no coincidence that 1803 represents a high watermark in the production and dissemination of single-sheet visual satires; as Alexandra Franklin has noted, more caricatures 'were published in 1803 ... than in any other year before 1815'.[3] Taken as a concentrated body of satire, these political prints are unusual in that they almost entirely eschew the partisan concerns by which they are

10.1   James Gillray, after Thomas Braddyll, *The King of Brobdingnag and Gulliver*, 26 June 1803 (BMC 10019)

animated at other moments; the fractious business and personalities of Westminster are put to one side as caricatures during the invasion scare instead direct their efforts to projecting reassuring and often bellicose fantasies of British consensus and indomitability – and, concomitantly, French weakness and Napoleonic delusion. This specific political climate of pervasive fear and (at least seeming) unanimity is the immediate context for *The King of Brobdingnag*. Published on 26 June, just over a month after the breakdown of the peace, it was etched by Gillray from a design by Captain Thomas Braddyll of the Coldstream Guards, who was at that moment engaged in defending southern England against the French.

Braddyll, the son and heir of the MP Wilson Gale Braddyll of Conishead Priory, was very much of the gentry. Evidently not lacking in confidence, in the first decade of the nineteenth century he was active and successful as both an amateur actor – playing Falstaff and King John in military performances at Rochester Theatre in 1802[4] – and an amateur caricaturist, with Gillray engraving four of his designs between 1803 and 1809 (all but one of which are anti-Bonaparte satires).[5] Writing from Portugal during the middle of the Peninsular campaign in late 1811, a fellow officer of the Coldstream Guards wrote to his mother that Braddyll, by then a Lieutenant-Colonel, was 'remarkably entertaining and clever', noting that 'you must have seen the caricature of the King holding Bonaparte in his hands, that is among his other productions'.[6] *The King of Brobdingnag* is, then, the work of an urbane, witty, and culturally engaged gentleman soldier that has been professionally etched, and possibly revised, by the most virtuosic of London's graphic satirists. This clarification of the image's authorship is important because any consideration of Gillray's caricatures must necessarily confront the thorny issue of their political disposition. Against the troubling fact of the pension Gillray received from the Pitt government between 1797 and 1801,[7] critics read his output in terms of its ambiguity, even its insistent ideological evasiveness. Contrariwise, part of my argument here will be that *The King of Brobdingnag* is, for all its playfulness, remarkably unequivocal in its political message.[8] Indeed, what is especially interesting about this caricature as an instance of Swiftian adaptation is the success with which Braddyll and Gillray fashion a comedic but stridently patriotic text (for graphic satires ought to be thought of as texts) out of a complex and always-shifting work of satirical fiction that famously undertakes to 'vex' its readers.[9]

The King of Brobdingnag is by no means exceptional in its mining of the literary canon. Georgian political caricature is an intertextual form that acquires structure and meaning through its obsessive citation of a wide range of cultural texts and objects.[10] So frequently do political prints of the period turn to and adapt literary works that such appropriation is perhaps best understood as not simply a recursive feature but almost a generic imperative. The texts most regularly seized upon by caricaturists are in many ways predictable: Shakespeare's plays, *Paradise Lost*, the Bible,

Hudibras, Don Quixote, and, of course, *Gulliver's Travels*. This is not just a matter of local allusion. Though brief references to and quotations from such texts are certainly legion in satirical prints, many caricatures engage with specific works in a more sustained and elaborate manner; in such cases a text is made integral to the design and satiric meaning of a print, with a notable scene or episode deployed to some extent allegorically and particular statesmen or public figures cast in the roles of identifiable characters.

Such caricatures exhibit features that Julie Sanders identifies with the processes of both adaptation, which often 'signals a relationship with an informing source-text or original', and appropriation, which 'frequently affects a more decisive journey away from the informing source into a wholly new cultural product and domain' – in this case, the medium of print engraving and the arena of politics.[11] More precisely, these caricatures can be understood as exercises in parody, a mode related to and overlapping with adaptation, but one in which, as Linda Hutcheon explains, 'imitation [is] characterized by ironic inversion, not always at the expense of the parodied text' and where repetition comes 'with critical distance'.[12] Such is the relationship between a satirical print and the text or texts it invokes. Graphic satire shows literary works functioning in this period as a political language or typology; their tropes, characters, and situations or narratives are taken up as a means of rendering a repertoire of political figures, groups, and ideologies legible for the public, and this appropriation usually involves a high and entirely self-conscious level of ironic play with a particular source.

The constitution of *Travels* as a fictional form and the relationship of Swift's book to the emergent genre of the novel are questions that continue to occupy us.[13] For caricaturists such as Gillray, however, there is no such generic confusion, for it is specifically the narrative-fictional qualities of Swift's text – the rich and extraordinary tapestry of situations and characters (or types) – that render it so quotable and adaptable for graphic satirists. And *Travels* shares with caricature a number of representational strategies and thematic concerns: it constitutes a kind of parody that, as Claude Rawson notes, 'transcends its immediate object';[14] it is written in a highly descriptive language that delights in hyperbole; its satiric effects pivot upon the elaboration of physiognomic peculiarity and juxtaposition; and it is manifestly concerned with issues of visual perspective and perception.[15] As Jeanne K. Welcher points out, 'for eighteenth-century imitators of Swift, the cartoon was a far more appropriate medium than were illustrations, with their staunch conventions and limited satiric techniques'.[16]

The Travels of *Travels*, 1726–1800

William Hogarth, for one, was astonishingly quick to recognize the visual potential of *Gulliver's Travels*. His print *The Punishment inflicted on Lemuel Gulliver* (BMC 1797) – which shows an assembly of Lilliputians forcibly administering an enema to the protagonist as a reprimand for his urination on the royal palace – was published in late December 1726, less than two months after Swift's book. Hogarth's imagined scene (it does not, of course, take place in the text) is a deft riff on the scatological humour of its source: as Gulliver extinguished the palace conflagration with his own bodily fluids, so the Lilliputians now exact homeopathic revenge by pumping water into his body using, appropriately, a fire engine. Graphic satirical appropriation of *Travels* therefore begins remarkably early; no other work of literature in the eighteenth century has such an immediate impact upon or provides such instant inspiration for caricature.

Yet Hogarth's image is a false start for Gulliverian satirical prints; sixty years would pass before the next caricature adaptation of Swift's text appeared. During this intervening period, the printseller John Bowles produced several engraved 'Lilliputian' sequences that show capering pigmy figures, but these satires are neither political nor appropriative; they rather anglicize an older Flemish grotesque tradition and testify in particular to the cultural uncoupling of the term 'Lilliputian' from its original Swiftian context.[17] Apart from a reissue of *The Punishment inflicted on Lemuel Gulliver* by Robert Sayer in 1757, now titled *The Political Clyster* (BMC 1797) and with a new gloss applying the satire to the incumbent Newcastle ministry, no political prints make noteworthy – that is, adaptive – use of *Travels* until James Sayers's *Gulliver Casting a Damper upon the Royal Fireworks at Lilliput* (1 March 1786, BMC 6919), which offers a parliamentary parody of Gulliver's urinary extinction of the fire in the Lilliputian palace (Part I, Chapter V).[18] Responding to a Commons debate about the need to reinforce fortifications at Plymouth and Portsmouth in which the Speaker Charles Wolfran Cornwall had cast the decisive, negative vote, Sayers's caricature imagines a huge Cornwall laying waste to the dockyard ramparts by discharging upon them a forceful stream of urine, labelled 'Casting Vote'. It is this print, rather than Hogarth's, that marks the beginning of an era of regular graphic satirical engagement with *Gulliver's Travels*. Over the next forty years, whether through brief quotation or more elaborate parody, at least thirty political caricatures appropriate Swift's text in some way.

It is not my intention here to survey exhaustively these Gulliverian political caricatures; such an exercise would little illuminate the dynamics and imperatives of graphic satirical adaptation with which I am concerned, and in any case Welcher's catalogue of visual imitations of *Travels* already provides a resource of this kind. Rather, through a close reading of the adaptive structures of the Braddyll-Gillray *King of Brobdingnag*, I consider what it means to put Swift's book to specific political use at a particular and unusually charged moment of cultural crisis, and what strategies of (mis)reading and ideological contortion are involved in pressing into patriotic service a fiction that we are accustomed to thinking of as resisting allegory and denying readers the comfort of stable meaning.[19] Before I do so, however, it is important to give a brief account of the status and mediation of *Gulliver's Travels* within the overlapping cultural economies of print, political discourse, and graphic satire at the close of the eighteenth century.

The print history of *Travels*, at least in Britain, has been thoroughly charted. The text was rapidly and repeatedly embellished with illustrations, usually one design for each part; Benjamin Motte published the first English illustrated edition in 1728, and by the turn of the century the best known such edition was that which appeared in 1782 as part of the series *The Novelist's Magazine*, with designs by Thomas Stothard.[20] Equally, *Travels* was subject to abridgement as early as 1727, but abbreviated versions that entirely omit Parts III and IV began to appear in the 1770s.[21] In particular, Francis Newbery's *The Adventures of Captain Gulliver* (1772), which was regularly reprinted for the next thirty years, offered an abridged account of the voyages to Lilliput and Brobdingnag that was written in the third person and supplemented with nineteen woodcut illustrations.[22] Marketed as one of Newbery's books 'for the Instruction and Amusement of Children',[23] this edition sold for just sixpence and significantly broadened the readership for Swift's text across the classes and generations. The years in which political caricaturists began to appropriate the *Travels* with some frequency thus coincided with a period in which the book underwent a fundamental transformation in terms of its audience, textual constitution, and visual proliferation. Tellingly, not a single political print makes reference to the voyages in Parts III or IV, thus at once reflecting and reinforcing the cultural excision of the second and more discernibly misanthropic portion of Swift's satire.

Yet alongside this sanitized refashioning of *Travels* as a popular – or children's – classic, we need to set a second, citational history, which sees pamphleteers and polemicists of the 1790s marshalling the tropes and characters of Swift's book with uncommon frequency. Lobbying for peace in 1797, Robert Heron asserted that to review the horrors of the war against revolutionary France was to encounter a procession more 'terrifying' and 'afflicting' than 'the ghostly train exhibited to the wondering Gulliver, in the magic palace of the governor Glubdubdrib' (Part III, Chapter VII).[24] Likewise, and implicitly invoking Swift as a defender of Irish interests, two anti-Union pamphlets of 1799–1800 referenced *Travels* as a means of ridiculing the British government's suggestion that union would commercialize the Irish economy. The first caustically compared the ministry's vision of a prosperous Ireland to 'the ingenious architect in Gulliver's voyage to Laputa, who contrived a new method of building houses by beginning at the roof' (Part III, Chapter V),[25] while the second dismissed the plan of the prime minister, Pitt the Younger, 'like another Gulliver . . . to drag the commerce, shipping *and all* of even our enemies to our shores!' (alluding to Part I, Chapter V).[26] These writers draw upon Swift's book as a repository of fantastical motifs that, by sardonic analogy, expose the absurdity of the Pitt government's policies and rhetoric.

Other commentators read *Travels* more precisely as a prescient sequence of political parables. In *Reflections on the Revolution in France*, Edmund Burke recommended his readers 'see Gulliver's Travels for the idea of countries governed by philosophers', thus comparing the revolutionary regime to Laputa;[27] in an essay concerned with British cultural decline, George Edwards praised Swift's book for its useful elaboration of 'ideas of civilization' and 'national perfection';[28] and in the second edition of his *Enquiry Concerning Political Justice*, William Godwin applauded *Gulliver's Travels* for its 'profound insight into the true principles of political justice' and lamented that 'a work of such inestimable wisdom failed, at the period of its publication, from the mere playfulness of its form, in communicating adequate instruction to mankind'.[29] That political thinkers as diametrically opposed as Burke and Godwin could accommodate *Travels* to their agendas suggests at once the political resonance and ideological pliability of Swift's book at the close of the eighteenth century. But these varied citations do share an understanding of *Travels* – one quite alien from our own critical concern with its strategies of ambiguity, evasion, and entrapment – as a pedagogical fiction that presents its reader with a series of alternately cautionary and exemplary fictional landscapes. And in at least one respect, *Travels* is invoked with discernible political consistency. Responding to and inveighing against the outbreak of war between Britain and revolutionary France in 1793, both Godwin's *Enquiry* and Henry Redhead Yorke's *Reasons urged against Precedent* quote at length from the description of human conflict and its causes that Gulliver offers the Master Houyhnhnm in Part IV, Chapter V,[30] while another pamphlet of the same year even republishes this excerpt as a discrete broadside entitled 'Thoughts on War, by Dr. Jonathan Swift'.[31] In radical discourse of the 1790s, then, *Travels* emerges as a cogent work of anti-war literature.[32]

That polemicists of the final decade of the eighteenth century cite all four parts of Swift's text makes it all the more striking that Gulliverian political caricatures of the same period attend almost exclusively to the voyage to Lilliput. With the exception of a brief allusion to Brobdingnag in a caricature of 1790 by William Dent, visual satirists take up and parodically adapt Part I alone.[33] Two prints by Isaac Cruikshank, for instance, depict William Pitt the Younger as Gulliver. The first, a response to the Seditious Meetings and Treasonable Practices Acts of 1795, imagines the prime minister as a colossal watchman suppressing – or rather, playing with the scene that inspired Sayers in 1786, 'extinguishing' – a Lilliputian crowd of opposition Whigs and radicals; in the second, a satire on the Union Bill that adapts Gulliver's rout of the Blefuscudian fleet (Part I, Chapter V), Pitt strides across the Irish sea, straining under the weight of the Dublin parliament that he is carrying back to Westminster with him.[34] In these caricatures, Gulliver the 'man-mountain' figures both the considerable personal authority wielded by the prime minister and the (coercive) power of the British state. Implicit to the satiric work performed by Cruikshank's prints is the recognition that to appropriate Swift's Lilliput is not only to make use of a fictional scenario but also to adopt the specific ironic perspective on contemporary politics embodied in Part I of *Travels*. In the 1790s as in the 1720s, that is, Lilliput serves as a distorted reflection of the incumbent government's machinations.

With these contexts in place we are now in a position to understand more precisely the adaptive strategy of *The King of Brobdingnag and Gulliver*. In drawing on *Gulliver's Travels*, Thomas Braddyll and Gillray are appropriating a work of fiction that – thanks especially to the Newbery abridgement – had a readership that spanned the classes; they are fashioning a patriotic image out of a text that had begun to acquire the status of an anti-war satire; and by parodically adapting material from the voyage to Brobdingnag they are manifestly breaking with the graphic satirical tradition of mining Part I of *Travels* alone. In the remainder of this essay, I will tease out the implications of each of these points, but I begin with the last and most significant of them, the turn from Lilliput to Brobdingnag, for attention to this innovation necessarily illuminates aspects of the caricature's audience and ideological outlook.

Napoleon in Brobdingnag, 1803–4

Braddyll and Gillray adapt a specific episode of *Travels* with greater care than may at first appear, and in casting Napoleon and George III as Gulliver and the King of Brobdingnag respectively, the print invites its reader to register the depth and wit of these parallels. Most especially, where Cruikshank's appropriation of Lilliput involves the harnessing of a syntax of political critique, Braddyll's taking up of Brobdingnag marshals a fiction that readily lends itself to panegyric. In stark contrast to the Emperor of Lilliput, the King of Brobdingnag is 'possessed of every Quality which procures Veneration, Love and Esteem; of strong Parts, great Wisdom and profound Learning, endued with admirable Talents for Government'.[35] As F. P. Lock notes, in his mental acuity and erudition the King vividly embodies the model of philosophical monarchy proposed in Plato's *Republic*.[36] Equally, he rules paternalistically over his nation, and as part of a balanced constitution that is protected by militia rather than a standing army. The depiction of George III as Swift's 'Prince of much Gravity, and austere Countenance' – features captured in Gillray's print – is thus unequivocally positive.

By 1803 George III had been celebrated and castigated in hundreds of prints across a period of almost forty years; caricaturists had a repertoire of familiar tropes at their disposal in treating the monarch. Representing Napoleon, on the other hand, was a different matter. As Stuart Semmel notes, Napoleon troubled the well-worn stereotypes through which the British understood France in the eighteenth century. Graphic satirists now had to grapple with a figure whose 'political, religious, even his ethnic identity did not seem clearly defined' and in whom 'elements of the old and new orders coalesced'.[37] Six months before the publication of *The King of Brobdingnag*, Gillray made an iconographic breakthrough with his *German-Nonchalance; or, the Vexation of Little Boney* (1 January 1803, BMC 9961), a print that established the satiric commonplace of deriding Napoleon for his stature and in 'Little Boney' created one of the most enduring figures of early nineteenth-century caricature. Braddyll's idea of showing the First Consul as Gildrig, the tiny '*Mannikin*' of Brobdingnag, is consonant with this new and more stable satirical representation of Napoleon.[38]

Yet the adaptation of *Travels* in *The King of Brobdingnag* does not only work, figuratively and graphically, to belittle Napoleon. The sustaining irony of Part II of *Travels* arises from the incongruity of Gulliver's brazen pride in his own and his country's accomplishments in the face of circumstances that emphatically underline his marked inferiority, as much culturally as physiognomically. The Napoleon-Gulliver of Braddyll's and Gillray's satire is a figure of absurd hubris. This point is made clear by the monologue given in a speech bubble to George III, which reproduces and only slightly adapts text from *Travels*:

> My little Friend Grildrig, you have made a most admirable panegyric upon yourself and Country, but from what I can gather from your own Relation & the answers I have with much pains wringed & extorted from you, I cannot but conclude you to be one of the most pernicious, little odious reptiles that nature ever suffer'd to crawl upon the surface of the Earth.[39]

Through this speech – itself an innovation, for no preceding Gulliverian caricature quotes at any length from the source text – the print locates us at a specific moment of *Travels*. Gulliver has just delivered a long and unashamedly laudatory description 'of the Government of *England*', and, having 'heard the whole with great Attention', the King responds in a point-by-point critique that exposes the unsavoury political realities so transparently varnished by Gulliver's account.[40] It is a scene of Swiftian ventriloquism: through the voice of the outsider the satirist exposes and excoriates the systemic corruptions of the British political order.

Of course, and as James Baker has argued with reference to the print's 1804 sequel, the inherent danger of Braddyll's and Gillray's appropriation of this episode is that it applies to France and Napoleon a satirical scenario that in the original text attacks contemporary England.[41] Yet we need to be wary of reading the intertextual operations of an image such as *The King of Brobdingnag*, which was produced under conditions of acute cultural alarm, as obviously or inevitably polysemous. As is demonstrated by the examples of polemical citation I offered earlier, writers of the period confidently applied the fictional landscapes of *Travels* to a range of political issues and events with considerable regard for the positive or negative nature of specific voyages but with no concern for the original targets of Swift's satire. In any case, if Gulliver speaks for the England that is, then Brobdingnag imagines an England that might be; eighty years after *Travels* had been published, George III, so often described as the 'father of his people', might easily be seen to have realized the image of benevolent monarchy outlined in Part II. Moreover, the text spoken by George III in Gillray's print omits the lines in which Swift's King details the problems of the English polity described to him – 'You have clearly proved that Ignorance, Idleness and Vice are the proper Ingredients for qualifying a Legislator' – while in further revisions the phrase 'a most admirable

Panegyric upon your Country' becomes 'a most admirable panegyric upon *yourself* and Country' (emphasis added), and the King's closing censure of Gulliver's 'pernicious Race' is tellingly rewritten as criticism of Gulliver alone.[42] That is, the print's reworking of the quoted text transforms a cultural critique into a personal one, almost as if to shut down the possibility of counterproductive inference.

In Part II, Chapter VI of *Travels*, Gulliver's puffed-up vision of his own nation – a picture of cultural superiority that is inseparable from his egotism – is shown to be to be a farcical delusion, and in adapting this scene Braddyll and Gillray take up a fictional scenario perfectly suited to their ridicule of Napoleon's bravado. *The King of Brobdingnag and Gulliver* is propaganda about propaganda, British patriotic sentiment about French patriotic sentiment; through a parody of *Gulliver's Travels* it constructs an image of British indomitability that encourages its viewer to laugh at the hollow fiction of Napoleonic indomitability. In this way, it is also a caricature about seeing or failing to see. Vision is one of the perennial tropes of eighteenth-century graphic satire, and countless prints from the 1760s to the 1790s show George III peering through a spy or quizzing glass or simply squinting as a means of deriding his political myopia.[43] *The King of Brobdingnag* compositionally repeats and updates one of the most mordant of Gillray's satires on George's short-sightedness, *A Connoisseur examining a Cooper* of 1792 (18 June 1792, BMC 8107). This print also depicts the King in profile from the waist upwards and carefully studying an opponent – a miniature of Cromwell by Samuel Cooper – in his right hand; here his eyes are barely open and his sight so poor that he holds the image, and the 'save-all' candle that illuminate it, exceptionally close to his face. The King, Gillray intimates, is equally blind to the virtues of art and the perilous nature of the political moment, with Cromwell representing the resurgent threat of regicide and republicanism in the wake of the French Revolution. For Welcher, *The King of Brobdingnag's* visual replaying of this earlier caricature implies a critique of George III, but such an interpretation misses one crucial difference between the two prints: in 1803 the King's eyes are wide open.[44]

As Vincent Carretta has argued, in the later 1790s 'George III's satiric character became a tactic rather than a target', with the King transformed by caricaturists into 'a comically positive figure'. Importantly, this representational shift recoded the satirical iconography that had developed around the King over the previous thirty years. George III continued to be shown using a spyglass or similar optical instrument, but, Carretta contends, citing *The King of Brobdingnag*, 'George no longer needs visual aids because of his own weakness: the insignificance of his opponents demands them'.[45] *The King of Brobdingnag* achieves this revaluation of the royal gaze by rechanneling the terms of *A Connoisseur examining a Cooper* through a specific adaptation of *Gulliver's Travels*. Swift's narrative is punctuated by acts of looking, of failing to look properly, and of looking where or at what one should not. In this 'drama of perception', as Pat Rogers aptly describes it, observation rarely attends or facilitates knowledge and understanding.[46] After his conversation with the King in Part II, Gulliver apologizes to the reader for the monarch's '*narrow Principles* and *short Views*', but the ringing irony of these words is that the scene has shown Gulliver to be the one whose vision is blinkered and whose judgement is warped by prejudice.[47] The King of Brobdingnag, by contrast, is a model of clear-sightedness and attentive scrutiny, and he immediately sees through Gulliver's fantasy. In *The King of Brobdingnag*, then, George III is as much the ideal spectator as the ideal monarch (for Swift, of course, the two are very much entwined). In its parodic adaptation of *Travels*, the caricature stages a comically mismatched encounter between a critically perceptive sovereign and an imposter blinded by his own arrogance.

And there is one further political dimension to the print's appropriation of this specific scene from Swift's book, for it also serves to cast Napoleon and George III as warmonger and peace-loving patriarch respectively. To corroborate his opinion of the King of Brobdingnag's '*confined Education*', Gulliver recalls offering to disclose to him the secrets of gunpowder and modern artillery. However, the King is horrified at Gulliver's detailed and gleeful description of the devastating effects of such military technology – 'which would rip up the Pavements, tear the Houses to Pieces, burst and throw Splinters on every side, dashing out the Brains of all who came near' – and, to Gulliver's bewilderment, refuses the offer.[48] In *The King of Brobdingnag*, George III is dressed in military uniform, but it is Napoleon-Gulliver who wields a weapon and adopts an aggressive posture. Six weeks after the breakdown of the Treaty of Amiens, the caricature posits Napoleon as the antagonist and Britain, embodied by its King, as a powerful nation more than capable of defending itself but nonetheless pacific in intent. In an audacious political move, Braddyll and Gillray actively harness the anti-war satire of *Gulliver's Travels* deployed by radical writers of the preceding decade. The most remarkable feature of this graphic satirical adaptation is thus the manner in which it quietly bends the Swiftian critique of warfare to its own propagandic and ultimately bellicose ends. This juxtaposition also carries an ideological charge: Gulliver recommends guns and gunpowder as a means by which the King can subdue any city that 'should pretend to dispute his absolute Commands'.[49] Modern artillery, like the prospect of a standing army for Swift, is associated with arbitrary rule.[50] Gulliver, at this moment in *Travels*, is the advocate of tyranny; conversely, the King of Brobdingnag is a just and enlightened sovereign who 'would rather lose Half his Kingdom' than countenance the use of such brutal force against his own people.[51]

I have elaborated in some detail the way in which *The King of Brobding-nag and Gulliver* responds to the invasion scare through a highly targeted adaptation, a political reshaping, of Swift's text; Braddyll and Gillray take up the ironies and cultural binaries staged in the conversation between Gulliver and the King in Part II, Chapters VI and VII and apply them to the contest between France and Britain. But the efficacy of the image's use of *Travels* lies in its equal appeal to the informed reader, who is equipped to draw the rich intertextual connections I have just made, and to the viewer who possesses little or no familiarity with Swift's book. That is, the print works at the levels of both sustained attention and immediate impression and is accessible to spectators across the broadest range of cultural literacy. As one historian put it in 1818: 'this playful effort of our caricaturist had a wondrous effect upon the opinions of the common people of England. Bonaparte had been painted to their imagination, by his admirers in this country, clothed in terror . . . John Bull laughed at his pigmy effigy strutting in the hand of the good King George'.[52] *The King of Brobdingnag* adapts a text that was especially accessible for an early nineteenth-century audience, in the sense that by 1803 it had long been available in cheap, abridged forms, including chapbooks, that could be read and bought by consumers spanning the range of classes and ages, but also in the sense that Gillray's print ridicules Napoleon by recourse to a Swiftian joke – 'nothing is great or little otherwise than by Comparison' – that might be enjoyed even by the illiterate.[53] Samuel Johnson's quip about *Travels*, 'When once you have thought of big men and little men, it is very easy to do all the rest', rings true.[54]

And to grasp the popular reach of this caricature we need only look at other prints that respond to the invasion scare. *The King of Brobdingnag* generated a level of response and imitation from other graphic satirists that was unprecedented in scale and immediacy. Versions of *The King of Brobdingnag* rapidly appeared in Spain and Germany,[55] and in Britain it directly inspired seven caricatures published in the second half of 1803, all of which look to Brobdingnag rather than Lilliput for satirical material.

In Temple West's *The Brodignag* [*sic*] *Watchman preventing Gullivers Landing* (December 1803, BMC 10130), Napoleon and his pigmy fleet reach the English coast only to find their way blocked by the towering presence of George III, while William Charles's *Gulliver and his Guide. Or a Check string to the Corsican* (August 1803, BMC 10051) directly reproduces the figure and scrutinizing pose of George III from the Braddyll-Gillray print but gives specific attention to the power of the British navy: the King inspects a tiny Napoleon as he climbs the steps towards the royal balcony, but the Consul is kept on a leash by a sailor and George happily acknowledges that his crown is 'protected – Hearts of Oak are our Ships Jolly tars are our men'.[56]

Where these caricatures are largely, indeed delightedly, derivative, two Brobdingnagian prints by Charles Williams engage with *Travels* in a more elaborate manner and politically parody specific moments from Part II, Chapter III, where Gulliver is repeatedly tormented by the Queen's Dwarf. The first of these caricatures, *The King's Dwarf plays Gulliver a Trick* (18 October 1803, BMC 10111), reworks the scene in which the Dwarf wedges Gulliver into a hollowed-out bone at the royal dining table and shows Sholto Henry Maclellan, Lord Kirkcudbright, a man known for being 'short in stature and deformed in person',[57] stuffing Napoleon into a bone and punningly exclaiming, 'There you little insignificant Pigmy, I've Bone'd you'. Published three days later, the second, *The Little Princess and Gulliver* (21 October 1803, BMC 10112), reimagines the Dwarf's dropping of Gulliver into a bowl of cream, with the role of Gulliver-Napoleon's persecutor now taken by the Prince of Wales's seven-year-old daughter Charlotte.[58] Though clearly inspired by *The King of Brobdingnag*, Williams's satirical diptych makes different use of Part II of *Travels*, patriotically appropriating the narrative less for its idealized image of paternalistic monarchy than for its insistent motifs of emasculation. Williams's Napoleon is very much Swift's Grildrig, a plaything who finds himself powerless not only in the face of true authority but even against the opportunistic cruelties of children and outsiders.

Fittingly, Braddyll and Gillray have the last word in this brief but intense period of patriotic Gulliveriana, and their sequel *The King of Brobdingnag and Gulliver (Plate 2d)* (fig. 10.2), published on 10 February 1804, is the last caricature to adopt the satirical strategy of depicting Gulliver-Napoleon among the giants of Brobdingnag. Citing, as the sub-title tell us, the scene of 'Gulliver manoeuvring with his little Boat in the Cistern' (Part II, Chapter V), the print shows Napoleon demonstrating his seafaring skills in a large tank of water before a court audience that

The KING of BROBDINGNAG and GULLIVER. *(Plate 2⁴)* — Scene. *Gulliver manœuvring with his little Boat in the Cistern* — Vide *Swift Gulliver*

I often used to Row for my own diversion, as well as that of the Queen & her Ladies, who thought themselves well entertained with my skill & agility. Sometimes I would, put up my Sail, and shew my art, by steering starboard & larboard; —However, my attempts produced nothing else, beside a loud laughter, which all the respect due to his Majesty from those about him, could not make them contain: —This made me reflect, how vain an attempt it is for a man to endeavour to do himself honour among those, who are out of all degree of equality or comparison with him !!! — Sw. Voyage to Brobdingnag !

10.2   James Gillray, after Thomas Braddyll, *The King of Brobdingnag and Gulliver. (Plate 2d)*, 10 Feb. 1804 (BMC 10227)

includes the enthroned George III and Queen Charlotte, four princesses, the Marquess of Salisbury (the Lord Chamberlain), and attendant pages and beefeaters. This work is considerably more elaborate in compositional terms and parodic conception than their original print. Gulliver informs the reader that 'Ladies gave me a Gale with their Fans; and when they were weary, some of the Pages would blow my Sail forward with their Breath', and the print renders these circumstances with care as part of its mockery of Napoleon's prowess as a naval commander.[59] On the one hand, *Plate 2d* is less satirically immediate than both its predecessor and the graphic satires inspired by that print; it yields its meaning only through more prolonged engagement and, perhaps, requires a greater degree of cultural proficiency on the part of its viewer. On the other hand, however, the discernible pictorial correspondences between *Plate 2d* and the woodcut illustrating the same episode in Newbery's *Adventures of Captain Gulliver* suggest that the caricature's parody was likely more accessible to an early nineteenth-century audience than we might at first assume.

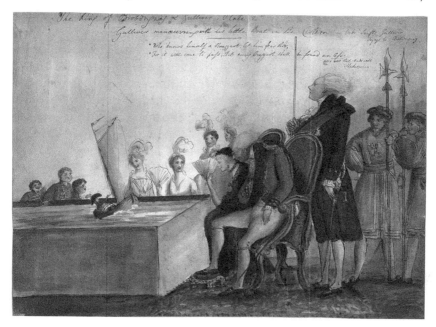

10.3　Thomas Braddyll, pen and watercolour sketch for *The King of Brobdingnag and Gulliver. (Plate 2d)*, 1803–4

Importantly, and unlike the 1803 *King of Brobdingnag*, Braddyll's original watercolour sketch of this caricature has survived (fig. 10.3), and we can thus compare Gillray's finished etching with the amateur's initial design: we can read Gillray adapting Braddyll adapting Swift. The assiduous fidelity with which Gillray engraves Braddyll's sketch is certainly striking, with the compositional arrangement, title, and subtitle retained without alteration. However, one revision is especially evident, for where Braddyll suggests a Shakespearean epigraph – 'Who knows himself a braggart, | Let him fear this; for it will come to pass, | That every Braggart shall be found an ass'[60] – Gillray instead includes, at the foot of the print, an extended passage from *Gulliver's Travels*:

> I often used to Row for my own diversion, as well as that of the Queen & her Ladies, who thought themselves well entertained with my skill & agility. Sometimes I would put up my Sail and shew my art, by steering starboard & larboard; – However, my attempts produced nothing else besides a loud laughter, which all the respect due to his Majesty from those about him could not make them contain. – This made me reflect, how vain an attempt it is for a man to endeavour to do himself honour among those, who are out of all degree of equality or comparison with him!!!

Gillray adapts and splices two different excerpts from *Travels* here, adding
to Gulliver's description of his sailing further sentences taken from a
slightly later point in the chapter, where, in the wake of his abduction
by a monkey, Gulliver's suggestion that he might have fought off the
animal is the cause of uncontrollable mirth at court.[61] In replacing
the Shakespearean aphorism with a longer citation from Swift's book,
Gillray lends the caricature a greater sense of parodic and narrative coherence and directs viewers towards the specific episode of *Travels* in question.
At the same time, the switch of quotations is a deft revision that at once
maintains Braddyll's satiric emphasis on the braggart while drawing particular attention to the 'loud laughter' occasioned by the empty bravado of
Gulliver-Napoleon. In the 1803 *King of Brobdingnag*, Napoleon elicits the
Englishman's curiosity and censure; in 1804, he evokes amusement and
ridicule. This print not only encourages but is *about* laughter.

Yet not everyone in the caricature is enjoying the joke, for in a subtle
and significant alteration Gillray's King – openly smirking in Braddyll's
design – looks intently and solemnly at Napoleon. As in the passage
quoted from *Travels* (and surely taking a cue from Swift), the King
maintains his composure while those 'about him' are unable to 'contain'
their mirth: George is not amused. Thus, the structural centre of *The King
of Brobdingnag and Gulliver (Plate 2d)* remains that of its 1803 predecessor:
the confrontation between the absurd egoist and the wise, beneficent, and
ever-alert monarch. But this encounter is now enveloped by a scene of
unbridled hilarity in which laughter spans and in some sense unites the
classes: princesses, pages, and beefeaters share the jest. Alongside the
critically attentive George and a swaggering Napoleon, the second
Braddyll-Gillray caricature now depicts a laughing British audience –
precisely the kind of public brought into being by their first Gulliverian
print. Folded into its anti-Bonaparte satire, *Plate 2d* offers a commentary
on the comic and political efficacy of the caricature to which it serves as a
direct sequel. In this follow-up print, Braddyll and Gillray not only return
to *Travels* but also seem to celebrate their own success in conscripting
Swift's book to diminish the spectre of Napoleonic invasion.

Notes

1 Wherever possible I identify the prints discussed in this essay, which were
   published as single sheets, according to the number they are given in Frederic
   George Stephens and M. Dorothy George, *Catalogue of Prints and Drawings in
   the British Museum: Political and Personal Satires*, 11 vols. (London: British
   Museum, 1870–1954), henceforth BMC.

2 George III reportedly took exception to the inaccuracy of his dress in the print: 'Quite wrong, quite wrong, no bag with uniform' (a bag-wig was not worn while in uniform). Quoted in Kenneth Baker, *George III: A Life in Caricature* (London: Thames and Hudson, 2007), p. 15.

3 Alexandra Franklin, 'John Bull in a Dream: Fear and Fantasy in the Visual Satires of 1803', in *Resisting Napoleon: The British Response to the Threat of Invasion, 1797–1815*, ed. Mark Philp (Aldershot: Ashgate, 2006), pp. 125–40 (126).

4 Letter from Sir Andrew Francis Barnard to his half-sister Isabella on 25 February 1802: *Barnard Letters 1778–1824*, ed. Anthony Powell (London: Duckworth, 1928), pp. 153–54, and *Monthly Mirror*, 13 (1802), pp. 219–20.

5 Besides *The King of Brobdingnag*, Braddyll was the satirist behind *The King of Brobdingnag and Gulliver (Plate 2d)* (10 February 1804, BMC 10227), *The Genius of France nursing her darling* (26 November 1804, BMC 10284), *St. George and the Dragon* (2 August 1805, BMC 10424), and *Farmer Giles & his Wife shewing off their daughter Betty to their Neighbours* (1 January 1809, BMC 11444).

6 Letter from John Mills to his mother, 13 November 1811: *For King and Country: The Letters and Diaries of John Mills, Coldstream Guards, 1811–14*, ed. Ian Fletcher (Staplehurst: Spellmont, 1995), p. 88.

7 According to William Cobbett, Gillray received an annual pension of £200. See *Cobbett's Political Register*, 30 May 1818, p. 625.

8 See especially Ronald Paulson, *Representations of Revolution (1789–1820)* (New Haven and London: Yale University Press, 1983), pp. 183–211; Ian Haywood, *Romanticism and Caricature* (Cambridge University Press, 2013), pp. 12–32.

9 Writing to Alexander Pope on 29 September 1725 about the progress of *Travels*, Swift stated: 'the cheif end I propose to my self in all my labors is to vex the world rather then divert it': Jonathan Swift, *Gulliver's Travels* (1726), ed. David Womersley, The Cambridge Edition of the Works of Jonathan Swift (Cambridge University Press, 2012), p. 592.

10 For good recent studies of Georgian graphic satire see Diana Donald, *The Age of Caricature: Satirical Prints in the Reign of George III* (New Haven and London: Yale University Press, 1996); Vic Gatrell, *City of Laughter: Sex and Satire in Eighteenth-Century London* (London: Atlantic, 2006); and *The Efflorescence of Caricature, 1759–1838*, ed. Todd Porterfield (Farnham: Ashgate, 2011).

11 Julie Sanders, *Adaptation and Appropriation* (London and New York: Routledge, 2006), p. 26.

12 Linda Hutcheon, *A Theory of Parody: The Teachings of Twentieth-Century Art Forms* (New York and London: Methuen, 1985), p. 6.

13 See, for instance, the essays in *The Genres of 'Gulliver's Travels'*, ed. Frederik N. Smith (Newark: University of Delaware Press, 1990), especially J. Paul Hunter's chapter, '*Gulliver's Travels* and the Novel', pp. 56–74.

14 Claude Rawson, *Gulliver and the Gentle Reader: Studies in Swift and our Time* (London and Boston: Routledge and Kegan Paul, 1973), p. 37.

15 John F. Sena makes many of these points in '*Gulliver's Travels* and the Genre of the Illustrated Book', in *Genres of 'Gulliver's Travels'*, pp. 101–38 (101).

16 Jeanne K. Welcher, *Gulliveriana VII: Visual Imitations of 'Gulliver's Travels' 1726–1830* (Delmar: Scholars' Facsimiles and Reprints, 1999), p. lxvii.

17 In the 1740s–50s, Bowles published three sets of twelve engravings entitled *The Lilliputian Dancing School, The Lilliputian Riding School*, and *Lilliputian Figures*, as well as a *Lilliputian Calendar*. See Jeanne K. Welcher, *Gulliveriana VIII: An Annotated List of Gulliveriana, 1721–1800* (Delmar: Scholars' Facsimiles and Reprints, 1988), pp. lxxii–lxxxviii.

18 In *Gulliveriana VII*, Welcher catalogues a number of mid-century satirical prints that allude to *Travels* indirectly. I would dispute her contention that representations of the colossus in political prints necessarily draw upon *Travels* (see pp. lxxxix–cx, 161–66).

19 See, for instance, Rawson, *Gulliver and the Gentle Reader*; Womersley in Swift, *Travels*, pp. lxxxvv–xcii; and Frederik N. Smith, 'The Danger of Reading Swift: The Double Binds of *Gulliver's Travels*', *Studies in the Literary Imagination*, 17:1 (1984), 35–47.

20 See David Lenfest, 'A Checklist of Illustrated Editions of *Gulliver's Travels*, 1727–1914', *Papers of the Bibliographical Society of America*, 62 (1968), 85–123; Robert Halsband, 'Eighteenth-Century Illustrations of *Gulliver's Travels*', in *Proceedings of the First Münster Symposium on Jonathan Swift*, eds. Hermann J. Real and Heinz J. Vienken (Munich: Wilhelm Fink, 1985), pp. 83–112; and Sena, '*Gulliver's Travels* and the Genre of the Illustrated Book'.

21 See M. Sarah Smedman, 'Like Me, Like Me Not: *Gulliver's Travels* as Children's Book', in *Genres of 'Gulliver's Travels'*, pp. 75–100; Welcher, *Gulliveriana VII*, pp. 44–45.

22 See Sydney Roscoe, *John Newbery and His Successors 1740–1814: A Bibliography* (Wormley: Five Owls Press, 1973), pp. 40–41.

23 *Morning Chronicle*, 10 June 1772.

24 Robert Heron, *A Letter from Ralph Anderson, Esq. to Sir John Sinclair, Bart. M. P. &c. on the necessity of an instant change of ministry, and an immediate peace* (Edinburgh: G. Mudie and Son, 1797), p. 80.

25 Robert Orr, *An Address to the People of Ireland, against an Union* (Dublin: J. Stockdale, 1799), p. 26.

26 Matthew Weld, *Constitutional Considerations, interspersed with Political Observations, on the Present State of Ireland* (Dublin: J. Moore, 1800), p. 37.

27 Edmund Burke, *Reflections on the Revolution in France* (1790), ed. Conor Cruise O'Brien (London: Penguin, 1968), p. 238.

28 George Edward, *The Great and Important Discovery of the Eighteenth Century, and the means of setting right the national affairs* (London: J. Ridgeway, 1791), p. 172.

29 William Godwin, *Enquiry Concerning Political Justice*, 2nd edn, 2 vols. (London: G. G. and J. Robinson, 1796), vol. 2, p. 202. For an extended consideration of Godwin's interest in Swift, see James A. Preu, *The Dean and the Anarchist* (Tallahassee: Florida State University Press, 1959).

30 Godwin, *Enquiry*, vol. 1, pp. 11–12; Henry Redhead Yorke, *Reason Urged against Precedent, in a Letter to the People of Derby* ([London]: [no publisher], 1793), pp. 24–26.

31 *Thoughts on War, Political, Commercial, Religious, and Satyrical* (London: Darton and Harvey, 1793), pp. 51–54.

32 For a consideration of *Travels* within the context of broader Augustan reflections on war, see Claude Rawson, *Satire and Sentiment 1660–1830: Stress Points in the English Augustan Tradition* (1994; New Haven and London: Yale University Press, 2000), pp. 29–97.

33 William Dent, *I. Frith the unfortunate stone-thrower, or a foolish throw for full pay. Wn the fortunate stone thrower, or a Wise throw for a full p-rd-n* (1790, BMC 7626).

34 Isaac Cruikshank, *The Royal Extinguisher or Gulliver putting out the Patriots of Lilliput!!!* (1 December 1795, BMC 8701) and *The Modern Gulliver removing the P-rl-t of Lilliput* (January 1800, BMC 9507).

35 Swift, *Travels*, p. 193.

36 F. P. Lock, *The Politics of 'Gulliver's Travels'* (Oxford: Clarendon Press, 1980), pp. 16–17, 131–32.

37 Stuart Semmel, *Napoleon and the British* (New Haven and London: Yale University Press, 2004), p. 6.

38 Swift, *Travels*, p. 135.

39 See Swift, *Travels*, pp. 188–89.

40 Swift, *Travels*, pp. 179, 182.

41 James Baker, 'Locating Gulliver: Unstable Loyalism in James Gillray's *The King of Brobdingnag and Gulliver*', *Image & Narrative*, 14:1 (2013), 130–47 (142). Baker's analysis of this 1804 print is problematic: he does not acknowledge it as a sequel to the 1803 caricature of the same name; he disregards the involvement of Braddyll; and his claim that 'Gulliver is the Georgian reader' (144) misreads the satire and irony of *Travels*.

42 Swift, *Travels*, p. 188.

43 See, for instance, *Farmer G—e, Studying the Wind & Weather* (1 October 1771, BMC 4883); James Sayers, *A Peep over the Garden Wall in Berkeley Square* (17 March 1794, BMC 8440).

44 *Gulliveriana VII*, p. 633.

45 Vincent Carretta, *George III and the Satirists from Hogarth to Byron* (Athens and London: University of Georgia Press, 1990), p. 317.

46 Pat Rogers, 'Gulliver's Glasses', in *The Art of Jonathan Swift*, ed. Clive T. Probyn (London: Vision Press, 1978), pp. 179–88 (185). See also David Oakleaf, 'Trompe l'Oeil: Gulliver and the Distortions of the Observing Eye', *University of Toronto Quarterly*, 53:2 (1983/84), 166–80; Deborah Needleman Armintor, 'The Sexual Politics of Microscopy in Brobdingnag', *Studies in English Literature 1500–1900*, 47:3 (2007), 619–40.

47 Swift, *Travels*, p. 193.

48 Swift, *Travels*, pp. 191–92.

49 Swift, *Travels*, p. 192.

50 See Womersley's long note on Swift's attitude towards the issue of standing armies in Swift, *Travels*, pp. 487–96.

51 Swift, *Travels*, p. 193.

52 *The Caricatures of James Gillray; with Historical and Political Illustrations, and Compendius Biographical Anecdotes and Notices* (London: John Miller, Rodwell and Martin, [1818]), p. 13.

53 Swift, *Travels*, p. 124.

54 James Boswell, *The Life of Samuel Johnson* (1791), ed. David Womersley (London: Penguin, 2008), p. 434.

55 A copy of the Spanish version is in the Curzon Collection at the Bodleian Library, shelfmark Curzon b.08 (150).

56 Three other prints are inspired by *The King of Brobdingnag* in that they make no allusion to *Travels* but do depict a pigmy Napoleon scrutinized by a giant King (or analogous figure). These are Piercy Roberts's *A Peep at the Corsican Fairy* (1803, BMC 10032); Temple West's *Amusement after Dinner, or the Corsican Fairy displaying his Prowess* (1803, BMC 10034); and *An Experiment with a Burning Glass* (15 September 1803).

57 *Annual Register ... of the Year 1827* (London: Baldwin and Cradock et al., 1828), p. 242.

58 Swift, *Travels*, pp. 151–52.

59 Swift, *Travels*, p. 170.

60 *All's Well that Ends Well*, IV.iii, ll.337–39.

61 Swift, *Travels*, pp. 170, 173–74.

Defoe's Cultural Afterlife, Mainly on Screen

Robert Mayer

Daniel Defoe's works are more frequently and more variously adapted or, more correctly, appropriated for the screen than those of any other eighteenth-century writer.[1] His closest competitor is Jonathan Swift; *Gulliver's Travels* (1726) has frequently been produced for film and TV, although not nearly as often as *Robinson Crusoe* (1719).[2] Several other works by Defoe have also been given screen treatment, yielding a body of responses to a major writer's work that has no parallel that I know of among eighteenth-century writers.[3] Most important, of course, there is a remarkable array of responses to *Crusoe*, including films by Luis Buñuel and Robert Zemeckis, but also less well-known cinematic treatments from 1903 onwards that feature, among others, the silent film star Douglas Fairbanks, Laurel and Hardy, and Peter O'Toole, not to mention several American television programmes that start from Defoe's most famous text and go in various directions, including science fiction (*Lost* [2004–10]), situation comedy (*Gilligan's Island* [1964–67]), and reality television (*Survivor* [2000–]).[4] There are also a number of significant reworkings of *Moll Flanders* (1722) for the screen, including one that never came about, although it was begun by the director Ken Russell. Russell's stab at *Moll*, which was produced by Bob Guccione, the publisher of *Penthouse*, ended badly, and the two men wound up in court. A television documentary about their failed association (discussed below) *was* completed, however, and shown on the BBC in 1987. There are also works produced for the screen based on *A Journal of the Plague Year* (1722), *Roxana* (1724), and even *A True Relation of the Apparition of one Mrs. Veal* (1706), the latter two for French and Spanish television respectively.[5] And there is, finally, a trilogy of important films by the contemporary British filmmaker Patrick Keiller, works that are by no means adaptations of texts by Defoe but, rather, filmic essays on contemporary Britain that make free and striking use of both *Robinson Crusoe* and *A Tour thro' the Whole Island of Great Britain* (1724–26).

In addition, Defoe's work is a touchstone for writers and artists around the world. One example of the continuing, extraordinary reach and influence of his writing is a 2013 exhibition in Hong Kong focused on, among other things, severe acute respiratory syndrome (SARS). Cosmin Costinas, the curator of the Hong Kong show – entitled 'A Journal of the Plague Year: Fear, Ghosts, and Rebels. SARS ... and the Hong Kong Story' – explains Defoe's relevance to the exhibition, which explored 'Hong Kong's complex political, social, pop cultural, and epidemiological history'. Costinas observes that the show highlighted Defoe because the organizers were interested in 'fear on an individual level but also fear overtaking a city, fear on a collective level' and 'this was very strongly present in the work of Defoe'.[6] In new media, film, and television, then, Defoe is a fruitful source for visual texts that appropriate his most famous narratives and use them to reflect upon contemporary society. My purpose in this essay is to treat a small number of the available works to explore why Defoe has been so important a source for screen artists in the last century and more. I shall do so by examining how Defoe's best-known works of fiction (and the *Tour*) have been used by twentieth- and twenty-first-century artists, demonstrating that key works by Defoe function as what Jan Assmann describes as 'figures of memory': 'fixed points ... of the past, whose memory is maintained through cultural formation ... and institutional communication'.[7] Assmann includes texts, 'recitation', and 'practice' among the examples of such activity, and Ann Rigney, in a recent book on the 'cultural afterlife' of Walter Scott and his novels, makes use of Assmann (among others) to locate 'the cultural memory of Scott's work' in 'the persistence of his texts across time' and 'above all in their reappearance in new guises in different places and media'.[8] This essay explores the cultural afterlife of Defoe's work, mainly by looking at works for the screen. Theorists have argued that cultural memory is 'a project of permanent rewriting', which is 'very much oriented toward the future', and indeed we see in the many appropriations of Defoe's texts that he has appealed to artists making use of the past to come to terms with the present or to attempt to shape the future.[9]

Consider, first, the case of *Moll Flanders*. Catherine Parke describes the first major film based on that book, *The Amorous Adventures of Moll Flanders* (1965), as a 'lightweight romp', primarily a vehicle for the American actress Kim Novak.[10] The movie was evidently an attempt to capitalize on the popularity of Tony Richardson's *Tom Jones*, released two years earlier and enthusiastically received by critics and audiences, in important part because of its 'bawdy licence'.[11] As such, the 1965

Moll Flanders participated in a small way in the loosening of standards for popular films in the late 1950s and early 1960s that eventuated, in 1966, in the end of the Production Code that had dominated American film-making for thirty years.[12] But, otherwise, it neither makes very interesting use of Defoe's original nor stands up, after fifty years, as the period comedy that it aimed to be.

However, *Moll* was approached very differently after the 1960s. Specifically, two screen versions appeared in the 1990s that were informed by feminist currents in Anglo-American society. The 1995 *Moll Flanders* by Pen Densham largely leaves Defoe's book behind in order to create the image of a woman who 'endures, thinks, and survives'.[13] Parke lists 'key narrative revisions' made by Densham 'in order to reconceive Moll's character as abused woman', but the film ends with typical Hollywood uplift (Moll [Robin Wright] is reunited with a beloved daughter) and with Moll's declaration of a 'great truth': that 'all men and women are created equal – we are all one being: humankind'.[14] A more interesting response to Defoe's book, and a more faithful adaptation, is ITV's 1996 version, *The Fortunes and Misfortunes of Moll Flanders*, directed by David Attwood and starring Alex Kingston. Attwood's *Moll Flanders* opens in Newgate with a condemned Moll looking dishevelled and miserable, but overall the film presents Defoe's heroine as a woman who unabashedly justifies her scandalous career. This Moll repeatedly asserts her determination to live life 'on my own terms and nobody else's'. Narrating the moment when she becomes a thief – described by her jailer as 'her final descent into vice and depravity' – she defends herself by arguing that as a thief she was just another 'merchant-adventurer' in a society awash with them and declaring 'I had to eat'. At the end of the film, Moll argues that 'we all want to be good, and we all want to prosper', observing: 'In truth, we do what we must, and get by any way we can'. Thus, Attwood's Moll is an empowered woman who makes her way in the world, an unapologetically sexual creature who is also, in the end, a worldly success. Parke correctly associates the films by Densham and Attwood with 'feminist politics'; they are works that use Defoe's narrative as a vehicle for constructing an image of woman that reflects and projects contemporary values.[15]

Perhaps the most striking response to *Moll Flanders* among the films made or projected after 1970 is the abortive Guccione-Russell collaboration. The BBC documentary *Your Honour, I Object* (1987), directed by Nigel French, lays out the dispute between the publisher and the director of *The Devils* (1971) and *Tommy* (1975), suggesting that Russell abandoned the project because his 'personal creative freedom' was hampered by the arrangement with Guccione, but also acknowledging that the contract between the two required Russell to make any changes requested by the producer. Surprisingly, the documentary suggests that although Russell was not particularly interested in bringing *Moll* to the screen, Guccione found Defoe's heroine personally meaningful.[16] Discussing Moll, the would-be producer argues:

> [T]he character ... is perennially interesting because it's the story of a little girl born in Newgate prison [with] everything in the world against her, and yet she succeeds through beauty, innocence, guile, and wit to become a woman of substance and means later on in life.

Guccione extracts a lesson from this narrative, asserting that one does not need parents and money behind one to succeed and finally declaring: 'she's evidence of it, I'm evidence of it'. He indicates, that is, that he turned to *Moll Flanders* as a quasi-autobiographical project. Guccione is not alone in seeing Moll as an illustration of the way we live now, and her story as a guide to how grit and determination can lead to success; among several others who use cyberspace to comment on Defoe's most famous heroine, Robin Bates describes Moll as a 'quintessential capitalist' and observes: '[w]hat is disturbing about *Moll Flanders* is how she is like us – or like what we might become if we were scrabbling hard to pull ourselves up in the world'.[17] Thus, in the late twentieth and early twenty-first century, Defoe's narrative about a woman who 'was Twelve Year a *Whore*, five times a *Wife* ... [and] Twelve Year a *Thief*' has repeatedly been construed in popular culture as an exemplary image of a strong woman and a determined competitor in a society dominated by the cash nexus.[18] As a reference point in the cultural memory of Anglo-American culture, Moll is not just a representation of historical significance, but also an ideological guidepost.

A Journal of the Plague Year also demonstrates that Defoe's works have been important to screen artists because of their relevance to contemporary experience. Clearly Defoe's account of the 1665 outbreak of the plague in London has not had the appeal to filmmakers that *Moll* or *Crusoe* have had. Still, there is at least one film indebted to the *Journal*, albeit a short one, but that film's focus on medical matters reminds us of how frequently Defoe's plague narrative figured in contemporary writers' responses to AIDS. *The Periwig-Maker* (2000), an animated short by Steffen and Annette Schäffler, is based on the *Journal*, although it gets its title and at least the occupation of its principal character from an observation in Pepys's diary. Given the film's length of fewer than fifteen minutes, the Schäfflers obviously had to be highly selective in their use of Defoe's text. What they chose to treat is revealing. Their film focuses on a man in London during the 1665 outbreak who records his thoughts in a diary. For the most part, the film's principal character does not roam the streets of the city during the 'Great Visitation'; what we learn about that event, we apprehend through the windows from which he looks out on his street as well as from his thoughts (voiced by Kenneth Branagh).[19] The film, then, views the plague from a limited perspective, but it manages nonetheless to reveal a great deal about the representation of the plague in the *Journal*. The book's reliance upon statistics is indicated in the film's opening scene in which we hear the wigmaker observe: 'The plague rages dreadfully, and the weekly bills of mortality must be higher than ever'. In this scene, too, the film raises the question of whether the origin of the plague is to be understood in terms of primary or secondary causes. After alluding to the mortality figures, the narrator considers whether the epidemic indicates 'that God [is] resolved to make a full end of the people of this city'. Shortly thereafter the film takes up the question of causation explicitly, when the wigmaker, like Defoe's H.F., rejects '*Turkish* Predestinarianism', according to which 'the contagion [is seen as] an immediate stroke from heaven without the agency of means'. While the film's protagonist declares that he does not wish to 'lessen ... the awe of the judgment of God', he insists that 'the plague is a distemper arising from natural cause'. Thus, *The Periwig-Maker* quickly stages a debate to which Defoe's book returns repeatedly and, like the original, generally comes down on the side of the more modern, 'scientific' explanation of the plague's onset.[20]

Much highly dramatic material in Defoe's narrative is omitted from the film; it does not, for example, show the protagonist visiting the 'great Pit' of Aldgate or tell the story of the Waterman.[21] In the place of such incidents the filmmakers substitute a single narrative of their own devising, a representation of the fate of a young girl living across from the wigmaker's establishment. We get our first clear view of the girl when a body is lowered from a second-story window so that it can be taken away by the collectors of corpses. Every element in the melancholy scene is drained of colour – the filmmaker's palette consists mainly of browns and greys – except for the girl's hair, which is red. She stands silently nearby as the body is loaded into a cart until an arm falls out and the girl cries out, 'Mother!' One of the men in charge of the cart pushes her aside, after which someone cries out, 'Lock her up', and the man who will become her 'Watchman' puts her indoors and shuts up her house with a padlock.[22]

This girl, at one point literally, haunts the seemingly detached wig-maker. She is seen at the window of the house in which she has been shut up and, later, when she escapes, we see her warming herself at a brazier set up by the guard. She also peers into the wigmaker's shop. The last time we see her at the shop-window, the watchman seizes her, locks her up again, and boards up the house. Throughout much of the film we see only the girl with red hair and her guard; otherwise the streets are empty and silent except for the occasional scream or call for dead bodies. Thus, the Schäfflers use the girl to represent all 'the terrible scenes of pain and death' in Defoe's 'disordered city'.²³ This character in *The Periwig-Maker* has been compared with the girl in the red coat in Steven Spielberg's otherwise black-and-white representation in *Schindler's List* (1993) of the liquidation of the Krakow ghetto, and it seems likely that the Schäfflers were aware of the precedent.²⁴ Whether they were or not, however, the girl with red hair in their film serves the same function: a focal point for the audience in a scene of general horror. After she has been locked up for the last time, the girl comes as a phantom to the wigmaker, announcing, 'I shall die tonight', and then asking, 'Are you disturbed by me?' When the man who has watched her from his shop-window remains silent, she concludes 'Then I'll go home and die there'. She does so, and in the next scene, as her body is deposited in a cart, the wigmaker puts his head into his hands, the only clear sign of grief in this emblematic observer of the plague.

Apart from the striking economy with which the Schäfflers use this story to represent the course of the plague and the desolation it brings, what is interesting about this element of the narrative is the way the film employs it to treat a surprising number of the issues explored by Defoe's *Journal*. Just after the wigmaker glimpses the girl for the first time, he begins to consider various 'remedies' for the plague, thinking, for example: 'I am burning great quantities of coals whose sulfurous and nitrous particles are assisting to clear and purge the air'. Then, as the mother's body is lowered into the cart, he wonders if he should follow 'Dr Berwick's advice and enter into another measure for airing and sweetening my room'.²⁵ Most notably, as we have seen, the film also uses the story of the girl with red hair to consider the 'shutting-up of houses' in which plague victims reside, the principal means of controlling the spread of the plague considered in both Defoe's text and the Schäfflers' film.²⁶ What is more, while the wigmaker watches the girl's unfolding drama, he considers the question of how the plague is spread, thereby implicitly weighing both the efficacy and the humanity or inhumanity of locking up everyone in a house once anyone becomes ill. We hear him assert, 'it is beyond question ... [that] [t]he calamity is spread by ... effluvia, by the breath or the sweat or the stench of the sores of the sick person', and he also expresses surprise 'that some people talk of infection being on the air alone'. David Roberts observes that, overall, 'H.F. is a contagionist'.[27] So too the film, which both registers the human reality of attempting to prevent the spread of the plague by locking people up and implicitly acknowledges its potential efficacy: if the disease is spread by 'effluvia', infected or possibly infected people should not be moving about the city. Thus, the Schäfflers' film seems as much if not more focused on what we would call public health issues embodied in Defoe's *Journal* as it is on striking material representing the fate of individuals caught up in the 1665 outbreak. A review of the film in *The New Republic Online* identifies Defoe first as '[t]he father of modern journalism' and then as a 'successful novelist'.[28] *The Periwig-Maker* suggests that the German filmmakers were drawn as much to the journalist in Defoe, or we might say the medical historian, as they were to the novelist.

The film's focus may well have developed out of the use of Defoe's text to report and reflect upon the AIDS crisis in the 1980s. Struggling to come to terms with the onset of a 'terrifying new disease' and trying to discuss what the epidemic meant and how it should be addressed, researchers in various academic disciplines as well as more popular writers like Susan Sontag (whose book, *AIDS and Its Metaphors*, was excerpted in *The New York Review of Books*) made regular use of Defoe as a guide to responses to earlier epidemics.[29] Discussing 'AIDS and the Duty to Treat' from a historical perspective, John D. Arras cites Defoe to illustrate his assertion that doctors who abandon 'their patients out of fear have been subjected to severe criticism from society', and a 1989 article in *Teaching Sociology* suggesting ways to teach about AIDS listed Deuteronomy, Defoe's *Journal*, and the 1987 history of sexually transmitted diseases, *No Magic Bullet*, as useful texts for discussing 'stigmatized illnesses'.[30] Indeed, the use of Defoe begins to seem somewhat proverbial by the late 1980s, a circumstance that appears to give rise to D. A. Miller's exasperated criticism of Sontag's book, in which he notes its deployment of texts and authors from the ancient world to the twentieth century (Thucydides, Defoe, Camus), decrying the fact that 'AIDS is diminished to an occasion for a *son et lumières* of such monuments'.[31]

More significant for an exploration of the cultural afterlife of Defoe's fiction than the academic (or high cultural) discussions making use of the *Journal* is the pair of articles (and the subsequent book incorporating them) that David Black published in *Rolling Stone* in 1985. Even Katie

Leishman, who is highly critical of Black's 1986 book, *The Plague Years: A Chronicle of AIDS, the Epidemic of Our Time*, acknowledges that he 'was one of the first journalists to appreciate the scope of the AIDS phenomenon'.[32] Black begins his discussion of responses to the onset of AIDS, which leads him to consider the vexed question of whether or not bathhouses in New York and San Francisco need to be shuttered, with a quotation from Defoe's *Journal* that might also have been used by the Schäfflers: 'all that could conceal their distempers did it, to prevent their neighbors shunning ... them, and also to prevent authority shutting up their houses'.[33] Thus, the use of Defoe to describe and think about AIDS was, by the early 1990s, widespread. It makes sense, therefore, that when the Schäfflers made their film based on Defoe's text, they rendered it, to an important degree, as an essay in epidemiology. The *Journal*, both in academic discourse and in popular publications and on screen, has been an element of cultural memory that allows writers and other artists in the age of AIDS to look simultaneously backwards and forwards as they consider a contemporary medical crisis.

The most recent example of this aspect of the cultural afterlife of Defoe's *Journal* is the work of the artists who focused on SARS in the Para Site 2013 exhibition in Hong Kong. The organizers found an 'uncanny connection' between London in 1665 and Hong Kong at the beginning of the twenty-first century and, as a result, posited a 'general recurrence of certain patterns of behaviour during an epidemic'. The exhibition set out to explore Hong Kong's experience but also to see the city's response to SARS as the most recent example of seemingly universal 'stories' of 'fear, exclusion, [and] the Other' in the face of real or imagined epidemics. One of the most striking images from the exhibition is Adrian Wong's 'Sak Gai (Chicken Kiss)' in which the artist addresses not only 'issues of contamination' but also corruption in mainland China that affected the response to SARS. Costinas suggests that Wong is seen 'dressed in the typical suit of a politician or businessman' as a reference to the poor official response by the Chinese to the onset of SARS in 2002 and 2003 and that his kissing the chicken references the more recent 'bird flu scare' of 2012. The particular ironies of Wong's photograph in the politico-medical context of Hong Kong would be difficult to stipulate without an extended account of both that context and the exhibition, but given the fact that avian flu is a disease that passes from birds to humans, the 'strong and direct visual impact' of the image is clear. 'Sak Gai' was first presented in a 2007 show entitled 'A Fear is This', at Embassy Projects, 'an experimental workspace' in Hong Kong; the show's website asked

'What is Hong Kong afraid of?' and indicated that in the show Wong sought to 'deconstruct phobias about the supernatural, luck, public health and personal safety'.[34] Wong's image must, then, have seemed perfectly suited simultaneously to address and ironize the epidemiological and political issues treated by Hong Kong's 'Journal of the Plague Year'. And the 2013 exhibition itself demonstrates that Defoe's *Journal* continues to resonate powerfully for artists responding to new illnesses in a globalized world.

Why is it that Defoe's texts are particularly suited to such explorations? Perhaps the best explanation is found in Defoe's defence of *Robinson Crusoe* in the preface to *Serious Reflections ... of Robinson Crusoe* (1720) where he argues that his fiction – 'Facts that are form'd to touch the Mind' – is offered 'for moral and religious Improvement'.[35] Defoe rarely, if ever, wrote without a practical end in view. Paula Backscheider points out that his education at Newington Green academy inculcated the view that 'knowledge' should be 'immediately useful and moral'. Writing about works published in the 1720s, Backscheider asserts that Defoe wrote 'to set his countrymen straight, to guide them, and to help them make distinctions'.[36] Not surprisingly, Backscheider assesses Defoe's fiction in instrumentalist terms. Thus, she observes that in the *Journal* 'Defoe turned observations about the 1665 plague into a comprehensive plan for lessening the spread and suffering of future plagues'.[37] Defoe, in short, used one outbreak of the disease as a 'fixed point' of the past useful for orienting oneself for present and future action. In a similar vein, Maximillian Novak discusses a host of works by Defoe that treated criminality, including *Moll Flanders*, as a response to a 'sudden surge in crimes of all sorts' from 1715 to 1725.[38] Thus, Defoe wrote to effect change and affect his contemporaries' thinking about crucial issues or crises. No wonder, then, that later artists and intellectuals have found his most famous narratives particularly productive 'figures of memory'.

Ian Watt, among others, has shown that no other work by Defoe has as notable a cultural afterlife as *Robinson Crusoe*, so it is fitting that the response by screen artists to that narrative is the most varied and the richest.[39] As I have shown elsewhere, the Crusoe story has been useful in the last fifty years and more for re-charting relations between the Occidental and the Other; before 1950, screen versions of *Crusoe* generally reproduced the representation of the Crusoe-Friday relationship in the novel in a more-or-less untroubled fashion. But starting in the early 1950s, with Buñuel's film, works for film and television increasingly viewed Crusoe's attitude towards or treatment of Friday critically. The key film in this critique of the Crusoe narrative is Jack Gold's *Man Friday* (1975), which views the Englishman as a pathological figure, bedevilled by religion and racism. But both before and after *Man Friday*, major post–World War II appropriations of the book by screen artists treat the Crusoe-Friday relationship as an element of Defoe's narrative that must be interrogated and, increasingly, revised.[40]

This approach to the novel in films and television series is by now well established and has, in fact, led in recent years to several fairly banal politically correct *Crusoe*s.[41] Far more interesting than those works are the uses to which Patrick Keiller puts the figure of Defoe, his most famous work of fiction, and his *Tour* in three films – *London* (1994), *Robinson in Space* (1997), and *Robinson in Ruins* (2010) – in which he develops a method that he comes to call 'Robinsonism' for considering crucial problems of contemporary life. This method entails journeys in which Keiller's Robinson explores first London and then England generally 'with the aim of developing novel definitions of economic wellbeing, based on the transformative potential . . . [of] images of landscape'. As Keiller explains his trilogy, 'in each film', the eponymous investigator 'attempted to better understand a perceived "problem" by looking at, and making images of, landscape'.[42] The journeys are undertaken by a man who in the first film is a part-time teacher at the fictional University of Barking, in the second a contract worker for 'a well-known international advertising agency' that asks him to undertake 'a peripatetic study of the *problem* of England', and in the final film, someone recently 'released from Edgcott open prison' who 'made his way to the nearest city, and looked for somewhere to haunt'.[43] From the first film to the last, Robinson is represented as a castaway on the island which he calls home; he both knows the landscape he explores and finds it strange and alien. Thus, Robinson and his companion in *London* and *Robinson in Space*, associated, in a way that is highly characteristic of Keiller's method, with the itinerants in August Sander's 1929 photograph, *Vagrants* (fig. 11.1),[44] explore England in the manner of Defoe's hero, who reports in his journal that some ten months after finding himself 'shipwreck'd . . . on this dismal unfortunate Island', he begins 'a more particular Survey of the Island it self'.[45]

To be sure, the wanderings of the Robinson of the films are inspired by myriad texts. In *London*, for example, one of the guiding spirits of the project is Alexander Herzen, the nineteenth-century Russian writer, whose critique of the city is quoted at length by the film's narrator, Robinson's unnamed and unseen fellow traveller (Paul Scofield). The Russian decries the ways in which London isolates its inhabitants – 'there is no town in the world which is more adapted for training one away from people and

11.1   © Die Photographische Sammlung/SK Stiftung Kultur - August Sander Archiv,
Köln/VG Bild-Kunst, Bonn and DACS, London 2014

training one into solitude than London' – but he also ruefully acknowledges his affection for the city: 'I came to love this fearful ant-heap where
every night a hundred thousand men know not where they will lay their
heads'. Other writers like Baudelaire, Poe, and Kafka are named by
Robinson as he travels, but Defoe and his works are constant reference

points. In *London*, Robinson and his friend visit Stoke Newington, looking 'for the place where Poe had gone to school', but find instead 'the house in which Daniel Defoe had written *Robinson Crusoe*'. This is the last event in the second 'expedition' in *London* (there are four in all), and the narrator opens his account of the next journey with the declaration: 'Robinson was devastated by this discovery; he had gone looking for the man of the crowd and found instead shipwreck and the vision of Protestant isolation'. This sense of desolation dominates all three films, each of which describes a voyage of discovery that is at best inconclusive. Iain Sinclair, in an important discussion of *London*, observes that Keiller's Robinson is 'marooned (Crusoed) in Vauxhall'.[46]

In *Robinson in Space*, the sense of loss and ruin proceeds from the examination of a 'particularly *English* kind of capitalism' that has produced 'the narrative of Britain since Defoe's time'. In this film the eponymous observer of English life and his friend undertake seven journeys (Defoe's *Tour*, of course, is also based on a series of 'Circuits *or* Journies'),[47] and what they mainly uncover is a strange, postmodern economic system typified by British Steel's Redcar plant, which 'produces 70,000 tonnes of steel a week ... and employs hardly any people'. As they do so, they repeatedly encounter Defoe. The 'method' of the 'project' described in the film, the narrator observes, 'had been suggested by ... [Robinson's] reading of Daniel Defoe's *Tour* ...', which is based on Defoe's travels as a *spy* for Robert Harley'. (Earlier the narrator reports that Robinson 'told me that he wished to become a spy, but was not sure who to approach'.[48]) In the midst of an extended consideration of Bristol (in the third journey), the narrator reports 'we visited the Llandoger Trow [a pub], where Defoe is supposed to have met Alexander Selkirk, the real Robinson Crusoe'. At Hull (Journey 6), the narrator notes both that 'Daniel Defoe was happy to welcome William III to England' and 'Robinson Crusoe sailed from Hull on September 1st 1651' as the camera captures first an equestrian statue of William III and then a frieze representing Crusoe in his goat-skin clothes.[49]

More telling than specific references to *Crusoe* is the deep kinship between Keiller's films, especially *Robinson in Space*, and the *Tour*, with its focus on what John Richetti memorably describes as 'the gear and tackle of everyday trades and common occupations, the techniques of industry and agriculture, and the paths, processes, and procedures of commerce'.[50] The films report the amount of rubbish shipped from 'the depots at Battersea and Wandsworth Bridge' (*London*), the fact that Malvern is 'a world centre for liquid crystals development and semi-conductor research' (*Robinson in Space*), and statistics on the production of rapeseed oil in the UK (*Robinson in Ruins*).[51] But, of course, like Defoe's *Tour*, the films do more than describe; they 'produce' the space they traverse and map, in the sense that they render it '*steeped* in its social and historical context', although the ideological cast of Keiller's films clearly sets them apart from Defoe's text.[52] Geoffrey Sill describes the motive for the *Tour* as 'a moral imperative pointing the way toward England's industrialization',[53] but *London, Robinson in Space*, and the tellingly named *Robinson in Ruins* worry about the apparent collapse of Britain's industrial economy and, more to the point, highlight the disparity between Britain's enduring industrial might and the failure of the new economy to provide jobs or, indeed, a viable way of life, for many Britons. Thus Middlesbrough, not far from Wynyard Park where Robinson and his fellow traveller see the Queen opening a Samsung plant, is described as having the highest unemployment in England, which, Robinson notes, 'has the least-regulated labour market in the industrialized world and the highest prison population of any nation in Europe'. And shortly after lamenting 'the passing of the *visible* industrial economy', the narrator reports that in Newbury, 'people were already living in the trees'.[54] In the final film in the trilogy, Robinson reports key moments in the financial collapse of 2008, encounters indications of Britain's nuclear industry and resistance to it, and notices signs of global climate change and considers the fate of the earth. Both the *Tour* and Keiller's films, then, construct a politically charged Britain, but one is 'triumphalist' while the other is a 'provoking reverie' on, among other things, 'the excesses of Thatcherism'.[55]

The kind of travel undertaken by Keiller's protagonist and his friend has been theorized by Michel de Certeau who describes a 'rhetoric of walking' that applies to all of Robinson's journeys; Certeau declares that '[w]alking affirms, suspects, tries out, transgresses, respects'. Such travelling is an imaginative feat in which sites defined by place names or other 'historical justifications' become 'liberated spaces' and are transformed into elements in a new, 'poetic geography'.[56] So, in *Robinson in Ruins*, as in the earlier films, the traveller makes surprising leaps, discovering historical connections that produce political and cultural meaning. A new (again unseen) narrator (Vanessa Redgrave) reports that Robinson has walked to 'Launton, near Bicester, in search of the site where a meteorite fell on 15 February 1830'; drawing on Robinson's materials, she reports that 1830 was a 'year of revolutions' not only in Belgium and France but also England, 'where the Captain Swing riots began at the end of August and continued through the autumn'.[57] She also observes that on 15 September of that year 'the Liverpool to Manchester railway was inaugurated'. Seemingly returning to the original purpose of this walk, she points out that '[t]he monument was half way up Poundon Hill', which was 'the site of a former Diplomatic Wireless Service transmitter used by Special Operations Executive during World War II'. But it turns out that the object – looking, in the film, untended and probably ignored, against a background of similarly untended foliage – 'was not meant to commemorate the meteorite', but was, instead 'a "Millenium Milepost"' (as we see in a close-up of the 'monument') on a 'National Cycle Network', one of a thousand funded by the Royal Bank of Scotland ('the world's largest bank'), which, Robinson read in the previous day's newspaper, 'was then the most vulnerable major bank in Europe'.[58] Thus in his walk to see a monument that was not there, Robinson brings together Luddite popular unrest, a major event in the first Industrial Revolution, an important example of 'extraterrestrial material falling from space',[59] World War II, the Millennium celebration (presided over by Tony Blair's New Labour government), and the Great Recession. The significance of these historical phenomena and the relationship among them are not stipulated, although they seem somehow crucial; later, reporting the collapse of Lehman Brothers and the hastily arranged sale of Merrill Lynch to Bank of America (over a four-and-half minute shot of a spider spinning a web), Robinson considers the possibility that 'this was no ordinary crisis and that some larger historic shift might be occurring'. At the beginning of the film, however, it is clear that Robinson's perspective goes beyond a possibly momentous political and economic transformation. 'He believed', reports the narrator, 'that he could communicate with a network of non-human intelligences that had sought refuge in marginal and hidden locations' that were 'determined to preserve the possibility of life's survival on the planet'. Minutes later, repeating a declaration in *London*, the narrator reports: 'Robinson had once said he believed that if he looked at the landscape hard enough, it would reveal to him the molecular basis of historical events and in this way he hoped to see into the future'. Keiller's characters, in short, undertake the kind of travelling that Certeau describes, in the course of which the walker does not so much make clear meaning as uncover 'possibilities': 'he makes them exist as well as emerge. But he also moves them about and . . . invents others'.[60]

I have elsewhere associated this movement in Keiller's films with 'drifting' ('free association in city space') and the results of such drifts, 'psychogeographies' ('*new emotional maps* of existing areas'), techniques of the Situationists, who envisioned the end of art and the transformation of society but who generally arrived at a sense of the impossibility of accomplishing their stated goals.[61] Keiller evokes all this in the midst of his trilogy when the narrator of *Robinson in Space* quotes one of the principal Situationists, Raoul Vaneigem:

> 'Reality ... sweeps me with it. ... I am always struck by the same basic contradiction: although I can always see how beautiful anything could be if only I could change it, in practically every case there is nothing I can really do. Everything is changed into something else in my imagination, then the dead weight of things changes it back again into what it was in the first place'.

As if illustrating Vaneigem's assertion, Robinson's wandering in the three films is repeatedly the occasion for visionary moments that lead nowhere: the possibility, in *London*, that the city might be transformed; the sense in *Robinson in Space*, when the travellers are in Blackpool, that they have arrived at a place that 'holds the key to ... [Robinson's] utopia'; and the fleeting sense in the last film that the financial crisis might produce a 'historic shift'. But all this comes to naught. By the end of the first film, Robinson is identifying the reasons for the 'failure of London', and in the second film, the travellers' contracts with the 'international advertising agency' funding their 'study' are abruptly cancelled and the narrator's last observation is: 'I cannot tell you where Robinson finally found his utopia'.[62] Finally, although the narrator reports in *Robinson in Ruins* that Robinson has 'a moment of experiential transformation' (on a visit to a 'ruined cement works'), in the end he simply disappears. Thus, Robinson's drifts end in failure. Robinsonism, then, may be inspired by, but it is also, in important ways, the undoing of, the 'circuits' of Defoe's *Tour*. And the image at the beginning of *Robinson in Ruins* of the eponymous researcher marooned in England like Defoe's Crusoe on his island – 'from a nearby carpark he surveyed the centre of the island on which he was shipwrecked' – is what remains at the end of that film and thus the whole trilogy.[63]

Once again, Defoe's writing is both a narrative and rhetorical model and a guidepost for an artist approaching contemporary problems. Keiller's attention to Defoe thus helps us grasp the significance of the afterlife of such texts as the *Tour* and *Crusoe*. The Robinson of the films sees Defoe as an observer who describes a country at the beginning of a great transformation, but Keiller's trilogy argues that in our time the 'narrative of Britain' has eventuated in a nation in 'ruins'. At the beginning of that historical arc, there is Defoe's *Tour* and its author's '"Enlightenment" ... values' as well as the hero of his best-known narrative, so important to, among others, Rousseau, but at the end there is only postmodern malaise for Keiller's Robinson.[64] Defoe, then, as a 'figure of memory' is an early modern writer whose interests and methods have made him useful to postmodern artists and writers confronting contemporary reality, who have taken up questions that Defoe's narratives essayed but have done so in a decidedly different register. Ann Rigney argues that in order to gauge the cultural afterlife of important writers, we need to describe and understand 'the social life of literary works', the ways, that is, in which writers and texts penetrate the cultures in which they endure. She observes in respect to the cultural afterlife of Scott: 'remembrance crystallizes into a limited number of sites of collective significance' – novels, characters, the figure of the author – 'by being repeated . . ., in different media and different forums which maximize their public presence'.[65] This examination of mainly visual works demonstrates that key Defoe texts – and the figure of Defoe himself – continue to be 'sites of collective significance' for writers, filmmakers, and conceptual artists. Those works show that such artists are not really interested in adapting Defoe's narratives; rather, they find him (as a crucial element in Anglo-American as well as post-colonial Anglophone cultural memory) useful for the collective 'permanent rewriting' of both the past and the future.

Notes

1 'Adapted' privileges text over image and overlooks the fact that, as Brian McFarlane argues, 'There are many kinds of relations . . . between film and literature, and fidelity is only one – and rarely the most exciting': McFarlane, *Novel to Film: An Introduction to the Theory of Adaptation* (Oxford: Clarendon Press, 1996), p. 11.

2 www.imdb.com lists twenty-three versions of *Gulliver's Travels* as well as two films derived from *A Modest Proposal* (1729), but the same source shows more than a hundred screen versions of *Crusoe* (accessed 15 July 2013).

3 Defoe is decidedly not as popular among screen artists as the big three – Shakespeare, Austen, and Dickens – but in terms of the variety of responses to his work, he may be second only to Shakespeare.

4 Robert Mayer, 'Robinson Crusoe on Television', *Quarterly Review of Film and Video*, 28:1 (2011), 53–65.

5 The latter two works are: *Lady Roxanne* (1991) for the French television series *Série rose*, featuring, according to www.imdb.com, 'male frontal nudity', and earning an NC-17 rating from the Motion Picture Association of America, indicating unsuitability for anyone under the age of 17; and *La aparición de la señora Veal* (1972), in the Spanish television series *Ficciones*.

6 CN/KN/HH, 'Hong Kong "Journal": Curator Cosmin Costinas tells the story of a city – interview', http://artradarjournal.com/2013/05/15/hong-kong-journal-curator-cosmin-costinas-tells-the-story-of-a-city-interview (accessed 15 July 2013).

7 Jan Assmann, 'Collective Memory and Cultural Identity', *New German Critique*, 65 (1995), 125–33 (129).

8 Ann Rigney, *The Afterlives of Walter Scott: Memory on the Move* (Oxford University Press, 2012), pp. 11, 12.

9 Klaus Poenicke, 'Engendering Cultural Memory: "The Legend of Sleepy Hollow" as Text and Intertext', *Amerikastudien/American Studies*, 43:1 (1998), 19–32 (20).

10 Catherine Parke, 'Adaptations of Defoe's *Moll Flanders*', in *Eighteenth-Century Fiction on Screen*, ed. Robert Mayer (Cambridge University Press, 2002), pp. 52–69 (58, 55).

11 The comment on *Tom Jones* is from *Time Out*, www.timeout.com/london/film/tom-jones (accessed 1 June 2014).

12 Kristin Thompson and David Bordwell, *Film History: An Introduction*, 3rd edn (Boston: McGraw-Hill, 2010), p. 476.

13 *Chicago Sun Times*, 1 June 1996, www.rogerebert.com/reviews/moll-flanders-1996 (accessed 27 April 2014).

14 Parke, 'Adaptations', p. 59; Densham is English, but the production companies for *Moll* were MGM and Spelling Productions, both American firms.

15 Parke, 'Adaptations', pp. 65, 64.

16 Russell indicates that he undertook the project to fashion a 'satire on eighteenth-century manners and morals à la Hogarth'. I am grateful to the staff of the Research Viewings section of the British Film Institute in London where I viewed *Your Honour, I Object!*

17 Bates is commenting on a class she is teaching: 'Moll Flanders, Quintessential Capitalist', 11 September 2013, www.betterlivingthroughbeowulf.com/moll-flanders-quintessential-capitalist/ (accessed 31 March 2014). See also 'Defoe's Moll Flanders as a Pragmatic Capitalist', 7 August 2012, http://fscafur.wordpress.com/2012/10/13, which describes Moll's behaviour as evidence of 'the same work ethic that contributes to success in a capitalist society' (accessed 31 March 2014).

18 Defoe, *Moll Flanders* (1722), eds. G. A. Starr and Linda Bree (Oxford University Press, 2011), p. 1.

19 Defoe, *A Journal of the Plague Year* (1722), ed. Louis Landa, intro. David Roberts (Oxford University Press, 2010), p. 2.

20 Roberts observes that '[u]ntil the very end, H. F. dismisses the theory that plague was the direct instrument of God's wrath': Defoe, *Journal*, pp. 215–16. The novel's discussion of '*Turkish* Predestinarianism' is at p. 165.

21 Defoe, *Journal*, pp. 52, 92.

22 Such men are referred to as 'Watchmen' in the 'ORDERS … *by the* Lord Mayor': Defoe, *Journal*, p. 34.

23 Maximillian E. Novak, 'Defoe and the Disordered City', *Publications of the Modern Language Association of America*, 92:2 (1977), 241–52 (241).

24 Jesse Lichtenstein, 'Films: Bringing Out the Dead', *The New Republic Online*, www.branaghcompendium.com/periwig.html (accessed 15 July 2013).

25 See Defoe, *Journal*, p. 29, for a reference to Berwick.

26 In an earlier version of his introduction to the *Journal* (Oxford University Press, 1990), Roberts describes 'the shutting-up of houses' as 'H. F.'s favourite subject': Defoe, *Journal*, p. xviii.

27 Defoe, *Journal*, p. 215, where Roberts also acknowledges that at times H.F. 'stretches his case' in respect to 'miasma theory'.

28 Lichtenstein, 'Bringing Out the Dead'.

29 Susan Sontag, *AIDS and Its Metaphors* (New York: Farrar, Straus and Giroux, 1988), p. 16. Sontag uses Defoe (pp. 47–51) in her discussion of 'plague', 'the principal metaphor by which the AIDS epidemic is understood' (p. 44).

30 John D. Arras, 'The Fragile Web of Responsibility: AIDS and the Duty to Treat', *The Hastings Center Report*, 18:2 (April–May 1988), 10–20 (16, 18), quoting the paragraph beginning 'Great was the Reproach' in Defoe, *Journal*, p. 200; Rose Weitz, 'Confronting the Epidemic: Teaching about AIDS', *Teaching Sociology*, 17:3 (July 1989), 360–64 (360).

31 D. A. Miller, 'Sontag's Urbanity', *October*, 49 (1989), 91–101 (99).

32 Katie Leishman, 'Two Million Americans and Counting', *New York Times*, 27 July 1986; www.nytimes.com/1986/07/27/books/two-million-americans-and-counting.html (accessed 15 July 2014).

33 David Black, 'The Plague Years' (part II), *Rolling Stone*, no. 446, 25 April 1985, p. 41; see also, Black, *The Plague Years: A Chronicle of AIDS, The Epidemic of Our Time* (New York: Simon and Schuster, 1986), p. 133.

34 See 'Embassy Projects. Adrian Wong, Works and Performances, 2005–2010', www.adrianwong.info/selected/?sak_gai (accessed 11 April 2014).

35 Defoe, *Serious Reflections During the Life and Surprising Adventures of Robinson Crusoe* (London: W. Taylor, 1720), sigs. [A6ᵛ], [A6ʳ].

36 Paula R. Backscheider, *Daniel Defoe: His Life* (Baltimore: Johns Hopkins University Press, 1989), pp. 19, 516.

37 Backscheider, *Life*, pp. 426–27.

38 Maximillian E. Novak, *Realism, Myth, and History in Defoe's Fiction* (Lincoln, Neb.: University of Nebraska Press, 1983), p. 123.

39 Ian Watt, *Myths of Modern Individualism: Faust, Don Quixote, Don Juan, Robinson Crusoe* (Cambridge University Press, 1996). Recent studies of the afterlives of *Crusoe* include Shawn Thomson, *The Fortress of American Solitude: 'Robinson Crusoe' and Antebellum Culture* (Madison, NJ: Fairleigh Dickinson University Press, 2009); Ann Marie Fallon, *Global Crusoe: Comparative Literature, Postcolonial Theory and Transnational Aesthetics* (Farnham: Ashgate, 2011); Joseph Acquisto, *Crusoes and Other Castaways in Modern French Literature: Solitary Adventures* (Newark: University of Delaware Press, 2012); Andrew O'Malley, *Children's Literature, Popular Culture, and 'Robinson Crusoe'* (Basingstoke: Palgrave Macmillan, 2012); Karen Downing, *Restless Men: Masculinity and 'Robinson Crusoe', 1788–1840* (Basingstoke: Palgrave Macmillan, 2014).

40 See Robert Mayer, '*Robinson Crusoe* in the Screen Age', in *The Cambridge Companion to 'Robinson Crusoe'*, ed. John Richetti (Cambridge University Press, forthcoming).

41 I refer here to *Robinson Crusoe*, dir. George Miller and Rodney K. Hardy (Miramax, 1997), with Pierce Brosnan; and *Crusoe*, dir. Michael Robison et al. (NBC, 2008–9).

42 Patrick Keiller, *The Possibility of Life's Survival on the Planet* (London: Tate Publishing, 2012), pp. 3, 9. There are three sources for the view of Robinson and Robinsonism developed here: Keiller's films; an installation at the Tate Britain in 2012, *The Robinson Institute*, which developed some of the themes and concerns of the films, especially *Robinson in Ruins*; and *The Possibility of Life's Survival*, which is, in important part, a print version of *The Robinson Institute*. See www.tate.org.uk/context-comment/video/tateshots-patrick-keiller (accessed 1 June 2014). Keiller describes the installation as 'a selection of its [the Tate's] images with historical and other works suggested by their subjects and their fictional cinematographer's concerns': *Possibility*, p. 3. I generally quote from *Robinson in Ruins*, but if the same language appears in *Possibility*, I cite that.

43 The prison, like the university, is apparently a fictional institution. On the former, see Keiller, *Possibility*, p. 5. In respect to Keiller's second Robinson film, I quote from the film and from Keiller's *Robinson in Space* (London: Reaktion Books, 1999), p. 6; the book reproduces some images and all of the narration from the film.

44 *The Robinson Institute* obliquely presents the photograph as an image of Robinson and his Friday. In *Robinson in Ruins*, the narrator identifies Robinson as a surrealist; Keiller, *Possibility*, pp. 3, 7 (the photograph), 45.

45 Defoe, *Robinson Crusoe* (1719), ed. Thomas Keymer (Oxford University Press, 2007), pp. 60, 84.

46 Iain Sinclair, 'Cinema Purgatorio', in *Lights Out for the Territory: 9 Excursions in the Secret History of London* (London: Granta, 1997), pp. 279–330 (311). In *London*, after the narrator notes 'an atmosphere of conspiracy and intrigue' in the city, there is a title card that reads simply 'VAUXHALL', introducing a discussion of where Robinson lives. Sinclair describes Keiller's Robinson as 'rescued from Kafka's *Amerika*, Defoe's Crusoe – displaced, condemned to internal exile': 'Cinema Purgatorio', p. 306.

47 Defoe, *A Tour thro' the Whole Island of Great Britain* (1724–26), abr. and ed. Pat Rogers (London: Penguin, 1971), p. 41.

48 Keiller, *Robinson in Space*, pp. 20, 173, 6. The travel in Defoe's *Tour* and Keiller's films was, in important part, invented; Rogers describes 'the structure of Defoe's "tour"' as 'the imaginative vehicle of a number of "circuits"', and Sinclair observes of Keiller, making *London*: 'he didn't walk … [t]he fiction walks instead'. Defoe, *Tour*, p. 18; Sinclair, 'Cinema Purgatorio', p. 309.

49 Keiller, *Robinson in Space*, pp. 102, 161. Both works are first shown headless (and the representation of Crusoe is never seen in full), and the narrator

declares: 'Robinson and I are proud to recollect our own experiences of *The Glorious Revolution*'.

50 John Richetti, *The Life of Daniel Defoe: A Critical Biography* (Oxford: Blackwell, 2005), p. 325.

51 Keiller, *Possibility*, p. 49. Keiller, *Robinson in Space*, p. 106, which notes that Defoe reported of 'Mauvern' that its mines might 'outdo Potosi'. See Defoe, *Tour*, p. 370.

52 Cynthia Wall, *The Literary and Cultural Spaces of Restoration London* (Cambridge University Press, 1998), pp. 104, 108; both Wall and Keiller cite Henri Lefebvre, *The Production of Space*, trans. Donald Nicholson-Smith (Oxford: Blackwell, 1991).

53 Geoffrey M. Sill, 'Defoe's *Tour*: Literary Art or Moral Imperative?', *Eighteenth-Century Studies*, 11:1 (1977–78), 79–83 (83).

54 Keiller, *Robinson in Space*, pp. 179, 90, 93. The comment about people living in trees is apparently an allusion to the Newbury Bypass Protest, which the Friends of the Earth describes as 'the UK's largest ever anti-road demonstration'; www.foe.co.uk/resource/press_releases/19970108103416 (accessed 4 August 2014).

55 Richetti, *Life*, p. 324; Sinclair, 'Cinema Purgatorio', p. 310.

56 Michel de Certeau, *The Practice of Everyday Life*, trans. Steven Rendall (Berkeley: University of California Press, 1984), pp. 100, 99, 104, 105.

57 The conceit of *Robinson in Ruins* is that the narrator is someone who is in possession of Robinson's research but has not travelled with him.

58 Keiller, *Possibility*, p. 53.

59 See 'Meteorites: Rocks from Space', www.oum.ox.ac.uk/learning/pdfs/meteors.pdf (accessed 4 April 2014).

60 Certeau, *Practice*, p. 98.

61 Robert Mayer, 'Not Adaptation but "Drifting": Patrick Keiller, Daniel Defoe, and the Relationship between Film and Literature', *Eighteenth-Century Fiction*, 16:4 (2004), 803–27 (814–16).

62 Keiller, *Robinson in Space*, pp. 1, 187, 203.

63 Keiller, *Possibility*, pp. 62, 14.

64 Richetti, *Life*, p. 83.

65 Rigney, *Afterlives*, pp. 11, 18.

CHAPTER 12.

Happiness in Austen's Sense and Sensibility and its Afterlife in Film

Jillian Heydt-Stevenson

Happiness and marriage are both afterlives, arriving after anticipation and emerging after courtship. And while we can distinguish between happiness and marriage, their linkage in courtship narratives is inevitable; such stories drive toward that proverbial state of 'happily ever after'. In Austen, wedded bliss is invariably projected into the novels' afterlives – what, that is, readers will never see, but can only imagine. Imagine they do: in sequels to the novels, in the bric-à-brac illustrating them, and in cinematic reincarnations. Assessments of film versions of Austen generally debate whether the novels' new lives transport them to hell or heaven.[1] I take inspiration, instead, from Robert Stam's more neutral and fruitful idea that '[a]daptations redistribute energies and intensities, provoke flows and displacements; the linguistic energy of literary writing turns into the audio-visual-kinetic-performative energy of the adaptation'.[2] The films provide the 'downstream contexts', to use Terence Cave's term, of our own era.[3] As Anna Holland and Richard Scholar have suggested, afterlives are 'revenant narratives, accounts of a haunting of the cultural imagination by figures and objects with a particular power to interest, disturb and move'.[4] As we watch the film adaptations of Austen's works, 'jumping over stiles', like Lizzy Bennet,[5] how do the cinema's restylings force our attention in new ways to the era's narrative innovations and the expectations they excite in readers? That is a specifically literary question, but a larger one is also at work here: what can these adaptations tell us about the history of happiness and pleasure?

Sense and Sensibility is my prime focus here. Both the 1995 film and the 2008 BBC mini-series use the technology available to film to supplement the 1811 novel, offering points of sensory ingress and bringing back to life what Austen's first readers would have already seen vividly in their own world – the geography, the locations, the clothes, the manners, and the presence of rural life.[6] For example, the 2008 BBC film's audio track dramatically conveys the rugged metonymies of beating hearts: pounding hooves and hammering waves.[7] The films also alter the novel: they build up Margaret's character, dramatize Edward's and Elinor's courtship, and eroticize the male leads.

These two versions share another decision: they make Marianne happy – very happy – and in a way that the novel allows only equivocally. This decision sheds light on modern notions of happiness in relation to those during Austen's era. In undertaking this genealogy of happiness, I will briefly survey the history of happiness: its classical antecedents and their late eighteenth-century afterlife. Then I discuss Austen's use of the word happiness in *Sense and Sensibility*, identifying how it echoes Aristotle's ideas in the *Nicomachean Ethics*. Finally, I turn to the two film versions of *Sense and Sensibility* to ask how, if courtship's afterlife is the bliss of marriage, these different narrative modes imagine and represent that happy state. In this section, I focus first on how the films, though effacing the novel's apparent cynicism, nevertheless re-establish some historical veracity in their emphasis on pleasure; and second, I explore the films' revisions of Marianne's character and her marriage: these highlight what in Austen seems to disturb us today – film-makers and scholars alike – her rendering of freedom and courtship as both more and less than happiness.

Afterlives of Happiness

Austen's novels, like Enlightenment and Romantic culture at large, are infatuated with happiness.[8] At the time, the word's meaning seemed both so broad a concept as to be indefinable, and palpably obvious, as in Pope's *Essay on Man*: 'Who thus define it, say they more or less | Than this, that happiness is happiness?'[9] Writers continued to deride such reductive tautologies. When Keats, in just one stanza of 'Ode on a Grecian Urn', extols the 'happy, happy boughs!', the 'happy melodist' and 'happy love! More happy, happy love!',[10] his repetition can imply, variously, an ironic signification or one relating to evanescence and permanence. The repetition reveals that each 'happy' might potentially mean something different from the last – good fortune, blessings, joy, bliss, pleasure, or chance – and in doing so, it confirms how many ways happy and happiness were defined in the late eighteenth and early nineteenth centuries.

The story of happiness is itself a series of afterlives, for when scholars narrate its history and try to define it, they generally begin with classical philosophers – Plato and Aristotle – and then move on to contrast those classical theories with later, modern (Enlightenment) incarnations. As Adam Potkay explains, the term happiness 'does not take wing until the eighteenth century, as a rendition of the Greek *eudaimonia*', which means flourishing; it is in fact 'neo-classical ..., expressing a secular ideal of rational contentment through ethical conduct'.[11] Ancient and modern notions of happiness differ in the importance they place on virtue, on whether happiness is objectively or subjectively determined, and on the question of when we know our happiness: at life's end or in the moment. The classical thinkers agree that the question of morality cannot be distinguished from the experience of happiness. Thus, for Aristotle, most 'are agreed about what to call [the good]: both ordinary people and people of quality say "happiness", and suppose that living well and doing well are the same thing as being happy'.[12] He goes on to explain that the 'function' of life is the 'activity of soul and actions accompanied by reason', and 'human good turns out to be activity of soul in accordance with excellence': happiness, then, 'is a kind of activity'.[13] For Aristotle, one only recognizes happiness at the end of life, when one can measure one's whole existence, a retrospective assessment made by gauging how rationally and thus virtuously one has lived.

In contrast, modernity calculates notions of happiness via daily life's shifting emotional barometer. As A. A. Long has said, the Enlightenment and its future system builders transmute happiness from virtue into ideas of 'excitement, ecstasy, or simple domestic comfort', to determine whether or not an individual is happy.[14] The subject, logically enough, measures this herself in the daily pulse of her inner feelings and sensations. John Locke describes this when he writes that because people chase happiness in so many ways, 'this variety of pursuit shows that every one does not place his happiness in the same thing, or choose the same way to it'.[15] To be sure, this epoch did not exclude virtue from happiness, but, as Austen reminds us, the most nefarious of characters can be quite happy in this modern sense of self-gratification. The John Dashwoods choose hedonism over virtue, but even more aberrantly they define their hedonism as virtue, thereby compromising the integrity of the latter word. Thus, John becomes an exemplary husband and father by defining generosity wholly in terms of fulfilling subjective desires.

Classical Happiness and Pleasurable, Romantic Afterlives

In her narratives of happiness triumphant, Austen is a kind of engineer who calculates the 'contact mechanics' of classical and more modern conceptions of happiness: are they 'deformed' under the load of their contact or elastic enough to bear each other's weight?[16] Where, in other words, do teleology and virtue stand in relation to happiness, subjectively defined? Certainly Austen acknowledges its idiosyncratic nature; after all, Mrs Jennings remains a picture of a contented self, despite imagining that her 'finest old Constantia wine' will restore the shattered Marianne's happiness.[17] Other characters' definitions of happiness are more reprehensible: Fanny Dashwood's greed, Lucy Steele's ambition, and Robert Ferrars's cottage dreams all spotlight how savagely they worship pleasure. In the most diminished sense, the pleasure-seekers are allowed belief in their own happiness, but in showing the consequences of a happiness derived from insatiability and narcissism, Austen tacitly criticizes how these characters obtained such happiness and questions the validity of their actions. Within the novel's scope, her exposure of the costs of this 'happiness' acts as a kind of proximate 'end of life' judgement, such as the one Aristotle advocates.[18] Their lives' telos manifests not in any closure at the novel's end, but in the misery they cause the ones they allegedly love. Regardless, the John Dashwoods remain self-satisfied, as does Robert Ferrars, who, by 'the happy self-complacency of his manner while enjoying so unfair a division of his mother's love and liberality, . . . earned only by his own dissipated course of life, . . . was confirming [Elinor's] most unfavourable opinion of his *head and heart*' (emphasis added).[19] In contrast, Austen defines the pursuit of happiness in Aristotelian fashion as action in the sense that 'happiness . . . is activity of soul'.[20]

Aristotle's ideas rematerialize in *Sense and Sensibility*, which consistently links merit and virtue to happiness, revealing that while the most immoral can experience some superficial species of happiness, the moral have to work at it, for it requires conscious effort and sacrifice: it involves putting aside one's own preoccupations to promote it in others and learning to relinquish one's own misery so as to participate in another's joy. The Dashwood women, for example, 'each for the sake of the others resolved to appear happy'.[21] The action required for happiness has a prehistory (or pre-life) in that it requires both self-knowledge and liberty and, by focusing on these qualities, Austen echoes Aristotle. Edward, surprisingly, powerfully states how liberty encourages happiness when, freed from Lucy, he says: 'I am grown neither humble nor penitent by what has passed. – I am grown very happy'.[22] Elinor's persuasion and his new happiness-induced courage permit him to visit his mother and receive the money necessary to marry. Aristotle links this liberty to the satisfaction of basic human needs: 'the one who is happy will also need external prosperity, in so far as he is human'; Elinor and Edward echo this in not being 'quite enough in love to think that three hundred and fifty pounds a-year would supply them with the comforts of life'.[23] Austen highlights another link between liberty and happiness:

> Elinor found every day afforded her leisure enough to think of Edward, and of Edward's behaviour[.] . . . There were moments in abundance, when . . . conversation was forbidden[.] . . . Her mind was inevitably at liberty; her thoughts could not be chained elsewhere; and the past and the future, on a subject so interesting, must be before her, must force her attention, and engross her memory, her reflection, and her fancy.[24]

Silence liberates Elinor so that she can be, paradoxically, more happily enchained by thoughts of Edward. Austen would never go as far as a Stoic like Cicero who claims that '[w]hile the virtues, one and all, move fearlessly onwards to suffer the torments of the rack, happiness, I repeat, will scorn to linger behind outside the prison gates'.[25] But Elinor's freedom arises from and presupposes what Aristotle would call 'human excellence', by which he means 'excellence of soul, not of body'.[26] Confinement constitutes liberty because her truest sense of freedom comes from knowledge of her inner independence. This, of course, does not belie the fact that she is happier knowing that Edward is single and hence marriageable.

The Happy Cinematic Afterlives of Austen's *Sense and Sensibility*

While the novel chafes against the conventional wisdom that happiness and pleasure prophesize domestic comfort, its film adaptations depict imagination and reality merging in companionate marriage. Roy Porter has stated that during the eighteenth century, 'As the business, profits and pleasures of temporal existence crowded out the mysteries of eternity, as the big issue turned from "Shall I be saved?" to "How shall I be happy?", a further question cast its shadow: "What is it, then, that I am?"' [27] For some, Austen collapsed the two questions into one, venerating love matches and offering few alternatives for happiness (or salvation) outside the wedded state. Yet they simultaneously cast the shadow of a doubt that happiness arises solely from the 'one-great-love-marriage'; Elinor, for example, reminds Marianne that 'after all that is bewitching in the idea of a single and constant attachment, and all that can be said of one's happiness depending entirely on any particular person, it is not meant – it is not fit – it is not possible that it should be so'.[28] Saturated in happiness, the 1995 and 2008 films embrace this 'bewitching . . . idea', and in doing so they call on another dimension of Austen's culture: that inalienable right to pursue pleasure.[29]

Though it may seem logical to differentiate pleasure and happiness – the former shallow, fleeting, and sensational and the latter attuned to deeper, long-lasting satisfaction – the eighteenth century often aligned them, almost rendering each of them essential to the authenticity of both. Indeed, pleasure often served as the sensation grounding any empirically minded system of moral philosophy. Though not a book one would call 'happy' or even one filled with many happy times, *Sense and Sensibility*'s plot nevertheless revolves around the hope for happiness and pleasure. Rowan Boyson argues that, during the eighteenth century, pleasure was considered as 'inherently communal rather than private or solipsistic'; it 'might register a feeling of collective dependence and interaction, and might be generated from a feeling of community'.[30] Austen fully exemplifies this in *Pride and Prejudice* (1813), where much happiness arises from the pleasure of conversation and sociability. In contrast, while the Dashwood women enjoy Willoughby's company, almost every other social occasion offers a sort of horror show.

Sense and Sensibility the novel resists pleasure, with the austere Elinor's rational worries dampening any chance of indulgent diversion. Perhaps this austerity signals a potential turn towards a classical emphasis on objectively accepted notions of virtue retrospectively accounted for, rather than subjectively determined contentment felt in the moment. Denise Gigante, in discussing Wordsworth and Shelley, points out that '[p]oetry gives pleasure to the human being conceived holistically, rather than as a unit of specialized expertise. Pleasure in fact *pulls* man together, as the pleasures of the imagination are synthetic'.[31] The 1995 *Sense and Sensibility*, directed by Ang Lee and with a screenplay by Emma Thompson, builds up that pleasure principle by creating an opening sequence of courtship between Elinor and Edward and by casting the charismatic Hugh Grant as the depressed hero. The novel, by contrast, forces us to take on faith that during the backstory – Elinor and Edward's courtship – the hero has what Lucy calls the capacity of 'making a woman sincerely attached to him'.[32] The plot and casting decisions bring superadded pleasures that 'pull' together the script, and perhaps the novel, by inviting us to experience pleasure and happiness together and by giving us a justification for Elinor's love and fidelity to a man who in the text only appears troubled. The film draws on the capacities of Grant's Edward to give more pleasure than Austen's distressed Mr Ferrars. This performance transforms Edward from a mostly silent and withdrawn character into a charming and sensitive man who understands grief and admires the Dashwoods' 'magnificent' library. The character's reserve becomes in the movie witty diffidence, which lightens the mood and increases pleasure and happiness. In the adaptation, Edward thereby gets a whole new life, drawing out the rebellious Margaret by teasing her about the source of the Nile. When, during Edward's and Elinor's courtship, their conversation becomes melancholy and veers toward hopelessness, he cheers them up: after explaining that his mother wants him to do something grand and dashing, he expresses a preference for the quiet country life, joking that he will 'keep chickens and give very short sermons', obviously not a line from Austen, but one that makes Elinor laugh.[33] Most strikingly, in the scene in which he reveals his bachelor status, when Elinor breaks down completely and everyone else leaves the room, he calmly and tenderly tells her that he loves her. This affable Edward pulls together pleasure and happiness – and love and courtship – into a coherent fullness.

In the novel, however, extreme happiness involves fragmentation of the self. Edward expresses his happiness in being able to tell Elinor he is not engaged, let alone married, by 'tak[ing] up a pair of scissors that lay there, and spoiling both them and their sheath by cutting the latter to pieces'.[34] In a gesture allying pain and pleasure, he expresses his freedom by destroying the sheath and anticipates his future happiness with Elinor, as he is now 'cut free' from the social and familial bonds previously 'sheathing' him from feeling whole. Significantly, Thompson's major alteration (the Margaret-Edward plot) becomes the de rigueur formula followed by the 2008 version, thus creating layered levels of imitation in its repetition of the varying joys unavailable to the novel's readers.

By transforming Edward into a handsome, funny, and charismatic man who plays well with children, both films render this hero a more proper object of amatory desire for modern audiences, thereby supplementing the novel's more meagre pleasures. In doing so, they follow a commercial but also historical logic. Freed from needing to see it as a mere impermanent sensation, the Romantic period allowed pleasure a new centrality in human happiness. Not yet, as Lionel Trilling claimed, did writers have to denounce pleasure for a deeper kind of spiritual aesthetic discipline. As Thomas Schmid and Michelle Faubert remark of Trilling's argument: 'Romanticism at large . . . registers the celebration of an embodied pleasure native to humanity and the lamentation for its inevitable loss'.[35] Austen's novels are built on the foundation of embodied pleasure as a prerequisite for happiness. Charlotte Collins (née Lucas), we therefore know, can never be happy, because her pleasure is embodied not in her own being, but in her 'home and her house-keeping, her parish and her poultry', external trappings which have 'not yet lost their charms'.[36] Both *Sense and*

Sensibility films reinforce the erotic undercurrent in Austen's courtship narrative by making this embodied pleasure not only sexual – the 2008 movie begins with Willoughby's fireside seduction of Miss Williams – but by making sexual desire a precondition for marriage, the heroes and heroines experiencing the chaste but amatory pleasures of mutual physical attraction. As I will discuss later in the essay, the 1995 and the 2008 films both require Marianne to fall in love before the wedding, not after.

The films, perhaps not surprisingly, voice their ardent faith in passionate attraction leading to and continuing a love match. To ensure this, the male heroes have to be 'cleaned up', so to speak, as Julian North has suggested: 'recasting [Edward and Brandon] as romantic heroes ... softens and eventually dissipates this critique ... of sexual impulsiveness'.[37] The films do not question the idea, which Austen dramatizes but also interrogates, that a companionate marriage provides the sure-fire prescription for a happy life and that one's family yearns to promote one's happiness. While motivations are always difficult to pin down, the films – in universally offering Edward and Brandon afterlives of considerable glory and in making substantial changes to the Marianne-Willoughby plot – revise what makes the novel difficult, what Claudia Johnson calls its 'unremitting ... cynicism and iconoclasm'.[38] Lee and Thompson's *Sense and Sensibility* takes Marianne's perspective regarding Willoughby insofar as it portrays him as a magnetic figure. He first appears on his impressive steed, which rears up dramatically. But the film also renders him far more sympathetic, showing him carrying Shakespeare's sonnets with him wherever he goes. Though he acts the rake, Willoughby is last shown posed as a gallant, sitting on a white horse atop a high hill. He is first shot from behind; the camera then focuses on his face as he looks down rather tragically at Marianne's wedding. After he turns his horse around, the camera returns to his face, framed behind that of the animal's, both projecting nobility. This arresting stance, highlighting his physical stature and his expression of devotion and loss, suggests that he is a figure worth admiring, and that their love was authentic and, at least for him, permanent.

The novel concerns itself less with the failure of first loves than with the loss of a life lived rationally and thus virtuously. Austen tells us that in hearing of Marianne's marriage, Willoughby merely feels 'a pang'.[39] The misfortune is not that these young lovers do not marry; instead, the tragedy lies in the 'irreparable injury' done to Willoughby in the novel's backstory, where 'too early an independence and its consequent habits of idleness, dissipation, and luxury, had made in the mind, the character, the happiness, of a man who, to every advantage of person and talents, united a disposition naturally open and honest, and a feeling, affectionate temper'.[40] When the narrator reveals that Mrs Smith believed that 'had [Willoughby] behaved with honour towards Marianne, he might at once have been happy and rich',[41] the novel further underscores the idea that, having lived virtuously, he would have been rewarded. The novel here also pays more attention to his potential – what he could have been if indulgence had not ruined him. In this sense Austen is more Aristotelian than Thompson and Lee: she explicitly exposes Willoughby as someone who could not put talent and goodness to work towards an energetic end, given that his pleasure calculus is based on the present moment rather than a holistic retrospective accounting.

Marianne's Happiness

The films find another source of pleasure in Marianne's relationship and eventual union with Brandon. In the novel, her family arranges her marriage, and her 'extraordinary fate' is that 'she was born . . . to counter-act, by her conduct, her most favourite maxims'.[42] The adoring advocate of consuming love embraces sober esteem. Not only filmmakers but also scholars (myself included) have found Marianne's marriage fraught since she, the ultimate advocate for the love match, becomes herself the subject of an arranged marriage, which could be interpreted as either a discomfit-ing economic exchange or a sign of her new-found maturity and self-awareness.[43] The films, however, eradicate the arranged marriage and consistently celebrate Marianne's open nature, no doubt revealing how romantic comedy slavishly observes conventional endings. Noting this adaptive feature, Julian North, hierarchizing novel over film, argues that these movies 'capitalize . . . on the fact that [Austen's subversiveness] can be so safely contained'.[44] Perhaps, though, Austen's subversiveness lies in being able to sustain multiple interpretive possibilities simultaneously: who is the 'real' Marianne? The passionate lover or wised-up wife – or both?

In reallocating Austen's energies by more predictably aligning Marianne's path to happiness, the films remind us what a modern audi-ence may find disturbing in Austen's novels or what might be difficult to achieve in that medium – her irony, doubleness, and ambiguity, much of which arises from the narrator's free indirect discourse, which, as Deidre Lynch and others have shown, infinitely complicates interpretation.[45] Helmut Müller-Sievers has argued that 'Human conscience does not allow for a position in which inside and outside, interpretation and description, empathy and criticism are conjoined. In this sense, free indirect speech is as in-human as the motions of industrial machines'.[46] Indeed, almost machine-like in chastising Marianne, the narrator, rather than announcing the heroine's marriage to Brandon as her own choice, tells us that it is her mother's

> darling object. Precious as was the company of her daughter to her, she desired nothing so much as to give up its constant enjoyment to *her* valued friend; and to see Marianne settled at the mansion-house was equally the *wish* of Edward and Elinor. They each felt *his* sorrows, and *their* own obligations, and Marianne, by general consent, was to be the reward *of all* (emphasis added).[47]

This passage invites us to ask if Marianne's marriage, like Lydia's (in Lady Catherine's words), is in its own way a 'patched-up business'.[48] Gone is the vibrant, headstrong Marianne who had taken to heart her mother's advice: 'Know your own happiness'.[49] In its place is a muted character apparently submitting to three people wrangling to marry her to Brandon so as to appease their debts to him. The language of economic exchange is not subtle: in frequently visiting her newly married daughter, Mrs Dashwood acts 'on motives of policy as well as pleasure', so as to bring Brandon and Marianne together as often as possible.[50] Marianne's company becomes an object to 'give' to 'her valued friend', and she, Edward, and Elinor consider Marianne to be Brandon's 'reward'; in short, they see her 'settled at the mansion house', as if she is the profit margin in the family budget, and will reimburse him for the 'obligations' they owe to him.[51] The narrator assures us that 'Marianne could never love by halves; and her whole heart became, in time, as much devoted to her husband, as it had once been to Willoughby'.[52] This, however, is a strange equivalence, since it implies that a short, youthful infatuation carries the same weight as the presumably more profound commitment of marriage.

It is also perfectly possible that, in marrying Brandon, Marianne joins the happy pantheon of Austen's other (later) heroines; yet if we acknowledge the ambiguity and mystery free indirect discourse stimulates, Austen's narrative technique and the history of happiness become more riveting than a positive assurance that Marianne is as happy with Brandon as she was with Willoughby. A return to the novel after a filmic interlude serves as a metaleptic intervention – that is, it is an act 'that consists precisely of introducing into one situation, by means of a discourse, the knowledge of another situation'.[53] The films 'forget' that in Austen's *Sense and Sensibility* Marianne's happy marriage draws primarily on a teleological model; and in a critical mediation, one could argue that this forgetting ultimately highlights Austen's narrative complexity, recalling how a passage such as this one incites the reader to question whether or not the fictional character has found a lucid balance between free will and sacrifice, whether she has abdicated her agency or actually had any to begin with. If the last case is valid, she would not have changed at all; in the end, she is as much an 'object' of her family's designs as she was a pawn of sensibility and 'irresistible passion'.[54] The novel's afterlives thus help unveil Austen's Aristotelian undercurrents and the way the story plays out the history of happiness. On the other hand, the novel raises a feminist issue, for evidently Austen's Brandon has eclipsed Marianne in significance: his sorrows and generosity are uppermost in the minds of her family.

If the novel 'corrects' Marianne ('She was born to discover the falsehood of her own opinions'[55]), the films celebrate her nature both by rewarding her with true love – rather than a husband she has to 'learn' to love – and by affirming the truth of 'her own opinions'. Both films unambiguously assert Marianne's happiness and obviate any potential gender bias favouring Brandon. Lee and Thompson guide us organically through Marianne's growing affection for Brandon. She thanks him on her sick bed, and as he leaves we see golden light shining on the door he has just closed. The 2008 film specifically speaks back to the novel, liberating Marianne from any hint of punishment. The films create a happy afterlife for Brandon's character as well, making him a powerful male figure. In the 2008 movie, for example, the Colonel confronts Willoughby about his intentions concerning Marianne, and then fights a manly duel with Willoughby while cross cuts propel us back and forth between the virile men striking swords and the abject Marianne, weeping silently at her writing desk, and then between the blood that flows from the vanquished Willoughby (Brandon's sword at his throat) and the liquid red wax that seals her letter.

The 2008 film blatantly inverts Austen's treatment of Marianne's happiness. There, we watch a conversation between Elinor and Marianne that echoes the one in *Pride and Prejudice* in which Jane, delirious with happiness, tells Elizabeth about her engagement with Bingley. Like Elizabeth, Elinor is miserable about her lost love and must rally forth to be happy for her sister. The mise-en-scène echoes the gap between the happy and dejected siblings by initially placing the girls at opposite ends of the room. The distance between them is echoed in lonely landscape sketches hanging on the wall.

MARIANNE: Elinor, Colonel Brandon has asked me to marry him.
ELINOR: And how did you answer him?
MARIANNE: I said that I would. Don't be angry with me.
ELINOR: Why should I be angry with you?
MARIANNE: Because I thought myself so much in love with Willoughby,
           because I have given you so much grief and trouble, because
           I shall be happy when you are unhappy.
ELINOR: Colonel Brandon is an excellent man and we owe him a great
           deal, but you should not marry him out of gratitude.
MARIANNE: I don't, Elinor. My feelings for him have changed so much.
           I love him.
ELINOR: Then I am very happy for you.
MARIANNE: I wish you could be happy too.
ELINOR: So do I; I must see if I can find myself a Colonel too.[56]

The conversation focuses on happiness, including the word 'happy' three
times and 'unhappiness' once. Instead of declaring, like the novel, that
'Marianne, by general consent, was to be reward of all' to appease the
family's debts,[57] the film's Elinor deliberately eradicates this possibility: she
emphasizes that although 'we owe [the Colonel] a great deal, ... you
should not marry him out of gratitude'. Further, the film's Marianne,
much like Austen's Elizabeth Bennet, actively declares her own happiness:
'My feelings for him have changed so much. I love him'. Notably, the
'change' has happened before marriage, not afterwards.

    In keeping with the romantic love plot's best conventions, both films
show Marianne falling in love before she marries, not after. From a
feminist point of view, one might see that the novel renders Marianne
lacking, given that she emerges as a kind of proto-angel in the house,
'restor[ing] [Brandon's] mind to animation, and his spirits to cheerfulness;
and that [she] found her own happiness in forming his, was equally the
persuasion and delight of each observing friend'.[58] From an Aristotelian
perspective, however, Marianne's happiness is complete, arising from the
sense the narrator gives of a virtuous life, which must be understood within
the context of social and familial life in full. In other words, the novel's
most subjectively centred character is transformed into the most objectively oriented member of a community. In the 2008 film clip that I quoted
above, we ultimately see the two sisters embrace physically, which is
doubled (to return to the passage) by Elinor's conversational caress: 'I
must see if I can find myself a Colonel too'. But, again, the film inverts the
novel insofar as it renders Elinor, not Marianne, the one who finds
happiness in making others happy.

What kind of afterlife is this? What kind of categorical imperative requires the metamorphosis of Marianne into an unmistakably happy character? Scholars have worked to categorize the different ways that material can be adapted from novel to film: certainly the 1995 and 2008 versions could be classified as '*celebrations*' of the novel,[59] less so perhaps in homage to the vicissitudes of concepts like happiness or institutions like marriage than in their visual-environmental authenticity (Linda Troost notes that in the Lee and Thompson movie '[n]o modern plants flower in the background'[60]). But cinematic treatments of *Sense and Sensibility* also fall under the branch of what has been called the 'liberating' adaptation: in the 2008 film we see a range of activities that are under erasure in the novel, from doing laundry to Willoughby undressing Eliza. Is Marianne's transformation into an unequivocally happy character an example of what Kamilla Elliott has called incarnation? That is, 'wherein the word is only a partial expression of a more total representation that requires incarnation for its fulfilment'.[61] Or is it what Thomas Leitch calls 'colonization', in which the screenwriter sees 'progenitor texts as vessels to be filled with new meaning. Any new content is fair game, whether it develops meanings implicit in the earlier text, amounts to an ideological critique of that text, or goes off in another direction entirely'.[62] Austen, like many of her peers, encourages readers to rethink, reframe, and participate in determining narrative modes and meanings; adaptations, in their 'redistributions of energy', do something similar, and this, too, can encourage the interrogatory aspect of reading, watching, and re-reading. It is nothing new to say that the adaptations of Austen's novels most often transform paradoxical narrations into conventional ones such as the 'megaplex' demands, so as, in Dianne Sadoff's words, to capture a 'crossover, multigenerational, mixed-sex audience'.[63] Deborah Cartmell and Imelda Whelehan want viewers of adaptations to 'enjoy' the 'traces' of the literary text, to discover how 'an adaptation, particularly a successful one, inhabits and imprints itself upon the notional "original"'.[64] In other words, a movement between the original and its afterlives, which can take viewers/readers over 'shifting thresholds, each of which re-calibrate the relation between "after" and "life"',[65] helps us recognize with more nuance our own cultural moment as well as Austen's.

Austen's novel and the 1995 and the 2008 films look to define what constitutes happiness. If the narrator 'corrects' Marianne's notion of happiness, perhaps the films 'correct' the narrator – or maybe it would be better to say that the films try to answer the conundrums that the text invites us to ponder: what is happiness, and how do we find it?

The questions remain immanent. The narrator affirms Marianne for 'earning' her happiness by 'working' at love, but in the film, happiness is a 'self-evident' truth, an 'unalienable right', rather like it is in *Pride and Prejudice*. The link to modern-day culture reminds us that when producing a film adaptation, in Linda Hutcheon's words, 'the contexts of creation and reception are material, public, and economic as much as they are cultural, personal, and aesthetic'.[66] To effect this contextual shift, the movie has to fill up the hole in the novel's middle: the love story that does not work out. So the film transforms this – it finds a centre in Marianne's happiness and her ability to choose freely based on principles of individual assertion rather than pure acquiescence to larger social demands. In doing so, she satisfies herself and the community without needing to sacrifice anything. Her happiness therefore becomes 'public happiness', wherein the 'civic, social and material conditions' of her marriage invite everyone to flourish.[67] In the novel, however, we are left pondering the question of agency and happiness: if power is wrenched from a character, can any conduct ensuing from that lead to happiness? And what role does sacrifice play in maintaining the community's happiness?

* * *

I have argued that *Sense and Sensibility* lacks much sustained pleasure or happiness. At the text's end, however – where happiness generally occurs in novels of this period – happiness takes on ecstatic tones.[68] If domestic happiness is the aspiration of life, perhaps it is not surprising that when Austen describes the attainment or seeming fulfilment of this everyday happiness, she resorts to the language of the ineffable. When Marianne finds she will be able to go to London, her 'joy was almost a degree beyond happiness, so great was the perturbation of her spirits'.[69] Adam Potkay sees this line as evidence that the eighteenth century differentiated crisply between happiness and joy, but what interests me here is Austen's use of 'almost', which suggests that happiness has a broad emotional scope. Though Potkay argues that happiness does not 'close down narrative, like intense joy or ecstasy, by being unspeakable',[70] in *Sense and Sensibility* happiness comes to have something of a sublime quality, causing distress, sleeplessness, and speechlessness. In the previous passage, Marianne's happiness perturbs 'her spirits'. When Mrs Dashwood arrives at Cleveland, thinking her daughter is dying, Elinor gives her 'joyful relief; and her mother, catching it with all her usual warmth, was in a moment as much overcome by her happiness, as she had been before by her fears'.[71] The characters' reactions to Edward's news that he is unmarried follow the same tenor: 'Marianne could speak *her* happiness only by tears . . . [A]nd her joy . . . was of a kind to give her neither spirits nor language'; Elinor 'was everything by turns but tranquil . . . – she was oppressed, she was overcome by her own felicity; – and happily disposed as is the human mind to be easily familiarized with any change for the better, it required several hours to give sedateness to her spirits, or any degree of tranquillity to her heart'.[72] Hearing the news, Elinor famously 'could sit it no longer'. Here her happiness becomes ecstatic as she seems, in the literal sense of the word, to be outside of herself but also feeling her body for the first time. Her emotion violates the normal control she exerts, as does the narrative voice, both seeming to have reached a point beyond language, beyond narration itself: the 'it' is indeterminate (her passion, her happiness, her control, her reason?). Edward, as I mentioned earlier, having ruined a pair of scissors and its sheath, falls 'into a reverie, which no remarks, no inquiries, no affectionate address . . . could penetrate, and at last, without saying a word, quitted the room'.[73] Ultimately he is 'one of the happiest of men', a statement that takes him into the realm of 'more than': he is 'more than commonly joyful', and he has 'more than the ordinary triumph of accepted love to swell his heart[.] . . . He was brought . . . from misery to happiness'.[74] If we return to Roy Porter's statement that wanting happiness can also 'cast its shadow', inviting the further question, '"What is it, then, that I am?"',[75] we see how their happiness rattles their sense of identity.

Such ecstasy may surprise readers, given the control Edward and Elinor have exerted, but I would argue that in the novel their extreme emotion is not repression released but happiness embodied. Thus when happiness does emerge in this social wasteland, it is felt 'in the blood, and felt along the heart'[76] – and it feels not like an unalienable right, but *strange*. The novel remedies this strangeness by offering a postnuptial look at both couples, defying Hegel's claim that 'history is not the soil in which happiness grows. The periods of happiness in it are the blank pages of history'.[77] Austen, however, fills in some of those 'blank pages', explaining that it is not long before Edward and Elinor 'had in fact nothing more to wish for, but the marriage of the Colonel and Marianne, and rather better pasturage for their cows'.[78] Perhaps Marianne and Brandon's marriage provides the prerequisite for better pasturage for said cows, which would be taking the Bildungsroman from organic union – willingly giving up so as willingly to find harmony – all the way to the organic: the happiness of livestock. And Marianne of course must learn to love, an 'unromantic' decision, but not a blank page. The cinematic versions of *Sense and*

Sensibility, more along Hegel's line, provide the soil for romance to germinate, but not to continue to flower in the afterlife of marriage. Instead the films so compress and intensify the desire courtship engenders that they imprint an oath on viewers' sensibilities that nothing could possibly go wrong in the future and that courtship is permanent. In ways less 'romantic', Austen's novels also promise that courtship *must* have a happy afterlife in marriage, but the prosaic end to *Sense and Sensibility* suggests that after ecstasy, the social harmony of two friendly sisters and their husbands makes them all 'more than commonly joyful'.[79] Walter Benjamin has said that 'The kind of happiness that could arouse envy in us exists only in the air we have breathed[.] ... [O]ur image of happiness is indissolubly bound up with the image of redemption'.[80] In these two films, this is the redemption of the couple; in *Sense and Sensibility* it is redemption of the family. And in having both film and novel, we breathe Austen's air and ours simultaneously, craving her happiness as well as our own.

Notes

1 See *Jane Austen on Screen*, eds. Gina Macdonald and Andrew F. Macdonald (Cambridge University Press, 2003), pp. 9–21.
2 Robert Stam, 'Introduction: The Theory and Practice of Adaptation', in *Literature and Film: A Guide to the Theory and Practice of Film Adaptation*, eds. Robert Stam and Alessandra Raengo (Oxford: Blackwell, 2005), pp. 1–52 (46).
3 *Pre-Histories and Afterlives: Studies in Critical Method for Terence Cave*, eds. Anna Holland and Richard Scholar (London: Legenda, 2009), p. 2.
4 *Pre-Histories and Afterlives*, p. 8.
5 Jane Austen, *Pride and Prejudice* (1813), ed. Pat Rogers, The Cambridge Edition of the Works of Jane Austen (Cambridge University Press, 2006), p. 36.
6 *Sense and Sensibility*, dir. Ang Lee, screenplay by Emma Thompson, perf. Emma Thompson and Kate Winslet (Columbia Pictures, 1995); *Sense and Sensibility*, dir. John Alexander, screenplay by Andrew Davies, perf. Hattie Morahan, Charity Wakefield, and David Morrissey (BBC, 2008).
7 For a rich analysis of the 'thematic shaping in film of Austen's stories', see Penny Gay, '*Sense and Sensibility* in a Postfeminist World: Sisterhood is still Powerful', in *Jane Austen on Screen*, pp. 90–110 (90).
8 On Austen and happiness, see Terry Castle, 'Introduction', in Jane Austen, *Emma* (1815), ed. James Kinsley (Oxford University Press, 1998), pp. vii–xxviii; Nicholas Dames, 'Austen's Nostalgics', *Representations*, 73 (2001), 117–43; Mary Favret, 'Free and Happy: Jane Austen in America', in *Janeites: Austen's Disciples and Devotees*, ed. Deidre Lynch (Princeton University Press, 2000), pp. 166–87; Claudia Johnson, *Jane Austen: Women, Politics, and the Novel* (University of Chicago Press, 1988); Claudia Johnson, *Equivocal Beings: Politics,*

Gender, and Sentimentality in the 1790s (University of Chicago Press, 1995); Stefanie Markovits, 'Jane Austen and the Happy Fall', *Studies in English Literature 1500–1900*, 47:4 (2007), 779–97; Patricia Meyer Spacks, 'Emma's Happiness', *Association of Departments of English Bulletin*, 84 (1986), 16–18.

9 Alexander Pope, *An Essay on Man* (1734), ed. Maynard Mack, The Twickenham Edition of the Poems of Alexander Pope, 11 vols. (London: Methuen, 1938–68), vol. 3, p. 130.

10 John Keats, 'Ode on a Grecian Urn' (1820), *Keats's Poetry and Prose*, ed. Jeffrey Cox (New York: W. W. Norton, 2008), pp. 461–62.

11 Adam Potkay, *The Story of Joy: From the Bible to Late Romanticism* (Cambridge University Press, 2007), p. 21.

12 Aristotle, *Nicomachean Ethics*, trans. Christopher Rowe, intro. Sarah Broadie (Oxford University Press, 2002), p. 97.

13 Aristotle, *Nicomachean Ethics*, pp. 102, 105.

14 A. A. Long, *Epictetus: A Stoic and Socratic Guide to Life* (Oxford: Clarendon Press, 2002), p. 193.

15 John Locke, *An Essay Concerning Human Understanding* (1689), ed. Peter H. Nidditch (Oxford University Press, 1979), p. 268.

16 Although Brian Michael Norton does not discuss Austen, he confirms that Austen's concerns were part of a larger crusade when he writes that 'while eighteenth-century thinking about happiness was deeply shaped by classical eudaimonism, the new understanding of happiness could only uneasily be contained within the framework of eudaimonist ethics. No longer seen as self-evident, the relation between virtue and happiness now demanded demonstration. Treatises on happiness arose, in part, to fulfill this task': *Fiction and the Philosophy of Happiness: Ethical Inquiries in the Age of Enlightenment* (Lewisburg: Bucknell University Press, 2012), p. 134.

17 Jane Austen, *Sense and Sensibility* (1811), ed. Edward Copeland, The Cambridge Edition of the Works of Jane Austen (Cambridge University Press, 2006), p. 224.

18 We cannot know for certain whether Austen knew of Aristotle's works. Sarah Emsley argues that Austen 'inherits the tradition of the classical and theological virtues primarily through her reading of . . . the works of Shakespeare, Samuel Johnson, and Henry Fielding'. Emsley thoroughly canvases the possibilities for Austen's knowledge of Greek, Latin, and the classical authors: *Jane Austen's Philosophy of the Virtues* (Basingstoke: Palgrave Macmillan, 2005), pp. 12, 17–20. Gilbert Ryle suggests that Austen's 'Aristotelian ethic-cum-aesthetic' potentially came from Shaftesbury: 'Jane Austen and the Moralists', in *Critical Essays on Jane Austen*, ed. B. C. Southam (London: Routledge and Kegan Paul, 1968), p. 121, quoted in David Gallop, 'Jane Austen and the Aristotelian Ethic', *Philosophy and Literature*, 23:1 (1999), 96–109 (106). Gallop's useful article summarizes several ways that 'Aristotle's ethics can be read as an uncanny anticipation of [Austen's]'; he briefly touches on the subject of happiness (p. 98).

19 Austen, *Sense and Sensibility*, p. 337–38 (emphasis added).

20 Aristotle, *Nicomachean Ethics*, p. 109.

21 Austen, *Sense and Sensibility*, p. 33.

22 Austen, *Sense and Sensibility*, p. 421.

23 Aristotle, *Nicomachean Ethics*, p. 253. In this passage, Aristotle specifically refers to the link between reflection and happiness ('happiness will be a kind of reflection' [p. 253]), which dovetails with the novel given that both Elinor and Edward seek a quiet country life and he seeks a career in the Church. Austen, *Sense and Sensibility*, p. 418.

24 Austen, *Sense and Sensibility*, p. 121.

25 Marcus Tullius Cicero, 'Discussions at Tusculum', *On the Good Life*, trans. Michael Grant (Harmondsworth: Penguin, 1971), p. 95.

26 Aristotle, *Nicomachean Ethics*, p. 109.

27 Roy Porter, *Flesh in the Age of Reason: The Modern Foundations of Body and Soul* (New York: W. W. Norton, 2004), p. 23.

28 Austen, *Sense and Sensibility*, p. 298.

29 Though he does not discuss the addition of pleasure into the film, William Galperin argues that 'In striving for coherence in a text where confusion and discontent are linked, the Lee/Thompson adaptation "saves" the novel in lieu of its ability, apparently, to save itself': 'Adapting Jane Austen: The Surprising Fidelity of *Clueless*', *The Wordsworth Circle*, 42:3 (2011), 187–193 (187).

30 Rowan Boyson, *Wordsworth and the Enlightenment Idea of Pleasure* (Cambridge University Press, 2012), p. 1. See the 1802 preface to *Lyrical Ballads*, where Wordsworth links both the exertions of the poet and the man of science to pleasure but maintains that the poet's pleasure is universal and communal, while that of the man of science is personal and private: William Wordsworth and Samuel Taylor Coleridge, 'Preface', *Lyrical Ballads: 1798 and 1802*, ed. Fiona Stafford (Oxford University Press, 2013), pp. 95–115.

31 Denise Gigante, 'Foreword', in *Romanticism and Pleasure*, eds. Thomas Schmid and Michelle Faubert (Basingstoke: Palgrave Macmillan, 2010), pp. ix–xv (xiii).

32 Austen, *Sense and Sensibility*, p. 150.

33 Lee and Thompson, *Sense and Sensibility*.

34 Austen, *Sense and Sensibility*, p. 407.

35 *Romanticism and Pleasure*, p. 1.

36 Austen, *Pride and Prejudice*, pp. 239–40.

37 Julian North, 'Conservative Austen, Radical Austen: *Sense and Sensibility* from Text to Screen', in *Adaptations: From Text to Screen, Screen to Text*, eds. Deborah Cartmell and Imelda Whelehan (London and New York: Routledge, 1999), pp. 38–50 (pp. 47, 46).

38 Johnson, *Jane Austen*, p. 72.

39 Austen, *Sense and Sensibility*, p. 430.

40 Austen, *Sense and Sensibility*, p. 375.

41 Austen, *Sense and Sensibility*, p. 430.

42 Austen, *Sense and Sensibility*, p. 429.

43 Jillian Heydt-Stevenson, 'Narrative', in *A Handbook of Romanticism Studies*, eds. Joel Faflak and Julia M. Wright (Malden: Wiley-Blackwell, 2012), pp. 159–76 (168–70). See also Alistair Duckworth's argument that 'Marianne's marriage to the rheumatic Colonel Brandon is a gross over-compensation for her misguided sensibility': *The Improvement of the Estate: A Study of Jane Austen's Novels* (Baltimore: Johns Hopkins University Press, 1971), p. 104. Sarah Emsley defends the marriage, seeing Marianne's 'education' as involving 'both the classical regulation of governing her feelings and improving her temper, and the Christian imperative of contrition': *Jane Austen's Philosophy*, p. 79.

44 North, 'Conservative Austen', p. 49.

45 Deidre Shauna Lynch, *The Economy of Character: Novels, Market Culture, and the Business of Inner Meaning* (University of Chicago Press, 1998), pp. 212–15, 231, 234, 236–38. Kathryn Sutherland points out that Austen's 'sophisticated aural figuration', her use of free indirect discourse, and her 'blurring of character with character and narrator ... are almost impossible to achieve in film': *Jane Austen's Textual Lives: From Aeschylus to Bollywood* (Oxford University Press, 2005), p. 341.

46 Helmut Müller-Sievers, *The Cylinder: Kinematics of the Nineteenth Century* (Berkeley: University of California Press, 2012), p. 153.

47 Austen, *Sense and Sensibility*, p. 429.

48 Austen, *Pride and Prejudice*, p. 396.

49 Austen, *Sense and Sensibility*, p. 120.

50 Austen, *Sense and Sensibility*, p. 428.

51 Austen, *Sense and Sensibility*, p. 429.

52 Austen, *Sense and Sensibility*, p. 430.

53 Gérard Genette, *Narrative Discourse: An Essay in Method*, trans. Jane E. Lewin (Ithaca: Cornell University Press, 1980), p. 234.

54 Austen, *Sense and Sensibility*, p. 429.

55 Austen, *Sense and Sensibility*, p. 429.

56 Alexander and Davies, *Sense and Sensibility*.

57 Austen, *Sense and Sensibility*, p. 429.

58 Austen, *Sense and Sensibility*, p. 430.

59 Thomas Leitch, *Film Adaptation and its Discontents: From 'Gone with the Wind' to 'The Passion of the Christ'* (Baltimore: Johns Hopkins University Press, 2007), p. 96.

60 Linda Troost, 'The Nineteenth-Century Novel on Film: Jane Austen', in *The Cambridge Companion to Literature on Screen*, eds. Deborah Cartmell and Imelda Whelehan (Cambridge University Press, 2007), pp. 75–89 (83).

61 Kamilla Elliott, *Rethinking the Novel/Film Debate* (Cambridge University Press, 2003), p. 161.

62 Leitch, *Film Adaptation and its Discontents*, p. 109.

63 Dianne F. Sadoff, *Victorian Vogue: British Novels on Screen* (Minneapolis: University of Minnesota Press, 2010), p. 246. Sadoff argues that 'Thompson adapts the atmosphere and perspective of Austen's novel to depict a deep cultural anxiety about the difficulty of 1990s sexual arrangements' (p. 60).

64 *Screen Adaptation: Impure Cinema*, eds. Deborah Cartmell and Imelda Whelehan (Basingstoke: Palgrave Macmillan, 2010), p. 12.

65 *Pre-Histories and Afterlives*, p. 5.

66 Linda Hutcheon with Siobhan O'Flynn, *A Theory of Adaptation*, 2nd edn (London and New York: Routledge, 2013), p. 28.

67 Potkay, *Story of Joy*, p. 22.

68 Potkay makes this point: 'Thus most writers reserve happiness, like death, for the end of narratives': *Story of Joy*, p. 23.

69 Austen, *Sense and Sensibility*, p. 180.

70 Potkay, *Story of Joy*, p. 23.

71 Austen, *Sense and Sensibility*, p. 378.

72 Austen, *Sense and Sensibility*, pp. 411, 412.

73 Austen, *Sense and Sensibility*, p. 408.

74 Austen, *Sense and Sensibility*, pp. 409–10.

75 Porter, *Flesh*, p. 23.

76 William Wordsworth, 'Lines Written a few miles above Tintern Abbey, on revisiting the Banks of the Wye during a Tour, July 13, 1798', Wordsworth and Coleridge, *Lyrical Ballads*, pp. 87–91 (88).

77 G. W. F. Hegel, *Lectures on the Philosophy of World History. Introduction: Reason in History*, trans. H. B. Nisbet (Cambridge University Press, 1975), 'Second Draft' (1830), p. 79.

78 Austen, *Sense and Sensibility*, p. 425.

79 Austen, *Sense and Sensibility*, p. 410.

80 Walter Benjamin, 'Theses on the Philosophy of History', *Illuminations: Essays and Reflections*, ed. Hannah Arendt, trans. Harry Zohn (New York: Schocken Books, 1969), pp. 253–64 (254).

CHAPTER 13

Refashioning The History of England: *Jane Austen and* 1066 *and All That*

Peter Sabor

Jane Austen completed her miniature *History of England* on 26 November 1791, three weeks before her sixteenth birthday. She wrote it as a parodic response to Oliver Goldsmith's four-volume *History of England* (1771), of which her brother James owned a copy and which she annotated extensively with a mocking marginal commentary (confined almost entirely to the third and fourth volumes), probably shortly before creating a history of her own.[1] Goldsmith claimed to narrate English history in a detached, impartial fashion; his work would, he declared, be 'a plain unaffected narrative of facts, with just ornament enough to keep attention awake, and with reflection barely sufficient to set the reader upon thinking'.[2] Austen, in contrast, set out to write an overtly arbitrary and bigoted account, with the Stuarts as the heroes and Elizabeth I as the principal villain of her story.

Like all of Austen's juvenilia, *The History of England* remained unpublished in her lifetime. First appearing in print only in 1922, its afterlife, although a far cry from that of Austen's novels, has been remarkably diverse. Illustrated by her sister Cassandra, it has also attracted the attention of modern artists: new designs were added in editions of 1963 (by Joan Hassall), 1966 (by Paulette Riches), 1978 (by Suzanne Perkins), and 1995 (by Juliet McMaster).[3] Part of the text was incorporated into John Barton's historical drama *The Hollow Crown*, first performed by the Royal Shakespeare Company at the Aldwych Theatre, London, in 1961 and since revived on numerous occasions.[4] And in Patricia Rozema's 1999 film adaptation of *Mansfield Park* (1814), in which Austen's heroine Fanny Price becomes a version of the author in her youth, among the pieces that we see her writing is *The History of England*.

Over thirty years before Barton's theatrical adaptation or Hassall's visual illustrations, moreover, *The History of England* was refashioned in a form akin to its own: burlesque history writing. In 1930, W. C. Sellar and R. J. Yeatman published *1066 and All That: A Memorable History of England*, a bestseller at the time and still popular today. Several critics have been struck by the resemblances between the two works. Deirdre Le Faye, for example, finds *The History of England* 'uncannily prophetic' of *1066 and All That*, while Daniel Woolf believes that it is 'anticipatory' of Sellar and Yeatman's 'much later parody'.[5] I suggest, in contrast, that there is nothing surprising about the parallels between the histories: their resemblance is not uncanny if Sellar and Yeatman, as I believe, were among the early readers of Austen's astonishingly precocious work. They had, after all, eight years in which to study the techniques of their youthful predecessor, and in *1066 and All That*, as its subtitle, 'A Memorable History of England', indicates, they put *The History of England* to good use.

The most obvious source for *1066 and All That*, as several readers have noted, is the illustrated history of England by the Scottish children's writer Henrietta Elizabeth Marshall, *Our Island Story: A History of England for Boys and Girls* (1905).[6] Replete with anecdotes, many of them apocryphal, it contained a wealth of stirring stories that Sellar and Yeatman could recast in comic and often surrealist form. In doing so, they were mirroring Austen's abusive treatment of Goldsmith; while Marshall provided Sellar and Yeatman with copious material to parody, Austen furnished many of the satirical techniques that they deployed.

I

For many years after her death in 1817, the existence of Austen's early writings, as well as her later manuscript works, was known only to members of her family and a few close family friends. These writings included three manuscript notebooks containing twenty-seven separate items, an epistolary novella 'Lady Susan', and two unfinished novels, 'The Watsons' and 'Sanditon'. Some public notice of the juvenilia was made for the first time in *A Memoir of Jane Austen* (1870) by Austen's nephew James Edward Austen-Leigh, in which he mentioned briefly the existence of 'several tales, some of which seem to have been composed while she was quite a girl'.[7] More information about the juvenilia appeared in the second edition of the *Memoir* (1871), in which Austen-Leigh also printed, for the first time, 'Lady Susan' and 'The Watsons', as well as a much abridged version of 'Sanditon'. The juvenilia, however, were represented only by one of Austen's miniature comic plays, 'The Mystery'. All of the other early writings, including 'The History of England', remained unknown to the reading public.

With the publication of *Jane Austen: Her Life and Letters, A Family Record* (1913), by William and Richard Arthur Austen-Leigh, the titles of several items in the first manuscript notebook and of both stories in the third were revealed for the first time. Until 1922, nothing at all was known of the contents of the second notebook. In that year, it became the first of the three to be published, under the title *Love & Freindship and Other Early Works*, with a preface by the novelist and literary critic, G. K. Chesterton. Chesterton had previously expressed his admiration for Austen's novels in an amusing clerihew of 1905, beginning 'The novels of Jane Austen | Are the ones to get lost in', as well as in his *The Victorian Age in Literature* (1913) and in an essay on *Emma* (1917).[8] His preface to *Love & Freindship*, however, was much the most influential of his writings on Austen, with insights into her juvenilia that remain of interest today.[9] The volume was a commercial and critical success, going through three impressions within a month, a fourth impression in 1923, and a reissue in 1929, as well as four impressions of an American edition in 1922.[10] Prominent critics such as Virginia Woolf, Augustine Birrell, and J. C. Squire (writing as 'Solomon Eagle') reviewed the collection favourably, and both R. Brimley Johnson and Annette B. Hopkins gave the title story, 'Love and Freindship', sustained attention.[11]

The title given to the collection, either by Chesterton or by the publisher, Chatto & Windus, *Love & Freindship and Other Early Works*, was misleading. Austen herself entitled it simply 'Volume the Second', with 'Love and Freindship' appearing first in order, followed by 'Lesley Castle', 'The History of England', 'A Collection of Letters', and finally several shorter pieces collectively entitled 'Scraps'. The ordering approximates the chronology of composition, with several dates provided by Austen herself; 'Love and Freindship', the earliest of the items, was completed on 13 June 1790. Chesterton clearly found this story much the most impressive part of the volume. His preface is largely devoted to 'Love and Freindship', which was, he contended, 'a thing to laugh over again and again as one laughs over the great burlesques of Peacock or Max Beerbohm'.[12]

Chesterton does not, surprisingly, so much as mention 'The History of England'. He does, however, draw attention to the existence in the manuscript of medallion portraits, 'the work of [Austen's] sister Cassandra'.[13] These watercolour portraits, thirteen in all, grandiloquently signed 'C E Austen pinx' (painted, *pinxit*, by Cassandra Elizabeth Austen), depict the English monarchs who feature in Austen's text. In the manuscript, they are inserted beneath the heading for the respective monarchs. They are, as Le Faye observes, 'as deliberately misleading as the text, portraying the monarchs not as royal heads of state but as contemporary and sometimes disreputable-looking ordinary people'.[14] In Chesterton's edition, twelve of the portraits are reproduced in colour on the endpapers, with that of Richard III mysteriously omitted, presumably through the publisher's inadvertence. Nonetheless, the portraits' prominent place on the endpapers draws attention to the work that they illustrate.

In 1922, the year in which 'The History of England' was first published, two young men graduated from Oriel College, Oxford with history degrees: Walter Carruthers Sellar (1898–1951) and Robert Julian Yeatman (1897–1968). Both were avid readers, and given the popularity of Chesterton's edition, it seems fair to assume that they would have become familiar with a newly discovered piece of mock-historical writing by a famous English novelist. The 1920s was a key decade both in the rise of Austen's reputation and in an increased awareness of the extent of her manuscript writing. 1923 saw the publication of R. W. Chapman's elaborate collected edition of the six novels the first scholarly edition of Austen or of any English novelist. *The Watsons*, with an introduction by A. B. Walkley, appeared in the same year; *Lady Susan* and *Sanditon*, both edited by Chapman, followed in 1925; and two more Chapman editions of Austen's manuscript writings, *Plan of a Novel* and the two cancelled chapters of *Persuasion* (1818), in 1926. All of these editions were the subjects of essays by leading reviewers, including E. M. Forster, J. Middleton Murry, and Virginia Woolf.[15] Woolf had also reviewed, in 1920, a memoir of Austen by her great-niece Mary Augusta Austen-Leigh, entitled *Personal Aspects of Jane Austen*. In this book, Austen-Leigh printed, from the volumes then in her possession, a few of Austen's hitherto unpublished marginalia on Goldsmith's *History of England*. As Woolf observed, these strident remarks by the teenage Austen include pro-Jacobite musings, such as 'Dear Balmerino! I cannot express what I feel for you!'[16] on the execution of the Jacobite leader. Katherine Mansfield was also struck by what she termed 'fiery outpourings' on Goldsmith's *History*, which 'revive Jane Austen's own voice'.[17] It is possible, I believe, that Sellar and Yeatman might also have read these intriguing comments by Austen on Goldsmith's work.

Another indication of Austen's increasing stature in the 1920s was Rudyard Kipling's short story 'The Janeites', first published in magazine form in 1924 and then in his collection *Debits and Credits* (1926).[18] 'The Janeites', which has received much attention from recent critics, concerns the experiences of British soldiers fighting in the trenches in

World War I and their therapeutic reading of Austen's novels. Its epigraph is a quatrain expressing the reverential sentiments for Austen that the term 'Janeites' conveys:

> Jane lies in Winchester – blessed be her shade!
> Praise the Lord for making her, and her for all she made!
> And while the stones of Winchester, or Milsom Street, remain,
> Glory, love, and honour unto England's Jane![19]

Both Sellar and Yeatman served in the army during the war: Sellar as a second lieutenant in France and Germany and Yeatman as a lieutenant in the Royal Field Artillery. Yeatman was severely wounded in battle and awarded the MC in 1916. If Kipling's story is any indication, they could have been reading Austen during their army years, before their matriculation at Oxford on the same day, 29 April 1919.

After graduating from Oxford, both Sellar and Yeatman began writing for literary journals, including the best-selling humorous and satirical magazine *Punch*, to which Sellar became a contributor in 1925 with Yeatman following suit a year later. In the late 1920s, they began to collaborate on the book that would make them famous: *1066 and All That*. Excerpts began appearing in *Punch* in September 1930; the book was published by Methuen a month later, a day after *Punch* published its final excerpt. By 1935, it had reached a twentieth edition; later reprints include an elegant Folio Society edition, with an introduction by Ned Sherrin, and a lavishly illustrated edition with an introduction by Frank Muir.[20] *1066 and All That* was also adapted twice for the stage: in a version of 1932 by Michael Watts and then as a musical comedy with lyrics by Reginald Arkell and music by Alfred Reynolds, first performed in 1935 and revived on several occasions. Sellar and Yeatman published three further collaborative works – *And Now All This* (1932), *Horse Nonsense* (1933), and *Garden Rubbish* (1936) – none of which achieved anything like the critical and popular success of *1066 and All That*.[21]

II

Referring to a remark in Sellar and Yeatman's preface, 'History is not what you thought. *It is what you can remember*',[22] Le Faye contends that Austen's 'approach is identical – accepting that for most people the only memories of their history lessons will be a few names and anecdotes of kings and battles, jutting out like rocks from a vast sea of forgetfulness'.[23] There are, though, some substantial differences between *The History of*

England and *1066 and All That*. Sellar and Yeatman's work, occupying 116 pages in the first edition, is some ten times the length of Austen's diminutive history, and it covers a much longer period: from Caesar's invasion of Britain in 55 BC to the end of World War I. Austen, in contrast, begins with Henry IV's ascension to the throne in 1399 and ends with the beheading of Charles I in 1649: a span of precisely 250 years. Sellar and Yeatman provide five 'test papers', parodying those set in school examinations at the time and containing mock admonitions to the students, such as 'Which do you consider were the more alike, Caesar or Pompey, or *vice versa*? (Be brief)', or 'Which came first, A.D. or B.C.? (Be careful)'.[24] The subtitle of *1066 and All That*, 'A Memorable History of England, comprising, all the parts you can remember including one hundred and three good things, five bad kings, and two genuine dates', suggests something of its self-confident, breezy tone, like that of an amused schoolmaster addressing a hopelessly befuddled pupil. Austen, in contrast, concludes her history with a pro-Stuart address to 'every sensible and well disposed person whose opinions have been properly guided by a good Education'.[25] Unlike Sellar and Yeatman, who emphasize the distance between themselves and their readers, Austen claims to be writing for a readership with views and sympathies akin to hers. Another innovation in *1066 and All That* is a series of prefatory items: a 'Compulsory Preface (This Means You)'; another preface ostensibly to the second edition but in fact published in the first; mock acknowledgments; spoof press opinions; a genuine 'authors' note', acknowledging previous publication of parts of the book in *Punch*; and finally three 'errata', including '*For* Pheasant *read* Peasant, throughout'.[26]

1066 and All That does, however, make significant and adroit use of its precursor. On her title page, Austen terms herself 'a partial, prejudiced, and ignorant historian'. Here she is parodying the preface to Goldsmith's *History of England*, which concludes with the hope that 'the reader will admit my impartiality', and indicating, in doing so, her belief that such pretensions of even-handedness are absurd. Sellar and Yeatman, similarly, take mock pride in their own cavalier approach, declaring in their 'compulsory preface' that 'all the History that you can remember is in this book, which is the result of years of research in golf-clubs, gun-rooms, green-rooms, etc.' They also claim that '2 out of the 4 Dates originally included were eliminated at the last moment, a research done at the Eton and Harrow match having revealed that they are *not memorable*'. Austen likewise alerts her readers that 'There will be very few Dates in this History'.[27]

Like Austen, too, Sellar and Yeatman furnish their work with a mock dedication. Austen's history is dedicated to its illustrator, her sister Cassandra, 'eldest daughter of the Revd George Austen', to whom 'this Work is inscribed with all due respect'.[28] The term 'Work' would be more appropriate for a full-length published history on the lines of Goldsmith's four volumes than for Austen's brief manuscript, while the phrase 'with all due respect' suggests an address to a powerful patron, rather than a seventeen-year-old elder sister with no influence at all. Sellar and Yeatman's dedication is an enigmatic tag: 'absit oman'.[29] The phrase, like so much of *1066 and All That*, is a play on words, combining the Latin 'absit omen' ('may no evil result') with the name of the distinguished military historian Sir Charles Oman, Chichele Professor of Modern History at Oxford and also a Conservative MP. He is a figure to whom a 'work' might have been dedicated 'with all due respect'.

Both *The History of England* and *1066 and All That* are furnished with illustrations designed to heighten the humour of their respective works. In one instance, as Jan Fergus remarks, Cassandra seems to have taken the lead in the collaboration between author and artist. At the head of her section on Elizabeth I, Jane Austen wrote the monarch's name and left space, as usual, for a satirical portrait. Cassandra, however, chose to include a portrait of Jane's beloved Mary Stuart, placed directly beside that of Elizabeth and contrasting with her in every way. The portrait of Elizabeth I, as Fergus observes, 'is abusive, almost a caricature; that of Mary Stuart is conventionally pretty and *reflects* conventional images – including the wimple that became a hallmark of Mary's portraits'.[30] On another occasion, Austen draws attention to her sister's work in describing Edward IV as 'famous only for his Beauty and his Courage, of which the Picture we have here given of him, and his undaunted Behaviour in marrying one Woman while he was engaged to another, are sufficient proofs'.[31] Part of the joke here is that 'the Picture', depicting an ill-dressed and unprepossessing military recruit, is neither of a monarch nor by Cassandra, who copied it from a 1780 satiric print, 'Recruits', by Henry Bunbury.[32] Sellar and Yeatman make no such textual references to the many line drawings of their illustrator, John Patrick Reynolds, but they do provide captions suggesting that the trio worked in close collaboration. Reynolds's frontispiece, for instance, depicts a king ogling a fetching queen, with the caption 'Magna Garter'; the outrageous pun is supported by a garter forming a prominent part of the queen's costume. Another of Reynolds's drawings, depicting a Roman soaking in a sunken bath, has the witty caption 'Roman occupied'.[33] Henry Summerson contends that

Reynolds's illustrations 'are as sharp and economical as the accompanying text, and no one who has seen his pictures of King John losing his clothes in the wash or Morton applying his fork is ever likely to forget them'.[34]

Like all histories, Jane Austen's relies on a variety of sources. Her principal debt is to Goldsmith. In addition, she alludes to a multitude of literary works; one of Austen's comic strategies is to enlist writers of fiction and drama as authorities for what purports to be a historical account. In the first of her short chapters, on Henry IV, she refers to 'a long speech' made by the king and 'a still longer' one by his son, the Prince of Wales, 'for which I must refer the Reader to Shakespear's Plays'.[35] In the same chapter on Henry IV, Austen claims that 'it is not in my power to inform the Reader who was his Wife',[36] on the grounds that neither of the king's two consorts figures among the characters in either part of Shakespeare's *Henry IV*. Most of Shakespeare's other history plays also figure in Austen's work: *Richard II*, *Henry V*, *Richard III*, the *Henry VI* trilogy, and *Henry VIII*. So too do plays by eighteenth-century dramatists: Nicholas Rowe's *The Tragedy of Jane Shore* (1714) and R. B. Sheridan's comedy *The Critic* (1779), although Rowe's play, we are told, 'is a tragedy and therefore not worth reading'.[37] There are also allusions to Sophia Lee's historical novel *The Recess; or, A Tale of Other Times* (1785), Charlotte Smith's first novel *Emmeline* (1788), and a letter contributed by Austen's brother James to his Oxford periodical *The Loiterer* (1789–90), under the name of Bluster. William Gilpin, one of Austen's favourite modern authors,[38] appears here as one of the 'first of men' because of his sympathy for Mary Queen of Scots; in his *Observations, Relative Chiefly to Picturesque Beauty* (1789), Gilpin commends 'that unfortunate princess ... whose beauty, and guilt have united pity, and detestation through every part of her history'.[39]

Shakespeare plays as large a part in *1066 and All That* as in Austen's *History of England*. The chapter on Henry IV, for instance, is entitled 'Henry IV. A Split King', and the monarch, 'Henry IV Part I', is said to have 'very patriotically abdicated in favour of Henry IV, Part II'.[40] Like Austen, Sellar and Yeatman allude to a scene dramatized by Shakespeare in *Henry IV, Part 2*: Prince Harry's youthful offence of striking the Lord Chief Justice, William Gascoigne. On assuming the crown, in Austen's history, Henry V is said to have grown 'quite reformed and Amiable, forsaking all his dissipated Companions, and never thrashing Sir William again'.[41] In Sellar and Yeatman's account, after 'hitting a very old man called Judge Gascoigne', Henry V 'determined to justify public expectation by becoming the *Ideal English King*'.[42] Elsewhere, like Austen, Sellar and Yeatman refer overtly to one of Shakespeare's history plays, *Henry VIII*, as a source. In their comic version of Thomas Cromwell's execution by Henry VIII, they declare that 'In the opinion of Shakespeare (the memorable playwriter and Top Poet) his unexpected defeat was due to his failure to fling away ambition'.[43] In her sketch of the dying Cardinal Wolsey, Austen quotes his words to the Abbot of Leicester Abbey 'that "he was come to lay his bones among them"'.[44] The line is taken from Goldsmith's history, which in turn is indebted to a report of Wolsey's words in *Henry VIII*:

> O father abbot,
> An old man, broken with the storms of state,
> Is come to lay his weary bones among ye.[45]

Sellar and Yeatman quote the same lines but with an ingenious twist, combining them with Mark Antony's famous words in Shakespeare's *Julius Caesar*: "'Father Abbot, I come to lay my bones among you, Not to praise them.'"[46] Another virtuoso use of Shakespeare occurs in Sellar and Yeatman's chapter on Robin Hood, in which we hear of 'the famous Friar Puck who used to sit in a cowslip and suck bees, thus becoming so fat that he declared he could put his girdle round the Earth'. The legendary Friar Tuck is thus spliced together with Ariel in *The Tempest*, singing 'Where the bee sucks, there suck I', and Puck in *A Midsummer Night's Dream* ('I'll put a girdle round about the earth').[47]

In addition to Shakespeare's plays, Sellar and Yeatman draw on a wide variety of literary works. As Summerson observes, *1066 and All That* contains allusions 'to writing by Milton . . . Pope, Gray, Keats, Tennyson, and Newbolt', while its title is indebted to Robert Graves's autobiography, *Goodbye to All That* (1929).[48] There are many other literary allusions not mentioned by Summerson: one to Jonathan Swift's *Gulliver's Travels* (1726), for instance, in a remark on 'how to make an egg stand on its wrong end', one to Emily Brontë's *Wuthering Heights* (1847), when Mary Queen of Scots is said to have been put 'in quarantine on the top of an enormous Height called Wutheringay', one to Robert Browning's poem 'Pippa passes', and an outrageous one to Victor Hugo, the 'romantic leader' of the Hugonauts.[49] Francis Bacon appears in a footnote as 'author of Shakespeare, etc'.[50] Pepys and Evelyn are conjoined in risqué fashion: Pepys, we are told, 'is memorable for keeping a Dairy and going to bed a great deal', while 'his wife Evelyn . . . kept another memorable Dairy, but did not go to bed in it'.[51] Horace Walpole, in turn, 'lived in a house with the unusual name of Strawberry Jam and spent his time writing letters to famous men (such as the Prime Minister, Walpole, etc.)'.[52] Rousseau is transmuted into 'Madame Tousseau, the French King's mistress, who believed in everyone returning to a state of nature and was therefore known as *la belle sauvage*'.[53] Havelock Ellis, the pioneering student of human sexual behaviour, appears as 'Generals Havelock, Ellis, etc.'[54] Oscar Wilde and Aubrey Beardsley are brought together with another risqué pun: Wilde 'wrote very well but behaved rather beardsley'.[55]

Sellar and Yeatman had a precedent for their use of bawdy jokes of this kind: the teenage Austen's sexually uninhibited mock history. Consider, for example, her chapter on James I, with its slew of homosexual puns – such as the remark that Henry Percy's 'Attentions' were 'entirely Confined to Lord Mounteagle', and an observation on the king's 'keener penetration' in his male friendships: as Christopher Kent notes, 'the word "penetration" seems carefully chosen'.[56] The chapter concludes with a charade on James's Scottish favourite, Sir Robert Carr: 'My first is what my second was to King James the 1st, and you tread on my whole'.[57] The answer to the riddle is 'carpet', with Austen thus depicting Sir Robert as the putatively homosexual king's domestic 'pet'.

In their chapter on the two impostor claimants to the throne during the reign of Henry VII, Perkin Warbeck and Lambert Simnel, Sellar and Yeatman seem to be directly indebted to Austen. In *The History of England*, Austen creates a bizarre sexual fantasy through a rhetorical question: 'if Perkin Warbeck was really the Duke of York, why might not Lambert Simnel be the Widow of Richard'.[58] Sellar and Yeatman, developing Austen's interest in gender and identity confusion, suggest that the two impostors 'were really the same person (i.e. the Earl of Warbeck)'. Later in the chapter they become 'Perkin Warmnel', 'Perbeck', 'Wimneck', 'Warmneck', 'Lamkin', and finally 'Permnel'.[59]

Sellar and Yeatman seem also to have been struck by Cassandra Austen's illustration of Elizabeth I, depicting her, in contrast to the beautiful Mary Queen of Scots, as a repulsive crone with a hooked nose and a massively protruding chin. In the text, Jane Austen recounts Elizabeth's cruel treatment of Mary 'in confining for the space of nineteen years, a *Woman*'.[60] By underlining Mary's femininity, Austen implies that Elizabeth's behaviour, like her portrait, is unwomanly – and Sellar and Yeatman follow suit, asserting that 'this memorable Queen was a man'.[61] They also draw on Austen's panegyrics on Mary, whom Austen ingeniously draws into her history on every possible occasion: Lady Jane Grey, for example, is said to be 'inferior to her lovely Cousin the Queen of Scots', while the Duke of Somerset, beheaded during the reign of Edward VI, 'might with reason have been proud, had he known that such was the death of Mary Queen of

Scotland'.[62] In *1066 and All That*, Mary becomes 'The Queen of Hearts', who 'was too romantic not to be executed'.[63]

Austen's contempt for Queen Elizabeth and intense admiration for Mary Queen of Scots are not merely eccentric: as the mother of James I, Mary was the head of the house of Stuart, which Austen, at least in her teenage years, believed had been wrongly dispossessed from the throne. Her chapter on Charles I begins with some egregiously circular reasoning: 'This amiable Monarch seems born to have suffered Misfortunes equal to those of his lovely Grandmother; Misfortunes which he could not deserve since he was her descendant'.[64] The pro-Stuart fervour that permeates the *History* echoes Austen's marginalia on her copy of Goldsmith's history, including her declaration that the Stuarts were 'a Family, who were always illused, Betrayed or Neglected Whose Virtues are seldom allowed while their Errors are never forgotten'.[65] Sellar and Yeatman hold no such brief for the Stuarts, summarizing the Civil War as 'the *utterly memorable Struggle between the Cavaliers (Wrong but Wromantic) and the Roundheads (Right but Repulsive)*'.[66] For Austen, in contrast, the Parliamentarians were 'the original Causers of all the disturbances, Distresses and Civil Wars in which England for many years was embroiled'.[67]

Elsewhere, however, Austen's wild prejudices are echoed by those of Sellar and Yeatman. Consider, for example, their respective treatments of Sir Francis Drake. In Austen's zany account, this 'ornament of his Country and his profession' is depicted as the precursor of his namesake, Austen's brother Francis:

> Yet great as he was, and justly celebrated as a Sailor, I cannot help foreseeing that he will be equalled in this or the next Century by one who tho' now but young, already promises to answer all the ardent and sanguine expectations of his Relations and Freinds, amongst whom I may class the amiable Lady to whom this work is dedicated, and my no less amiable Self.[68]

Francis Austen, aged seventeen, was then a lowly midshipman, serving on the thirty-eight-gun HMS *Minerva*. He was knighted in 1837 and would eventually, at the age of eighty-nine, become Admiral of the Fleet in 1863, far into 'the next Century', but without, of course, ever achieving anything like the renown of Drake. Austen's mock tribute has the effect of trivializing Drake's exploits, as though he too had depended on the 'ardent and sanguine expectations' of his sisters rather than his own prowess.

For Sellar and Yeatman, Drake's storied career affords fine opportunities for comedy, as they scramble and recompose some of the myths surrounding him. In their version:

> The Spaniards complained that Captain F. Drake, the memorable bowls-
> man, had singed the King of Spain's beard (or Spanish Mane, as it was
> called) one day when it was in Cadiz Harbour. Drake replied that he was in
> his hammock at the time and a thousand miles away.[69]

The first two references are obvious enough: Drake proverbially described
his raid on Cadiz in 1587 as singeing the King of Spain's beard (here, in
another outrageous pun, the 'Spanish Mane'), and his insistence on
finishing a game of bowls while awaiting the arrival of the Spanish armada
in 1588 is a celebrated, though probably apocryphal, story. Sellar and
Yeatman also work in the first line of a celebrated poem by Sir Henry
Newbolt, 'Drake's Drum' (1897): 'Drake he's in his hammock an' a
thousand miles away'. The poem builds on a legend: that at times of
national danger Drake's drum, carried with him on his ships, will beat,
summoning the heroic sailor back from the dead to the defence of his
country. Here, in a wild twist, Drake himself uses the line as a prosaic alibi:
he could not have 'singed the King of Spain's beard' when he was
'a thousand miles away'.

It is also instructive to compare the respective treatments of the Earl of
Essex in *The History of England* and *1066 and All That*. For Austen, Essex
was 'equally conspicuous in the Character of an *Earl*, as Drake was in that
of a *Sailor*'. She likens 'this noble and gallant Earl', in one of her many
literary analogies, to Frederic Delamere, the hero of Smith's *Emmeline*,
with Queen Elizabeth as a counterpart to Emmeline, who in the
novel breaks off her engagement to Delamere and marries another suitor.
Delamere's abusive treatment of Emmeline, which includes abducting her
to Scotland, fully justifies her actions, but Delamere's wonderfully attractive name, as well as his impetuous character, makes him a natural parallel
to Austen's version of Essex. In her account, 'he was beheaded on the
25th of Febry, after having been Lord Leuitenant of Ireland, after having
clapped his hand on his Sword, and after performing many other services
to his Country'.[70] Notable here is Austen's provision of the precise date of
Essex's execution, despite her boast that 'there will be very few Dates in
this History'. The sentence structure adroitly turns the famous incident
of Essex's clasping his sword after having his ear boxed by Queen Elizabeth
into a heroic exploit, yet another of his 'services to his Country', rather
than an affront to decorum.

Sellar and Yeatman also furnish a bizarre account of Essex's execution,
after first conflating him with Robert Dudley (whom they spell as
'Dudleigh'), Earl of Leicester, another aristocrat romantically linked to
the queen. In their version, which adapts the highly overwrought account

of Essex in Marshall's *Our Island Story*, Essex 'had a secret arrangement with Queen Elizabeth that he was to give her a ring whenever he was going to be executed, and she would reprieve him'. Instead, though, of the ring being misdelivered, as in *Our Island Story*, Sellar and Yeatman have Essex failing to connect with a telephone call ('give her a ring'): 'he was given the wrong number and was thus executed after all, along with the other favourites'.[71]

Neither Marshall nor Austen is so much as mentioned in *1066 and All That*. There is a page of Acknowledgments but, like so much of the book, it is a spoof. Sellar and Yeatman here give thanks to the editors of four publications 'in which none of the following chapters has appeared'. This eclectic group of non-sources is *The English Historical Review*, a highly respected historical journal founded in 1886; *Bradshaw*, a guide to railway timetables; *La Vie Parisienne*, a popular French weekly magazine; and *The Lancet*, an august medical journal founded in 1823. Sellar and Yeatman (of whom only Sellar was then married) also thank 'their wife, for not preparing the index wrong. There is no index'.[72]

These ingeniously unhelpful acknowledgments efficiently cover the authors' tracks. There is no mention, here or elsewhere in *1066 and All That*, of Robert Graves, for his contribution to the book's title; of Helen Marshall, whose work is its primary object of satire; or of Jane Austen, whose *History of England* had shown how effective such satire could be. This silence has a precedent in Austen herself. The only historian mentioned anywhere in her work is John Whitaker, author of *Mary Queen of Scots Vindicated* (1787). Oliver Goldsmith, author of the four volumes that she recreated as *The History of England*, is never named. And Austen, in turn, would not be mentioned in the book that recreated her mock history in the twentieth century: *1066 and All That*.

Notes

1 See Peter Sabor, 'Jane Austen: Satirical Historian', in *Swift's Travels: Eighteenth-Century British Satire and Its Legacy*, eds. Nicholas Hudson and Aaron Santesso (Cambridge University Press, 2008), pp. 217–32 (218–19).
2 *Collected Works of Oliver Goldsmith*, ed. Arthur Friedman, 5 vols. (Oxford: Clarendon Press, 1966), vol. 5, p. 338.
3 *Shorter Works by Jane Austen*, intro. Richard Church, decorations by Joan Hassall (London: Folio Society, 1963); Jane Austen, *The History of England*, illustrated by Paulette Riches (Toronto: Aliquando Press, 1966); Jane Austen, *Love and Freindship and Other Early Works*, intro. Geraldine Killalea, illustrated by Suzanne Perkins (London: Women's Press, 1978); Jane Austen, *The History*

of England, eds. Jan Fergus et al., illustrated by Juliet McMaster (Edmonton: Juvenilia Press, 1995). McMaster discusses her illustrations of *The History of England*, and of Austen's other juvenilia, in a chapter of *Young Jane Austen: Studies in Her Early Fiction* (Farnham: Ashgate, forthcoming).

4 John Barton, *The Hollow Crown: An Entertainment By and About the Kings and Queens of England* (London: Samuel French, 1962), rev. edn (London: Hamish Hamilton, 1971).

5 Jane Austen, *The History of England*, intro. A. S. Byatt, ed. Deirdre Le Faye (Chapel Hill: Algonquin Books, 1993), p. xi; Daniel Woolf, 'Jane Austen and History Revisited: The Past, Gender, and Memory from the Restoration to *Persuasion*', *Persuasions*, 26 (2004), 217–36 (226).

6 See, for example, Rosemary Mitchell, 'Marshall, Henrietta Elizabeth (1867–1941)', *Oxford Dictionary of National Biography*, www.oxforddnb.com/ view/article/57458 (accessed 10 September 2014); H. E. Marshall, *Our Island Story: A History of England for Boys and Girls* (London: T. C. and E. C. Jack, 1905).

7 James Edward Austen-Leigh, *A Memoir of Jane Austen* (London: Richard Bentley, 1870), p. 59.

8 Chesterton's clerihew was first published in Edmund Clerihew Bentley, *Biography for Beginners* (London: T. Werner Laurie, 1905), n.p. See also Chesterton, *The Victorian Age in Literature* (London: Williams and Norgate, 1913), pp. 92, 105, 109; and Chesterton, 'The Evolution of *Emma*', *New Witness*, 10 (1917), 274–75.

9 Margaret Anne Doody, contending that 'Chesterton in 1922 had more of an eye for what is going on in Austen's earlier writing than most critics have had', suggests that he 'read and approved this youthful expressionistic Austen, who shows us that form itself is an arbitrary but delicious play, depending on rules that can be amazingly broken from moment to moment, if the writer is daring and deeply knowing' (intro. to Jane Austen, *Catharine and Other Writings*, eds. Margaret Anne Doody and Douglas Murray [Oxford University Press, 1993], pp. xxxii, xxxvi).

10 See David Gilson, *A Bibliography of Jane Austen* (Oxford: Clarendon Press, 1982), pp. 371–73.

11 Virginia Woolf, 'Jane Austen Practising', *New Statesman*, 15 July 1922, pp. 419–20, rpt. in *The Essays of Virginia Woolf, Volume III: 1919–1924*, ed. Andrew McNeillie (London: Chatto and Windus, 1988), pp. 331–35; Augustine Birrell, *The Times*, 12 June 1922, pp. 15–16, rpt. in his *More Obiter Dicta* (London: William Heinemann, 1924), pp. 36–42; 'Solomon Eagle' [J. C. Squire], *Outlook*, 49 (1922), 509; R. Brimley Johnson, 'A New Study of Jane Austen (interpreted through *Love and Freindship*)', prefixed to Léonie Villard, *Jane Austen: A French Appreciation* (London: G. Routledge, 1924); Annette B. Hopkins, 'Jane Austen's "Love and Freindship": A Study in Literary Relations', *South Atlantic Quarterly*, 24 (1925), 34–49.

12 Jane Austen, *Love & Freindship and Other Early Works*, preface by G. K. Chesterton (London: Chatto and Windus, 1922), pp. x–xi.

13 Chesterton, preface to *Love & Freindship*, p. xi.

14 Austen, *The History of England*, ed. Le Faye, p. ix.

15 E. M. Forster, 'The Six Novels', *Nation and Athenaeum*, 34 (1923–24), 512–14, rpt. in Forster, *Abinger Harvest* (1936), ed. Elizabeth Heine (London: André Deutsch, 1996), pp. 142–45; Forster, '*Sanditon*', *Nation and Athenaeum*, 36 (1925), 860, rpt. in *Abinger Harvest*, ed. Heine, pp. 145–48; J. Middleton Murry, review of *The Watsons*, intro. by A. B. Walkley, *Nation and Athenaeum*, 32 (1922–23), 824; Virginia Woolf, review of *The Watsons*, *New Statesman*, 10 March 1923, pp. 662, 664.

16 Mary Augusta Austen-Leigh, *Personal Aspects of Jane Austen* (London: John Murray, 1920), p. 27; Virginia Woolf, 'Jane Austen and the Geese', *Times Literary Supplement*, 28 October 1920, p. 699, rpt. in *Essays of Woolf, Volume III*, ed. McNeillie, pp. 268–71.

17 Katherine Mansfield, 'Friends and Foes', *Athenaeum*, 3 December 1920, pp. 758–59, rpt. in Mansfield, *Novels and Novelists*, ed. J. Middleton Murry (London: Constable, 1930), pp. 302–4.

18 Rudyard Kipling, 'The Janeites', *Story-Teller*, May 1924, pp. 139–50, rpt. in Kipling, *Debits and Credits* (London: Macmillan, 1926), pp. 147–74, followed by a poem, 'Jane's Marriage', pp. 175–76.

19 Kipling, 'The Janeites', p. 147.

20 Sellar and Yeatman, *1066 and All That*, intro. Ned Sherrin (London: Folio Society, 1990); *1066 and All That*, intro. Frank Muir (Stroud: Alan Sutton, 1993).

21 For information on Sellar and Yeatman's lives and work, I am indebted to the *Oxford Dictionary of National Biography* entry on Sellar by Henry Summerson and to the introductions by Sherrin and Muir.

22 Sellar and Yeatman, *1066 and All That* (London: Methuen, 1930), p. vii.

23 Austen, *The History of England*, ed. Le Faye, p. xi.

24 Sellar and Yeatman, *1066*, p. 15.

25 Austen, *The History of England*, in Jane Austen, *Juvenilia*, ed. Peter Sabor, The Cambridge Edition of the Works of Jane Austen (Cambridge University Press, 2006), p. 189.

26 Sellar and Yeatman, *1066*, p. xii.

27 Sellar and Yeatman, *1066*, p. vii; Austen, *Juvenilia*, p. 176.

28 Austen, *Juvenilia*, p. 176. Austen dedicated three more of her early writings to Cassandra; see Peter Sabor, 'Brotherly and Sisterly Dedications in Jane Austen's Juvenilia', *Persuasions*, 31 (2009), 41–45.

29 Sellar and Yeatman, *1066*, p. [v].

30 Austen, *History of England*, ed. Fergus et al., p. ix.

31 Austen, *Juvenilia*, p. 178. Annette Upfal and Christine Alexander suggest that 'Cassandra may have inserted the image under the chapter heading for this monarch before Austen transcribed the slightly modified text'. They postulate 'a much closer collaboration between the two sisters' than is generally assumed, suggesting that 'Cassandra began with the painstaking work on the images before Austen had time to transcribe all the text so that the sisters were

working on the MS almost simultaneously': *Jane Austen's The History of England & Cassandra's Portraits*, eds. Upfal and Alexander (Sydney: Juvenilia Press, 2009), pp. 26, 28.

32 This was first noted by Fergus (*History of England*, ed. Fergus, p. iv), who also observes that the same print by Bunbury furnished Cassandra with her portrait of Henry V.

33 Sellar and Yeatman, *1066*, p. 4.

34 Henry Summerson, 'Sellar, Walter Carrruthers (1898–1951)', *Oxford Dictionary of National Biography*, www.oxforddnb.com/view/article/39442 (accessed 10 September 2014).

35 Austen, *Juvenilia*, p. 177. The allusion is to *Henry IV, Part 2*, in which the king's speech begins 'Thy wish was father, Harry, to that thought', and his son's reply begins 'O, pardon me, my liege' (IV.v, ll.92, 138).

36 Austen, *Juvenilia*, p. 177.

37 Austen, *Juvenilia*, p. 179.

38 In his 'Biographical Notice of the Author' prefixed to the first edition of *Northanger Abbey* and *Persuasion*, Austen's brother Henry remarks that 'At a very early age she was enamoured of Gilpin on the Picturesque' (J. E. Austen-Leigh, *A Memoir of Jane Austen and Other Family Recollections*, ed. Kathryn Sutherland [Oxford University Press, 2002], pp. 140–41).

39 Austen, *Juvenilia*, p. 182; William Gilpin, *Observations, Relative Chiefly to Picturesque Beauty*, 2 vols. (London: R. Blamire, 1789), vol. I, p. 92.

40 Sellar and Yeatman, *1066*, p. 44.

41 Austen, *Juvenilia*, p. 177.

42 Sellar and Yeatman, *1066*, p. 45. The link between *The History of England* and *1066 and All That* here is noted by Fergus (*History of England*, ed. Fergus, p. 24).

43 Sellar and Yeatman, *1066*, p. 55.

44 Austen, *Juvenilia*, p. 180.

45 William Shakespeare, *Henry VIII*, IV.ii, ll.20–22.

46 Sellar and Yeatman, *1066*, p. 56; Shakespeare, *Julius Caesar*, III.ii, l.76 ('I come to bury Caesar, not to praise him').

47 Sellar and Yeatman, *1066*, p. 27; Shakespeare, *The Tempest*, V.i, l.88; Shakespeare, *A Midsummer Night's Dream*, II.i, l.175.

48 Summerson, 'Sellar'.

49 Sellar and Yeatman, *1066*, pp. 52, 60, 105, 60

50 Sellar and Yeatman, *1066*, p. 63.

51 Sellar and Yeatman, *1066*, pp. 72–73.

52 Sellar and Yeatman, *1066*, pp. 81–82.

53 Sellar and Yeatman, *1066*, p. 88.

54 Sellar and Yeatman, *1066*, p. 104.

55 Sellar and Yeatman, *1066*, p. 111.

56 Austen, *Juvenilia*, pp. 186, 187; Christopher Kent, 'Learning History with, and from, Jane Austen', in *Jane Austen's Beginnings: The Juvenilia and 'Lady Susan'*, ed. J. David Grey (Ann Arbor: UMI Research Press, 1989), pp. 59–72 (67).

57 Austen, *Juvenilia*, p. 187.
58 Austen, *Juvenilia*, p. 179. Upfal and Alexander note that Austen's 'absurd conjecture ... calls Richard's sexual preferences into question' (*Jane Austen's History*, p. 30).
59 Sellar and Yeatman, *1066*, pp. 50, 51, 52.
60 Austen, *Juvenilia*, p. 184.
61 Sellar and Yeatman, *1066*, p. 58.
62 Austen, *Juvenilia*, pp. 180, 182.
63 Sellar and Yeatman, *1066*, p. 60.
64 Austen, *Juvenilia*, p. 187.
65 Austen, *Juvenilia*, p. 337.
66 Sellar and Yeatman, *1066*, p. 63.
67 Austen, *Juvenilia*, p. 188.
68 Austen, *Juvenilia*, p. 185.
69 Sellar and Yeatman, *1066*, p. 59.
70 Austen, *Juvenilia*, pp. 185, 186.
71 Sellar and Yeatman, *1066*, p. 61; Marshall, *Our Island Story*, ch. 73.
72 Sellar and Yeatman, *1066*, p. ix.

Select Bibliography

Anderson, Emily Hodgson, *Eighteenth-Century Authorship and the Play of Fiction* (London: Routledge, 2009).

Barchas, Janine, *Matters of Fact in Jane Austen: History, Location, and Celebrity* (Baltimore: Johns Hopkins University Press, 2012).

Barker, Gerard A., *Grandison's Heirs: The Paragon's Progress in the Late Eighteenth-Century English Novel* (Newark: University of Delaware Press, 1985).

Benedict, Barbara M., *Framing Feeling: Sentiment and Style in English Prose Fiction, 1745–1800* (New York: AMS Press, 1994).

  Making the Modern Reader: Cultural Mediation in Early Modern Literary Anthologies (Princeton University Press, 1996).

Blewett, David, *The Illustration of 'Robinson Crusoe', 1719–1920* (Gerrards Cross: Smythe, 1995).

Bourdeau, Debra Taylor and Elizabeth Kraft (eds.), *On Second Thought: Updating the Eighteenth-Century Text* (Newark: University of Delaware Press, 2007).

Brewer, David A., *The Afterlife of Character, 1726–1825* (Philadelphia: University of Pennsylvania Press, 2005).

Bruhn, Jørgen, et al. (eds.), *Adaptation Studies: New Challenges, New Directions* (London: Bloomsbury, 2013).

Budra, Paul and Betty A. Schellenberg (eds.), *Part Two: Reflections on the Sequel* (University of Toronto Press, 1998).

Cartmell, Deborah and Imelda Whelehan (eds.), *The Cambridge Companion to Literature on Screen* (Cambridge University Press, 2007).

  (eds.), *Adaptations: From Text to Screen, Screen to Text* (London and New York: Routledge, 1999).

Cave, Terence, *Mignon's Afterlives: Crossing Cultures from Goethe to the Twenty-First Century* (Oxford University Press, 2011).

Chandler, James and Maureen McLane (eds.), *The Cambridge Companion to British Romantic Poetry* (Cambridge University Press, 2008).

Cook, Daniel, 'On Genius and Authorship: Addison to Hazlitt', *The Review of English Studies*, 64 (2013), 610–29.

  'Authors Unformed: Reading "Beauties" in the Eighteenth Century', *Philological Quarterly*, 89:2–3 (2010), 283–309.

Cox, Philip, *Reading Adaptations: Novels and Verse Narratives on the Stage, 1790–1840* (Manchester University Press, 2000).

Davis, Lennard, *Factual Fictions: The Origins of the English Novel* (New York: Columbia University Press, 1983).

Dickie, Simon, *Cruelty and Laughter: Forgotten Comic Literature and the Unsentimental Eighteenth Century* (University of Chicago Press, 2011).

Donaldson, Ian, 'Fielding, Richardson, and the Ends of the Novel', *Essays in Criticism*, 32:1 (1982), 26–47.

Doody, Margaret Anne and Peter Sabor (eds.), *Samuel Richardson: Tercentenary Essays* (Cambridge University Press, 1989).

Dow, Gillian and Clare Hanson (eds.), *Uses of Austen: Jane's Afterlives* (Basingstoke: Palgrave Macmillan, 2012).

Elliott, Kamilla, *Rethinking the Novel/Film Debate* (Cambridge University Press, 2003).

Fiske, Roger, *English Theatre Music in the Eighteenth Century*, 2nd edn (Oxford: Clarendon Press, 1986).

Flynn, Carol Houlihan and Edward Copeland (eds.), *Clarissa and Her Readers: New Essays for the 'Clarissa' Project* (New York: AMS Press, 1999).

Ford, Richard, *Dramatisations of Scott's Novels: A Catalogue* (Oxford Bibliographical Society, 1979).

Forry, Steven Earl, *Hideous Progenies: Dramatizations of 'Frankenstein' from Mary Shelley to the Present* (Philadelphia: University of Pennsylvania Press, 1991).

Freeman, Lisa, *Character's Theater: Genre and Identity on the Eighteenth-Century English Stage* (Philadelphia: University of Pennsylvania Press, 2002).

Gallagher, Catherine, *Nobody's Story: The Vanishing Acts of Women Writers in the Marketplace, 1670–1820* (Berkeley: University of California Press, 1994).

Gerard, W. B., *Laurence Sterne and the Visual Imagination* (Farnham: Ashgate, 2006).

Girdham, Jane, *English Opera in Late Eighteenth-Century London: Stephen Storace at Drury Lane* (Oxford: Clarendon Press, 1997).

Haywood, Ian, *Romanticism and Caricature* (Cambridge University Press, 2013).

Holland, Anna and Richard Scholar (eds.), *Pre-Histories and Afterlives: Studies in Critical Method for Terence Cave* (London: Legenda, 2009).

Humphreys, Anne, 'The Afterlife of the Victorian Novel: Novels about Novels', in *A Companion to the Victorian Novel*, eds. Patrick Brantlinger and William B. Thesing (Oxford: Blackwell, 2002), pp. 442–57.

Hunter, J. Paul, *Before Novels: The Cultural Contexts of Eighteenth-Century English Fiction* (New York: W. W. Norton, 1990).

'Serious Reflections on Farther Adventures: Resistances to Closure in Eighteenth-Century English Novels', in *Augustan Subjects: Essays in Honor of Martin C. Battestin*, ed. Albert J. Rivero (Newark: University of Delaware Press, 1997), pp. 276–94.

Hutcheon, Linda with Siobhan O'Flynn, *A Theory of Adaptation*, 2nd edn (London and New York: Routledge, 2013).

Hutcheon, Linda, *A Theory of Parody: The Teachings of Twentieth-Century Art Forms* (New York and London: Methuen, 1985).

Keymer, Thomas (ed.), *The Cambridge Companion to Laurence Sterne* (Cambridge University Press, 2009).

Sterne, the Moderns, and the Novel (Oxford University Press, 2002).

(published as Tom Keymer), *Richardson's 'Clarissa' and the Eighteenth-Century Reader* (Cambridge University Press, 1992).

Keymer, Thomas and Peter Sabor, *'Pamela' in the Marketplace: Literary Controversy and Print Culture in Eighteenth-Century Britain and Ireland* (Cambridge University Press, 2005).

(eds.), *The Pamela Controversy: Criticisms and Adaptations of Samuel Richardson's 'Pamela', 1740–1750*, 6 vols. (London: Pickering and Chatto, 2000).

Kewes, Paulina, *Authorship and Appropriation: Writing for the Stage in England, 1660–1710* (Oxford: Clarendon Press, 1998).

Leitch, Thomas, *Film Adaptation and its Discontents: From 'Gone with the Wind' to 'The Passion of the Christ'* (Baltimore: Johns Hopkins University Press, 2007).

Loveman, Kate, *Reading Fictions, 1660–1740: Deception in English Literary and Political Culture* (Aldershot: Ashgate, 2008).

Lupton, Christina and Peter McDonald, 'Reflexivity as Entertainment: Early Novels and Recent Video Games', *Mosaic: A Journal for the Interdisciplinary Study of Literature*, 43:4 (2010), 157–73.

Lynch, Deidre (ed.), *Janeites: Austen's Disciples and Devotees* (Princeton University Press, 2000).

The Economy of Character: Novels, Market Culture, and the Business of Inner Meaning (University of Chicago Press, 1998).

Macdonald, Gina and Andrew F. Macdonald (eds.), *Jane Austen on Screen* (Cambridge University Press, 2003).

Maruca, Laura, *The Work of Print: Authorship and the English Text Trades, 1660–1760* (Seattle: University of Washington Press, 2007).

Maxwell, Richard and Katie Trumpener (eds.), *The Cambridge Companion to Fiction in the Romantic Period* (Cambridge University Press, 2008).

Mayer, Robert, 'Robinson Crusoe on Television', *Quarterly Review of Film and Video*, 28:1 (2011), 53–65.

(ed.), *Eighteenth-Century Fiction on Screen* (Cambridge University Press, 2002).

Mayo, Robert D., *The English Novel in the Magazines, 1740–1815* (Evanston: Northwestern University Press, 1962).

McFarlane, Brian, *Novel to Film: An Introduction to the Theory of Adaptation* (Oxford: Clarendon Press, 1996).

McGinnis, Reginald (ed.), *Originality and Intellectual Property in the French and English Enlightenment* (New York: Routledge, 2009).

McKeon, Michael, *The Secret History of Domesticity: Public, Private, and the Division of Knowledge* (Baltimore: Johns Hopkins University Press, 2005).

The Origins of the English Novel, 1600–1740 (1987; Baltimore: Johns Hopkins University Press, 2002).

McMurran, Mary Helen, *The Spread of Novels: Translation and Prose Fiction in the Eighteenth Century* (Princeton University Press, 2010).

Mirmohamadi, Kylie, *The Digital Afterlives of Jane Austen* (Basingstoke: Palgrave Macmillan, 2014).

Newbould, M–C., *Adaptations of Laurence Sterne's Fiction: Sterneana, 1760–1840* (Farnham: Ashgate, 2013).

Oakley, Warren, *A Culture of Mimicry: Laurence Sterne, His Readers and the Art of Bodysnatching* (London: MHRA, 2010).

Paige, Nicholas, *Before Fiction: The Ancien Régime of the Novel* (Philadelphia: University of Pennsylvania Press, 2011).

Parisian, Catherine M., *Frances Burney's 'Cecilia': A Publishing History* (Farnham: Ashgate, 2012).

Parker, Kate and Courtney Weiss Smith (eds.), *Eighteenth-Century Poetry and the Rise of the Novel Reconsidered* (Lewisburg: Bucknell University Press, 2014).

Parrill, Sue, *Jane Austen on Film and Television* (Jefferson: McFarland and Co., 2002).

Price, Leah, *The Anthology and the Rise of the Novel: From Richardson to George Eliot* (Cambridge University Press, 2000).

Pucci, Suzanne R. and James Thompson (eds.), *Jane Austen & Co.: Remaking the Past in Contemporary Culture* (Albany: State University of New York Press, 2002).

Rawson, Claude (ed.), *The Cambridge Companion to Henry Fielding* (Cambridge University Press, 2007).

Satire and Sentiment 1660–1830: Stress Points in the English Augustan Tradition (1994; New Haven and London: Yale University Press, 2000).

Richetti, John (ed.), *The Cambridge Companion to the Eighteenth-Century Novel* (Cambridge University Press, 1996).

Popular Fiction before Richardson: Narrative Patterns, 1700–1739 (Oxford: Clarendon Press, 1969).

Rigney, Ann, *The Afterlives of Walter Scott: Memory on the Move* (Oxford University Press, 2012).

Rose, Mark, *Authors and Owners: The Invention of Copyright* (Cambridge, MA: Harvard University Press, 1993).

Sanders, Julie, *Adaptation and Appropriation* (London and New York: Routledge, 2006).

Schellenberg, Betty A., *The Conversational Circle: Re-Reading the English Novel, 1740–1775* (Lexington: University Press of Kentucky, 1996).

Seager, Nicholas, 'The 1740 *Roxana*: Defoe, Haywood, Richardson, and Domestic Fiction', *Philological Quarterly*, 89:1–2 (2009), 103–26.

'*Gulliver's Travels* Serialized and Continued', in *Reading Swift: Papers from the Sixth Münster Symposium on Jonathan Swift*, eds. Kirsten Juhas et al. (Munich: Wilhelm Fink, 2013), pp. 543–62.

Shepherd, Lynn, *Clarissa's Painter: Portraiture, Illustration, and Representation in the Novels of Samuel Richardson* (Oxford University Press, 2009).

Smith, Frederik N. (ed.), *The Genres of 'Gulliver's Travels'* (Newark: University of Delaware Press, 1990).

Spencer, Jane, *Aphra Behn's Afterlife* (Oxford University Press, 2001).

The Rise of the Woman Novelist: From Aphra Behn to Jane Austen (Oxford: Blackwell, 1986).

Stam, Robert and Alessandra Raengo (eds.), *Literature and Film: A Guide to the Theory and Practice of Film Adaptation* (Oxford: Blackwell, 2005).

Starr, G. Gabrielle, *Lyric Generations: Poetry and the Novel in the Long Eighteenth Century* (Baltimore: Johns Hopkins University Press, 2004).

Stern, Simon, '"Room for One More": The Metaphorics of Physical Space in the Eighteenth-Century Copyright Debate', *Law and Literature*, 24:2 (2012), 113–50.

Sutherland, Kathryn, *Jane Austen's Textual Lives: From Aeschylus to Bollywood* (Oxford University Press, 2005).

Swindells, Julia and David Francis Taylor (eds.), *The Oxford Handbook of the Georgian Theatre, 1737–1832* (Oxford University Press, 2014).

Temple, Kathryn, *Scandal Nation: Law and Authorship in Britain, 1750–1832* (Ithaca and London: Cornell University Press, 2003).

Terry, Richard, *The Plagiarism Allegation in English Literature from Butler to Sterne* (Basingstoke: Palgrave Macmillan, 2010).

Townshend, Dale and Angela Wright (eds.), *Ann Radcliffe, Romanticism, and the Gothic* (Cambridge University Press, 2014).

Warner, William B., *Licensing Entertainment: The Elevation of Novel Reading in Britain, 1684–1750* (Berkeley: University of California Press, 1998).

Watt, Ian, *The Rise of the Novel: Studies in Defoe, Richardson and Fielding* (London: Chatto and Windus, 1957).

Welcher, Jeanne K., *Gulliveriana VII: Visual Imitations of 'Gulliver's Travels' 1726–1830* (Delmar: Scholars' Facsimiles and Reprints, 1999).

Wiles, R. M., *Serial Publication in England before 1750* (Cambridge University Press, 1957).

Index